I0605047

SEVEN RIVERS

Vanessa Taylor is a historian of rivers, water and the environment at the University of Greenwich. She has published extensively, written for *BBC History Magazine* and appeared on Channel 4, and is one of the foremost experts on the history of the river Thames. She was raised in the watersheds of the Mersey, Thames, Los Angeles and Stour rivers, and now lives in London.

SEVEN RIVERS

A Journey through the Currents of Human History

VANESSA TAYLOR

PEGASUS BOOKS
NEW YORK LONDON

SEVEN RIVERS

Pegasus Books, Ltd.
148 West 37th Street, 13th Floor
New York, NY 10018

First Pegasus Books cloth edition September 2025

ISBN: 978-1-63936-863-1

10 9 8 7 6 5 4 3 2 1

Printed in the United States of America
Distributed by Simon & Schuster
www.pegasusbooks.com

To Lisa

Contents

Introduction

> '(I often wonder what it will be like
> To have one's soul required of one
> But all I can think of is the Out-Patients' Department –
> "Are you Mrs. Briggs, dear?"
> No, I am Scorpion.)'
>
> Stevie Smith, 'Scorpion' (1972)[1]

There are about 1.39 billion cubic kilometres of water in the world, we're told. That amount doesn't change – it just gets redistributed. Sometimes the water is flowing through our bodies; sometimes it's in the rice field, or in the rows of plastic bottles on supermarket shelves. Most of it, by far, is in the world's oceans: nearly 97 per cent. River flows, amazingly, constitute only around 0.0002 per cent of the world's water at any given time. That is less than the amount found in glaciers, groundwater, permafrost, lakes, or in the atmosphere; even swamps hold more water than rivers.[2] Yet rivers are water at its most historical. They are the familiar flows through our landscapes, shaping our named territories and our home turfs. Rivers are also where we get most of our water – the lifeblood of our historical civilisations, from Jericho in the Jordan Valley 10,000 years ago to the Indus culture of 7000 BCE and onwards. When they dry up, societies die.

Rivers have served basic needs for drinking water, navigation routes and trade. But basic needs have only ever been part of the story, and are always inextricably bound up with questions of power and wealth: who commands the irrigation systems, the canals and the gunboats at the river mouth? Water flows by gravity but it also, as Marc Reisner said in *Cadillac Desert*, 'flows uphill to money'.[3] Very many of our rivers are hybrids: natural streams of water that have been adapted by people and their technologies over time. Environmental historians capture this feature of rivers through metaphors such as the 'organic machine' of Richard White's vision of the Columbia River, and Sara Pritchard's Rhône as a 'confluence' between 'nature and nation'.[4] For humans, like beavers, adapting rivers is what we do to make our world more liveable. This has been going on for a very long time, as shown by the stories here: the building of dams, levees and fish traps, canals, water mills and irrigation channels for the intensive use of water. These adaptations have frequently had their downsides. Rivers are the historical record of our successes as well as our failures and injustices: the dry riverbeds, displacement of people and destruction of ecosystems.

I'd like to say that my own interest in rivers arose from their importance for our civilisations or some such thing, but it is less noble than that. As a child, I wanted to be a rabbit living in the ground; then to be a water rat and watch the world flow by from inside a riverbank. One day, when I was about eight, my older brothers started digging in our garden: they were going to build an underground swimming pool. An excellent idea, I thought. I knew they wouldn't want me to help so, a few feet away I began digging an underground pool of my own. Mine would have coloured lanterns, like in the book *Nicky and His Forest Friends*. How I was going to get the hosepipe down to the muddy hole at the bottom of the garden, or secure the ceiling, or achieve the crystalline tiled floor the pool surely deserved, were matters I didn't face head-on. The absence of a practical streak was something we siblings shared at that time. As I recall, there was only ever a dim realisation that this job might be more than I could manage. The digging sessions got shorter and then stopped after a few days, but my fascination with water, rivers and underground spaces remained.

Some version of this feeling about water and rivers seems to be universal; only the stone-hearted can resist a river. Their mysterious, spiritual quality is always there, alongside their implacable capacity for flooding and destruction. From the holy springs of Anglesey to the subterranean Puerto Princesa in the Philippines, rivers are enduringly seductive.

Every river deserves its own history. And an infinite number of stories could be written. Sometimes rivers are drab water channels, like 'Mrs Briggs', and sometimes they are 'Scorpion', as in Stevie Smith's poem of that name, or, like people, they can be both at the same time. All rivers have compelling stories. I have chosen the seven rivers in this book because they magnify the common qualities of these great natural arteries that run through our lives. They are 'world rivers' by virtue of the roles they have played in our history. They have served as the power bases for empires and been fought over as frontiers. Their river basins – those great systems of tributaries and groundwater all flowing to the main river – have been plundered for their gold, timber, salt, oil, rubber and people. Vast trading networks have been forged between them such as the deadly 'middle passage' of the slave trade linking the Niger and Mississippi basins. Alongside this, rivers seem to have generated in humans an infinite capacity for invention: the elites with their pantheons of river gods, lotus pools and hanging gardens; fishing rituals and creation myths with their sources lost in the mists of time; the infinite everyday power struggles and subtle rebellions on main rivers and distant tributaries. And rivers themselves have always had their own logic: their natural beauties, their floods, droughts, water-borne diseases and mosquitoes, their tendency to silt-up and mutate into marshland, their marshy subsidence beneath city streets, their changes of course, tipping points and disappearances. These rivers have shaped our lives, just as we have shaped theirs.

This book is inspired by the rise of environmentalism which has provided new ways of looking at nature. Environmentalism has many roots. Some trace it to the moment the Cuyahoga River in north-east Ohio – birthplace of Rockefeller's Standard Oil – caught fire in 1969, captured in *Time* magazine; some to the moment 'Spaceship Earth' was first seen from the moon; some to the 1967 SS *Torrey Canyon* disaster, spilling millions of gallons of crude oil off Britain's south-west coast, further affecting France, Guernsey and Spain; or further back to the 'dawn of green' when earnest Victorians opposed reservoirs in the Lake District, or to Henry David Thoreau's mystical naturalism; or much further back to the veneration of the natural world in Hinduism.[5]

The seven rivers that follow – the Nile, Danube, Ganges, Thames, Mississippi, Niger and Yangtze – each span three chapters in a broadly chronological order, exploring distinct facets of the rivers and their watersheds. Some chapters start from the geological origins of the rivers and some from the time of their place in human history.

Certain themes recur across the seven rivers. There are rivers as highways and as ecosystems; rivers connecting geological time and human time, and during climate change; rivers as water sources and navigation channels; rivers and taxation systems; rivers as polluted drains; as borders and streams that connect 'involuntary neighbours'; rivers as metaphors for nationhood or empires, or for human existence; rivers as gods and goddesses; rivers as sacred or as portals to other worlds; rivers transformed by dams and augmented by canals and pipelines. There are river names, hydronyms and layers of language through time; rivers as corridors for people, wildlife and pathogens, and as wetlands and stopping posts for flyways; rivers as anchors for human memory and as places where memories are lost with shifting baselines and extinctions; and rivers as places for adaptation and reinvention.

This is also a story of seven river basins. There are the famed main river channels from source to sea, but also their watersheds gathering all the rain that falls, all the tributaries and their tributaries in turn, the groundwater, ponds, seasonal pools, dried-out riverbeds, former wetlands now drained and turned into farmland or cities, and once mighty rapids subdued beneath great lakes.

This is a story of us, in seven rivers.

River 1: Nile

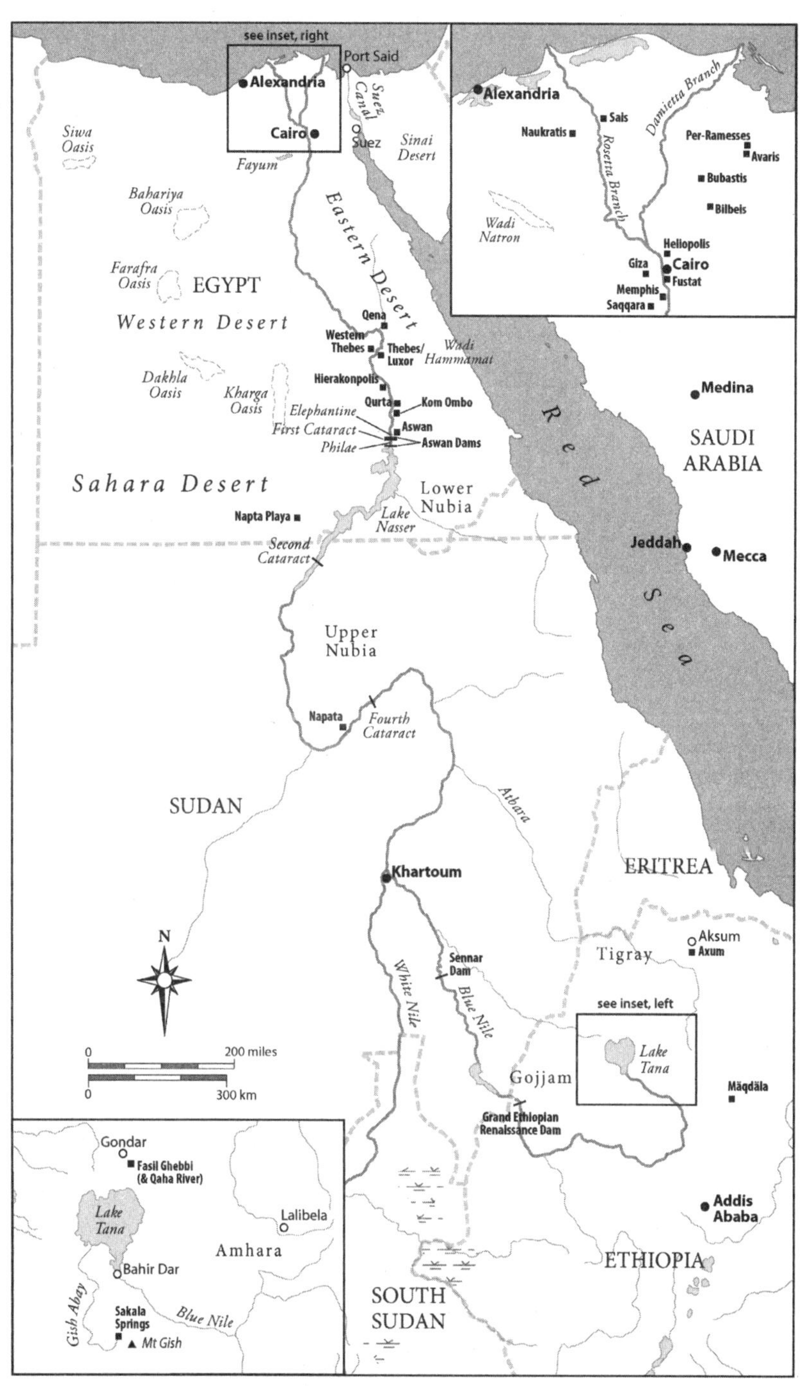

see inset, right
Port Said
Alexandria
Cairo
Suez Canal
Suez
Siwa Oasis
Sinai Desert
Fayum
Bahariya Oasis
Eastern Desert
Farafra Oasis
EGYPT
Western Desert
Qena
Western Thebes
Thebes/ Luxor
Wadi Hammamat
Dakhla Oasis
Hierakonpolis
Kharga Oasis
Qurta
Kom Ombo
Elephantine
Aswan
First Cataract
Philae
Aswan Dams
Red Sea
Sahara Desert
Lower Nubia
Napta Playa
Lake Nasser
Second Cataract
Jeddah
Mecca
Medina
SAUDI ARABIA
Upper Nubia
Napata
Fourth Cataract
Atbara
SUDAN
Khartoum
ERITREA
N
Aksum
Axum
Tigray
Sennar Dam
White Nile
Blue Nile
see inset, left
Lake Tana
Gojjam
0
200 miles
0
300 km
Mäqdäla
Grand Ethiopian Renaissance Dam
Addis Ababa
ETHIOPIA
SOUTH SUDAN
Alexandria
Sais
Naukratis
Rosetta Branch
Damietta Branch
Per-Ramesses
Avaris
Bubastis
Bilbeis
Wadi Natron
Heliopolis
Giza
Cairo
Fustat
Memphis
Saqqara
Gondar
Fasil Ghebbi (& Qaha River)
Lake Tana
Lalibela
Amhara
Bahir Dar
Gish Abay
Sakala Springs
Blue Nile
Mt Gish

1

Ancient Ecosystems and the Art of Recycling

'I have not snared the water-fowl of the gods.
. . .
I have not turned back water at its springtide.
I have not broken the channel of running water.'
The Egyptian Book of the Dead, trans. E.A. Wallis Budge (1895)[1]

The Ancient Egyptians loved a hippopotamus. Their hippopotamus deity, Taweret, was the goddess and protector of pregnant women and their babies. You can see her in museums, in blue-glazed and rock crystal amulets from at least the fifteenth century BCE – standing on hind legs, pregnant, with hanging breasts, the back of a crocodile and feet of a lion, but recognisably a hippo's head and a ferocious set of fangs.[2] A bundle of powerful beasts. The mighty *Hippopotamus amphibious* – once native to the River Nile in Egypt – were hunted as well as venerated: for sport, for their meat and for their ivory teeth. There is also a cuddlier-looking hippopotamus artefact from the Middle Kingdom with a bright blue glaze, no bigger than a child's hand, decorated with lotus flowers and, crucially, its mouth is shut.[3] There must have been hundreds of these figurines in their heyday and thousands more of the real thing. They came for the water and the mud in the deep silty river that lay between the Nile at Aswan in southern Egypt and its delta on the eastern Mediterranean coast. Hippopotami were part of the region's culture from its very beginning. They are there in rock art from 15,000 years ago, alongside images of wild cattle and wetland birds, east of the river at Qurta and in ancient streams. Hippopotamus remains have been found right across the Sahara from these 'pluvial' years when the desert too was a savannah. These were the days before the rains stopped (around 5000 to 3500 BCE) and the Nile River corridor became Egypt's liveable zone for people and the creatures of the natural world they exploited and worshipped as deities.[4]

The Egyptian Nile was by no means the world's first great river civilisation. There were complex societies at least as ancient on the Tigris, Euphrates, Indus and Yellow rivers. The hieroglyphic script that developed in Egypt from the early 3000s BCE may have been inspired, for example, by the writing system of Mesopotamia: the 'land between two rivers' (Tigris and Euphrates) of today's Iraq.[5] But no single river culture retained such a formidable presence for so long, harnessing nature to flourish over thousands of years. This chapter asks how the thirty dynasties of Ancient Egypt sustained the trappings of rule along the Nile over 3,000 years. How did the people of these earliest civilisations on the Egyptian Nile work with nature on the river? Their annual calendars, spiritual life, labour force and irrigation systems – their command of oases as well as the river – all these were geared to the production of food, drink and massive surpluses for the rich to keep things going for another year. How did they do it, the Egyptians, the Greeks and the Romans who followed them?

The chapter looks at three aspects of this ancient world on the Nile. The first is the challenge for rulers that came with managing a river that was always a bit too long. The second is the intensity of exploitation of the natural world: most famously, though not only, the ability to harness the Nile flood. The third is the art of recycling. Like all rivers, only on a grander scale, the Nile embodies a sense of timelessness. Partly this is an illusion as we look back from a distant future, but it was an illusion also projected by the elites on the ancient river. Maintaining a sense of continuity was important for those aiming to exert control and authority over the Nile. They did this by recycling the past: the materials, the river management and the cultural traditions of those who came before them.

To turn to the first feature: the Nile, as everyone knows, is very long: the world record holder at 4,238 miles from source to sea.[6] It has never been controlled by a single power. Egypt itself occupies the last thousand miles or so of the river: a line of water sandwiched between the deserts of the Sahara. North of Cairo, in pharaonic time the line of river split apart like the fingers of an outstretched hand as the delta branches of the Nile flow into the Mediterranean Sea. The southern boundary of the Egyptian Nile was for much of the time located around Aswan, as it is today. This is just downstream from the white-water cataracts that once formed a natural boundary, at the border with today's Sudan (then Kush). Just above the border, a cavern on the island of Elephantine was revered as the source of the Nile flood.[7] This was the home of Hapi, the androgynous god of the flood, with his hanging breasts and stomach, lotus flowers and dripping papyrus. Everyone knew that the river itself flowed from somewhere far to the south, but this seems to have made no difference: this symbolic source put down a marker to show where the most important stretch of the Nile began. The Egyptians called the Nile 'iteru' (*jtrw*), meaning 'river'.[8]

The famous Dynastic Era of Egypt starting around 3000 BCE was a unified kingdom stretching from Aswan to the sea, founded by violent conquest and binding people along the river whether they liked it or not. For a long time before the era of recorded kings there were two kingdoms. Upper Egypt extended from the southern border at Aswan northwards to the base of the delta: the region of the famous pyramids at Giza and the early capitals of Heliopolis and Memphis. Lower Egypt referred to the delta region up to the Mediterranean coast. These two kingdoms had their own cultures and symbolism. Lower Egypt was represented by the papyrus, the wetland sedge found in great profusion along the silty waterways of this northern kingdom. Its counterpart, the aquatic lotus flower, represented Upper Egypt.[9]

The first to achieve the unity of Upper and Lower Egypt is traditionally understood to be Narmer (c. 3000 BCE). A famous piece of silt stone found at Hierakonpolis depicts Narmer, on one side, wearing the White Crown of Upper Egypt, shaped like a tall, slanted bowling pin. On the other side, the king wears the Red Crown of Lower Egypt, the delta land he had just defeated; beside him are the beheaded bodies of his enemies. From this point, wearing the 'Dual Crown' (*pschent*) – White and Red at the same time – was the aspiration of every Dynastic ruler.[10] To truly merit the Dual Crown meant maintaining control and authority across this long river kingdom. Rulers of the thirty dynasties over the next 3,000 years displayed wildly different abilities in this respect: from Narmer or later the highpoint of the New Kingdom in the second millennium BCE to the fragmentation of the so-called 'Intermediate Periods', when pharaohs killed or fled from each other in quick succession. At times, there were several claimants at once to the Dual Crown, including 'every feather-wearing chief of Lower Egypt', as an eighth-century BCE Kushite pharaoh once described his northern rivals.[11] The Twenty-Fifth Kushite Dynasty itself is an example of several dynasties that originated from outside Egypt's borders and which ruled over the country for a time.

For all dynasties, projecting power along the whole river corridor was a major challenge. The base of the delta was the strategic key to the Egyptian Nile for thousands of years. This was the site of the earliest capitals, such as Memphis to the south of today's Cairo, with its cities of the dead at Saqqara and Giza, where the pyramids rose above the floodplain. Along the river, too, there were 'nomes' (administrative units) for everyday management, each with its own deity: twenty-two of them in Upper Egypt and twenty in Lower Egypt.[12] But each dynasty had its preferred power base; capitals shifted up and downstream over time. An abiding power base through many transfers of power was located on the Nile's Qena Bend, hundreds of miles south of the delta. Here on the east bank stood the great temple complex of Karnak in Thebes (today's Luxor): the epicentre of the worship of Amun, who with his golden river barque had become fused with the earlier sun god Ra. At times the Theban high priests were more powerful than pharaohs; some pharaohs based themselves here. Having been endowed with great riches and with its own strategic advantages in Upper Egypt, Thebes was a place to be reckoned with by anyone seeking to maintain the Dual Crown. This challenge was approached through a mixture of diplomatic gamesmanship, appeasement and homage, and episodes of raw violence.

One New Kingdom papyrus illustrates a curious case of power being projected along the river through sheer brinkmanship. It is a tale of two rulers and some hippos during one of the fragmented 'Intermediate Periods' (mid-second millennium BCE). One ruler was Apepi of the foreign Hyksos Fifteenth Dynasty, at that time based in the delta city of Avaris. The other was Seqenenra Taa II, ruler of the simultaneous and rival Seventeenth Dynasty, based down in Thebes. One day, Apepi sent a messenger south to Thebes to convey a complaint and an instruction to Seqenenra. Apepi claimed that he was being kept awake at night by 'the hippopotami from the swamp . . . in the eastern waters of the city [of Thebes], because they do not allow that sleep come to me, day or night, because their noise is in his ear!' Seqenenra was instructed to 'expel the hippopotami'. The papyrus fragment breaks up at the moment that shows Seqenenra pondering this strange complaint from 300 miles away, and we don't know what happened next. Scholarly interpretations abound as to what Apepi was trying to achieve. Was the implication that Seqenenra couldn't even control the hippopotami – a basic skill for any self-respecting pharaoh? We do know that Seqenenra was later killed in battle, possibly by the Hyksos, but also that the Hyksos were ultimately defeated by Seqenenra's descendants: the all-conquering Eighteenth Dynasty of the New Kingdom. So this story may have had a happy ending for New Kingdom audiences. It suggests at the very least some ingenious methods for projecting power along the river. It also conveys, perhaps, the importance of controlling the natural world. A long-standing component of Egyptian kingship was the ritual hunt and killing of hippopotami, demonstrating a kind of power over chaos.[13]

This ability to control nature is the second feature of the ancient Nile. Harnessing the Nile flood and keeping the harvests rolling in was as important to controlling the river corridor as defence against usurpers or an ability to exude pharaonic authority. The very earliest visual image of artificial irrigation so far discovered comes from Egypt some five thousand years ago, from the 'pre-dynastic' period just before Narmer. This carving on a stone mace head (a kind of ceremonial bludgeon) depicts the so-called 'Scorpion King', named after the scorpion symbol at his side. On his head sits the White Crown of Upper Egypt and, wielding a hoe, he appears to be engaged in the ritual opening of an irrigation canal.[14] Demonstrating a measure of control over the Nile waters has been an important part of rule in Egypt ever since.

All being well, the Nile flood made its appearance from June each year, when the swollen floodwaters started to rise downstream reaching the time of the 'plenitude' in September, when it drowned the floodplains. Then as floodwaters slowly ebbed away, seeds for the harvest could be sown. In good years this supported two harvests a year; Egypt could then export wheat and barley, serving as the 'breadbasket' of a wider world.[15] But only about three-quarters of annual floods achieved this ideal. Too little or too much water meant either drought or the wrong kind of flood, which in turn led to famine and disease.

Rulers couldn't control the volume of water arriving from thousands of miles upstream but instead relied on a mixture of propitiation of the gods, informed predictions, and blind hope. All along the riverside from Aswan to Memphis, there were 'Nilometers' that measured rising water levels as the flood made its way northwards. These took many forms, from simple lines carved into the riverbank marking water levels, such as those at Elephantine near the southern border, to the elaborate structures incorporated into riverside temples of Kom Ombo and Luxor. The domain of temple priests, Nilometers were used to decide when to announce the plenitude and what tax levels to set for the harvest, so that the wealth of the flood could be distributed upwards. Sixteen cubits at the southern border was considered the ideal river depth for the plenitude (one cubit being around the length of a man's forearm).[16] In addition to water that irrigated the crops, water supply was raised from the Nile and its waterways by means of the *shaduf*, a levering device with a long pole, until after the pharaonic period when the Persian Wheel or *saqia* arrived, typically turned by a pair of oxen.[17]

A successful harvest also relied on the ability to command a well-functioning system of *corvée* (forced) labour. This ensured that when peasants weren't quarrying, building or fighting Egypt's enemies, they were growing food. Perhaps 200,000 peasants supported a population of three million people in the Nile Valley in the second millennium BCE.[18] These vast resources of corvée labour and raw materials also enabled powerful rulers to secure their place in the afterlife. It may have taken between 20 to 30 thousand men at a time to build the Great Pyramid of Giza (Fourth Dynasty), constructed from over two million limestone blocks. Labouring people were as expendable as other parts of the natural world. Many thousands died during building, quarrying and mining work for the pharaohs. One estimate suggests perhaps 10 per cent of the workforce was routinely lost, rising to 50 per cent in more dangerous mining operations which employed convicts or enslaved workers, such as those from Kush.[19]

The great human cost involved in construction works, river maintenance and canal building is a pervasive feature of all powerful societies right up to the modern era. Sometimes this has relied on imperial power over others and systems of slavery, and sometimes on feudal hierarchies, but it is a feature of most of the rivers in this book from the Nile to the Yangtze and the Mississippi.

Gods have been especially helpful in this task of corralling the manual labour of the people and legitimising it symbolically. Rulers on the Nile did not rely solely on their own human powers but worshipped and propitiated a natural world that was alive with gods. The greatest of all of these – the falcon-headed sun god Ra – controlled day and night, life and death. He sailed in his barque for all eternity across the sky during the twelve hours of daylight and through the underworld for the twelve hours of night, to return the next day. There were hundreds of animal gods: from the other falcon-headed sky god Horus to the moon god

Thoth, represented by a baboon or by the ibis, the sacred wading bird with its elongated and regal beak. Anubis, with the head of a jackal, stood at the passage to the underworld. The lowly dung beetle, or scarab, symbolised rebirth and the morning sun.[20]

Little in nature went unused. Papyrus reeds from the Nile delta were the paper of the ancient world. The word 'paper' (in English) comes from the Latin 'papyrus' and perhaps before that from the Egyptian *pa-en-per-aa* (or 'that which belonged to the king').[21] 'Fossil water' from the great Nubian Sandstone Aquifer left over from rains that fell on the Sahara hundreds of thousands of years ago created oases in the western desert. These were used as outposts for Egypt's defence against incursions from the west, as well as places of exile and sometimes of escape.[22] The teeth and tusks of great beasts could be transformed into delicate ivory objects, like the pintail duck cosmetic box from the New Kingdom now in a Baltimore museum, or a hippopotamus ivory knife adorned with images of its living self as Taweret, goddess of childbirth, used to ward off evil in Middle Kingdom nurseries.[23] The humble donkey and mule were beasts of burden though, like the peasantry, they did not make it into the realm of gods.[24]

Dry riverbeds, or wadis, that once flowed into or out of the Nile provided land routes of trade, conquest and mining expeditions from the Nile River to the Red Sea.[25] The waterless Wadi Hammamat between the Nile and the Red Sea was quarried for the siltstone formed from ancient river sediment that had hardened over millions of years to provide a limitless supply of stone coffins (sarcophagi).[26] Natron bubbling out of pale saline lakes in the Wadi Natron (west of the Nile) was used in making the blue glaze faience for amulets such as Taweret's and the scarab beetles such as those produced in a delta factory. Natron was also the key drying agent used to mummify both the dead and the food they would need in the afterlife. This posthumous meal alone was a huge guzzler of resources. In a single and quite ordinary New Kingdom tomb, the occupant was laid to rest with nineteen 'victual mummies': the bodies of ducks, geese and turtle doves.[27]

The Aswan region of stone quarries was the source of some of Egypt's most famous monuments and the site of long-term power struggles with Kush. Here, below the southern border the 'cataract Nile' flowed from a land abundant in gold, timber, ivory and people to enslave. But only the most powerful rulers could navigate the rapids that led into Kush,[28] because this meant conquering the rock-strewn bed itself. Canals (or trenches) began to be dug into this stony riverbed from at least the time of the Old Kingdom, as recorded in the third millennium BCE when inscriptions were left at the scene proclaiming the magnificence of the pharaoh. These also told of subject Kushite chiefs who supplied the wood from acacia trees used to build vessels to ship blocks of Aswan stone northwards for the pharaoh's pyramid.[29] The boulders must have kept tumbling downstream because five hundred years later, a Middle Kingdom Pharaoh (Senusret III/Khakaura) dug a new trench. The name of the canal – 'Beautiful are the Ways of Khakaura living forever' – was preserved on a stone for posterity. Nearby rocks contained inscriptions to the gods of Elephantine: the Lord of the Cataract, Khnum, with the head of a ram and powers over the annual flood, his consort the goddess Anukis (or Anuket), and their daughter Satet.[30] These goddesses were no feminists. They oversaw the destruction of men and women with the same stone-cold approval. As Khakaura said elsewhere of his exploits in Kush: 'I have carried off their women and brought away their relatives, emptied their wells and driven off their cattle, cut down their grain and set fire to it.'[31]

Later still, the New Kingdom Pharaoh Thutmose I had to start trench-digging again, as did his grandson Thutmose III, who sensibly left an instruction for the fishermen of Elephantine to keep the river clear. It was during this New Kingdom era that Egypt's empire reached its greatest extent: from the Kushite city of Napata (Gebel Barkal) in the south, above the Fourth Cataract, to the far bank of the Euphrates River in Mesopotamia (today's Iraq) at its north-eastern edge.[32] Egypt's famous female 'King' Hatshepsut (r. 1473–1458 BCE), widow of Thutmose II, considered herself all-powerful across the globe. On obelisks she erected at the Theban temple of Amun-Ra – from whom ultimately her power flowed – she declared: 'There is no rebellion against me in any land; . . . All foreign lands are my subjects. He made my boundary at the limits of heaven; Everything the Orb encircles works for me.'[33] Such a tight grip on the river kingdom and its neighbours was exceptional. And, needless to say, temporary. But part of the job of a pharaoh was to convey the message that the gods of the natural world were specifically and forever shining down upon them. This meant somehow smoothing out ruptures between successive or rival dynasties.

This brings us to the third feature. One of the secrets to the longevity of Egyptian culture was the recycling of the epic materials and traditions left behind by those who had come before. The Nile and its riverside provided a stage for scenes of violent rupture to take place while the newcomers acted as if nothing had changed. Every new arrival wanted to set in stone suitably pharaonic images of himself and his family beside the most prestigious of gods: *Time* magazine 'Man of the Year' for all eternity. But not every ruling dynasty could afford all the trappings – the stone quarried from scratch, the capturing of slaves, the acacia trees. So this was also about literal recycling.

Even the super-rich early Ramessides of the New Kingdom were not above reusing materials and adding their own names to monuments created by earlier dynasties, though the vast monuments built for their delta capital at Pirammes set new heights of wealth and grandeur that almost matched the pyramids of the Old Kingdom. Nothing was permanent, and when the Ramessides' glory days were over, their delta capital too fell prey to natural forces. Around 110 tonnes of silt are estimated to have been carried downstream to the delta each year from the Blue Nile on its journey from the Ethiopian highlands. This raised the delta ground by over a centimetre each century and perhaps as much as 1.5 metres every thousand years. Maintaining clear waterways amid the shifting streams of mud and water required money and stable governors.[34] By the Third Intermediate Period (from 1069 BCE), the eastern Pelusiac delta branch that had been home to the Ramesside capital had long ago silted up; its monuments were being raided as raw materials by later rulers. This is how a giant palm-leaf column showing the god Seth blessing Ramesses II (thirteenth century BCE) ended up on a totally different delta branch in a temple dedicated to the cat-goddess Bastet, built by the Libyans of the Twenty-Second Dynasty.[35]

Even more than material recycling, this was also a matter of cultural recycling to keep the pharaonic traditions afloat. An example of this, found in the temple rituals of Thebes, shows the importance both of cultural continuity and of maintaining a pharaonic presence in the temple complex. The best way for new rulers to manage the city of Thebes, radiating such awesome symbolic capital, was to appropriate it and absorb its powers by participating fully in its rituals.

One day in March 656 BCE, the princess Nitiqret, daughter of the Saite king of the Twenty-Sixth Dynasty, set off from the delta on a sixteen-day river journey upstream to Thebes. Probably little more than a child, she was 'clothed in linen and adorned with new turquoise'. Along the way the great flotilla of ships that accompanied her, commanded by a Saite general, was met by the representatives of nomes lining the route, who supplied them with 'every good thing'. Nitiqret also carried with her a bequest of thousands of acres of estates from her father the king, solemn promises of regular supplies of 'bread, beer, milk, cake, vegetables, oxen and geese from Theban officials', and pledges of sacks of emmer wheat from miscellaneous temples.[36]

This journey to Thebes was a centuries-old tradition. From at least the New Kingdom, pharaohs had appointed family members to join the Theban temple hierarchy in worshiping the god Amun. The so-called 'God's Wife of Amun' became especially high status – typically a role allocated to the pharaoh's daughters. We don't know if this life of celibate devotion was a dubious privilege or a lucky escape for those appointed, while their sisters were married off to half-brothers or strangers in strategic alliances.[37] It must have had its attractions. Temple halls were filled with music: singers, flautists, harpists and dancers. The God's Wife of Amun is rarely seen in iconography without her sistrum (*shesest*): often an iron rattle with tiny cymbals and adorned with the cow goddess Hathor, goddess of fertility and, perhaps no coincidence, of drinking.[38] But the fate of a God's Wife was dependent on the standing of her Pharoah. If he was deposed, God's Wife would stay on in Thebes but would be obliged to 'adopt' the new pharaoh's appointee as a 'daughter' who would in time replace her.

This journey of the Saite princess Nitiqret was therefore part of a ritualised handover of power following the defeat of the Kushite Twenty-Fifth Dynasty in 656 BCE. This is described on a huge 'stele' of pink granite now standing in the Cairo Museum.[39] The Saite faction from the delta had aligned with the Assyrians under the powerful Ashurbanipal to bring an end to a period of Egyptian rule by the Kushites from the south. In 663 BCE, together they may have sacked the city of Thebes (or may not have: experts disagree), a stronghold of the Kushites who, as it happens, were genuinely ardent Amun worshippers. Then the Saite shook off the Assyrians and took power themselves, but eventually they put things right in Thebes.[40] This river journey of Nitiqret in 656 BCE was the orderly handover of God's Wife of Amun from the Kushites to the Saite Dynasty (664–525 BCE). When Nitiqret arrived at the Thebes quayside, the Kushite God's Wife, Shepenwepet II, must have had a good poker face as she watched her status drain away. According to the stele, Shepenwepet II when she 'saw her, was pleased with her and loved her more than anything'. Nitiqret in time became God's Wife of Amun, succeeded by her own great-niece Ankhnesneferibre on her death in 586 BCE. But the whole cycle of sacred wives seems to have ended with the arrival of the Persians in 525 BCE.[41]

The Persian Twenty-Seventh Dynasty (525–404 BCE) – or 'the hated Persians' as they are often called, though venerated in modern-day Iran – took a different approach to Egyptian rituals of cultural recycling. They were half-hearted pharaohs in comparison with other invaders, though the conqueror Cambyses II (r. 530–522 BCE) and later Persian kings paid some homage to Egyptian traditions of rule, such as adopting an Egyptian royal name.

The kingdom on the Nile was now for the first time absorbed into something much bigger than itself: the Achaemenid Persian Empire, with its own ancient culture and capital at Persepolis.[42] The Persians did the same as subsequent imperialists on their arrival at the Nile, pivoting its river and resources towards the centre of their own empire by means of canals and trade routes. Darius I (r. 522–486 BCE) is remembered for building or possibly completing the first 'Suez Canal': a waterway linking the eastern Nile delta and the Red Sea to the east.[43] Much of what we know of Egypt from Herodotus comes from his visit during this first Persian occupation around 450 BCE.[44] But the Persians lost their grip on the Nile only a few decades later. They returned for just ten years in the 340s BCE, causing the flight of the pharaoh of the Thirtieth Dynasty, Nectanebo II – often referred to as 'the last native king of Egypt' – before Egypt and the rest of the Achaemenid Empire were swallowed up whole by Alexander the Great of Macedon (r. 336–323 BCE).[45]

This Greek conqueror Alexander adopted a more traditional approach, fully embodying the trappings of power on the Nile for his new subjects. The city of Alexandria – the first Egyptian capital on the coast – showed where the new ruler's priorities lay, turning Egypt around to face the Mediterranean Sea. But from the start, Alexander took pains to integrate himself. Following his victory in 331 BCE over the Persian Darius III, Alexander went first to the oracle of the Temple of Amun at Siwa Oasis in Egypt's Western Desert.[46] Although this was no doubt a bid for legitimacy, Greek and Egyptian culture had been fused for some time. Amun by now had an alter-ego in Zeus Ammon. The oasis temple at Siwa had been built on traditional Egyptian lines but by Greek architects possibly from a trading post on the North African coast, commissioned by the Saite Dynasty who also employed Greek mercenaries and allowed Greek traders to establish a port city of Naukratis in the delta.[47] But Alexander was also an Egypt enthusiast. Images of him at the shrine of the sacred barque of Amun in Thebes – which he commissioned – show him in full pharaonic garb: the kilt and broad collar, the Red Crown of Lower Egypt, and, in his hand, the *ankh* or symbol of life. Facing him is Amun-Ra, wearing the Dual Crown of Upper and Lower Egypt.[48]

Ultimately though, Alexander's role in Egypt was that of an absentee landlord. Like many ambitious rulers, he aspired to a royal flush of rivers across South Asia and the Middle East. After his conquest on the Nile, he headed east with his men until at the Indus River they refused to go any further. Alexander turned back and died at Babylon on the banks of the Euphrates in 323 BCE. When his empire collapsed after his death, Egypt passed to general Ptolemy I as a rump of the Macedonian Empire, and Ptolemy's descendants and their officials continued the long tradition of fusion and recycling, as a settled hierarchy within Egyptian culture over the next 300 years.[49]

The last of the ruling Ptolemies, the famous Queen Cleopatra VII (r. 51–30 BCE), has left an eternal legacy without the aid of a tomb. Few certain images remain of her, apart from on coins of the era.[50] Into this semi-void, the twentieth century gave us Cleopatra's Hollywood good looks, Caucasian vibes, heavy use of kohl eyeliner, and an ongoing debate about her status in Black African history. Her political and personal entanglements with the Roman rulers circling Egypt's coastline ended in defeat and Cleopatra's suicide, with Egypt absorbed into the Roman Empire under Octavian (Augustus Caesar) in 30 BCE.

Like earlier foreign rulers on the Nile, the Romans looked for the benefits that could flow to their heartland: the mineral wealth and the harvest on its fertile riverbanks. There was no talk of barbarians, as heard on the banks of the Roman Danube, Rhine and, later, Thames.[51] The Romans were enamoured with this Graeco-Egyptian world. Many avidly adopted the paraphernalia of Egyptian kingship in the newly conquered land, commissioning images of themselves as pharaohs on the temples they built to Amun, Isis and other local gods. The New Kingdom obelisks ('Cleopatra's Needles') that were shipped many centuries later to London and New York were probably initially moved from Heliopolis to adorn Roman Alexandria at the command of Octavian himself. Obelisks also started to leach towards Rome; perhaps over forty of these were removed from the Nile during the Roman centuries.[52]

The river, or *iteru*, was known to the Romans as *Nilus* from the Greek *Neilus,* and images of the Nile god himself became suitably Romanised. Gone was the half-crocodile, androgynous Hapi (god of the flood) adorned with dripping reeds and birds, replaced by a masculine reclining Roman river god, with sixteen cherubs representing the sixteen cubits of the optimal Nile flood. Images of Nilometers appeared on Roman coins, mosaics and textiles.[53] A mosaic floor far away at Palestrina near Rome (second century to 20 BCE) depicts a watery Nilotic landscape. In the background are wild rocky heights, black Africans (probably Kushites) with bows and arrows, lions and snakes. The Nile flows down to a foreground of boating, hippopotami being stuck with harpoons, lounging women and Roman soldiers.[54] The westward spread of the Nile's fame had begun. This kind of material and cultural recycling by Egypt's incoming new elites both transformed and perpetuated the Nile's ancient traditions.

Despite the appearance of long continuity, the Nile was a place where cultures, faiths and languages merged and mutated, through recycling and shared traditions and appropriation. There was no single moment at which Ancient Egypt died. The culture of the Ancient Egyptian Nile persisted into the future in many threads, like the distributary streams that flow out from an estuary near its journey's end. The next chapter looks at what happened to these streams of river and culture when Byzantium lost control of the Nile in Egypt and the river passed into a new historical era. The Nile continued to be a place of continuity, alongside some profound changes and ultimately a radical overhaul of the river itself in the modern age.

2

Regime Change on the River

> 'The Nile River and its delta look like a brilliant, long-stemmed flower in this photograph of the southeastern Mediterranean Sea, as seen from the International Space Station.'
>
> NASA, 'Nile River Delta at Night' (20 April 2011)[1]

When in 639 CE the Arab general 'Amr ibn al-'As defeated the Byzantine Christian rulers in Egypt, he surveyed the scene before him on the river. 'The periods of its rise and fall are as regular as the courses of the sun and moon,' he observed. 'Egypt offers by turns the image of a powdery desert, a liquid and silvery plain, a black and slimy marsh, a green and waving meadow, a garden blooming with flowers, or a field covered with yellow harvests. Blessed be the creator of so many wonders.'[2] The arrival of the Rashidun ('Rightly Guided') Caliphate on the lower Nile, fewer than ten years after the death of the Prophet Muhammad – a companion of 'Amr ibn al-'As – brought another ingredient to the cocktail of faiths that sustained the annual flood and harvest. Islam was to last on the river. It wasn't true, though, that the river's rise and fall was so predictable. A failure of the flood could help to topple a regime.

This conquest was not about destruction. Egypt's granary, wealth and strategic location were the key attractions, as with those who had come before. The second Rashidun Caliph of Medina moved on Egypt as part of a growing ascendancy following the defeat of Byzantine Syria.[3] All empire-builders eyeing up the regions of the eastern Mediterranean, Arabian Peninsula or South

Asia over the next fourteen centuries had an Egypt-shaped jigsaw piece in their plans. This chapter explores the fortunes of the Nile after Ancient Egypt. What did the handover period look like after the Arab conquest? What happened to the old ways on the Nile? And how has the Nile River, or *Bahr al-Nil* (sea of Nile) in Arabic, itself been affected by those in charge from the time when Rome lost its power to today?[4] The regime changes that followed the arrival of 'Amr ibn al-'As do not form part of a convenient dynastic set. Suffice it to say that from the time of General 'Amr in the seventh century to Gamal Abd al-Nasser in the 1950s there were broadly five named Caliphates, a period of Mamluk control (the slave army turned warlords), four centuries of Ottoman rule that eventually became caught in the web of British imperialism, then fully independent Egypt from the 1950s. We begin with the second Rashidun Caliphate under 'Umar ibn al-Khattab (r. 634–44) and what they encountered on arrival.

The forces of 'Umar were not completely unwelcome on the Nile. By this time, the centre of gravity in the Roman Empire had moved away from Rome itself in the fourth century to the eastern capital of Constantinople on the Bosphorus linking the Mediterranean and Black Sea. And the Greek-influenced Byzantine Empire helped to shape the life of the Nile for the next three centuries. The invaded country was ruled from Byzantium (Constantinople: Istanbul, today), though with an increasingly faltering grip. Egypt itself was run by the Copts: a Christian elite of mixed Greek/Egyptian descent. At the point when General 'Amr arrived, the Patriarch of the Coptic Church in Egypt was hiding out from church authorities in Constantinople over a doctrinal disagreement. The letter of surrender that the Patriarch sent to the invaders may reflect relief at impending release from the 'Byzantine yoke', making for a surprisingly helpful transition.[5]

The polytheistic pagan world of the Nile had gradually faded, as Christianity moved from the persecuted margins to being the religion of emperors by the fourth century. The Egyptian language had also evolved: its written form changing from hieroglyphs through a long period of 'hieratic' script on papyrus, to a 'shorthand', simplified script derived from these earlier forms, known as Demotic (meaning 'popular').[6] By the second century CE, the locals were speaking Coptic: a mix of spoken Egyptian and imported Greek 'loanwords'. Their Christian scholars and officials used Greek script when writing, in place of the overly pagan Demotic script. This was the strange mixture later found on the Rosetta Stone, a routine tax instruction issued in three scripts by the teenage ruler Ptolemy V Epiphanes in 196 BCE. At the top were Egyptian hieroglyphs; in the middle, the commonly used Demotic script; at the bottom, Greek – the enduring written language of the Ptolemaic ruling class that would eventually provide the key to the other two scripts.[7]

Egyptian hieroglyphs were a rarity by the late fourth century, with the old gods of the Nile perhaps enduring longest in Kush and Egypt's southern border.[8] The last hieroglyph that has been found was on the river island of Philae below Elephantine, in the form of graffiti carved by a priest on the Gate of Hadrian at the Temple of Isis, dated 24 August 394 CE. This reads: 'Before Mandulis son of Horus, by the hand of Nesmeterakhem, son of Nesmeter, the Second Priest of Isis, for all time and eternity.'[9]

The practice of mummification was also dying out by this time, replaced at first by shallow burials of bodies sprinkled with the drying agent natron. Some of the very last mummies found are those of Coptic monks from the seventh and eighth centuries, laid to rest in monasteries occupying the site of the riverside Theban complex formerly dedicated to the god Amun.[10] This was the slow death of Ancient Egypt. Knowledge of Ancient Egyptian culture would later spread to the West through a net of Greek and the Latin of the Roman Empire: words like 'pyramid' and 'hippopotamus' (horse of the river). Ancient Egyptian may have also have been preserved via words such as 'oasis' (possibly from the Coptic *ouahe* for dwelling-place), 'pharaoh' (from Egyptian for 'great house'), and the river name itself, though its meaning is uncertain, the 'Nile'.[11]

When General 'Amr arrived at the *Bahr al-Nil*, he selected as his capital a place located just south of the foot of the Nile delta, on the east bank, which became known as Fustat. According to one legend, the natural world itself welcomed the newcomers: the city of Fustat grew on the site of General 'Amr's tent, which he left standing when he went north to conquer the port city of Alexandria. Finding that a dove had prophetically laid her eggs in the tent, here, 'Amr decided, he would build his new city.[12]

But this was a place with a long-standing strategic pre-eminence. Fustat, like the later capital of al-Qahira, is now part of Greater Cairo. The island of Roda made for easy access across the river at this point, which at times was bridged by a pontoon of boats. This location was probably earlier occupied by the Persians. It was here too that the Romans had built the fortress and harbour they called Babylon, where Emperor Trajan had brought the Red Sea Canal back into use (112 CE). The name 'Fustat' itself may have derived from *phossaton*, the Greek word for 'ditch', possibly referring to this ancient waterway. At any rate, General 'Amr carried out orders from the Caliph in Medina to clear out the silt and get water flowing once more along this eastward channel.[13] Mosques, civic buildings and public fountains went up in Fustat and other cities. A new burial ground was created below the Muqattam Hills east of the capital, where General 'Amr himself was laid to rest, in land that was once the domain of the fertility goddess Hathor.[14]

A new hierarchy took shape within Egyptian society. From the start there were advantages for Arab settlers, who were exempt from a tax levied on non-Muslims and allocated favourable land above the floodplain of the river. Tax and other inequalities led to Coptic uprisings from the late 600s and proved an incentive for conversion to Islam gradually over the centuries to come.[15] The Caliphates at first retained Coptic elites as administrators and Greek continued to be used for business. But after a couple of generations, Arab officials were favoured and Arabic became the language of official business.[16] Even the Egyptian-speaking, Greek-alphabet-using Christian Copts could not weather-proof themselves forever from the mist of Arabic all around them. Coptic ceased to be heard on the streets of Egypt somewhere around the eleventh century, though to this day the spoken language of first-millennium Egyptian is preserved in Coptic Church services in the Nile region.[17]

Under the Caliphates, the riches of the Nile's annual flood were re-orientated once again, now pivoted eastwards. Along with Egypt's grain, revenues from valuable estates such as the vineyards of the Fayum marshes began to flow to the treasury of the ruling Caliph. Grain, still sown and harvested by corvée labourers, could now be shipped via the Red Sea Canal to Mecca, Medina and other cities of the Arabian Peninsula, at least until a revolt in the east in the 740s led the Umayyad Caliphate to shut off the canal.[18]

The Nile flood retained its dominance in the lives of Egypt's people. The important job of measuring and predicting the Nile flood continued with the aid of Nilometers along the river. A new Nilometer (*al-Miqyas* in Arabic) was built on Roda Island (Cairo) by the Umayyad Caliphate (661–750). And when this was damaged by heavy flooding during the Abbasid era (750–969), it was replaced by a magnificent new Nilometer designed by the astronomer Alfraganus, with a hereditary (possibly Coptic-convert) guardian appointed.[19] This Nilometer was restored over the centuries and still stands today. A stone column measuring nineteen cubits occupies the centre of a giant well that would fill up as the Nile flood reached its height. Steps lead down to the base where the last puddles of water lingered when the flood subsided. Its walls are adorned by Qur'anic passages on themes of nature and abundance. A painting of the interior by the Italian Luigi Mayer in 1800, from the late Ottoman period, shows a viewing gallery that allowed the guardians to watch the rising flood and calculate tax levels for the harvest. Above this is an ornately patterned dome, circled by windows for a 360-degree view of the daylight and the stars.[20]

While the seasonal cycles endured, the calendars and Nile River festivals became tangled up. The ancient solar calendar on the Nile was joined by the Islamic lunar calendar, with its moveable New Year in the month of Muharram, while Egyptian Copts continued to use the Egyptian calendar, with its New Year in Thoth (September): the first month of the Nile plenitude.[21] Many ancient celebrations on the Nile persisted, and became assimilated by the Arab settlers, just as Coptic Christianity had earlier adapted ancient sacred ceremonies relating to the Nile plenitude. The Fatimids (969–1171), for example – the first Caliphate to base their empire in Egypt – are especially known for their sometimes enthusiastic participation in the popular celebration of the plenitude, with the Caliph processing to the Nilometer on Roda Island each year during this time of *wafa' al-Nil*. Under their rule, too, a mosque was built alongside this Nilometer. And later an elaborate plenitude ceremony was developed, involving 'the perfuming of the Nilometer' with musk and saffron, the recitation of verses from the Qur'an and the full immersion of an official.[22]

A Coptic festival marking the early rising of the Nile flood in May with the ritual sacrifice of a Christian martyr also brought people together in boats on the river and along the banks, as a box containing the martyr's finger was flung into the waters of the Nile. Known in Arabic as *id al-shahid*, this custom persisted into the 1300s. In the feast of Epiphany (around 18/19 January), known as *al-ghitas* (submersion) in Arabic, Christians in the eastern Orthodox traditions commemorate the baptism of Christ in the River Jordan by his cousin John. The Coptic Christian practice of submersion in the River Nile was another celebration that brought crowds of Christians and Muslims together on the river, at least into the Fatimid period.[23] When this ritual was later suppressed, its practitioners would continue it inside the churches. Epiphany water tanks stood in for the Nile, like one that survived into the 1880s at the church of St Shenoute in Old Cairo. It is thought that the flood season festival of Abu Hajjaj today, commemorating a thirteenth-century Sufi sheikh, preserves the Ancient Egyptian *Opet* procession of the barque of Amun-Ra upstream between the temples of Thebes.[24]

In comparison with the rulers who came before them, the Arab ruling elites had little interest in the ancient pharaonic trappings of the Nile. They did not adorn their capitals with pharaonic obelisks overwritten with their own names, though they freely raided and recycled existing materials to build their own cities.[25]

Stone with inscriptions from ancient Heliopolis helped build the city of Fustat and can still be found in the walls of Old Cairo and in the tenth-century Al-Hakim Mosque, just as Fustat itself was later raided for al-Qahira (Cairo) in the turbulent years of the mid-eleventh century.[26] Some materials have gone through many cycles. The heavy stone coffin of Nectanebo II, Egypt's last pharaoh who fled the Persians in the 340s BCE, was found more than two thousand years later at the Attarin Mosque in Alexandria, which itself had replaced the Coptic Church of St Athanasius.[27] Someone during this interval drilled twelve drainage holes into the sarcophagus, as if for a water basin: whether for a suppressed Epiphany ritual or for ablutions before Islamic prayers, we may never know. It now sits in the British Museum in London.

Egypt remained a strategic prize and envied granary during the centuries after the arrival of General 'Amr's army and was marked by rapid regime changes. The time of the Rashidun Caliphs was short (632–61), and the Nile soon became part of a great empire stretching from Arabia to southern Spain under the Umayyads (661–750); a succession of other realignments followed.[28] But the power of Nile conquerors was always tied both to the fortunes of their wider empires and to prosperity within Egypt itself. Devastation caused by low floods in the Nile in the 960s helped bring down the ailing Sunni Abbasids Caliphate (750–969).[29] Under their conquerors, the Shia Fatimids (969–1171), Egypt also endured terrible famine resulting from some of the lowest river flows on record during the 1060s and 1070s, a time known as the al-Shidda al-'Uzma or 'massive calamity', and possibly traceable to a global climate shift, the 'Medieval Warm Period', from the eleventh to thirteenth centuries. It was during this time that the Fatimids may have sent envoys upstream to Ethiopia to dissuade them from impeding the flood.[30]

At this point we must leap-frog over successive players on the Nile. No change would be as profound as that in the 'river regime' itself that began in the twilight years of the Ottoman Empire. A father and son – one grim, the other magnificent – began the Ottoman ascent to becoming the world's most powerful empire. Selim the Grim captured Egypt in 1517, followed by his son Suleyman the Magnificent, who expanded the Ottoman Empire westwards along the Danube. The Egyptian Nile became absorbed into an empire that at its height in 1650 covered 3.4 million square miles. Ottoman conquests occupied a great trapezoid from Algiers on the south-west of the Mediterranean coast, through the Balkans and Central Europe to the region above the Black Sea in the north-west; across to Baku and the Caspian Sea in the north-east, and sweeping down through Iraq to Basra where the combined waters of the Tigris and Euphrates flow to the Persian Gulf in the south-east, and spanning both sides of the Red Sea.[31] Egypt's wealth now flowed to the Ottoman 'Sublime Porte' in Istanbul and helped to cross-subsidise less lucrative parts of the empire, such as the beleaguered city of Budapest on the Danube.

But still, the Nile itself could not be relied on, with its annual flood dependent on the rainfall over Ethiopia's distant 'water tower', as it is known. A series of low Nile floods from the 1780s to 1810 brought drought, famine and disease to the land. In dire necessity, the peasants (*fellahin*) of Ottoman Egypt sold their labouring animals or ate them for food: the oxen, water buffalo and donkeys. Waterwheels that normally turned the grain mills and raised river water stood still.[32] This was also a time of waning Ottoman authority and circling European powers. A brief occupation by Napoleon's French forces was terminated by combined Ottoman and British forces on the Battle of the Nile (1798), though not before French soldiers dug up and were forced to surrender the famous granodiorite Rosetta Stone that had been repurposed for Ottoman fortifications on the Rosetta branch of the delta.[33]

The period that followed, however, saw not decline but a resurgence of Egyptian power. Holding European forces at bay was the powerful figure of Mehmed Ali (r. 1805–48),[34] Pasha of the Eyalet of Egypt from 1805. Mehmed Ali was an archetypal multi-national Ottoman: a Turkish-speaking Albanian born in the Macedonian Balkans and based in Cairo. In principle he answered to Istanbul, but instead he intended to be master of his own destiny, eventually declaring himself hereditary Khedive of Egypt. 'I am well aware that the [Ottoman] Empire is heading day by day towards its downfall . . .', he is reported to have said in the 1820s: 'But upon its ruins I shall build a vast kingdom.' He had prepared the way for his heir: 'My son, the Victorious, shall . . . go to fulfil his destiny on the banks of the Euphrates and the Tigris . . .'.[35]

The key to this was Mehmed Ali's determination to build a modern Egypt with a home-grown textile industry by harnessing the waters of the Nile, through a series of irrigation canals transporting water for cotton and flax fields. His workforce stretched Egypt's canal network from around 500 miles to 1,200 miles, bringing 18 per cent more land under cultivation and lengthening the growing season. This task required perpetual dredging of waterways that were fed by silt-laden delta streams.[36] These upgrades rested on distinctly un-modern corvée labour. Egypt's peasants had to work sixty days a year as payment to the Khedive. Death tolls on these projects were astonishingly high. Perhaps as many as 100,000 (a third of the labour force) died in one building project alone during these years, when a canal linking the Rosetta delta branch to the coastal city of Alexandria was resurrected.[37] As Mehmed Ali said in the 1830s, 'driving all the men to dykes and canals is difficult for them but is necessary'.[38]

Mehmed Ali's successors as Khedive lacked his skill in maintaining Egypt's independence in the face of rising European geopolitical strength. The project of expanding the country's economic and territorial dominion ran aground. Major water projects that followed on the Nile and at Suez acted as stepping-stones first to Egypt's (re)colonisation and then to independence and, above all, to a project that permanently changed the Nile. These developments were on the face of it separate but they became closely tied. The first, the opening of the Suez Canal in 1869, pulled the Nile region firmly into global geopolitical rivalries that initially at least undermined its own power. Egyptian and French funded, this French-engineered waterway, built with corvée labour, cut southwards from the Mediterranean coast to the Red Sea via the Gulf of Suez. In addition, a newly built freshwater canal conveyed drinking water from the Nile in Cairo to Port Said and other staging posts on the shipping canal.[39] The Suez Canal gave Ottoman Egypt easy access to the Arabian Peninsula, including the cities of Mecca and Medina, but also dramatically cut shipping routes between Western Europe and the Indian Ocean that had formerly rounded South Africa's Cape of Good Hope. The journey between Britain and India was reduced by around 77 per cent. When in the mid-1870s an indebted Khedive of Egypt had to surrender his shares in the canal, the British government snapped them up like a hungry crocodile.[40] It was in large part British desperation to protect its Suez Canal majority shareholder interests from rising Egyptian nationalism in the early 1880s that drove its naval bombardment of Alexandria and declaration of Egypt as a 'protectorate' at that time, while retaining a nominal Ottoman-appointee as Khedive.[41]

Wherever Britannia went during this high point of empire, she brought her Union Jack shield, of course, but also a giant mangle to squeeze every last drop of water and cultivatable land out of her colonised territories to grow cash crops, especially cotton to supply Lancashire's textile mills. No single development in its history affected Egypt's ancient river as fundamentally as the Aswan Low Dam (1899–1902).[42] This spelt the beginning of the end for the Nile flood. This dam of rubble and granite stretched right across the mile-wide river at Egypt's southern border. During the months of the summer inundation, the river continued to flow freely through sluice-gates that had recently been perfected on England's Liverpool-Manchester Ship Canal.[43] When low-water season approached, the dam gates were shut to store up a reservoir of water. The Island of Philae and its ancient temples now lay partially drowned for several months each year beneath this lake, and later dam enlargements fully submerged the island for part of the year.[44] In Cairo, the celebration of the cutting of a dyke on the Khalji Canal with the arrival of the inundation came to an end in the 1890s.[45]

The Ottoman Empire died around a century after Mehmed Ali's prediction of its destruction, having backed the losing side in the First World War. Within Egypt, continuing nationalist uprisings forced the British government to recognise Egyptian independence under a new king, but they maintained a military presence in the region and continued to develop dam and cotton projects upstream in what they called 'Anglo-Egyptian Sudan'.[46] After the Second World War, things started out on familiar enough lines. The British (now flanked by the Americans) supported Egyptian government plans in the early 1950s to build a bigger and better dam at Aswan along with a hydroelectric power station. But in a few short years, the Aswan High Dam and Suez Canal would become fused in a way that caused both to slip from their hands. In 1952 a 'Free Officers' coup d'état brought to power Gamal Abd al-Nasser, who would become a major figure in Pan-Arab, Pan-African and anti-colonial politics. This brought the Aswan High Dam to the heart of the Cold War. American officials in the early 1950s are said to have considered that Britain's 'colonial and imperialistic policies are millstones around our neck', but the two nations were sufficiently aligned that in the mid-1950s amid tensions over Nasser's relations with the Soviet bloc, the United States and Britain withdrew their funding offer for the Aswan High Dam.[47] In response, Nasser abruptly nationalised the Suez Canal to help finance the dam, later also closing it off by sinking a series of 'blockships' across the canal bed.[48] The Soviet Union stepped in with a loan to the Egyptian government instead. Fifty years earlier, British warships would have settled the matter. But this moment has been seen as the symbolic end to British imperial authority, when humiliatingly, a joint British, French and Israeli attack on Port Said was opposed not only by the USSR, but also by their American ally. Britain and France were obliged to withdraw altogether from the Suez and Nile region.

The Aswan High Dam and reservoir, which opened in 1970, finally terminated the natural flood of the Nile, replacing it with a regulated flow of water all year round. Turbines in the dam generated what at that time was the greatest kilowatt capacity in Africa, though today it is only one source of the brilliantly lit flower of the Nile seen from space.[49] As the entire pharaonic landscape of Aswan was about to be submerged under the vast Lake Nasser, this proved a route to some diplomatic repair work for Britain and France.[50] A flank of countries came to the aid of Egypt in the 1960s, through UNESCO, the cultural wing of the United Nations, helping to lift some of its epic archaeology above the shoreline of the lake. Egypt's riverside monuments in the process became rebranded as global property, opening up new tensions. As Amadou-Mahtar M'Bow, the Senegalese Director-General of Unesco put it: '. . . our generation is the first in history to perceive the totality of these works as an indivisible whole, each of them being considered as an integral part of a single universal heritage'.[51]

The Aswan Dam's construction uprooted over 50,000 Nubians, Egyptians and Sudanese from their homelands, a trend of displacement experienced on dammed rivers across the world as hydro-electricity became the master key to modern industrial development.[52] This has persisted as a feature of all the major rivers of this book – the huge human sacrifice in hard labour, enslavement, displacement and death that has gone into making waterways (natural and artificial) and irrigated land work effectively for national or imperial economies. From the Yangtze and Grand Canal to the Ganges and Mississippi, riverside communities have been subjugated in the name of the gods, empire, nation, 'the people', development, or other outsized concepts. Increasingly too the ecological costs of these river works have become clear.

The past two centuries have transformed the land, waterscapes and ecosystems of the Egyptian Nile. At some point in the nineteenth century, the last hippopotamus of the Egyptian Nile region had already quietly slipped away. The sacred ibis (*Threskiornis aethiopicus*) is also gone.[53] The many streams of the delta have been reduced to just two – the Rosetta and the Damietta branches. The year-round water from the Aswan Dam has allowed agriculture to expand many miles in both directions, from the arid lands west of Alexandria and eastwards towards the Sinai desert. While in some places land has been 'reclaimed' from the water for productive farming and urban expansion, other wetland ecosystems have emerged.[54] Along the Nile riverside once inundated for several months each year, plant-free sandy banks have given way to reedy swamp: now a winter home for the richly feathered purple heron

(*Ardea pururea*) and the elusive little bittern (*Ixobrychus minutus*), which in the springtime hides in the reedbeds and marshlands of the Danube and other northern rivers. The 340-mile-long Lake Nasser at Aswan now provides a huge freshwater refuge during winter months for birds from Eurasia and North Africa, and home to flocks of Egyptian geese (*Alopochen aegyptiacus*).[55]

The volume of silt journeying downstream has been drastically reduced by the Aswan High Dam, a situation compounded by lower rainfall in the Ethiopian highlands. One estimate suggests that the first Low Aswan Dam had already reduced the silt load each year from 200 million to 160 million tons. And when the Aswan High Dam first became operational in 1963, this number plunged further to 126 million tons. This period has seen the reversal of the process by which sediment-filled streams of the Nile delta raise land levels on the coast (progradation). Delta land is now sinking and the shoreline is in retreat, a phenomenon echoed but not yet fully understood on the Yangtze, Mississippi and other dammed rivers in recent decades. As coastal land subsides and sea levels rise, the life of the river and the fortunes of delta communities are closely tied.[56]

3
Source

'O World, how could you so conveniently have forgotten
that I, your first fountain, I your ever Ethiopia
I your first life still survive for you?'

Tseqaye Gabre-Medhin, 'Nile' (1997)[1]

When the Greek historian Herodotus met an Egyptian scribe who claimed to know the source of the Nile, he thought the man was joking. According to this scribe, the Nile rose between two mountains near Egypt's southern border. Flowing from 'springs . . . which are bottomless', these waters rose to the surface then divided into two, it was said: some headed north through Egypt; the rest streamed southwards towards Ethiopia. Armed with tales from his visit to Egypt around 450 BCE along with 'theories . . . of certain Greek thinkers', Herodotus concluded that the Nile started somewhere in the Sahara Desert. The source of the Nile was unknown, he said, only because the desert was so empty of people. 'The idea that it rises in snowy regions makes no sense at all,' he considered, 'as anyone capable of rational thought could realise.'[2] About 1,500 years later, the Arabic geographer Al-Biruni (973–c. 1052) also considered that at the source south of Egypt there could be 'no freezing of moist substances at all'. 'Falling dew' must be responsible for the water at its source in the 'Mountains of the Moon'. But there was only so much dew to go round. The upper Nile was linked to the rivers of Mesopotamia (Iraq): when the Nile water was high, it followed that the waters of the Tigris and Euphrates must be low.[3] As we have seen, Ancient Egyptians believed in a symbolic source at their southern border even though they knew that this stream arrived there from lands far away upstream. Contradictory, simultaneous ideas about the Nile are not confined to the distant past but are a persistent feature of the way people think about rivers. This is part of their symbolic richness and of their potential for political conflict.

This chapter is about the Nile River as a place where many different origin stories meet. Tales of the source of the Nile have become interwoven with others about the creation of the world and the baptism of Christ, celebrated each year at Epiphany. Nowhere do these streams meet more vividly than in the highlands of Ethiopia: the location of the source of the Blue Nile and the subject of this chapter.

The actual source of the world's longest river was a mystery until the nineteenth century. The Nile, we now know, has two sources in fact: a watery fork. The first, the White Nile (*Bahr al-Jebel*), rises far to the south-west in Uganda's great Lake Victoria.[4] Equatorial rains and highland springs keep the flow of the White Nile steady on its journey northwards until the South Sudan plains where it meets the Sudd ('blockage', in Arabic), a huge swamp over 35,000 square miles in size in the wet season, with a lattice of navigable channels: home to the antelope and Nile crocodile, the African buffalo and hippo – over a hundred species of mammals, a hundred of fish, and a vast array of birdlife. Many tonnes of water here evaporate into thin air in the summer sun. The water that remains takes many months to move through the swamp and into the White Nile to continue its journey northwards.[5]

The Blue Nile (*Abay*) approaches from the south-east, flowing out of Lake Tana in the Ethiopian highlands, another large lake, shallow and fringed with papyrus, over 1,200 square miles in area, with thirty-seven islands that are today home to 15,000 people.[6] Being fed by monsoon rains, the Blue Nile is far less predictable than the White Nile but provides around 60 per cent of the combined waters of the Blue and White that reach Aswan at Egypt's southern border.[7]

For a long time, the vast, complex geography of the Nile cast a spell that hid its origins. The Nile waters below Egypt's southern border created barriers both to knowledge and to military expansion. First, there were the hundreds of miles of rocky cataract river that hampered navigation upstream. And below Khartoum in the south-west was the 'water divide' of the Sudd. It was said that when Emperor Nero sent his Roman soldiers up the White Nile in the autumn of 61 CE, they turned back when they reached the Sudd, bearing tales of impassable clumps of floating vegetation.[8] So there was a lot of guesswork. Maps of Africa from medieval Europe showed speculative channels of the Nile running through the centre of a blank continent. The western headwaters appeared to be flowing through lakes from a source to the south, in the fabled Mountains of the Moon. Portuguese maps from the early 1500s also featured the rotund figure of Prester John: a legendary Christian king living in north-east Africa, reputedly descended from one of the Three Wise Men and ready to help the Crusaders in the Holy Land, if only he could be found. The distant mountains and lakes, the multiple streams, the moon, even a Christian king: these rumours may have been started by reliable narrators back in the mists of time.[9] But the myths took centuries to unravel. The course of the White Nile between Lake Victoria and the Nile in Egypt was finally traced by rivalrous British explorers John Hanning Speke and Richard Burton, in the 1850s.[10]

The source of the Nile was only half a mystery. The connection between the Nile in Egypt and the Blue Nile upstream in Ethiopia was known much earlier. There was long established traffic and trade between the upstream Blue Nile region and the Egyptian Nile. And there are old tales of Ethiopian kings threatening Muslim rulers downstream in Egypt. During a terrible famine in 1200–1201, the Sultan in Egypt is said to have sent a plea to Ethiopia to release the floodwaters the Ethiopians were thought to be holding back. In 1321 an Ethiopian envoy was sent downstream with a demand for the ruler to restore the churches of the Copts and a threat that the Nile waters would otherwise be diverted from his land. The emperor of Ethiopia in 1704 boasted that he could cut off the water to the Ottoman Pasha of Egypt.[11] In the next century, an English biblical geographer, C.T. Beke, sent unheeded warnings to the British prime minister about the consequences for British interests in Egypt should the Ethiopian headwaters fall into the wrong hands.[12] So a working knowledge of the upstream Nile as the source of Egypt's water supply long pre-dated modern hydrology, even if this also overestimated the powers of upstream rulers before the era of modern dam technology.

But the Nile was never just a water source. Long ago – nobody knows when – the upper Nile became fused with another kind of source: the story of the creation of Adam and Eve in the Garden of Eden from Genesis. The first book of the Hebrew Bible, Genesis may also have been the earliest to be written (around the early to middle second millennium BCE), and it fused origin stories of the Israelites with myths of Mesopotamia and Western Asia.[13] In Genesis, the Garden of Eden was watered by a river that 'when it left the garden it . . . branched into four streams', which were named. But only two of the named rivers could be identified with any certainty by a later audience: the Tigris and Euphrates of Mesopotamia (the land 'between two rivers' in today's Iraq). For a long time, people have tried to fill in the blanks of this semi-mythical waterscape. The mysterious Pishon, 'which encircles all the land of Havilah, where the gold is', has defied location. Then there was the Gihon, 'the one which encircles all the land of Cush'. References to the biblical Gihon as the Nile date back at least to the first century CE.[14] The Nile was also referred to as Gihon in early medieval maps. It appears as one of the four rivers of paradise on the mid-fifteenth-century Catalan-Estense map.[15] Was Kush in today's Sudan the biblical Cush? Was Ethiopia Cush?

Many other traditions ultimately flowed out of this Genesis story. In some Islamic traditions, the Nile was one of four rivers near, if not in, paradise. According to one tradition reported by an Egyptian Sunni Muslim scholar in the early 1400s, the Prophet Muhammad spoke with the Angel Gabriel at the farthest end of earthly knowledge, where he was shown the "'the Lote-tree beyond which none may pass'". Here, the Prophet said:

> There were four rivers, two hidden and two visible. I asked, 'What is this, O Gabriel?' He said, 'The two hidden rivers are rivers in Paradise. The two visible rivers are the Nile and the Euphrates.'[16]

The Venetian Marco Polo (1254–1324) recorded from his travels in Central Asia, India and China that the Gihon, Tigris and Euphrates flowed into the Caspian Sea, stemming from an Islamic tradition that identified the Gihon as the Amu Darya River (though none of these rivers flow to the Caspian Sea).[17]

Associations between Gihon and the Nile must have resonated early in Ethiopia, where Christianity first took root in the fourth century. According to a Byzantine tradition, one day in the early 300s two young Christian boys were travelling with a merchant and his men from the port city of Tyre (Roman Syria) when they were shipwrecked on the west coast of the Red Sea, then controlled by Ethiopia's powerful northern kingdom of Axum (or Aksum), in today's Tigray region. The merchant and his men were killed at once. But the two boys, Frumentius and Aedesius, were spared and taken to the Ethiopian court where they were kept on in the service of the king. When the Axumite king died, the queen asked the boys to remain until her son Ezana came of age, which they did. Aedesius later left Ethiopia but his companion, Frumentius (c. 300–c. 380), stayed on as a Christian missionary. Frumentius was later appointed as the first bishop (*abun*) of the Ethiopian Orthodox Tewahedo Church by the Coptic Patriarch in Alexandria on the Egyptian coast. Later still he was canonised as Saint Frumentius.

King Ezana (approximately r. 320–50), his most strategically important convert, established Christianity as Ethiopia's official religion, forging lasting religious and trade connections with Alexandria and the Greek-speaking world of the eastern Mediterranean. Translations of the Bible from Greek into Ethiopian *Ge'ez* followed in the fourth and fifth centuries.[18] And over time the Ethiopian Church navigated the changing regimes of its neighbours, including the Arab conquest in the 640s and the slow spread of Islam southwards into Nubia along the Nile and on the Red Sea coast. Axum's influence declined during the 600s, and the ruling dynasty shifted southwards around 800 CE to the Ethiopian highlands, taking Christianity with them.[19] This relocation coincidentally brought them close to the source of the Blue Nile.

The mountainous headwaters of the Blue Nile are an utterly different world from the desert-fringed Egyptian Nile. Here in Ethiopia's 'water tower', monsoon rains fall between April and September, beginning their journey northwards towards the Sudan and Egypt.[20] By the seventeenth century, the Ethiopian Emperor Susenyos (r. 1607–32) dominated the country from this highland region. As a member of the Solomonid Dynasty, Susenyos claimed a matchless lineage from Hebrew kings. Although established in the 1270s, this dynasty traced their descent over two thousand years from the Queen of Sheba and King Solomon, son of David (1 Kings 10:1–13). According to this tradition, the marriage of the queen and Solomon produced a son who travelled to Ethiopia taking with him the Ark of the Covenant.[21] But at this point in the seventeenth century, Susenyos needed military assistance. He turned to the Portuguese, who were offering their services to Christian Ethiopia in struggles with Ottoman forces. Portuguese firepower was accompanied by the soft power of merchants and Roman Catholic Jesuits. Susenyos' reign in the early 1600s saw a second wave of Iberian Jesuit priests and a charm offensive at his court, led by the (Spanish) Jesuit Pedro Páez. Emperor Susenyos furthered the alliance by converting to Roman Catholicism around 1612 and allowed Páez to build Catholic churches in his domain. The resourceful Páez also helped to build a palace for the king on the shore of Lake Tana. Stonemasons were imported from the west coast of India, where Portugal had a trading colony at Goa.[22]

Another palace built for Susenyos at Azäzo, south of Gondar, had fruit trees, a fountain and a water tank or sunken pool used for swimming and fishing; the whole was possibly inspired by India's Mughal palaces. Ingenious hydraulics caused water to flow down the walls and windows of a pavilion set in the middle of the pool. The Portuguese Jesuit Manoel de Almeida, in charge of the building, wanted the palace to seem like an earthly paradise (*fazer paraiso*).[23] We do not know whether this water tank was also used for Christian rituals of the court. In these small pools of water – like the water tanks of Coptic churches on the Egyptian Nile or the tanks and step wells of Islamic and Hindu elites in India – the symbolism of water and of rivers merge in ways that can't easily be pinned down. But somehow this only adds to water's symbolic richness. The mythic status of the Blue Nile has been built up over the centuries by thousands of stories.

Seductive tales of the Blue Nile region issued from Iberian travellers and writers during the early years of the European presence in Ethiopia. Francisco Alvarez, part of a Portuguese embassy in the 1520s, described to incredulous readers the rock-hewn churches of Lalibala (built by the twelfth- and thirteenth-century Zagwe Dynasty).[24] And in the early 1600s Iberian priests and officials began publishing eyewitness accounts of the ultimate source of the Blue Nile beyond Lake Tana: the Sakala Springs rising in Mount Gish to become the Gish Abay River, which flows up into the south-western shore of the great lake. It is said that the Jesuit Pedro Páez visited the Sakala Springs with Emperor Susenyos around the year 1615.[25] Soon afterwards also, the Jesuit Father Lobo provided a description: two springs 'a stone's cast distant from each other' issued from a hole in the mountainside. One spring was just over five foot in depth, wrote Lobo, or 'at least we could not get our plummet farther, perhaps because it was stopped by roots, for the whole place is full of trees'. The other spring was fathomless, like the one talked of long ago by the scribe of Herodotus: 'with a line of ten feet we could find no bottom, and were assured by the inhabitants that none ever had been found'.[26]

The Sakala Springs are still considered today a key source of the Nile. Gish Abay, or Gilgel Abay as it is called downstream, flows for over 50 miles and is estimated by hydrologists to supply around 60 per cent of the water reaching Lake Tana. Around forty other rivers and streams also flow into the lake, but its sole outlet is the Blue Nile, exiting near its south-eastern tip. Lake Tana provides about 8 per cent of the water that ultimately collects in the Nile on its journey northwards at Aswan.[27] Given these percentages, it takes an act of imagination to see the Sakala Springs as *the* source of the Nile, but this origin story has managed to withstand the scrutiny of science. Also tangled up in this story, though less susceptible to proof or disproof, is the Gihon River of the biblical garden. Another tradition has long held this river – Gish/Gilgel Abay – to bear the name of Gihon rather than the Nile itself.[28]

Accounts of the Ethiopian highlands and the headwaters of the Blue Nile flowed in rivulets out of Africa to distant audiences. One influential account of Ethiopia published by the Spanish Dominican Friar Luís de Urreta in the 1610s was based entirely on conversations with an Ethiopian traveller he met in Valencia, who went by the name of Don Juan Balthazar. Ethiopia was so full of riches, Urreta assured his readers, that in some places the ground shone with gold after rain.[29] These descriptions of Ethiopia's Mount Amara, it is thought, in turn formed part of the desk-based research for the writings of two Anglican clergymen: Samuel Purchas (c. 1577–1626) and Peter Heylyn (1599–1662). The visions of earthly paradise in these works subsequently found an echo in the account of Adam and Eve's fall and expulsion from Eden in *Paradise Lost* (1667/74) by the English Puritan poet, John Milton.[30] In this epic, allusion-filled description of the garden at the dawn of creation, only the most ardent reader can follow the labyrinthine journey through all the places where Eden was and where it was not. This Ethiopian paradise was listed by Milton under the places where Eden was not, while being identified as the source of the Nile:

> Nor where Abassin kings their issue guard,
> Mount Amara, though this by some supposed
> True Paradise under the Ethiop line
> By Nilus' head, enclosed with shining rock,
> A whole day's journey high, but wide remote
> From this Assyrian garden.[31]

While Europeans were weaving Ethiopia into their symbolic

landscape, back in the Lake Tana region Emperor Susenyos faced rebellion against his Catholic conversion and Portuguese alliance. At the highest level, Orthodox Christians and Roman Catholics were not on speaking terms. Doctrinal differences had pushed the two churches – one headquartered in Byzantium, the other in Rome – ever further apart until by 1054 they had excommunicated each other, and it stayed this way until the liberalising Vatican Council in 1965.[32] Resistance to foreign Roman Catholicism from Emperor Susenyos' subjects and the local Orthodox clergy was fierce and the conflict left many dead.[33] When Susenyos abdicated and gave way to his son Fasilides, this brought both the source of the Nile and the biblical Gihon back into Orthodox Christian hands.

The new Emperor Fasilides (r. 1632–67) kicked out the Portuguese Jesuits. Around 1636 he established the House of Gondar at the new palace of Fasil Ghebbi, north of Lake Tana in today's Amhara region. The palace survives to this day as a famed site for the Ethiopian celebration of Timkat (Epiphany). Here, Fasilides installed a large sunken bath, 50 by 30 metres, fed by a canal leading from the Qaha River (one of the streams flowing into Lake Tana's northern shore).[34] This may have always been intended for Epiphany, when the Orthodox Church celebrates the baptism of Jesus in the River Jordan (baptism being from the Greek, 'to dip, plunge, bathe').[35] In the time of Fasilides' grandson, Iyasu I (1682–1706), a French visitor to the court described a Timkat ritual as 'Gottas' or 'The Day of Washing' (probably from *id al ghitas*, or Arabic for Epiphany, which we saw on the Egyptian Nile). On this day, he said, the emperor went with his court to a palace near Gondar 'where there is a magnificent bason [sic] of water which serves for that pious ceremony'.[36]

The political influence of Gondar waned during the 1700s, but its sacred importance remained. In the reign of Emperor Tewodros II (r. 1855–68), the Solomonid imperial capital was moved south-east from Gondar to Dabra Tabor, with a fortress at Maqdala (today's Amba Mariam). In the 1880s, one in every six people in Gondar is said to have been a priest; there were forty-four churches in the city.[37] The very fabric of its buildings was sacred, according to a chronicle of the region during the time of the Solomonid emperor's declining relations with the Orthodox Church, with Gondar, and with the British. According to this *Goğğam Chronicle*, one day soldiers from the army of Emperor Tewodros came to Gondar and stripped its buildings for materials, even taking the crosses from the roofs of its churches. The chronicler saw this action as responsible for what happened next. When in 1868 Tewodros went to war with the British government, on the morning of the Battle of Maqdala, the chronicle relates that he and his men waited at the fortress gates with a newly forged cannon. But it failed to discharge as the British army approached. This was, says the chronicle, 'due to the anger of the arks of the Covenant, for it was made from the sacred utensils of Gondar'.[38] For context, Tewodros' men also faced over 13,000 soldiers from the British and Indian armies.[39] Tewodros shot himself rather than be taken alive.

This episode reminds us that it isn't only the Nile that is symbolically charged. Anything can be invested with meaning and magical properties, and equally become a source of conflict. The past confers a sacred 'aura': from sunken baths and 'sacred utensils' to artefacts raided from Maqdala still held by the British Museum, to the locks of hair taken from Tewodros and recently handed back to Ethiopia by Britain's National Army Museum, to Solomonid claims of a dynasty stretching back to the biblical King David, to the 1,700-year-old obelisk removed from Axum by occupying fascist Italian forces in the 1930s and returned in 2005; or the Egyptian obelisks still bringing their New Kingdom glamour to the banks of the Seine, Thames and Hudson rivers.[40] But none provide a continuous stream of magical connection to the past so effectively as rivers, with the Nile being perhaps the king of all sacred streams.

The poem 'Nile' published in 1997 by the Ethiopian writer Tseqaye Gabre-Medhin conveys this sense of Ethiopia as the source of all creation: 'I, your first fountain, I your ever Ethiopia'. This was written in the wake of spectacular discoveries of early hominins in the country reaching back over four million years ago, bringing a new creation story to Ethiopia as the 'cradle of humanity'.[41] But the poem also complains of a world that is careless with its debt to the Nile's sacred source. Even its neighbour downstream has embraced soulless hydrology:

> O Sudan, born out of the bosom of my being,
> how could you so conveniently count down
> in miserable billions of petty cubic yards
> the eternal drops of my life-giving Nile to you?[42]

But always sitting alongside the sacred history of the Nile has been a thoroughly utilitarian history. The creation of canals for trade or conquest was quite compatible, as we saw, with devotion to the gods of the river in Ancient Egypt. And Roman emperors on the Danube, Rhine and other rivers brought martial river gods to a new level, as we shall see in the next chapter. In our industrial and partially secular age, rivers have been harnessed relentlessly to irrigate cash crops and create energy to an extent that the titans of the ancient world could not have imagined. The damming of rivers is synonymous with economic development, and today there are over 35,000 dams across rivers on every continent except Antarctica.[43]

Ethiopia has been no more able to ignore the potential of rivers for energy and irrigation than any other country. Lake Tana was eventually engineered in the 1990s; its waters now enter the channel of the Blue Nile through Chara Chara weir, though its islands are still dotted with monasteries, including St Stephen's on Daga Island, where Emperor Fasilides lies alongside his ancestors.[44] The largest dam in Africa is currently nearing completion on the Blue Nile in Ethiopia, just south of its border with the Sudan. With the arrival of this Grand Ethiopian Renaissance Dam, Egypt can realistically be worried by the impacts of upstream water management. Around 90 per cent of Egypt's water supply comes from the Nile River (55 billion cubic metres each year).[45]

Even now, though, the Nile is not fully disenchanted. Dams started to go up on the Blue Nile in the twentieth century. British officials and cotton growers built the Senner Dam on the Blue Nile in Sudan in the 1920s to irrigate the region's rich 'black cotton' soil, and then turned their attentions to Lake Tana. Even as they did so, the British envoy Robert Cheeseman was visiting the sacred Sakala Springs and writing scholarly articles about the lake's religious history.[46] William Willcocks, the British water engineer behind the Aswan Low Dam (1899) and other colonial projects, was not only a scientist. While working in Iraq and Syria, he searched for the Garden of Eden in his spare time, casting an expert eye over the 'whole length of the Euphrates to see where a garden could be placed which could be irrigated by free flow through the twelve months of the year'.[47]

Today, great care is taken to maintain the Christian identity of the Sakala Springs that flow into Gish Abay as it begins its journey north to Lake Tana. Local priests act as gatekeepers. One of the springs has been encased in a metal pipe running through a church enclosure. Only those who are fasting and pure can enter this space, it is said, at risk of death.[48] Things are freer a short distance downstream. Here, within another church, the same spring is used for ablutions by both women and men; people come from all around with plastic containers to collect the holy water. Meanwhile, north of Lake Tana, at Fasilides' sunken bath, Christians of the Ethiopian Church still come at Timkat (Epiphany) to celebrate the baptism of Jesus in the Jordan, with the walls around the bath draped in the red, gold and green of the nation's flag.[49] At the other end of the Nile in Egypt, Coptic Christians today comprise 10–15 per cent of the population alongside a Sunni Muslim majority. Many still celebrate *Eid el Ghettas*, or the 'feast of immersion', at Epiphany by plunging into the waters of the Nile or neighbouring canals, at midnight on 19 January. Within living memory this has been a popular ritual shared among those of different faiths on the river, but current hostilities against Christians make this a potentially hazardous public ritual.[50]

The Nile still flows through different symbolic worlds, across dam technologies and across religious, ethnic borders and national borders. There are violent conflicts along stretches of the river and in the wider river basin. The Ethiopian government has recently been pitted against forces in Tigray, north of Amhara, and there is civil war in Sudan. The Nile River is part of global geopolitical forces that help to shape life and death along its banks. The river as the biblical Gihon sits uncomfortably with all this complexity. But tales of the source of the Nile and the paradise garden at the dawn of time do what origin stories are meant to do: simplify and tidy up the mess of history. Before drought, floods and violence, and before people make all the mistakes they will inevitably make, there is the perfect garden and the perfect spring. A single source for the Nile isn't true to hydrology or history but it remains a powerful vision for harmony.

River 2: Danube

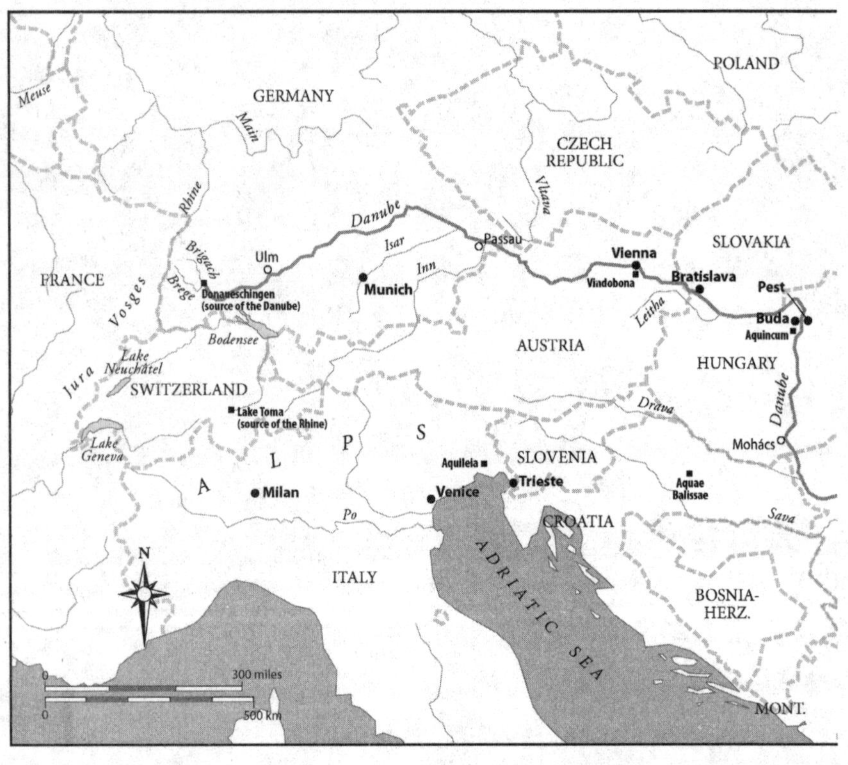

POLAND
GERMANY
Meuse
Main
CZECH
REPUBLIC
Vltava
Rhine
Danube
Passau
SLOVAKIA
Brigach
Isar
Ulm
Vienna
Inn
Bratislava
FRANCE
Munich
Vindobona
Pest
Vosges
Brege
Donaueschingen
(source of the Danube)
Leitha
Buda
Aquincum
Bodensee
AUSTRIA
Lake
Neuchâtel
HUNGARY
Jura
SWITZERLAND
Danube
Drava
Lake Toma
(source of the Rhine)
Lake
Geneva
A
L
P
S
Mohács
Aquileia
SLOVENIA
Trieste
Aquae
Balissae
Milan
Venice
Po
CROATIA
Sava
N
ITALY
ADRIATIC SEA
BOSNIA-
HERZ.
0
300 miles
0
500 km
MONT.

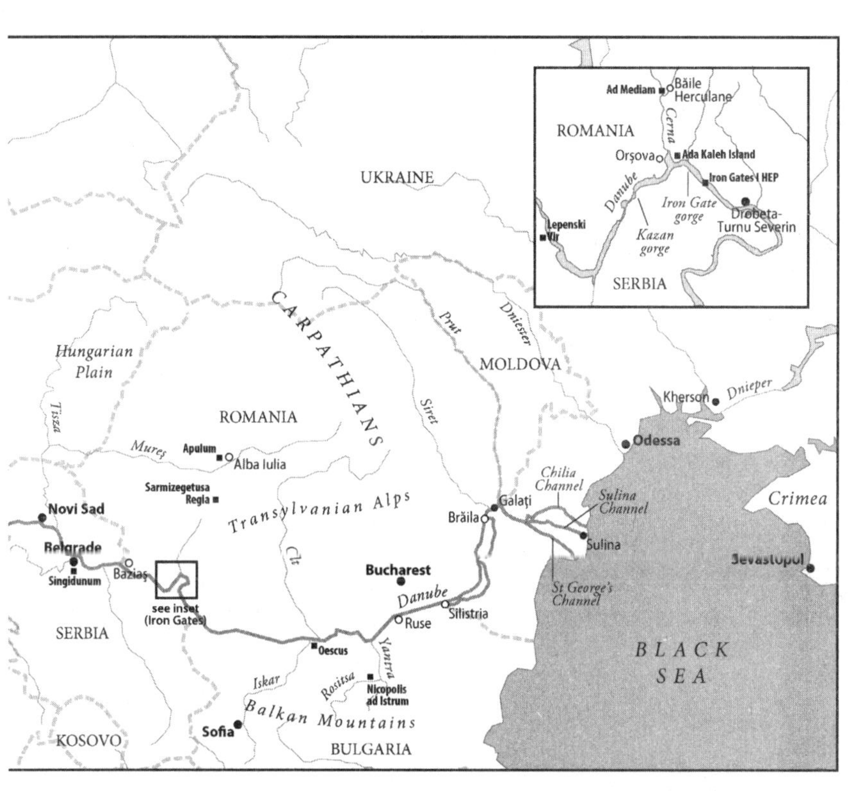

UKRAINE
MOLDOVA
ROMANIA
CARPATHIANS
Hungarian Plain
Tisza
Mureş
Apulum
Alba Iulia
Sarmizegetusa Regia
Transylvanian Alps
Novi Sad
Belgrade
Singidunum
Baziaş
see inset (Iron Gates)
SERBIA
KOSOVO
Olt
Bucharest
Danube
Ruse
Silistria
Oescus
Iskar
Rositsa
Yantra
Nicopolis ad Istrum
Balkan Mountains
Sofia
BULGARIA
Prut
Siret
Dniester
Brăila
Galaţi
Chilia Channel
Sulina Channel
Sulina
St George's Channel
Kherson
Dnieper
Odessa
Crimea
Sevastopol
BLACK SEA
Ad Mediam
Băile Herculane
Cerna
Orşova
Ada Kaleh Island
Iron Gates I HEP
Iron Gate gorge
Drobeta-Turnu Severin
Lepenski Vir
Kazan gorge
SERBIA

4
Corridors and Frontiers

> 'Germany is separated from Gaul, Rhaetia, and Pannonia, by the rivers Rhine and Danube; from Sarmatia and Dacia, by mountains and mutual dread.'
>
> Tacitus, *Germania* (97–98 CE)[1]

The Danube rises from two springs – Brege and Brigach – that meet near the town of Donaueschingen in the Black Forest in south-west Germany. Today the source is commemorated by a classical stone pool. Like a toddler prince in his shorts and blazer, this is the improbable infancy of a river that has grown up to cause much territorial heartache. Upstream lies a rival, 'hydrological' source of the river and a reclining stone god, Danuvius. From there, the river flows east, crossing first into Austria north of the Alps, with its northern tributaries bringing water from the mountains, and along the Hungary-Slovakia border towards Budapest. Dropping southwards through the Hungarian Plain and into Serbia, it then passes through a series of spectacular deep gorges known collectively as the Iron Gates, with Romania and the Carpathian Mountains to the north and the Balkans to the south-east.[2] It forms Romania's border with Bulgaria, before heading northwards to form a southern tip for Moldova and finally Ukraine where its three-part delta meets the Black Sea.

Although the river flows from the west, when people first came to the Danube region they probably arrived from the east, but little is known about them. The earliest settlements found on the Danube are at the great Djerdap Gorge, part of the Iron Gates, dating back to the mid-6000s BCE, on the Danube's southern, right bank (in direction of flow) in present-day Serbia. These were the hunter-gathering villagers of Lepenski Vir, who laid fish-like stone heads in the floors of their houses. They may have lived on this spot for up to eighty generations. What happened to them next we do not know. For thousands of years, people crossed in all directions through the Danube region, leaving only the barest traces of who they were or their direction of travel.[3]

On the bridge between this prehistory and early recorded history, some white noise developed about cultural distinctions between east and west, north and south. Western Europeans in the past few centuries of imperial success tended to make claims about being at the vanguard of civilisation. Partly to redress the balance perhaps, recent scholars have tended to stress the east-to-west direction of cultural travel, with Europe as 'the westerly excrescence of the continent of Asia', as archaeologist Barry Cunliffe put it, or 'the dregs of Eurasian history', in the words of the historian Felipe Fernández-Armesto.[4] The early evolution of farming and science, of writing, of the world religions: all rose in the east and spread westwards. For Cunliffe though, the intricate networks of rivers and long coastline of Europe were the making of it, encouraging mobility and technological innovation.[5] The Danube and its riverside occupies a key place in this picture as the 'middle European corridor', as an ancient path for migration and cultural exchange between the Black Sea and Atlantic Ocean, and with connected routes from perhaps as far away as the Yellow Sea on China's Pacific coast.[6]

For legal scholar Stephen Gorove in the 1960s, the Iron Gates were the 'historic gateway' through which 'the East' (Soviet Bloc) had 'come to challenge the West', while 'waves of Occidental culture and tradition' had 'penetrated . . . the depths of the mystical Orient'. This Cold War era was just the latest iteration of geopolitical tensions and rival cultural identities along the Danube. Frequently the left/right bank axis was also an important dividing line. The Iron Gate gorges, with their sublime stone walls rising from the river, were only one of many portals between different worlds along the Danube, between south and north, east and west. And like the cataract of the Nile, for much of the time this long rocky stretch of river was as much a barrier as a gateway.[7]

This chapter explores the way in which boundaries and corridors spread across the Danube during the Roman years, and what this meant for the inhabitants and territory along the river. The Danube was a meeting place and battleground for people vying for power. Rivers are a double-edged sword, especially for the locals. They provide water supply for humans, animals and agriculture, a transport route for trade and armies, and a level of defence. But as natural frontiers, they are also the obvious place to have a fight. And the Danube, flowing 1,770 miles across Europe, has been a magnet for warring parties.[8] It is less than half the length of the Nile though longer than the Egyptian portion of the Nile, and it too has never been occupied by a single power. This Roman era was also the time when the Danube, Rhine and other rivers became part of a web of cultural and imperial distinctions that continue to exert power up to today.

The names of rivers promise to provide clues to their early history that they don't always deliver. River names or 'hydronyms' are considered to be among the oldest words found in existing languages. But there is rarely agreement about their true meanings or origins, as in the case of the Thames and the Nile.[9] The Danube is one of the select few river names about which there seems to be a consensus. The root _*deh$_a$nu_ is said to be a Proto-Indo-European source for the word 'river'. This is found in the Sanskrit *Dānu* (river goddess), the Iranian *dānu*, and the names of the rivers Danube, Dnieper and Don. These Proto-Indo-Europeans were a group of people who spoke a common language, living perhaps 5,000 years ago or more. No one knows what they looked like, where they lived, or whether they were a group at all but simply traded with each other. There is no homeland or river to attach to them. Some say they were early farmers in Anatolia; others that they lived in the forest steppes of Ukraine and southern Russia. But nobody knows for sure. At some point they split up and went their separate ways. The only reason we know they ever existed is due to the many traces they left in languages scattered across Eurasia, from the Atlantic coast of Ireland to Asia. More than twelve language groups have been traced back to this single ancestral group, among them Celtic, Germanic (including English), Greek, Latin (including all the Romance languages), Slavic (Russian, Serbian and Ukrainian among others), Anatolian (Hittite), Sanskrit (including Hindi and Urdu), Iranian, and Tocharian from Central Asia's Silk Road.[10]

The argument for a common early language was first proposed on the banks of the Hooghly River in 1780s Calcutta, in a talk by the British official and Sanskrit expert, Sir William Jones.[11] Since this time, scholars have worked backwards through these languages to trace hundreds of root words that became diffused among the languages. So a Proto-Indo-European root connects 'estuary' or 'river mouth' in English to the Latin *ōstium* and the Russian *ustĭje*. The 'beaver' (English), once ubiquitous on rivers across Eurasia, is related via the shared Proto-Indo-European *bhébhrus* to the *bebru* of the Celtic Gauls, though in the Sanskrit *babhrú* in India refers to the mongoose. The *weh*$_x$*p*-, or 'body of water', of Proto-Indo-European is linked to *ùpė* in Lithuanian (Baltic) and to *wappu*- for 'wadi' or 'riverbank' in ancient Hittite, the oldest of the Indo-European languages.[12] 'Water' itself is one of only sixteen words thought to be shared (as so-called 'cognates') across all of the twelve main language groups from an ancient original: **wódr̥*.[13]

It seems likely that the Danube once flowed through this world of prehistoric words. But by the time we pick up this story in the Roman era, the descendants of the Proto-Indo-Europeans were strangers who couldn't understand each other. The Greeks had coined the term 'barbarian' for those who didn't speak Greek, and the Romans were using it liberally for those beyond their borders and their uncivilised ways, and to subject people within their own empire. Even the rivers of Rome's empire came to be seen as superior to other rivers, such as the waters of 'the barbarian Neckar and Main', as one Roman writer called these right-bank Rhine tributaries, though these too partly flowed through the empire.[14]

Rome was an obscure city until the sixth century BCE, dominated by the Etruscans to the north. But Romans came to eclipse all their neighbours. By the time they headed north out of the Italian Peninsula into the lands beyond the Alps and into the eastern Mediterranean in the first century BCE, they had already conquered Greece and the stronghold of Carthage on North Africa's coast. Between 58 and 51 BCE, Julius Caesar claimed Gaul (the territory between the Pyrenees mountains in the south and the River Rhine in the north) for Rome.[15] It was from here that he sailed to Britain in 55 and 54 BCE, leaving a challenge for later rulers to follow up, as we shall see in the chapters on the Thames. Caesar returned to Italy from Gaul in 49 BCE brimming with confidence, famously 'crossing the Rubicon' with his army – the river in north-east Italy where it was customary to disband – and moving on to Rome, where he assumed imperial powers and transformed Roman leadership forever. It was Octavian (later, Augustus Caesar), Caesar's adopted successor, who shortly after Caesar's assassination in 44 BCE took Rome to the Danube. Defeating his rival Mark Anthony and Cleopatra to conquer Egypt in 30 BCE, Octavian and his successors moved into regions south of the Danube over the next decades, securing the Alpine region of Raetia, together with Noricum, Pannonia and Moesia, an area roughly between the Drina (a right-bank tributary of the Danube) and the Black Sea, in which the long-forgotten settlement of Lepenski Vir lay buried by the riverside.[16]

The Danube River became interlocked with the Rhine as Rome's heavily fortified northern frontier, or 'limes', snaked along their banks. Plugging the gap between these two rivers was an occupied region: the *Agri Decumates*.[17] Only strong resistance from local tribes prevented Roman colonisation of lands north of the Rhine and along the Elbe River in the first century CE. Roman power became concentrated especially south of the Rhine and south of the Danube.

Like other conquerors of the ancient world, Romans used rivers to measure their imperial reach across these vast territories. And they too were prone to exaggeration. As a speech in praise of the Emperor Maximian put it in the 290s CE:

> The Rhine, the Danube, the Nile and the Tigris with its twin the Euphrates and the two Oceans where the sun sets and rises and whatever lands, rivers and shores are between them are as . . . common to you as the daylight . . .[18]

These weren't simply channels of water. By the time Romans encountered the rivers of their vast empire, many already had a long history of myth and legend inherited from the Greeks, their conquered heroes. Much of this pantheon of river gods, or *potomai*, was recorded in the *Theogeny*, written in the late 700s/ early 600s BCE by Hesiod who, like Homer, may have been part of the very first generation of Greek writers to write down stories from oral traditions. The *Theogeny* listed the lower Danube – the 'beautiful-flowing Ister' – alongside the Nile and other rivers descended from Tethys and Ocean, the Titan offspring of the union of Earth and Sky. Over time, the Ister came to be recognised as the same river that the Romans called Danuvius, upstream.[19] While the people of the ancient Nile worshipped localised river gods who lived right there on their own river, such as Hapi in his cave and the deities of the island of Elephantine, the Romans were more like the Greeks, who collected river gods like souvenirs during their conquests and wove them into a wider symbolic universe. By the time Octavian was expanding into the Danube region, the Roman poet Ovid (43 BCE–17/18 CE) was writing stories of these gods in his *Metamorphoses*, while in exile on the Black Sea coast at Tomis (today's Constanta, south of the Danube delta). The rivers in Ovid's dangerous world of overbearing Graeco-Roman gods were shapeshifters. There is the 'clearest stream in Phrygia', formed by tears shed by woodland creatures when Apollo was flayed alive by the satyr Marsyas; or the nymph Arethusa – goddess of fountains – changed by the goddess Diana first into a fog, then a stream, then rising a great distance away as a sacred spring to escape the relentless attentions of the river god Alpheus. When

Phaëton insists on driving the chariot of his father Apollo – the sun god – and loses control of it when flying too close to the sun, the Ister is one of several famous rivers, along with the Ganges and 'Euphrates in Babylon', to be set alight by the scorching heat of his flailing wings. Egypt's river runs dry and conceals its source:

> Nile flees in fear to earth's most distant place
> and hides his head, which still remains concealed.
> Its seven mouths fill up with dust and empty,
> seven beds without a stream.[20]

By contrast, in the hands of Roman emperors, sculptors and coin makers, the river gods of their conquered Roman territories became a corporate brand. They acquired a homogenous quality, typically represented, like Danuvius, as the reclining figure of a bearded statesman with flowing hair, a six-pack of abdominal muscles, and a priapic cornucopia of harvest fruit, though some possessed additional characteristics, like the 'two-horned Rhine', or Nilus with his sixteen cherubs. And, like the Nile gods of Dynastic Egypt – but unlike Ovid's deities – Rome's river gods were always on the side of the powerful.[21]

Roman control of the land south of the Rhine and Danube allowed them to co-opt existing trade routes that passed through this region. They were able to command the trade in amber (*glesum* in Germanic), for example, by which the unworked material was transported south from the Baltic Sea along the ancient 'amber roads'; the well-travelled streams and valleys of the Elbe, Oder and Vistula rivers. The city of Aquileia on the Adriatic Sea became the epicentre for skilled amber carvers. Writing in *Germania* (c. 98 CE), the Roman politician and historian Tacitus claimed that amber '[f]or a long time . . . lay amidst the other jetsam, until our luxury made its reputation'. Of those gathering amber on the Baltic's south coast, he noted an industriousness and 'patience quite unusual among the typically lazy Germans' (referring to people between the Rhine and the Baltic). They were, he said, the 'only people to collect the amber . . . in the shallows'; although, he added, '[a]s you would expect of barbarians . . . they never asked . . . what it is or how it is produced'. In fact, the trade in amber between the Baltic and Mediterranean dated back at least to 1600 BCE, though the Romans took the trade to new levels. So great was their love of this resin that a craze for amber-coloured hair to match their jewellery swept through the ranks of women from first-century Roman high society.[22]

With their written language, the Romans had a great advantage over the people they encountered in Europe with their mostly oral cultures, in their ability to 'control the narrative'. There is nothing approaching the prodigious material culture left by the Egyptians on the Nile to tell us what those who lived around the Danube and other rivers of the Roman Empire thought and believed about their world. Their occupation buried or Romanised much of what came before. It is easier to pin down the geographical outlines of the Roman provinces and their fortifications than to understand the people who lived there. Old maps of the Roman Empire, like those in Shepherd's *Historical Atlas* (1911), show the names of regional pre-Roman groups that may be semi-mythical: from the Batavians at the Rhine estuary by the North Sea to the Getae of the lower Danube.[23]

At sacred springs it is possible to see glimpses of the people who were there before the Romans. The thermal spring of Ad Mediam in today's Romania retains evidence of settlement and worship long before the Romans occupied Dacia. Before and after the Romans developed the thermal springs at Aquae Balissae (between the Sava and Drava rivers in Croatia), Latin-inflected personal names found on inscriptions suggest a settlement of the Pannonian-Celtic *Iasi* people. The Roman city of Aquincum (today's Budapest, situated at a cluster of hot and cold springs) was probably already a settlement of the Celtic *Eravisci* people.[24] Romans developed pre-existing sacred springs all across the empire, such as those of *Dea Sequana* at the source of the River Seine near Dijon (Burgundy), where 400 pre-Roman votive wooden body parts – heads, limbs and stomachs – have been found in the wet ground, by which people may have appealed for relief from pains and disease of every kind.[25]

But the stamp of Roman culture on the Danube and other rivers of the empire was laid down brick by brick, making it hard to see what was there before. Many of today's major Danubian cities sit on fortresses built for Roman legions on the riverbanks: from Singidunum in Moesia (today Serbia's capital, Belgrade) to Aquincum (Budapest) in Lower Pannonia and Vindobona in Upper Pannonia (Vienna), the plague-ridden base where Marcus Aurelius fought the Marcomanni, or 'border' people, north of the Danube.[26]

Water infrastructure for drinking, bathing and irrigation was also a key feature of this Roman real estate. Public baths were plumbed into every Roman fort and city, with water sometimes transported over great distances.[27] Over 1,300 Roman aqueducts have been identified across the Mediterranean region by a recent survey.[28] The most famous are arched, multi-tiered structures spanning river valleys with effortless grandeur, like the Pont du Gard of southern France. But aqueducts went up everywhere from Crocodilopolis in Egypt's marshy Fayum to Longovicium in England's County Durham; from Carthage on the Tunisian coast to the subterranean Gadara Aqueduct in Jordan. The Romans exploited river water, well water and hot springs or thermae in Bulgaria, fed by deep set thermo-aquifers.[29]

No single Roman left more of a mark on the Danube River than the Andalucian-born Emperor Trajan (r. 98–117), the same ruler who had also revived the Persian canal between the Nile and the Red Sea. Rome's borders expanded under this pugnacious leader, reaching as far east as Northern Mesopotamia. The Trajan era was therefore the worst time for Dacian forces on the Danube's north bank to launch a series of raids across the river into Roman territory. Trajan personally saw to it that the Dacians (approximately from today's Romania) were crushed in battle in 106 CE.[30] A column with over a thousand tonnes of Luna marble stands in Rome today in what was once the Temple of the Divine Trajan, designed by Apollodorus of Damascus. Topped by the bronze figure of Trajan himself, near its base is the god of the Danube, his arms resting on the rippling surface as he watches the march of Roman legions across a pontoon bridge to the north bank. Above this are scenes of fighting and the surrender of the Dacians; their severed heads presented to the emperor; the suicide of their leader Decebalus; and the loading of Dacian women and children onto boats towards unknown fates south of the river. A Trajan-era coin shows the god Danuvius standing with one knee pinning down the cowering female figure of Dacia, with one hand around her throat.[31]

All Dacia's riches thereby fell into Roman hands: their slaves and salt works, rivers and mountain passes, the gold and salt route from the Carpathian Mountains to the Tisza River on Dacia's western border. Dacia was one of Rome's more short-lived territories and its only province wholly north of the Danube.[32] But there are relatively few inscriptions in the region to suggest the survival of Dacian elites or their participation in administering the new colony, as happened elsewhere. Traces of a Dacian language are found in some place names and personal names. But this was overlain by the Romance, Latinised language that survives today like other regions with a much longer Roman occupation. Perhaps up to 25 Dacian words have been linked so far to the earlier Indo-European.[33] A veil of obscurity descended over the belief systems of the conquered people over time. Pre-Roman traces left today, such as the apparently sacred site at Sarmizegetusa Regia in the Carpathian Mountains, have become a focus of national pride and intensive archaeology in Romania. The deities of the Roman world poured into Dacia, though along with the Roman staples – like Jupiter and Diana – were the fusion gods of Rome's multi-ethnic armies, such as Jupiter Dolichenus, an echo of a Syrian god, and Mithras the bull-slayer, possibly of Persian origin. No fewer than fifty Mithraic structures have been found at Roman-era Apulum (today's Alba Iulia) on Romania's Mureş River.[34]

To tame the Danube and the people on its north bank, Trajan determined to develop the region below the Iron Gates. From Apollodorus of Damascus he commissioned a bridge here where the river became shallow and wide, and using skilled Moesian units he renewed a military road and towpath cut into the rocks along the southern riverside. Upstream, he built canals to bypass the rapids of the gorge region. A stone from this era, the *Tabula Trajana* commemorating the emperor's work, is fixed by the riverside today. Another tablet found during the building of a hydroelectric power station at the Iron Gates in the 1960s celebrates the canal of Trajan, which 'because of the danger of cataracts diverted the river and made navigation on the Danube safe'. These memorials have mostly outlived the structures they recorded.[35] South of the river, Trajan built a new city, *Nicopolis ad Istrum* (Victory on the Danube), to defend the region between the Danube and the Balkan Mountains. No fewer than three aqueducts supplied this thriving centre. Ister, god of the lower Danube, was displayed on coins struck in the city. Atilla the Hun would later destroy Nicopolis, this city of victory, in the 400s.[36]

Just as river borders helped to create the Roman Empire, their dissolution was part of its unravelling. Rome's river boundaries on the Danube and Rhine held more or less for over 350 years, though the province of Dacia north of the river was abandoned in the 270s to consolidate Rome's northern boundary.[37] But river crossings into Roman territory from the late fourth century have become key set pieces in the story of the fall of the Roman Empire, though there are competing accounts of these events. Who crossed the rivers, and why? What caused the crumbling of Roman defences all over Europe after the late 200s? Was the Rhine frozen over in the deep midwinter of 406? Did the empire fall or was it pushed? For some, Persian pressure on Rome's borders caused the empire to divide between Western and Eastern wings in 395, leaving it vulnerable. Some consider that armies of Huns in the late 300s and early 400s may have created a crush of people on the empire's northern river borders of the Rhine and Danube, before different groups eventually broke through.[38] Some say climate change played a part. Rising temperatures in the fourth century caused drought and political upheaval in China and the Huns' westward shift away from the arid Mongolian steppe, under the brutally effective Attila

(r. 434–53), knocking down dominoes across central and western Europe. Others believe that Rome brought about its own collapse. Internal rivalries eventually fractured the empire.[39]

The identity of the people who crossed Rome's border rivers is also much debated. One tradition has it that the fourth and fifth century was a period of great migration in the region: tribes with cohesive identities were on the move. Some say groups of ethnically 'German' people expanded across the Rhine and upper Danube region, settling down to become the core of 'successor states' and Germanic medieval kingdoms. For others, 'Germanic' ethnicity, like that of 'the Celt', is the stuff of historical myth, based on stereotypes and speculations from Roman writers. Those who crossed the rivers instead had mixed, fluid, and probably at this point unknowable ethnic identities; they were swept up in the wake of short-term military alliances and border skirmishes, with little lasting impact. Disagreements about long-past migrations are all the sharper because of Nazi Germany's claims to a historic Germanic ethnic identity, which continue to live on today.[40]

The Danube crossings may have happened something like this. In the year 376 CE, groups of Goths moved south across the Danube into Roman territory. The Goths (another group with an Indo-European language) are of disputed origins but may have moved from the Black Sea region into post-Roman Dacia. They seem to have crossed the river by agreement with Roman officials, but then rebelled.[41] The Gothic Wars saw a crushing defeat of Roman forces at the Battle of Adrianople in 378 in their province of Thracia (later Turkey's Erdine) and the death of the Emperor Valens. Looking for land and *la dolce vita* within the empire, the Goths established a temporary peace. Then under the Gothic-Roman leader Alaric the Visigoth (r. 395–410) they rebelled once more, sacking Rome and stripping its riches: the first conquest of the Eternal City but not the last. In time, groups of Goths settled in Gaul (roughly, France) and then moved on to Spain, until they were unseated by the rising power of the Umayyads (already established by then as Egypt's ruling Caliphate).[42]

The second crossing of the Danube, that of 31 December 406 (or 405) CE, saw armed groups crossing the Rhine into Gaul. This one took the imperial army by surprise, preoccupied by a thousand distractions. Tradition records these river crossers as Alans, Sueves and Vandals, possibly followed by Franks and Burgundians.[43] Whoever they were, by this point effective Roman river limes had passed out of living memory. Rome itself was to be attacked once again in 455 by the infamous Vandals (whose origins, too, are uncertain but perhaps they came from North Africa). Two decades later, in 476, the last of the Roman emperors, Romulus Augustulus, was overthrown, bringing an end to the Western Empire, while in the east the Byzantine Roman Empire continued for another thousand years at Constantinople (today's Istanbul).[44]

Rome's 'barbarians' and Romanised subjects living in the former Danube-Rhine borderlands forged new alliances and enmities in the centuries that followed. The rivers of the region became part of origin stories for new ethnic identities and ambitious nation states, from French (Bourbon and Napoleonic) claims to Gaul's historic northern limit at the Rhine, to nineteenth-century arguments for the Rhine (both sides) as 'Germany's river', and Romania's recent invocation of an ancient Dacian identity along the Danube and its northern tributaries. In 2004 a gigantic 40-metre head of Decebalus, the vanquished Dacian strongman, was carved into rock at the Iron Gates, reviving a half-dead tradition of cartoon-like images of military strength on the Danube.

Debates about identity and civilisation are today very much still alive on this long river flowing across Europe to the Black Sea at the symbolic boundary between Europe and Asia. The next two chapters look at how the Danube evolved as a transboundary river and place of rival empires up to the present day.

5
Gods of the Transboundary River

'The rashness of the Turks seemed to me quite remarkable; they never hesitated to continue their voyage in spite of the densest darkness, the absence of any moon and the violent gales. . . . In fact, on one occasion part of the deck was carried away with a loud crash, which caused me to spring from my bed and admonish the sailors to be more careful. Their only reply was to shout out "*Alaure*", that is, "God will protect us" . . . .'

Journey from Buda to Belgrade in *The Turkish Letters of Ogier Ghiselin de Busbecq Imperial Ambassador at Constantinople 1554–1562*, trans. Edward Seymour Forster (1927)[1]

On the morning of 27 September 1896, three monarchs stepped onto an imperial steamer from a quay on the Danube at Orşova, the south-west Romanian town just upstream from the Iron Gates gorge. The first was the Habsburg Emperor Franz Joseph of Austria-Hungary. From Romania, on the Danube's left (north) bank, was King Carol I Hohenzollern-Sigmaringen, a monarch imported three decades earlier from a German royal family. Here he was dressed in the uniform of his Austro-Hungarian regiment. From Serbia, on the river's right (south) bank, was King Alexander I (Obrenović).[2] Flying in 'immense profusion' on the Romanian bank were the flags of Austria, Hungary, Romania and Serbia and cannons fired from all sides. The steamer set off with a flotilla of vessels downstream past a fortress on the river island of New Orşova, where the soldiers of an Austro-Hungarian garrison offered a salute. Two flags fluttered above their heads. On the island fortress was the flag of the house of Habsburg. Hoisted from the mosque nearby was the star and waning crescent moon of the Ottoman Empire.

The occasion was the opening of the Iron Gates canals, built by Austria-Hungary, also known as the Habsburg 'Dual Monarchy' which had ruled as one since 1867. These were mile-long navigation channels dug out from the riverbed, one along each bank and separated from the main river by a low wall. They were built to overcome the treacherous rocks of the Danube through the miles of the gorges that plagued navigation between the middle and lower river. The ceremony also marked a new moment in power struggles along the Danube that had been ongoing between the Ottomans and Habsburgs since the 1300s. The island of New Orşova – known as Adakale (castle island) to the Ottomans – may have been first occupied by them in the early 1400s; it changed hands many times between the Habsburgs and Ottoman rivals over the centuries.[3] Since 1878 it had been under occupation by Austria-Hungary. The Congress of Berlin of that year had granted shipping taxes to the Habsburgs to fund the Iron Gates canals.[4] It had also formally recognised the independence of Romania and Serbia from Ottoman control. For the Ottoman soldiers looking on from the island, this spectacle of flags and cannons must have been a galling sight.

On board the steamer, a benediction for the canals was given by a Hungarian Roman Catholic bishop, though in this part of the river they were deep in Orthodox Christian territory. The royal steamer passed through a garland of flowers into the canal on the downstream side. Emerging at the other end, the monarchs proceeded to a banquet at the site of ancient springs the Romans had called *Ad Medium*, and now the spa palace of *Herkulesbad* (Baths of Hercules) on Romania's Cerna tributary. There, Emperor Franz Joseph welcomed his fellow monarchs from 'the two friendly States whose shores, washed by the waters of the Danube, symbolise in their mutual proximity the community of our interests'.[5] Like Emperor Trajan many centuries before him, Franz Joseph confidently announced the end of the Iron Gates navigation problem: '[t]he last hindrances which stood in the way of free traffic along the course of this great stream are removed'. It was later reported that Austria-Hungary was aware of design weaknesses in the canals but hadn't fixed them since the Romanian and Russian grain trade were likely to be the main beneficiaries. For now, the monarchs sealed their friendship with toasts drunk from goblets of gold provided by the Hungarian government, and then went their separate ways.[6]

This apparent harmony unravelled badly over the next twenty years. By 1903, King Alexander of Serbia was dead, assassinated along with his wife by officers from his own army due to his excessive deference to Austria-Hungary.[7] On 28 June 1914 the Emperor Franz Joseph's nephew, and heir to the Austro-Hungarian throne, Archduke Franz Ferdinand and his wife Sophie, Duchess of Hohenberg, were shot dead on a visit to Sarajevo (Bosnia-Herzegovina) by the student Gavrilo Princip, a Bosnian Serb nationalist. One month later, the First World War began. On one side were Austria-Hungary, Germany and, strangely, the Ottoman Sublime Porte. On the 'Allies' side at various points were Britain, France, Italy, Romania, Russia, Serbia and (from 1917) the United States. In the conflict that followed, 1.2 million men died fighting on the Austro-Hungarian side.[8] Although the causes of the First World War are notoriously complex, some of the tensions that led to it were played out on the Danube River in the previous centuries. This chapter looks at how the shifting borders and allegiances of the Danube contributed to these unfolding events.

Some rivers have become part of the national identity of the countries through which they flow. The Volga is 'Russia's river'. In literature, art and music, its people and boatmen (even women) were part of Russia's unifying nineteenth-century myth, a natural artery that sanctified its imperial expansion to the south.[9] The Thames is often called 'England's River', however annoying this is for those living near other English rivers. The people of the Danube have always had to share their river and this has rarely been achieved on equal terms. Some 1,400 years after the fall of the Western Roman Empire in 476, the Danube was still a world of borders and fortresses, but with different frontiers, actors and rules of the game.

This chapter explores the Danube as a transboundary river, a fragmented territorial and cultural space. Water expert David Kinnersley once referred to people living along rivers as 'involuntary neighbours': showing how they are tied together by shared water supplies, flood hazards, flows of pollution and transport routes. The word 'river' itself is a root for 'rival', deriving from the Latin '*rīvālis*', defined by the *Oxford English Dictionary* as '(originally) person living on the opposite bank of a stream from another, person who is in pursuit of the same object as another'.[10] The 'shores, washed by the waters of the Danube' referred to by Franz Joseph did create a community of a kind but not a 'community of our interests'. This was more frequently a case of competing interests nestled along the banks.

The chapter looks firstly at the two dominant land empires of the early modern Danube: Habsburg Austria-Hungary and the Ottoman Empire. Secondly, it explores how the geopolitical world around the river shifted as new players arrived, including imperial Russia on the Danube basin's eastern flank, new riparian nation states and competing Western European powers. Thirdly, it returns to the island of Adakale where we started, as both land empires headed for a fall.

We begin in Rome in 1651, as Pope Innocent X saw his new sculpture – Gian Lorenzo Bernini's *Fountain of the Four Rivers* – go up in the Piazza Navona. At its centre was a granite obelisk dating from the time of Roman rule on the Nile – a copy of an Egyptian original that had been commissioned by the Emperor Domitian. This pagan obelisk had been reinvented, topped by a dove from the family arms of the Pope. At its base were four stone river gods in the classical Roman style, representing the known continents of Africa (Nile), the Americas (Rio de la Plata), Asia (Ganges) and Europe – represented not by Rome's own River Tiber but the Danube. From its seat in Vienna on the banks of the Danube, the Habsburg Holy Roman Empire had been at the heart of the recent Catholic defence against Protestant forces in the Thirty Years War (1618–48). The god of the Danube, reaching back to touch the papal arms, was claimed understandably enough for the Catholics. What this ignored, however, was the presence of Muslims on the river just downstream from Vienna.[11] The lower Danube was an Ottoman river that had very little to do with the Pope. Over time, too, new identities, homelands and power blocs emerged or became more visible, involving not just Roman Catholics and Sunni Muslim Ottomans, but also Orthodox Christians, Jews, Pan-Slavs and fervent nationalists.

The Danube River was woven into the histories of two great Central European empires across six centuries from the 1300s to the 1900s. Upstream were the Habsburgs, a wildly successful ruling family who had begun their dynastic life at the Habsburg Castle in Switzerland's upper Rhine River basin in the ninth century. They ended up with two family wings from the 1500s. There were the Spanish Habsburgs, a great beast that incorporated among other places the Low Countries on the North Sea coast and the Spanish America. And there were the Austro-Hungarian Habsburgs who married and fought their way to the crowns of Central Europe. Their Habsburg Empire and the Holy Roman Empire – an ambiguous, high-status Roman Catholic territory dating back to King Charlemagne – both radiated out from Vienna on the left bank of the middle Danube for many centuries. When Hungary (and, with it, Croatia) demanded autonomy in 1867, Austria-Hungary became the so-called Dual Monarchy; two semi-detached royal houses separated along the Leitha tributary, with Austria in the driving seat.[12]

The Ottomans had already begun their move on the lower Danube by the time they captured the Roman Empire's eastern capital at Byzantium (Constantinople) on the Black Sea in 1453. Early Ottoman fortresses were built on the right-bank cities of Silistria and Ruse in the late 1300s, in today's Bulgaria. The Balkan regions – what would later become Serbia and Bosnia-Herzegovina – were partially secured by the mid-fifteenth century, and the two fertile territories on the lower Danube's left bank: Wallachia and Moldavia.[13] It was Suleyman the Magnificent who led the

Ottomans deep into Central Europe. The personable Suleyman was known for his fine ways. Foreign ambassadors standing before the Sultan's throne at the Sublime Porte couldn't help but be distracted by the seat beside him, occupied by a golden helmet, Venetian-made, encrusted with diamonds, rubies, pearls, turquoise and emerald, and topped with technicolour plumage.[14] Just a few years after his father's Ottoman conquest of the Nile, Suleyman took Belgrade (Serbia) at the Danube-Sava confluence on the right bank: 'the key to all Central Europe'.[15] The miraculous capacity of the Ottomans at this time to exploit any weakness was described by the sixteenth-century Habsburg ambassador, Ogier Ghiselin de Busbecq, like 'mighty rivers, swollen with rain, which, if they can trickle through at any point in the banks, spread through the breach and cause infinite destruction'.[16] The next to fall were Hungarian cities, including Buda facing Pest across the Danube: a massive blow at the heart of Habsburg Central Europe. Ottoman westward advances stalled at the gates of Vienna in 1529 and again in 1683, but they remained embedded in the middle Danube – especially on its southern shore – and the two empires had to share the Danube.[17] But their approach to it was strikingly different.

At Budapest, the Ottomans rebuilt the city to their own liking, installing mosques and baths at the ancient geothermal springs. On Buda's hilly right bank, Ottoman officials lowered themselves into pools of warm sulphurous liquid all year round, even when the water outside slowed to a halt in the ice-bound Danube. The small-scale holy war rumbling away on this part of the river is suggested by a map of Buda made for the Flemish-German atlas *Civitates Orbis Terrarum* (1617). This bird's-eye view shows the walled cities of Buda and Pest linked across the Danube by a pontoon bridge of boats. Rising above Buda is a mosque. Formerly the Church of the Holy Virgin, this was now a site of 'Mohammedan abominations' according to the map's commentary. In the foreground above Pest a finely dressed Pasha, in a cobalt-blue turban bigger than the matching blue domes of the mosques, speaks with a subordinate, his temple pierced by feathers, an animal-skin cape slung over his shoulder and a sabre in his belt. The subordinate is a Deli, we are told – the Ottoman bodyguards known for acts of mad daring and loyalty – or as the map's cartouche put it 'a barbaric tribe among the Turks'. Beyond Buda's fortified walls vineyards climb lush hills to the west; and on the right-hand side of the map, the river flows upstream round an orderly pastoral scene on Margaret Island. Cannon fire from fortresses on the walls of Buda suggest a city under threat – the main reason why the wealth of Egypt was needed to cross-subsidise this hard-to-defend city.[18]

The balance of power on the Danube River was altered by the Habsburgs' formation of new alliances in the late 1600s, in the form of the so-called 'Holy League', comprised of the Habsburgs, Venice and Russia, among others.[19] Together the League defeated Ottoman forces at Budapest in the 1680s and pushed their stronghold downstream on the river, transforming the world of the middle Danube.

In the centuries that followed, the Austrian state put a significant amount of investment into the river. From the 1820s and 1830s, commercial operations linked riverside cities as steamboats puttered between Vienna and Pest (left bank), taking in the majestic Danube Bend at 10 to 12 miles an hour downstream; half the speed for the return journey against the current.[20] By the 1820s steamboats were churning up rivers all over the world, gobbling trees and later coal as transport entered the carbon age: part of a wide tourist network that included the steamboats with enslaved crews plying the rivers of the Mississippi basin. Travel tips were published for international audiences. As an 1833 *Pocket Book for Conversation* put it: 'Travelling in steam boats is very agreeable . . . particularly so for parties of pleasure, on large rivers such as the Rhine, the Danube, the Loire, the Thames, the Delaware, the Ohio, &c.' Passengers could sleep comfortably, lounge in cabins with carpeted floors, write letters home, dress for dinner before full-length mirrors. Ladies' cabins were thoughtfully 'below deck as being the most retired place'. Small talk offered in six languages in the *Pocket Book* – 'You are grown fat, sir'; 'How, madam, you are already going?' – was interspersed with hints of the violent backdrop to this leisured world: 'A great many lies are circulated';

'The Margrave . . . has been killed by a canon ball' [sic].[21] With its own steamship line, Vienna became part of a network of desirable international destinations. A new railway sponsored by the Austrian Lloyd Steamship Company from the 1850s took tourists from Vienna south across the Alps to Trieste, one of Austria's Italian-speaking possessions on the Adriatic Sea. From this 'Austrian lake', travellers could proceed by steamship across the Mediterranean to Alexandria on Egypt's coast where, the advertisements suggested, palm trees, pyramids and women of seductive charms awaited them.[22]

But these steamboats could only travel so far on the Danube, as they were unable to ride rapids or scrape along the rock-strewn waters of the Iron Gate gorges. Always downstream were the Ottomans, who had no reason to help Vienna create a bustling passenger trade or military highway to the Black Sea. Thanks to the Iron Gates, the lower Danube remained impassable and many thought the Sublime Porte preferred it this way. In response to one of many Austrian appeals to Istanbul in the 1830s, the Ottomans declared themselves afraid to clear rocks from the river that God had placed there at the moment of creation. With Russian assistance, Austria managed to wear down Ottoman opposition and blasting of rocks took place in 1834.[23] It was not until 1878, when the Congress of Berlin gave the Austro-Hungarians rights over the lower Danube, that they could start to invest in the Iron Gate canals. By this time, Istanbul had lost its upper hand.

For this shifting power relationship, we need to turn to our second focus: the emerging imperial presence of Russia on the lower Danube. If Russia helped to bolster Habsburg power on the middle Danube in the late 1600s, a century later they became even more active on the lower Danube and in the Black Sea region. At this point, imperial Moscow expanded south-west, capturing Kiev and other parts of the Ukraine. Over the next decades the Russian Empire set its sights on warm-water ports on the Black Sea and on the lower Danube River itself. All of this was Ottoman territory. But in 1774 a Russian military victory over the Ottomans in Bulgaria and the Treaty of Küçük-Kaynarca ended Ottoman control of the Khanate of Crimea and Russia lost no time in taking over and developing these lands.[24]

Empress Catherine the Great announced her arrival in this 'New Russia' with a grand river journey in a style befitting the ancient pharaohs. With her lover and fixer Prince Grigory Potemkin, Catherine in 1787 set out from St Petersburg on the icy eastern shores of the Baltic, heading towards Kiev in a sledge-borne carriage flashing gold across the snow. At Kiev they waited for the ice to melt on the Dnieper River, then embarked downstream in a flotilla of vessels, stopping to inspect Potemkin's new riverside towns along the way. When they reached the lower Dnieper on their way to the Black Sea, there were Ottoman fighting ships in the estuary. The Empress and her party were obliged to leave the river at Kherson and travel by land east across the Crimean Peninsula to view her new Black Sea fleet at Sevastopol. Within a few years Russia began to neutralise the threats in this region and was able to annex the Crimean Peninsula.[25]

Russian expansion was only part of this changing landscape of the lower Danube and Black Sea region. European powers far to the west of the Danube were also gravitating to the river during the century that followed, while along the river and across the wider Balkan region, enmities and loyalties only partially suppressed by Ottoman sovereignty were rising to the surface. One by one territories were breaking free from Ottoman control, with Greece famously among the first in 1830 with the conclusion of its War of Independence, followed by a succession of emerging nation states. Another Russian defeat of the Ottomans and the Treaty of Adrianople in 1829 gave Russia a toehold on the Danube itself for the first time, as Wallachia and Moldavia on the left bank swapped Ottoman control for Russian 'protection'.[26]

These years saw Danubian territories, states and allegiances reshuffled, and also forced migrations and mass expulsions. Although outsiders, Russians could claim a shared, paternalistic religious and ethnic identity with many of those on the lower Danube through Orthodox Christianity and Pan-Slavism.[27] But change was also brought about by armed conflict including combatants far from the river. British and French determination to prevent Russian expansion on the Danube and in Crimea culminated in their joint action with the Ottomans in the Crimean War of the 1850s. With Russia's defeat, Wallachia and Moldavia were prised from its hands and united as one province: the 'Danubian Principalities', later becoming the nation state of Romania (as first constituted).[28] Following Russia's support for Bulgaria against the Ottomans and its failed siege of Silistria in 1854 on the Danube's southern shore, thousands of Bulgarians fled Ottoman reprisals; thousands more were killed in Bulgaria following revolt in the 1870s. But in one of the many reversals of these years, Russian victory in their war against Turkey in 1877 created the territorially massive state of Bulgaria, only for this to be cancelled at the Congress of Berlin the following year.[29] Overseeing these proceedings was Otto von Bismarck. One of the people for whom the word 'bestrode' was invented, Bismarck dominated the diplomatic world of Europe at this time. With his trenchant and no-nonsense walrus moustache, he was the force behind the Prussian-led rise of unified Germany until his dismissal by the young Kaiser Wilhelm II, of the perfectly coiffed 'Imperial' moustache, who later led Germany into the First World War. Germany in the 1870s made no direct move on the lower Danube but through Bismarck it helped to re-landscape its riverbanks to its own geopolitical ends. The Congress confirmed Bulgarian independence though with a much-reduced territory, as well as the independence of Serbia and Romania.[30]

The Danube of the late nineteenth century was an increasingly Christian river. On the left (north) bank, the new nation state of Romania (roughly the region of Dacia many centuries earlier) shook off not just foreign overlords but the perceived foreign elements within, refashioning itself as a Christian nation.[31] Persecution and famine triggered a mass emigration of Jewish Romanians: the *fusgeyers* (wayfarers) began to leave their homeland in search of better lives. Moving on foot, then by train, and from river ports on the Danube, they headed for the sea ports of Hamburg on the Elbe and Rotterdam on the Rhine, and from there to the Thames and the Atlantic world beyond.[32]

Ottomans had been on the southern (right) bank of the lower Danube or *Tuna* (its Ottoman name) for around 500 years by the time of their war with Russia in 1877, and the river was a key to their identity. 'The Danube is for us the water of life,' the hero had cried in a famous play by the Ottoman playwright Namık Kemal: *Vatan Yahut Silistre* ('Fatherland or Silistria', 1873), set during the events of the (failed) Russian siege of Silistria in the Crimean war. 'If the Danube were to go, our *vatan* could not live,' he said.[33] But this *vatan* (fatherland) came to an end in 1877 after a replay of this siege, when 160,000 Russian troops crossed to the south bank of the Danube. Ottomans and Greeks with deep roots on the southern riverside were ejected from Bulgaria following this Russian victory.[34] The pain of Ottoman expulsion from the Danube lasted well into the twentieth century. 'If a river exists in the heart of a Turk, that river is the Danube, if there is a mountain, it is the Balkan range,' declared Yahya Kemal Beyatlı in 1921 – a Turkish politician-poet of the newly established Turkish Republic.[35] 'Tuna Türküsü' ('The Song of the Danube') was written by Hasan Âli Yücel, a twentieth-century politician-poet who lived far from its shores: born in Ottoman Istanbul and dying in the same city.[36]

This brings us to the third part of these unfolding events: back in the middle of the river on the island of Adakale, downstream from Orşova, where we began this chapter. This island was to be the last Ottoman outpost on the Danube. Adakale was one of many thousands of islands receiving the shifting silt of the Danube and its 300 tributaries. On the Austrian Danube alone there are thought to have been around two thousand islands before hydroelectric dams arrived. The Romanian Danube has 194 islands by a recent estimate. Establishing the sovereignty or ownership of river islands is often difficult. Where rivers form boundary lines, islands midstream need to be allocated to one or other territory. Typically international law allocates them according to where they sit in relation to an imaginary line midstream called the *thalweg*. The island joins the territory of whichever bank it is situated closest to. But islands can also shift within a river, as they accumulate or lose land with the movement of silt. They can appear from nowhere or disappear. This impermanence was one of the problems with the Partition of India in the Ganges delta, as we shall see. In the late nineteenth century Romania and Bulgaria squabbled over a pair of morphing river islands.[37]

But in the case of Adakale, the niceties of international law and river morphology proved of little importance, as the island was reduced to a mere stepping-stone in the rising tensions between Austria-Hungary and territories on the Danube's southern shore. By the late nineteenth century, the key perceived threat was rising nationalism in Serbia on the southern shore, which was backed by Russia. Serbia's neighbour Bosnia-Herzegovina, still nominally under Ottoman control, was subject to its proprietorial concern while Austro-Hungarian moves downstream chipped away at Ottoman territories.[38] A note on the 'Blessing of the Water in Bosnia' in the Serbian newspaper *Novosti* summed up this neighbourly concern at Epiphany in January 1914, on the eve of the First World War: 'Even in places which lie under the foreign yoke,' it read, 'the Servians [sic] preserve their customs against the day when in glorious joy the day of freedom dawns.'[39] Austria-Hungary, for their part, were anxious to prevent the island of Adakale and, more importantly, Bosnia-Herzegovina, from being dragged ever further into the orbit of neighbouring Serbia.[40]

Adakale, strangely, had been excluded from the 1878 Congress of Berlin: forgotten about, it is often said, though this seems unlikely given its acrimonious history. Perhaps it was deferred to 'any other business' after the next war, which is more or less what happened.[41] But under terms agreed at Berlin, Austria-Hungary had sent troops into Bosnia-Herzegovina in 1878, and decided to occupy Adakale at the same time.[42] When in 1908 they went one step further and annexed Bosnia-Herzegovina, while leaving its citizens still subject to their Ottoman feudal obligations, this drove a wedge between the Habsburgs and Russians that would contribute directly to war.[43] The annexation of the island of Adakale followed in May 1913, a 'piratical trick', according to the Serbian newspaper *Tribuna*: 'It is a thief who, when he cannot steal a whole sack of gold, contents himself with one dinar.'[44] From a safe distance, some in the British press considered Adakale a quaint relic by this time; a 'musical comedy island'.[45]

Following the assassination of Archduke Franz Ferdinand in late June 1914, Austria-Hungary declared war on Serbia one month later on 28 July.[46] That night the Danube was the scene of what some consider to have been the first shots fired in the First World War. Serbian soldiers blew up a railway bridge across the Sava River near its confluence with the Danube at Belgrade and were fired at by Dual Monarchy soldiers from a small gunboat, the SMS *Bodrog*, still afloat today as a rusty hulk on the river at Belgrade.[47] At the other end of Europe the government in London was equally provoked by a river crossing by Austria-Hungary's powerful ally Germany. When the Kaiser's forces, heading for France, crossed the River Meuse into neutral Belgium on 4 August, this escalated the international conflict. Their occupation of Belgium and the Netherlands – with their interlinked Rhine-Meuse-Scheldt estuaries facing London and the Thames estuary – was a treaty breach and considered a direct threat to Britain and its navy. The British government declared war the same day.[48]

In the end, the Ottoman and Habsburg empires crashed and burned together. The Dual Monarchy was dissolved, with Austria suffering massive territorial losses after the First World War. The 600-year-old Ottoman Empire came to an end with the Treaty of Lausanne of 1923, with the much smaller Turkey as its successor state. The Ottomans held out to the end for Adakale, but the island went instead to Romania. The three hundred Muslim Ottomans then living on the island joined hundreds of thousands of people forced to leave their lands in the mass-population swaps after the war. A few stayed on; some joined Turkish communities in Dobruja in Romania; some went to Turkey.[49] Today the island of Adakale lies submerged in the reservoir of the Soviet-era Iron Gates dam, like the canals of Franz Joseph and the original site of Lepenski Vir.

This chapter has shown how rivalries along the Danube during these centuries reshuffled its involuntary neighbours. Some groups became freer and more powerful; others became weaker or lost their homes on the riverside world altogether. The next chapter will look at how problems embedded in the Danube stream itself became a focus of geopolitical conflict.

6

The Case of the Undredged Delta

'. . . the Flags of all Nations shall be treated on the footing of perfect equality'.

Treaty of Paris, Article XVI (1856)[1]

In the 1830s, complaints began about the condition of the Danube's delta that led into the Black Sea. The delta, it seemed, was developing a treacherous ridge of sand. The depth of water in the Sulina shipping channel was said to have dropped from 16 feet to just 10 feet in recent years; its shores were now 'strewn . . . with the wrecks of ill-fated merchantmen'.[2] This chapter explores how an apparently simple maintenance issue on a river can become caught up in major geopolitical conflicts, and how mechanisms to manage the Danube became instruments of domination.

The problem appeared to lie with the Russians – newcomers on the Danube. Under the 1829 Treaty of Adrianople, Russia had managed to get the Ottoman court to cede their navigation rights on the lower Danube. Worse, they had also gained control over the Danube delta with access to the Black Sea and Bessarabia, a major bread-producing region with humus-rich soil north of the delta that was watched over beadily by all European powers.[3] The Russians were now able to quarantine and tax foreign ships entering the delta from the Black Sea, a right they enjoyed to the full for the next twenty-five years. Russia, it was said, was exacting maintenance duties but failing to dredge the sandbar. This provoked, in time, an outpouring of nostalgia in the British press for the old Ottoman dredging rake. By this 'simple, and effective . . . process', as the Preston *Chronicle* put it in 1853, every vessel passing from the delta to the Black Sea had been obliged by the Ottomans 'to tack to her stern a good iron rake, and by that means each . . . performed her share of the necessary scavenging'.[4] British politicians claimed to have seen these rakes with their own eyes. They were lying idle in the port town of Sulina, a place now packed with lightermen, river pilots and taverns: the lighters (flat-bottomed barges) for vessels to offload their cargoes before passing over the sandbar; the pilots to help them navigate the shifting sands; and the taverns to mop up the sailors' wasted days.

Was the sandbar really worse than in the 1820s or was it that this was now a Russian sandbar? We don't know, but the Russian foreign minister Count Nesselrode was unmoved by the sturdy rakes. He pointed to their new English steam-powered dredger as a sign of good faith, even though – according to British premier Lord Palmerston in 1853 – it broke down every two hours and had to be towed to the Ukrainian port of Odesa for repairs.[5] Meanwhile 'the size of our labourers' loaves varies with the depth of water on the bar of the Danube', a British observer complained.[6] In a single stormy night in December 1856, over eighty vessels – ships and lighters – were wrecked in the shallows of the Sulina channel, with more than 300 dead.[7] The spiralling tensions of these years arose from competition over the territories slipping out of Ottoman hands. Nesselrode counted on the British and French hating each other enough to prevent joint action against Russia, a mistake that was to cost him his job. The Crimean War (1853–6) left none of the powers covered in glory but ended in Russian defeat and their loss of Southern Bessarabia that had connected them to the lower Danube. The delta was handed back to the Ottomans under the Treaty of Paris following the war.[8]

Into the emerging vacuum on the Ottoman Danube came Russia and Austria-Hungary, as we've seen. But there were also new players on the Danube. The defeat of Russia at Crimea offered an opportunity to devise a power-sharing mechanism on this river that befitted the status of international players – specifically those based in London – who were a great deal further away from Sulina than Moscow was. The 1856 Treaty of Paris set up two international organisations to govern the Danube. The first, 'Riverain Commission', was intended to be permanent and in time responsible for the whole river.[9] The second river organisation, the 'European Commission of the Danube', oversaw the maritime river downstream as it flowed towards the Black Sea: initially a temporary body that would dissolve when its work improving the delta channels was complete. In principle, the Riverain Commission represented the riparian (i.e. riverside) states, including delegates from Habsburg Austria, the two upper Danubian German states of Bavaria and Württemberg, and the Ottoman Empire. Moldavia and Wallachia (the 'Danubian Principalities') and Serbia were then still formally 'vassal states' of the Sublime Porte, and so were represented by more junior officials.[10] International tensions on the upstream, fluvial river meant that the Riverain Commission was defunct within a few years. But the European Commission of the Danube lived on, representing Crimean War combatants: Britain, France, Habsburg Austria (later Austria-Hungary), Prussia, Russia, Sardinia and the Ottoman Sublime Porte.[11]

These arrangements were not created from scratch but modelled on earlier solutions on the neighbouring River Rhine in the 1815 Treaty of Vienna, which retained a powerful hold on later international relations. Napoleon's ambitious new political frameworks during the years of French territorial expansion had been so extensive in the Rhine region that after the war there was no going back. The River Rhine rises in the Swiss Alps and flows for around 760 miles through today's Switzerland, Germany – forming the German/French border for part of its journey – and into the Netherlands.[12] As it approaches the sea at Rotterdam, the Rhine becomes part of a sprawling delta entwined with the Meuse estuary to the north and the Scheldt estuary to the south.

Following his victory over Austria and Russia in 1805 at the Battle of Austerlitz, Napoleon had cancelled the legendary Holy Roman Empire of the Habsburgs and established in its place the Confederation of the Rhine (1806–13), a collective of German states allied to France. By this, Napoleon symbolically restored to France the prestige of the Holy Roman Empire from the time of the Frankish Charlemagne a thousand years before.[13] He also initiated what is seen as the world's first international river-based organisation, the *Magistrat du Rhin* (1808), to manage navigation along this waterway. The French emperor shared a long-standing French aspiration to claim the lands of Roman-era Gaul, stretching from the Pyrenees and Alps in the south to a northern border at the Rhine. This included territory that would later become Belgium and the southern Netherlands, and provoked indignation in the north. The German nationalist writer Ernst Moritz Arndt protested in 1813 that the Rhine was 'Germany's river, not Germany's boundary'.[14] Tension over the Rhineland boundaries, with rich coal and iron-ore resources, were to fuel French-German hostilities into the twentieth century.[15]

Some flamboyant claims about river rights had issued from Napoleon and his officials as French armies rolled across neighbouring territories. The first was about the River Scheldt, which flows through northern France, Belgium and the port of Antwerp, before entering the sea in the Netherlands. The 'Scheldt Decree' (1792) declared that '[t]he flow of rivers is a common asset, not given to transfer or sale, of all states whose waters feed them', a principle attributed to the earlier work of the Dutch scholar Hugo Grotius (1583–1645).[16] Asserting riparian rights all along the stream of a river and its tributaries in this case had the twin virtues both of denying Dutch claims to supremacy over the Scheldt estuary within their borders, and of excluding the distinctly non-riparian British, whose Thames estuary and Port of London were handily situated for trade with the Scheldt. A few years later came another and altogether stranger claim about the magical powers over the Scheldt River and its adjoining estuaries conferred by French occupation of their upstream waters. By this time, France controlled the United Provinces of the Netherlands (named the Batavian Republic by Dutch revolutionary 'patriots', after the Roman-era people of this territory).[17] Early harmony between the Dutch and their French occupiers had given way to a more overtly authoritarian approach. The Netherlands, Napoleon stated in 1795, were the natural possession of France; its entire territory was no more than 'an alluvium of some of the principal rivers of his empire'.[18]

Napoleon's ultimate loss of his river kingdoms became a source of mockery: a key French defeat at Leipzig in 1813 was captured in a popular cartoon. In it, Napoleon flees the city of Mainz at the Rhine–Main confluence, clutching a sceptre capped with the head of Charlemagne as scraps of paper spill out of his open rucksack: labels of his many losses, among them Holland, the mouth of the Rhine, and his beloved Confederation of the Rhine.[19] The precedent of shared riparian management created by the *Magistrat du Rhin* outlived Napoleon, however, and was expanded by the Treaty of Vienna in 1815. This established the Central Commission for the Navigation of the Rhine with headquarters at Mainz, still going and now based at Strasbourg. This 1815 settlement embodied the principle of free navigation on international rivers – free movement to all along the rivers – and also the rights and obligations of riparian states as custodians for these rivers.[20] These principles then bounced from river to river, though they were subject to wild extremes of interpretation.

This brings us back to the dredging problem in the Danube delta. The European Commission for the Danube turned the Sulina Channel into a navigable waterway in the late nineteenth and early twentieth centuries. There was nothing anyone could do about the ice that paralysed shipping in the lower river for up to three months each winter. The Commission succeeded in straightening and shortening the Sulina Channel by 12 nautical miles, turning it into something more like a canal. Fewer ships were lost on its sandbars. But the delta channel remained wayward. Only relentless dredging sustained the required 24-foot depth, at least up to the outbreak of war in 1914. The delta bed continued creeping eastwards into the sea day by day, as the river slowed and dumped the combined silt and detritus of the Danube and its tributaries. By the end of the First World War, Sulina's lighthouse, which had been built in 1867 on the Black Sea coast, could be seen blinking away in fog two-thirds of a mile from the travelling shoreline.[21]

Amid international tensions in the 1910s the European Commission of the Danube managed to retain a veneer of neutrality into the first years of the Great War. Representatives were still discussing dredgers and jetties while their sons were killing each other on the battlefields, but the entry of Romania into the war on the Allied side in 1916 ended this situation and the delta passed through the hands of warring parties till the end of hostilities.[22] The post-war settlement reconstituted the European Commission of the Danube from Brăila (Romania) to the Black Sea. This now represented Romania plus the Allied victors of the First World War – Britain, France and Italy, with the new League of Nations arbitrating in case of disputes, which brought the United States to the Danube.[23] Yet another organisation, an International Danube Commission, was established for the upper and middle ('fluvial') river from Ulm to Brăila, representing riverside states as well as members of the European Commission of the Danube.[24] A British admiral, Sir Ernest Troubridge, was placed in charge of the International Danube Commission.[25] For Troubridge, this administrative job was an ambiguous posting: the war had altered his fortunes, starting with a court martial in 1914 that left him exonerated but his reputation damaged, and ending with his wife Una leaving him for the writer Radclyffe Hall to become the first lesbian power couple. But with Austria-Hungary, Germany, revolutionary Russia and the Ottomans all out of the picture there was, in principle, money to be made on the Danube for the British.

Dredgers built in Scottish shipyards went back to work on the delta bed.[26] Boardrooms across Britain's east coast port cities filled with cigar smoke and a new capitalist machine chugged into action as shipping's heftiest players came together to create a River Syndicate: the Right Honourable Earl Grey of the shipbuilders Swan Hunter on the River Tyne; Sir Frederick William Lewis of Furness Withey on the Tees; Charles Barrie on the Tay at Dundee; and Lord Inverforth of Andrew Weir & Co. on the Clyde at Glasgow who, as Minister of Munitions, could help handle post-war reparation rules.[27] In 1920 the Syndicate (trading as the

Danube Navigation Company) acquired majority shares in the best-performing steamship companies of the defeated Austrians and Hungarians.[28] In theory, British shipping could now merrily dominate the Danube passenger and freight trade.

But free passage and free trade on the river proved elusive. Repairs along the war-torn river were very expensive. Many of the Austro-Hungarian steam vessels were scattered to the four winds and had to be hunted down. And if British investors reverted to amicable, lofty trading relations with those with whom they had just been fighting, relations between neighbours along the Danube itself were far more febrile. Where once the Austro-Hungarian Empire had provided a single 'customs union' along the 800 or so miles of river from Passau in Lower Bavaria to Orşova in south-western Romania, the successor states now imposed separate taxes all along the river.[29] Such was the mutual antipathy between the Hungarians and the Kingdom of Serbs, Croats and Slovenes (SHS, founded in 1918) that in some places they operated two separate customs and medical examination stations at their river border. Here people were searched twice for contraband and double-checked for infectious diseases. The Austrian and Hungarian shipping companies – though British owned – were denied access to the lower Danube ports of Romania on the left bank and of the Kingdom of Serbs, Croats and Slovenes on the right bank.[30]

The Romanian government on the 'maritime Danube' was not a pliable member of the European Commission of the Danube (EDC). It was Romanian grain harvests that provided most of the shipping fees to fund the EDC, but the harvests were variable, whereas the costs of maintaining the Sulina Channel kept rising. This was a problem for sovereignty.[31] Romania had shaken off the Ottomans and Austria-Hungary only to welcome Britain, France and Italy on their doorstep. Things did not go according to plan for the British River Syndicate in the end. Their expectations that Vienna would continue as a major financial hub on the Danube were not fulfilled. Their Danube Navigation Company sold its steamship interests in 1933, just in time for what came next.[32]

The rise of Nazi power in Germany in the 1930s changed everything, as international agreements on land and water were ripped up. In 1936, Germany occupied the Rhineland – a demilitarised zone along their Rhine border with France, Belgium and the Netherlands under the 1918 Treaty of Versailles. And the Germans began moving eastward along the Danube, renouncing their membership of the International Danube Commission.[33] By 1938, Germany had annexed Austria and invaded Czechoslovakia. With the support of its Italian ally, Germany gained admittance to the European Danube Commission in March 1939, though not before most of the Commission's powers and assets in the delta had been hurriedly transferred to Romania. A year into the Second World War, in September 1940, the Danube upstream from Bratislava (by now the capital of a pro-German Slovak Republic) was declared to be Germany's alone. For the river from Bratislava down to Brăila, a new 'Council of the Fluvial Danube' was announced.[34]

The Danube during these years was a dark place. Danubian states from the river's source to the Black Sea participated in the atrocities of the Holocaust; many hundreds of thousands of Jews from this region were deported and killed. The river port of Passau in Austria aided access to the site of the Mauthausen complex of concentration camps after 1938.[35] The Danube was used as a black hole to hide Nazi crimes. Massacres carried out by the Hungarian authorities, allied to Germany, include the killing in January 1942 of over three thousand Jews and Serbians, alleged partisans, in the port city of Novi Sad in today's Serbia. Many of these individuals had been rounded up and taken to the Strand – a tree-lined bathing spot from the Belle Epoque – where they were shot and thrown into the frozen river, the ice having been broken up with cannon fire. Some of the bodies were later seen downriver in Belgrade.[36] In Budapest during the final winter of the war, with Hungary now ruled by the fascist Arrow Cross Party, thousands of Jewish residents of the city were shot into the freezing water of the Danube, today memorialised on its embankment by the Shoes on the Danube Promenade (2005).[37] In Romania, allies of

Germany under the fascist wartime leader Ion Antonescu carried out massacres from 1941, while deportations to concentration camps led to the deaths of perhaps up to 400,000 Jews in Romania and territory to its east.[38]

The fall of Nazi Germany and the end of the Second World War saw reprisals across borders, acts of summary justice, and many more who escaped from justice.[39] After the unimaginable breakdown of humanity and international law, the global powers and leaders of Danubian states sized each other up. The political and territorial landscape had been once again radically reshaped. The British and French with their newly pre-eminent American ally tried to recreate a Danube commission with the now traditional mash-up of riparian states and powerful non-riparian players, but this time there was no escaping Russian might.

The USSR ignored Western proposals and successfully asserted authority over riparian states downstream from Bratislava (then Czechoslovakia), where the Iron Curtain began on the Danube. Nor were they interested in suggestions for a US-inspired Tennessee Valley-style Authority on the Danube. Instead a Soviet-sponsored event, the Belgrade Convention of 1948, created a new Danube Commission representing only the states situated along the riverbank. In the spirit of 1815, Soviet Russia with some justification called for 'The Danube for the Danubians'.[40] It was itself once again a riparian state, having taken the trouble to annex Bessarabia in June 1940.[41] The British and French representatives found themselves sidelined at the inaugural event in Belgrade and walked out; America's representative stayed on but was also powerless. The Viennese-born American legal scholar Josef L. Kunz saw in the Belgrade Convention the 'decline of good manners in diplomacy' and 'a new era of barbarism'.[42]

The political history of Europe has remained intimately tied to engineering decisions on the Danube, from canal-building to hydroelectric schemes. For the ancient navigation problem at the Iron Gate, the USSR adopted the blunt but effective solution of drowning the gorge region in a multi-purpose hydroelectric lake, an approach already adopted at Aswan and later seen on the Busa

Rapids on the Niger River, the Yangtze's Three Gorges and across all the world's major rivers. The immediate post-war years also saw the return of strategically bad dredging of the Sulina Channel. Operations carried out by Soviet Russia and Romania focused instead on the northern Chilia branch of the Danube delta.[43]

The Danube is still a barometer for wider pressures in the region. During the thaw in international tensions of the Khrushchev years (1953–64), upper Danube states began to join the Danube Commission such as Austria in 1960.[44] But the power struggles between riparian nation states still ripple along the Danube. In particular, Bessarabia (or Budjak), the coveted toehold on the Danube's maritime coast, has remained a place with jealous neighbours. Since 1991, this majority Russian-speaking region has been the sovereign territory of independent Ukraine, curling round the western coast of the Black Sea, past the port of Odesa down to the Danube's northerly Chilia branch. West of Ukrainian Budjak, there is some nostalgia in Romania for the borders of Greater Romania from the years after the Great War to the Nazi-Soviet Pact of 1940. In 2017 as a national holiday was declared by Romania's Chamber of Deputies to celebrate its former control of Bessarabia, a news report published a map showing Romania's 'natural borders' far beyond its eastern border today at the Prut River, extending right up to the Dniester River that runs through the Ukraine and Moldova. In principle, this would remove both Moldova and Ukrainian Bessarabia from the banks of the Danube.[45]

The Danube and its neighbouring rivers the Dnieper and Dniester are also strategic territory in Ukraine's struggle to maintain its borders since the Russian invasion from the east in February 2022. When in the autumn of that year the military commander General Sergei Surovikin issued an expressionless announcement of Russia's withdrawal from Kherson and its retreat to the left (east) bank of the Dnieper River, reports suggested that Russian-backed authorities had removed the body of Grigory Potemkin for its own safety from St Catherine's Church in Kherson. Shortly afterwards, the bronze figure of Catherine the Great, who had long gazed down on the streets of Odesa, disappeared behind a chipboard hoarding.[46] The rivers of the region have provided both a helpful line of defence and an inconvenient blockage to tactical retreats. Soldiers still get bogged down in riverside marshes, as in Russia's slow progress across the Donets River and Donbas region in the early months of the war. In May 2022, Kyiv repelled Russian forces by opening the floodgates on the Soviet-era Kozarovychi dam on the 'hero river' Irpin, a tributary of the Dnieper.[47] Dams, bridges, navigation channels and port storehouses have all proved effective tools in this war at the Danube intersection with the Black Sea, the site of some of the key ports for international food supply. The Ukraine and Russia together provided a third of the world's wheat supply before the outbreak of war, alongside the Ukraine's major exports of sunflower oil and corn. Whereas before the war six million tons of grain a month left the Ukraine's ports, this number was down to one million by June 2022.[48]

The Danube Commission membership too is still contentious. When the Commission celebrated its seventieth anniversary in Budapest in 2018, its origins as a Soviet-dominated institution were only faintly discernible in its public-facing website.[49] But Russia did not relinquish membership of the Commission when Ukrainian independence severed its Bessarabian link to the Danube in 1991, despite the complaints of Ukrainians who have not forgotten that the Commission still represents, in principle, the 'Danube for the Danubians'. On Russia's invasion of Ukraine in February 2022, the Danube Commission suspended the Russian Federation's membership 'until the restoration of peace, sovereignty and territorial integrity of Ukraine within its internationally recognised borders'. A press release questioned whether the Russian Federation, 'as a country with no bank of the Danube on its territory, can in the future continue to be a contracting state of the Belgrade Convention'.[50] Following Moscow's attacks on grain facilities at the Danube ports of Reni and Izmail and its withdrawal from the UN's Black Sea grain corridor in summer 2023, Russia was formally excluded from the Danube Commission in March 2024.[51]

The Danube River is a slender thread in the twenty-first-century world of long-range missiles, space satellites, troops from North Korea, and a background noise of nuclear escalation. But when the Ukraine war is over, Danubians will still need a collaborative body to manage the river. What form this takes is likely to mirror quite clearly the power relations that emerge from the conflict north of the Danube delta where it flows into the Black Sea.

River 3: Ganges

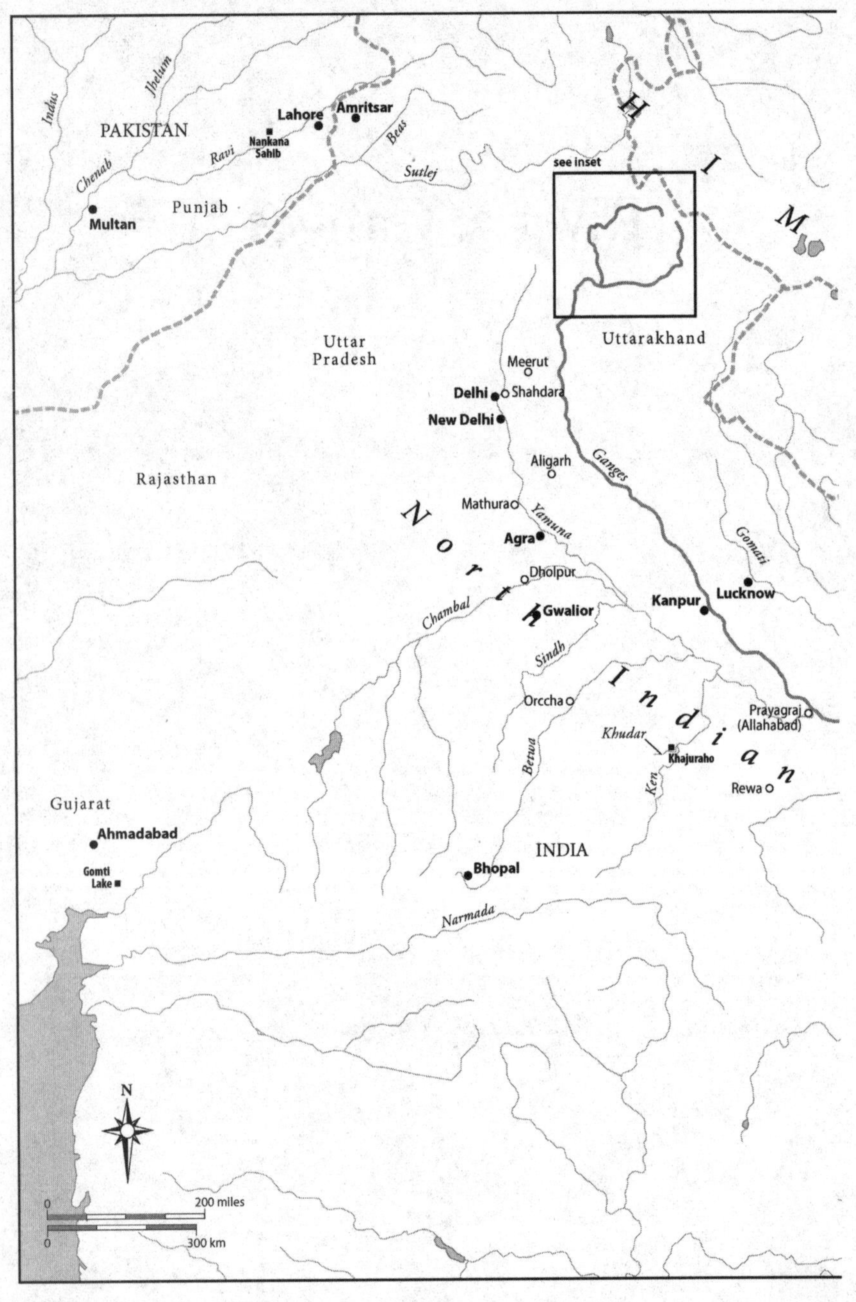

PAKISTAN
Indus
Jhelum
Chenab
Ravi
Lahore
Amritsar
Nankana Sahib
Beas
Sutlej
Multan
Punjab
see inset
H
I
M
Uttarakhand
Uttar Pradesh
Meerut
Delhi
Shahdara
New Delhi
Ganges
Aligarh
Rajasthan
Mathura
Yamuna
N o r t h
Agra
Gomati
Dholpur
Chambal
Gwalior
Kanpur
Lucknow
Sindh
I n d i a n
Orccha
Prayagraj (Allahabad)
Khudar
Khajuraho
Betwa
Ken
Rewa
Gujarat
Ahmadabad
Gomti Lake
INDIA
Bhopal
Narmada
N
0
200 miles
0
300 km

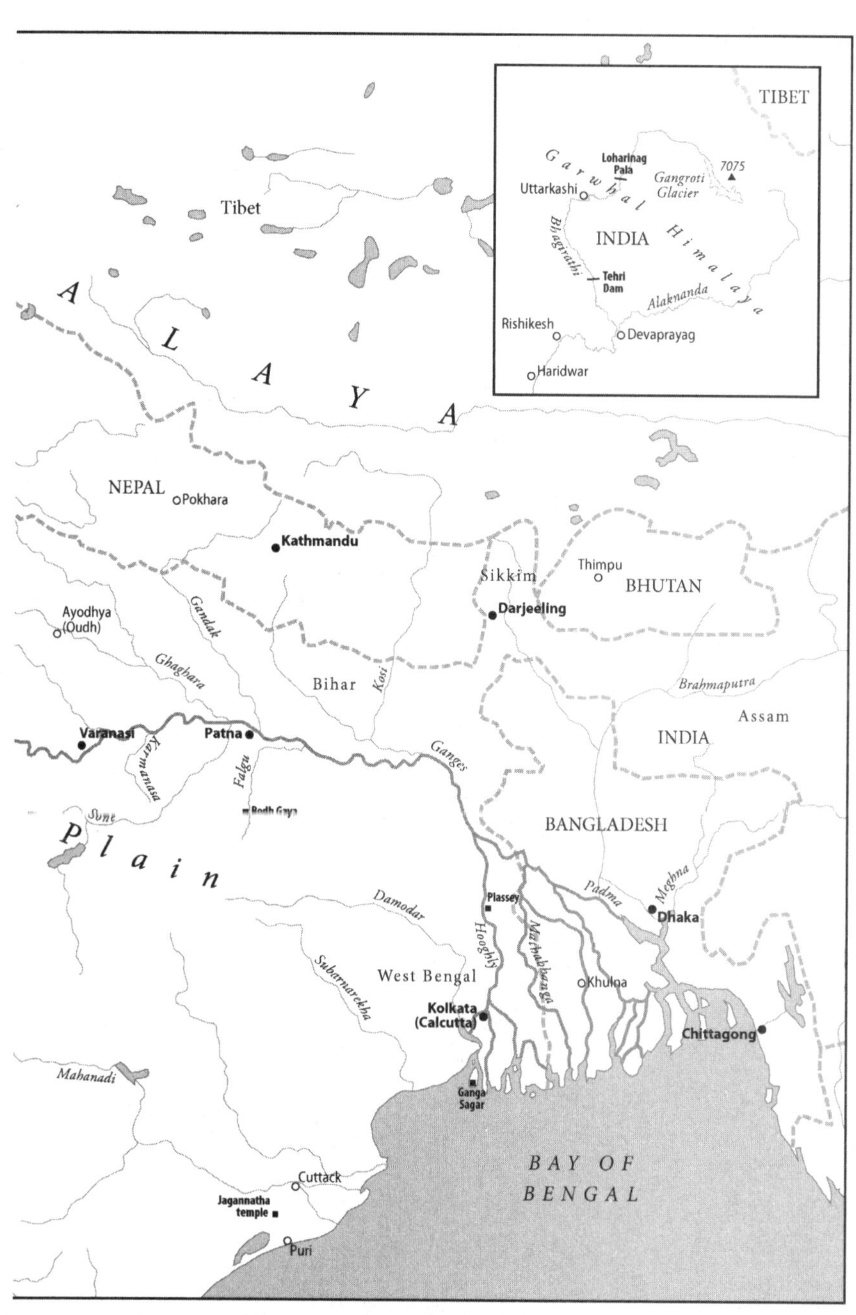
TIBET
Loharinag Pala
Garwhal Himalaya
Gangroti Glacier
7075
Uttarkashi
Bhagirathi
INDIA
Tehri Dam
Alaknanda
Rishikesh
Devaprayag
Haridwar
Tibet
A L A Y A
NEPAL
Pokhara
Kathmandu
Sikkim
Thimpu
BHUTAN
Darjeeling
Ayodhya (Oudh)
Gandak
Ghaghara
Bihar
Kosi
Brahmaputra
Assam
INDIA
Varanasi
Patna
Karmanasa
Falgu
Ganges
Bodh Gaya
Sone
P l a i n
BANGLADESH
Damodar
Plassey
Padma
Meghna
Dhaka
Hooghly
Mathabhanga
Subarnarekha
West Bengal
Khulna
Kolkata (Calcutta)
Chittagong
Mahanadi
Ganga Sagar
BAY OF BENGAL
Cuttack
Jagannatha temple
Puri

7
Numinous Rivers

'From the towering source of the world
In a thousand streams
Cascades the primeval blazing fountain,
Fragmenting silence,
Splitting its stone heart.'

Rabindranath Tagore, 'Brahmā-Viṣṇu-Śiva' (1883)[1]

In theory, there are two stories to tell about the path taken by the Ganges. One is about its physical source in the mountains and its course to the sea. The other is about its sacred source and sacred path across India. But these two stories are so intertwined that it isn't possible to talk about the history of India without talking about them both.

The River Ganges is fed by the Gangotri Glacier in the Himalayas, the mountain chain formed when South Asia – the breakaway piece of Gondwana – collided with the continent of Laurasia somewhere between 55 and 35 million years ago.[2] The river's starting point is normally seen as the place where the Bhagirathi River (which flows out of the glacier) meets the Alaknanda River at the first confluence at Devaprayag. From there, the Ganges flows for 1,557 miles from source to sea through Rishikesh and Haridwar towards the North Indian Plain, through Kanpur (Cawnpore) to Allahabad, where it meets the Yamuna River – the river on which Delhi sits.[3] Their combined waters flow eastward through Varanasi (Benares) and Patna towards the head of the delta. Here the Hughli (Hooghly) branches off as a distributary towards

Kolkata (Calcutta). Joined finally by the Brahmaputra River from the north-east, the many streams of the Ganges flow through the mangrove forest region known as the Sundarbans. Much of this delta region, including the city of Dhaka, now lies in Bangladesh.

Like all rivers, the Ganges is not just a single stream but a centipede with many legs. And each leg or tributary in this case has a rich history of symbolism. These waters also constitute the wider Ganges River basin: a watershed encompassing all the rainfall, glaciers, rivers and groundwater as a single hydrological system, over one million square kilometres in size. Even this vast basin is linked to another system, the Ganges-Brahmaputra-Meghna delta on the east coast, which forms a watery web across India, Bangladesh, China, Nepal and Bhutan. Some 1.7 million square kilometres in size, all the rivers of this greater basin ultimately drain into the sea through delta streams in the Sundarbans, where their cargo of sediment is carried through a vast fan delta into the Bay of Bengal.[4]

The holiest of seven sacred rivers in Hinduism, the Ganges is the embodiment of Mother Ganga. From its glacial source in 'the Abode of the Gods', its waters issue into the Bhagirathi from the 'mouth of a cow', a point of origin more famous than the source of the Blue Nile. Unlike the forlorn, unachievable search for the rivers of the Garden of Eden, no one is in any doubt about where 'the primeval blazing fountain' of Hinduism begins, invoked by Tagore's poem that opens this chapter. The Ganges and its tributaries are home to Hindu gods at every turn. The water is slowed by its flow through Shiva's hair. At Haridwar, Lord Vishnu left his sacred footprint.[5] Bathing in the river is a purifying act, with the confluences of rivers (or *prayags*) particularly venerated. The stories of this region are found from the earliest literature onwards, from the *Upanishads* of the Vedic period (around 1500 to 500 BCE) and the *Ramayana* and *Mahabharata*, dated around 500 BCE to 100 CE: epics handed down by oral tradition until recorded in a huge volume of texts written in Sanskrit.[6] These texts contain stories of the origins of the rivers themselves; sometimes they are competing accounts, from the *Ramayana* tale of Himalaya and his two daughters, Ganga and Uma, to the tale of the Yamuna river as the daughter of Surya, the solar god. The Ganges is always a goddess as well as a river, like her sisters, Yamuna and Saraswati.[7] And the river within Hinduism is also part of a much bigger picture. As Sunil Amrith has put it: 'the Ganges epitomizes liquid *shakthi*, the energy that sustains the universe. The Ganges is not alone, it stands at the apex of a land of sacred waters.'[8]

No other faith can compete with Hinduism in this symbolic water world. But even so, Hinduism is only one of the several religions that has evolved or been practised on the Ganges, which has been transformed by ruling dynasties of different faiths and cultures over thousands of years. Each has their own distinct and interwoven history of ideas about water, from Sikhism and Sufism to the Tirthankaras or 'ford makers' of Jainism who forged a path across 'the ocean of existence', to Islam and the family of the Prophet Muhammad himself: the guardians of a well and holy shrine at Mecca, situated near a sixth-century trade route by the Red Sea coast.[9]

This chapter follows the numinous Ganges through the many intersecting rulers and faiths that have spread through its region: from Hinduism, Buddhism and the arrival of Islam with the Delhi Sultanate in the 1200s, into the Mughal era from the sixteenth to nineteenth centuries. The centrality of religious faith and identity to the Ganges has shaped the political as well as cultural life of this region. How did people of different faiths interact around the waters of the Ganges? Partly this is a story of cultural fusion and co-existence. It is also one of conflict, competition and revenge. Often these strands have flowed side by side and are interlaced like wetland streams.

Syncretism, co-existence and suppression all have a long history on the Ganges. South Asia gave birth to two of the world's major religions: Hinduism and Buddhism. But, given the strikingly intimate relationship between the Ganges and Hinduism, the origins of this faith are strangely unclear. Many Hindus trace their religion to a time long before humans, as revealed to Aryans in the *Vedas*. Others argue that indigenous groups and others including

Aryans developed a set of beliefs that evolved into Hinduism. There is no complete consensus today.[10] By contrast, Buddhism is relatively simple. It was here in the Ganges region that Prince Siddhartha Gautama (Buddha, possibly around 490–400 BCE) is said to have found enlightenment sitting under the fig-bearing Bodhi Tree at Bodh-Gaya (Gaya, Bihar) on the banks of the Falgu (Phalgu) River, which joins the Ganges downstream from Patna.[11] From here Buddhism is thought to have been carried east along the Silk Roads to China and beyond by Central Asian traders somewhere around the first century CE.[12] At Dunhuang Oasis west of China, a crossroads on this journey, a series of caves has been unsealed to reveal thousands of Buddhist texts and images of Buddha, including the woodblock-printed *Diamond Sutra* (868 CE), the earliest printed book discovered so far. Among the many legacies of this diffusion are the 600-year-old Buddhist statues revealed by low water on a Yangtze River island near Chongqing during the 2022 drought.[13]

The Ganges River has provided a richly symbolic stage for both religious fusion and conflict. King Ashoka (c. 304–232 BCE) of the Mauryan Empire announced his conversion to Buddhism through a series of stone pillars inscribed with his edicts which he distributed across his empire, reaching from the Ganges basin to the far south on the Deccan Plateau.[14] Ashoka's pillars were to be moved from place to place by later rulers, like the obelisks along the Nile, gaining layers of prestige like barnacles.[15] Many centuries later, the ruler Harsha, a Hindu and follower of Shiva as a young man, called a conference at Prayag, the confluence where three holy rivers, or '*triveni sangam* (the intertwining braid of three)', of Hinduism meet – one of the sites of today's festival of Kumbh Mela.[16] Here Harsha in the seventh century CE invited a Chinese monk, Hsuan Tsang, to discuss Buddhist wisdom with high-status Hindu Brahmins. Hindu images were presented to the Brahmins, while a life-size golden image of Buddha was installed in a tower by the riverside, though the event seems to have had mixed results. The Buddhist tower was set alight and an attempt was made on King Harsha's life, followed by mass punishments.[17] It was also during the time of Harsha that the famous bodhi tree at Bodh-Gaya is said to have been cut down by the Bengali ruler Shashanka, his rival and a follower of Shiva.[18] It was the Buddhist Ashoka who Indira Gandhi referred to in her famous speech at the first UN environment conference in 1972: as the first and perhaps the only monarch, until very recently, to forbid the killing of a large number of species of animals for sport or food, foreshadowing some of the concerns of this Conference. 'Along with the rest of mankind, we in India – in spite of Ashoka – have been guilty of wanton disregard for the sources of our sustenance.'[19]

If conflicts over riverside territory and holy spots along the river were a focus for acts of usurpation or revenge, this was not always about competing faiths. Rivalries between Hindu groups divided by political or territorial allegiances could express themselves as acts of devotion. An image of the elephant god Ganesh was stolen back in the seventh century by a Pallava king from a temple in the capital of the Chalukya dynasty; half a century later, images of the deities Ganga and Yamuna were stolen away by Chalukyana forces from temples in northern India, and disappeared into the Deccan region.[20] Conversely, the waters of the Ganges were embraced across faiths by those living in the region. When Muhammad ibn Tughluq (r. 1325–51) of the Delhi Sultanate extended his rule from Delhi far to the south in the 1320s, he ordered Ganges water for his personal use to be conveyed to his new southern capital. For ablutions at their coronations, Bengal's seventeenth-century Muslim rulers used water from the Ganga Sagar in West Bengal: a place of Hindu pilgrimage near the entry of the Ganges into the sea.[21] Bahadur Shah II, the last of the Mughal emperors – deposed in the 1850s after the Indian Rebellion of 1857 – was said to drink only Ganges water, like the emperor Akbar, his sixteenth-century Mughal predecessor.[22]

A feature of the Ganges is that it can be highly mobile, like the River Jordan. Its waters can be transposed from place to place, literally and symbolically, by many ingenious means. Hindu rulers of the southern Chola Dynasty in the eleventh century had Ganges water transported in pots to their southern strongholds.[23] Today, every twelve years in the city of Kumbakonam, near the banks of the sacred Kaveri River in the state of Tamil Nadu, the waters of the holy rivers of India are brought to the Mahamaham Tank for a festival aligned, like the Hindu festival of Kumbh Mela, with the movements of Jupiter.[24] As we shall see when we look at the Thames, drops of Ganges water are used to transform rivers all over the world. Its numinous qualities are both its defining feature and impossible to pin down.

These qualities of water were not found only in rivers. They have flowed through waters of all kinds, including the profusion of ingenious methods used to abstract, store and convey water over thousands of years. These stemmed from the tanks and reservoirs of the very earliest Indus Valley settlements 9,000 years ago to water gathering in rock pools, stepwells (*baoris*), canals that linked temples and palaces to holy rivers, majestic water tanks and simple tube wells.[25] Whether the water was used for drinking, cooking, washing, ritual ablutions, or to beautify the worldly palaces of Indian elites, it became naturalised and sacred over time. Like the Ganges River itself, these waters embodied an infinite variety of symbolic meanings.

The conquering Mamluks of the Muslim Delhi Sultanate in 1206 changed the Ganges region for ever. Iconoclasm at Hindu sites may have begun early on. When the travelling judge and diarist Ibn Battuta, acting as emissary for Sultan Muhammad Tughluq, was on his way to China's Yuan court in the 1340s, he stopped at a place he called Kajarrā (possibly Kadwaha), west of the Betwa tributary of the Yamuna river, though this is often identified as the more famous Khajuraho temple complex to the east. Here there was 'a large tank, about a mile in length', with a red stone pavilion situated at each of its four corners. Some of the idols were said to have been already 'mutilated by the Muslims', but at the same time Ibn Battuta reported that Muslim disciples now came to the pavilions 'to learn their secrets' from 'a company of *jugis* who have matted their hair and let it grow until it has come to be as long as themselves'.[26]

The rulers of the Delhi Sultanate also brought their own culture, weaving water channels, artificial lakes and tanks into cities, palaces and pavilions, mosques and mausoleums. Above all, a succession of dynasties transformed the right bank of the Yamuna at Delhi. The waters of this sacred Ganges tributary flowed through the veins of their heartland of red sandstone.[27]

There is a tale of how the large tank Hauz-i-Shamsi, still to be seen in Delhi's Mehrauli Archaeological Park, came to be built in 1230 by an early Mamluk ruler, Sultan Shams U'ddin Iltutmish. One night the Prophet Muhammad came to the dreaming Sultan, riding on Buraq, his 'winged horse'. When he awoke the next morning Iltutmish hurried to the spot chosen by the Prophet only to find the imprint of a horse's hoof right there in the wet ground.[28] This tank (*hauz*), fed by rainwater and the Yamuna River, became a place of faith and charity. At its centre was a pavilion and mosque, to be reached by boat when the water was high, and on foot at other times. When the water was low, the poor could use the margins of the tank to 'sow sugar canes, gherkins, cucumbers, and green and yellow melons', according to Ibn Battuta.[29]

As dynasties came and went at Delhi, the sacred Hindu Yamuna River became ever more entwined with the city's many refurbishments and waterworks. Sultan Firuz Shah Tughluq (r. 1351–88) was famed for his public works: mosques, public baths, canals and reservoirs, joining Firuzabad, his new capital at Delhi, by canal to the Yamuna River. By means of this canal, too, he conveyed one of Ashoka's Buddhist sandstone pillars south from Topra (in today's Uttar Pradesh) to adorn the roof of his fortress. Some of the Sultan's canals provided irrigation and water transport from the Yamuna westwards to the Sutlej River, the closest of the five rivers of the Punjab in the Indus River basin, initiating the web of waterways that would later be scored through by Partition in the twentieth century. Beside the thirteenth-century water tank he restored (the Hauz-i-Khas), Firuz Shah placed his tomb.[30]

The Delhi Sultanate gave way to the Mughal Empire in 1526, which continued a tradition of imported cultures by harnessing water that transformed the rivers and water sources of the Ganges region. This was inaugurated by Zahir al-Din Mohammad Babur (1483–1530) of Kabul, known as Babur. Born in Uzbekistan and said to be descended from both Genghis Khan and the ruthless Timur (Tamerlane), Babur was a far more appealing character than either of his gruesome forebears.[31] Keeping a diary as he conquered his way across the Ganges plain, he noted his likes and dislikes in this new land beyond the Indus that was so different from his own: everything from the crocodiles of the Ganges and their human casualties to the porpoise, 'water-hog' or possibly river dolphin of the river, and the frogs that 'run 6 or 7 yards on the face of the water'.[32] Babur found the landscape of India 'greatly wanting in charm'. The ground was a 'dead level plain' and their orchards had no walls.[33] This flat world needed a sense of heavenly order.

Gardens, for the Mughals, should reflect paradise. That is, they should contain four streams and be enclosed by a wall, the word 'paradise' itself meaning 'walled garden' (*pairidaeza* in old Persian).[34] As Babur crossed the Ganges plain, swimming in its rivers, watching his men wrestle on the banks, praying and taking drugs, each time he reached a spring or strategic junction of a river he commanded the building of a new *charburgh* or 'fourfold, enclosed garden'.[35] When he took the city of Agra on the Yamuna River from the defeated Ibrahim Lodi in 1526, he sunk a stepwell three storeys deep into its fort. At Dholpur near the Chambal River (a Yamuna tributary), he spotted an outcrop of red sandstone and ordered a pavilion to be cut into it, complete with a formal garden and lotus pool.[36] This formal paradise garden was to find its grandest expression in the region under Shah Jahan with the Taj Mahal at Agra, a memorial for his late wife Mumtaz Mahal, built between 1632 and 1654.[37]

The Mughals would, like earlier rulers on the Ganges, select a site as if to absorb and supersede its sacred powers. This was the case at Allahabad in the northern province of Uttar Pradesh, a confluence that surpasses all others. At this meeting place, three sacred rivers converge: the Ganges, Yamuna (or Jumna) and a third, invisible river: the Sarasvati (or Saraswati). For some, this third river is a spiritual entity; others say it still flows, underground, and they can pinpoint the location. It was here at Prayag (today's Prayagraj) that Harsha had held his conference of Brahmins and Buddhism nearly a thousand years earlier. And here Babur's grandson, Akbar I (r. 1556–1605), chose to establish a city, renaming the place Illahabas meaning 'abode' of the 'divine' (later becoming Allahabad).[38] Into the city's new fort, Akbar incorporated a Buddhist pillar of Ashoka with its 1,800-year-old advice (edict V), written in third-century Prākrit, about all the creatures that must not be killed:

> . . . pigeons, bats, queen ants, terrapins, boneless fish . . ., the puputa [perhaps river dolphins] of the Ganges, skates, tortoises, and porcupines, squirrels, twelve-antler stags, bulls which have been set free, household animals and vermin, rhinoceroses . . .[39]

Akbar is known for his syncretism and embrace of different faiths. Perhaps more typical of the Hindu Ganges under Islamic rule was an uneasy balance of benign tolerance and authoritarian suppression of the conquered faith. Three cities in Uttar Pradesh demonstrate how peaceful co-existence could be tipped into suppression, with tensions that are still alive today: the cities of Mathura, Varanasi and Ayodhya. The close, literal association of specific places on the Ganges and its tributaries with episodes in the Hindu epics has at times sparked inter-faith conflict. But frequently conflict on the Ganges riverside was as much about power and politics as about faith. Religious fervour could be an expression of political rebellion and religious suppression could be a tool of political control.

One such place is the city of Mathura. During the time of Sikander Lodi (r. 1489–1517), one of the last Sultans of the Afghan Lodi Dynasty before defeat by the Mughals, the city of Mathura became a centre for rebellious Vishnu followers (Vaishnavism).[40] Around this time Mathura had become specifically associated with Lord Krishna. Some believe this to be his birthplace.[41] Lord Krishna, an avatar of Vishnu in the *Mahabharata*, was the charioteer and spiritual guide of Arjuna, one of the five Pandava brothers who battled with their cousins.[42] Devotees of Vishnu at this time believed that when Lord Krishna was finally victorious over his uncle, he rested at Mathura's Vishram Ghat, the very steps that lead down to the Yamuna River.[43] As a young man Lodi had been specifically advised by counsellors not to 'lay waste ancient idol temples. [I]t does not rest with you to prohibit ablution in a reservoir which has been customary from ancient times,' said one.[44] But there are stories of his conflict with rebellious Vishnu followers, and blocking their worship at Vishram Ghat.[45]

Mathura passed through many phases. In the early 1600s, the city benefited from the lavish investments of a loyal supporter of the fourth Mughal emperor Jahangir, Bir Singh Deo, Lord of Orccha on a bend of the Betwa River (a west-bank Yamuna tributary). In the early 1600s, Singh Deo donated an archway over Vishram Ghat at a cost equal to his own body weight in gold, along with a weighing machine for others to measure their charitable giving.[46] But this city remained a site of peasant rebellions and in the 1670s Aurangzeb, son of Shah Jahan, destroyed its Keshava Deva Temple, provocatively replacing it with a mosque and *id-gah* (open-air space for prayers at Eid). A later image of the site by Indian watercolourist Sita Ram shows a pool and fountain before an elegant red sandstone building set within a hilltop walled enclosure. The city of Mathura itself Aurangzeb renamed Islamabad.[47] This site, now known as Shahi Iedgah, has become a focal point for Hindu nationalism in recent years.[48]

Destruction of temples for Aurangzeb seems to have been politically contingent. At the holy city of Varanasi on the Ganges, he had shown early support, indicating that its temples, and the Brahmins in charge of them, should be protected. But when some years later news reached him that Hindu elites in the city had provided support to one of his enemies, he ordered its Visvanath temple to be destroyed.[49] This history is today a source of controversy in Varanasi, the constituency of Prime Minister Narendra Modi of the Bharatiya Janata Party (BJP). This is despite long centuries of co-existence between Hindus and Muslims in this Ganges-Yamuna region, known for its mixed culture or 'Ganga-Jamuni tehzeeb'.[50]

The third site of heightened tension today is Ayodhya (formerly Oudh) on the banks of the Ghaghara River, a left-bank tributary of the Ganges.[51] Ayodhya has a long association with Rama, hero of the epic *Ramayana*, sometimes appearing as an incarnation of the protector god, Vishnu, while his wife Sita is an avatar of Vishnu's wife, Lakshmi. In one version of the *Ramayana* story, Rama – heir to the throne of Ayodhya – is sent with his wife into the forest by his father the king, at the behest of his stepmother. In the forest the faithful Sita is abducted. But with the help of the monkey god Hanuman, Rama recovers Sita and he is eventually restored to Ayodhya where he takes the throne.[52] Divali, the autumn festival of lights, celebrates this outcome. But in the twentieth century, Ayodhya has become a place of great controversy. Some argue that its mosque – Babri Masjid, dating from 1528 in the time of Babur – was built on the site of an earlier destroyed Hindu temple. In the first year of Indian independence (1947) the mosque had to be cordoned off by the government of India. In 1992, violence erupted again and the mosque was destroyed by a mob in riots that led to the deaths of up to 2,000 people, including 1,700 Muslims.[53] After decades of a Hindu nationalist ('Hindutva') campaign to rebuild on the site of the mosque, in 2024 a temple was consecrated here, dedicated to Rama.

These are in part fights over real estate and ownership of specific holy places on the riverbanks of the Ganges region. The ancient sacred history and specific nature of the holy Ganges can make it hard to share with other faiths, like the holy land of Jerusalem. And these conflicts also reflect different ways of understanding the universe that extend well beyond disputes on the rivers of the Ganges region. In 2007 an official Indian archaeological team surveying Ram Setu, the ridge linking India and Sri Lanka, was for a time suspended. Their offence was to discuss this 18-mile underwater limestone ridge in geological terms rather than in the terms set out in the *Ramayana*: as the bridge built by Rama's monkey army to help him get back his wife Sita from the demon king.[54] Are the events in the Hindu epics literally true?[55]

These tensions were to be magnified a thousandfold when Partition in the 1940s divided up the land and waters of South Asia, drawing a line between homelands, waters and faiths that were thoroughly fused.

8

River under Occupation

'No inconsiderable addition to the Collector's work is entailed by the colonization and reclamation of these areas, once impenetrable tracts of thorny jungle, haunted by wild beasts and intersected by tidal streams, but now rapidly developing into a flourishing expanse of . . . cultivation . . . .'

Bengal District Administration Committee (1913–14)[1]

India had been the dream of European states for centuries. Reaching its shores, and those of China and the Spice Islands, was a driving force in the fifteenth-century dawn of maritime exploration. Finding a sea route to the riches of the east would cut out the many middlemen who added so much to the cost of spices and silks transported overland. Christopher Columbus believed he had achieved this when he stumbled on the 'West Indies' and the Americas in 1492. But it was the Portuguese – pioneers of the high seas – who got there first. After Vasco da Gama found a sea route round Africa's Cape of Good Hope, they secured a settlement on India's west coast at Goa from 1510. Other Europeans eventually followed, vying with established Arab traders and the Portuguese for a foothold on India's Spice Coast. Over time the list of desired commodities expanded, but the aim of European merchants in the east remained essentially intact: to extract resources and establish trading patterns designed for their own personal benefit and that of their national economies back home. The Ganges River was at the heart of these ambitions.

When the sculptor Bernini added the muscular Ganges and his punt-pole to the fountain of river gods at Rome's Piazza Navona in 1651, European merchants were already trading in the Ganges basin. But they were by no means in charge of the river or its surrounding territories – just another set of traders in a land of flourishing agriculture, manufacture and domestic and international markets. By the 1570s the Portuguese merchants had spread east to the River Hooghly (Hughli): an outlet of the Ganges and centre for cotton and silk. Next to arrive in Bengal, where the Ganges flows into the ocean, were the English East India Company – monopoly traders with their own army, sponsored by the Crown – and their mirror image, the Dutch East India traders. During these final years of the long reign of Akbar (the third Mughal emperor, r. 1556–1605) and those who followed, the Hooghly was a place of intense rivalries between the Europeans, but all were subject to lucrative trading duties payable to the local Nawab of Bengal and carefully watched by their Mughal overlords. Any change in fortunes between the traders was eagerly exploited: when in 1632 the Portuguese were temporarily ejected by the Mughals for a transgression, they were overtaken by the Dutch and then English East India Company.[2]

To the Mughals of the sixteenth and seventeenth centuries in their capitals upstream in Agra and Delhi, these coastal merchants were bit-part players. The Mughal Empire was then at the height of its powers, exerting authority over their Indian territory and still expanding. Only the most ruthless of imperial sons succeeded to its throne: Shah Jahan (r. 1628–58), the fifth Mughal Emperor and son of Jahangir, was typical in having confined and possibly murdered his brother to seal his succession. A 1628 portrait shows him as he wished to be seen: his head respectfully in profile and framed by a psychedelic halo, his robes enriched with silken flowers and precious stones. In one hand he holds a miniature portrait of himself, in the other a golden sword, and behind him the Yamuna River is flecked with boats – all symbols of his power.[3] But even Shah Jahan, 'Ruler of the World', was in time usurped by his own son, Aurangzeb (r. 1658–1707): the sixth emperor who expanded the Mughal Empire to its greatest extent. It was during the reign of Aurangzeb that the English East India Company gained a trading licence, purchasing land to build a settlement and fort on the Hooghly River: Calcutta and Fort William.[4]

Aurangzeb was the last of the formidable Mughals. Subsequent rulers proved unequal to the task of holding their empire together and resisting foreign incursions. It was only after his death that the East India Company forces started to find their power from their Fort William base, clashing first with the Nawabs of Bengal.[5] The tightening grip of the Company on India was achieved gradually in stages: establishing client states here, annexing territories there. Important turning points were the capture of Bengal through the battles of Plassey (Palashi) on the Hooghly River in 1757 and Buxar on the Ganges River seven years later, defeating the rulers of Bengal and Awadh, respectively, and the seventeenth Mughal Emperor based in Delhi.[6]

British supremacy in India was a frail beast that had to be sustained by constant vigilance against foreign competition. This took British forces to other distant lands and seas, from the Battle of the Nile against the French in 1798 to the struggles between Britain and Russia over Afghanistan and neighbouring territories in 'The Great Game'. There were also the Indian people themselves, who turned out to be more formidable. The most obvious problem – the occupation itself – was to remain the British elephant in the room for a very long time.

This chapter looks at the Ganges River drafted into the service of the British Empire. The river had many faces, which shaped the relationship between the Indians and the British. The Ganges was the main source of navigation through Northern India and the source of irrigation, while its heavy sediment load over the centuries had created the fertile lands between its rivers: the Ganges-Yamuna Doab.[7] The Ganges had multiple dimensions under the shadow of occupation: as a trading river, a river of taxation, a river of irrigation for cash crops, a river of rebellion and of allies, and ultimately a river and a people that could not be controlled.

On the morning of 13 September 1833, Vishwanath Singh, son of the Raja of Rewa, arrived at the sacred confluence of the Ganges and Yamuna rivers at Allahabad. Rewa, about a hundred miles south of Allahabad, was a troublesome state for the East India Company at this point and the prince, when later Raja himself, was to prove an intractable imperial subject, locking horns with the British authorities over their interference in his internal affairs, including their efforts to wipe out *sati* (the practice of burning widows on the death of their husbands). On this occasion, there was no chance of the prince arriving at the confluence unnoticed. Accompanying him were 200 foot-pilgrims, 40 elephants, 200 camels, 300 horses and 20 palanquins (covered litters carried by servants).[8]

The prince and his party set up camp and proceeded to bathe and perform their holy ablutions. Afterwards they were approached by a British revenue official for the sum of nearly 5,500 rupees: the Pilgrim Tax due for bathing at the confluence under Regulation 18 of 1810. The prince 'declined on the ground that he did not bathe *at* the junction' of the rivers, only near the junction.[9] Refusal to pay the tax was a ritual regularly performed on the river. Members of princely houses tended to refuse to pay the tax and were then to be found exempt. Generally, authority for exemption was then requested from British officials higher up. But on this day, the Allahabad revenue officer was also upset by the choice of the princely bathing spot outside the designated zone. If unchecked by the British government, the 'officiating Brahmins' might be 'allowed to exercise their casuistry in determining the places along the banks of the river which may be considered equally holy'. The tax would then 'doubtless be evaded, and many places . . . be found as holy as that marked off by Government officers'.[10] The exemption was eventually confirmed by the Government of India's Council of Directors. No comment was made on the threat of creeping Brahminical powers up the riverbank.

This was the place that Akbar had taken over around 1575 and, in a spirit of reinvention, renamed it Illahabas: both holy and the perfect place to build a fort. Its use by Hindus for bathing, collecting holy water and worship at the temple had continued unabated during Muslim rule. But at various points Hindu pilgrims had become subject to a tax on their activities. When the British took over Allahabad and other pilgrimage sites along the Ganges in the early 1800s, it seems they weren't quite sure what to do. At first, they withdrew the tax, disapproving of Hindu 'superstitions', but then they reinstated it. After some decades of ambivalence, the unpopular pilgrim tax was to be discontinued altogether in 1840.[11]

What the merchants of the East India Company really came for were the profits of this trading river. The region between the Ganges and Yamuna rivers (the 'Ganges-Yamuna Doab') was one of the most fertile in all India, supporting crops both in summer (monsoon-fed) and winter.[12] Under the British, commercial crops were intensively cultivated and exported: rice, cotton, wheat, jute, indigo and opium. Saltpetre (potassium nitrate) from Calcutta and Patna was prized for its use in gunpowder and fertiliser.[13] The Company's presence in India allowed the British government to directly control Indian exports and imports that had previously required legislation to engineer. The Calico Acts of the early eighteenth century – restricting cotton textile imports into Britain – had been about protecting British trade from the popularity of Indian cottons among consumers at home. Once in India, Britain utterly transformed its cotton market. Indian farmers became producers of raw cotton for British textile manufacturers. The cotton textiles were then shipped back to India for their consumer market. By the eve of the First World War, 60 per cent of goods imported to India were British. Over 33 per cent of these were textiles manufactured in Britain that were entering India with preferential duties.[14] Cotton – so unassuming in comparison to more exotic silks and spices – has also been a relentless driving force in development policies from the Mississippi to the Nile, Niger and Yangtze rivers.

But India also offered other riches. The East India Company merchants were now free to try to cultivate Indian tea to sell to their consumers at home and undermine the wildly popular Chinese tea trade. The famed tea trader Richard Twining (1772–1857) and other growers worked hard to identify Indian teas that tasted as good as Chinese varieties. Promising growing regions identified were rainy Assam in eastern Bengal – where tea was already growing wild – and Darjeeling, the favourite summer refuge in the Bengal highlands (Sikkim, between Nepal and Bhutan).[15] Cheap, indentured labour was used in both places: Indian labourers who had agreed to be bound for a set period of labour – typical of colonial agricultural labour relations. Darjeeling in 1898 was to become the first place in India to receive a public hydro-electricity supply, fed by the Himalayan headwaters of the Teesta and Rangeet rivers of the Brahmaputra basin, providing both electric lighting and power for the tea factories.[16]

The Ganges was a gift to merchants: both the major transport artery of northern India and the source of agricultural riches.[17] Flowing for a thousand miles through the fertile Ganges plains, it carried timber from the forests of the Himalayas, wheat, rice and indigo, sugar, saltpetre and stone – heading eastward to the port of Calcutta. It was also a river of great changes. During the dry season, boatmen used bamboo punt-poles to steer their vessels along a sluggish and shallow river at a rate of perhaps no more than three miles an hour. Many of the tributaries were impassable for all but the small country boats. The monsoon rains made a huge difference, adding as much as 35 feet to the level of the river below Allahabad and doubling the speed of the river flow.[18] Time was money, of course, though the rains could be a mixed blessing for cargoes of grain or rice that in the smaller boats were open to the elements. In the deep Hooghly River at the port of Calcutta seasonal fluctuations were far less dramatic: great ocean vessels came and went all year round. The top of the navigable river was at Haridwar in the state of Uttarakhand, where the plains meet the Himalayan mountains. Above Haridwar, timber was floated downstream from the Garhwal forests. No one fought their way upstream from there, so boats heading north gave way to pack animals, sometimes the boatmen bringing their own in vessels lined with bamboo and straw. From here the horses and donkeys were loaded with high-value, lightweight goods and would pick their way across the mountains on the long journey north to

Afghanistan and Tibet.[19]

Calcutta had become India's main economic, political and maritime hub under the British. Formerly prosperous cities were overshadowed – such was the fate of the textile metropolis of Dacca (Dhaka) on the Buriganga, or 'Old Ganges' River, in the north of the delta complex.[20] Other private merchant monopolies had crystallised around the port alongside the East India Company and, by 1830, 65 per cent of its major trading vessels were owned by only six merchant companies ('Agency Houses').[21] Many of these merchants were born and lived among the traders of Calcutta, Indians as well as British. The carbon age arrived on the Ganges in the 1820s, with the first steamship, the Thames-built SS *Enterprise*, reaching the river via the Cape of Good Hope after a long journey. The British had managed to persuade the pliable Nawab of Awadh (Oudh), Ghazi-ud-din Haider (r. 1819–27), to join a small group of investors funding the enterprise, but it was the East India Company and a series of private British companies that were to run the regular steamship services that followed. Powered by coal from the local Burdwan coalfield or from Calcutta's English coaling station, steamships cut journey times dramatically. The 800-mile trip from Allahabad to Calcutta could now be made in just eight days (and three weeks to get back upstream), compared to forty days or more in the dry season without steam, or twenty days in the rainy season.[22]

But steam-powered river journeys gave way, over time, to the steam railways opening up from the 1860s. Six railway bridges spanned the Ganges by 1905, with those at Allahabad and Benares (Varanasi) over 3,000 feet long.[23] In that same year, 15,000 vessels were estimated to be on the Ganges, which sounds a lot but over 45,000 boats were at that time plying the rivers of Assam, where railways came later. Railways offered both the freedom of new strategic routes and, in theory, more controllable conditions. A 'chaos of petty competition' was how one commentator described the Ganges trade in the 1930s.[24] But boat trade endured on the river, from the seasonal rhythms of the boatmen and their families to the well-trodden routes of the lumbering pack-bullocks – linking rivers and distant markets.

Inseparable from British economic expansion was military power. 'Gunboat diplomacy' was conducted not just on the coasts and open seas but also on the rivers of their formal and informal empire, and no single trade is more associated with this than the opium trade, which links three rivers in this book: the Ganges, Yangtze and the Thames. Although the Victorian age is remembered for its moral rectitude, for much of the nineteenth century the consumption of mind-altering drugs was perfectly normal and the trade in opium was a key part of the treasury profits. Before the East India Company gained control over the Ganges riverside trade, opium was already imported from Turkey and other places for the domestic market, valuable for its medicinal and narcotic qualities. Thoroughly upstanding wholesalers, like those of the Worshipful Company of Apothecaries or the Quaker chemists Allen & Hanbury, would go down to the customs warehouses on the Thames to inspect consignments arriving with the City's opium merchants.[25] And when the East India Company and British government saw an opportunity to use the opium grown at Patna and Benares on the Ganges to sell to the nearby Chinese market, they found a way to force their way in. In order to exploit their access to Indian opium, the British turned their guns on the Qing Dynasty forces. When the Qing Emperor brazenly resisted their efforts to break the promisingly vast Chinese market in the 1830s, the British navy blockaded their ports and enforced rights to 'free trade' on preferential terms (the Opium Wars of 1839–42). This policy underpinned the East India Company's intensive opium business at Patna at the confluence of the Ganges and Gandak rivers, and at Benares (Varanasi): from here issued a constant trickle of opium balls, the size of a grapefruit and weighing around 3½ pounds, wrapped in dried poppy petals. Opium comprised more than 40 per cent of the value of India's export market at this point.[26]

A pictorial feature in *The Graphic*, a British weekly illustrated newspaper, showed the East India Company's opium factory in Patna, looking like an IKEA warehouse. Balls of opium were stacked five to a shelf and twenty shelves high. The shelves were linked above the aisles by a series of walkways. In another image, '[a]n opium Fleet of native boats' passed down the Ganges through Bihar state towards the sea: a scene worthy of 'the world's first "narco-military" empire', as Britain has been called. This was 'preceded by small canoes, the crews of which sound the depth of water, and warn all boats out of the Channel by beat of drum, as the Government boats claim precedence'. Alongside was a raft of floating timber cut from the forests of Nepal to be used to pack the opium.[27] From the Bay of Bengal, ships headed south-east through the narrow Malacca Straits below Singapore and up into the South China Sea. The cargo would be unloaded at Canton and make its way through the rivers and towns of southern China up to the Yangtze for transport into the interior.[28]

The Ganges was also crucial for water supply (irrigation) as well as transportation for cash crops, and for maximum efficiency this meant augmenting the rivers with artificial waterways. Crop failures couldn't be ignored, but the East India Company and their government backers also got drawn into questions of subsistence farming and public service. When a severe famine in the middle Doab region (the Agra famine) in the late 1830s was badly handled – some would say caused – by the colonial authorities, around 800,000 people are estimated to have died.[29] Decisions taken about grain-storage policies, grain exports and food distribution couldn't be divorced from wider economic priorities and cultural values. Victorian attitudes to relief and charity underlay what the East India Company were prepared to do to help: both in anticipating future droughts and in their responses to famines as they were unfolding.

There were broadly two schools of thought about what to do about poverty or 'want' at this time. One was that people should be assisted as much as possible. Another view – held by increasing numbers of British politicians and officials in the Malthusian world of the late eighteenth and nineteenth centuries – was that providing 'indiscriminate alms' demoralised the poor. This was a guiding principle of Britain's own hated Poor Law and workhouse reforms of the 1830s. It was there also in Westminster's responses to the Agra famine of 1837–8 and the Irish famine in the 1840s, attitudes laced with a sense of racial superiority over the Indians and Irish respectively. This was at odds with established values of 'obligations' to the peasantry still held by Indian elites and the patrician Mughals.[30]

Not all Indians knew what moral code they were up against with the British. In one highly respectable appeal for charitable assistance in 1860, for example, there was a clear expectation of paternalist support. Kishan Lall, a former police officer and graduate of Agra College, wanted help from Lord Canning, Governor General of India, with a water tank. Lall had built a tank at Allygurh (Aligarh, Uttar Pradesh) with charitable subscriptions from local Hindus. This 'Uchal Tank' had soon become a 'place of pilgrimage' and Lall presented a series of requests to Canning. Firstly, he patiently asked that the British troops and 'camp followers' passing the tank on the Cawnpore Road be prevented from felling banyan trees and killing the peafowls and monkeys. Secondly, the subscribers were funding a dispensary for the poor at the tank but they couldn't fund the free food. Lord Canning was requested to provide the food for their patients at the tank. Thirdly, Lall asked that the tank's water supply be linked to the nearby Ganges Canal. 'Government Patronage' was 'solicited for support and protection'.[31] There is no record in the India Office file of an answer to any of this, but it represented a hopeless culture clash given the horror with which the British upper classes viewed 'begging'. British officials considered water pipes to be more effective weapons against hunger than food.

It is no surprise then that, following the Agra famine of the 1830s, the British sent in the water engineers. The resulting Ganges Canal was funded by the East India Company and ran from Haridwar to Cawnpore (Karnpur), dug by what the canal engineer described as 'tribes of a wandering class whose chief, if not entire occupation is digging tanks and watercourses'.[32] At around 900 miles in length, this was the longest single canal structure in the world when it opened in 1854. It was capable of providing water for 1½ million acres of land if the monsoon rains failed. The Ganges region now had three irrigation canals, including the western and eastern 'Jumna' canals built or restored under British supervision in the 1820s (connected to the Yamuna River) – a sign of genuine investment. Although some dismissed these earlier canals as 'noisesome and pestilent swamps', they had nevertheless defended people living nearby during the Agra famine.[33] Likewise, the Ganges-Yamuna region was later to escape the worst of 'the great famine' that killed many millions of people in Southern India in the 1870s.[34] Canals and irrigated terrain or wetlands, though, created their own problems due to the swarms of malarial mosquitos they attracted. In 1908 an epidemic of malarial fever killed up to two million people in the irrigated Ganges-Jamuna Doab and eastern-central Punjab.[35]

As soon as construction began on the Ganges Canal it got drawn into the otherworldly dimensions of water in Hinduism. At the start of construction, Hindu priests in the holy city of Haridwar at the top end of the canal were concerned at the way the canal would block the waters of the Ganges. The canal engineer Sir Proby Cautley responded by leaving a small opening for Ganges water to stream through, while also (it is said) hosting a ritual for the new canal in honour of Lord Ganesh, 'God of Beginnings'.[36] This was not mentioned at the official canal opening ceremony in April 1854, which was a strictly Christian affair. Here, the Europeans present were situated in a 'special enclosure' where prayers were held, then the Lieutenant Governor opened the canal gates to release the 'majestic flood'. In the next moment, as reported by the *Illustrated London News*, the general populace along the banks of the canal responded with 'a frenzy gradually rising till massy crowds flung bodily into the flood, and ere long the channels were full of delighted swimmers'.[37]

The diplomatic Cautley had in addition arranged to install ghats (flights of steps leading down to the river) for pilgrims at Haridwar hoping, as he put in an 1860 report, that these would 'be received by the Hindoo as some atonement for the liberties taken with the Ganges, as well as with the tutelary deity of the ghat upon the site of which these works were constructed'.[38] At the southern end of the canal at Cawnpore he had installed a pair of plinths ready for 'a sculpture emblematical of the Ganges River'. (There were Trafalgar Square-style lions at the Haridwar end.) For this, Cautley suggested 'Nundi's cow', facing upstream (possibly referring to Nandi, Shiva's Bull).[39] Just two years after the Indian Rebellion and events at Cawnpore this suggestion was unlikely to find favour.

The Ganges was also a stage for some of the underlying hostility that divided India's people and their occupiers. The Indian Rebellion of May 1857 began – like many other rebellions – in a small, unremarkable way then gathered momentum and crashed like a great wave, eventually ending both the East India Company and the Mughal Empire. It started among the Indian rank and file of the Bengal army stationed at Meerut, north-west of Delhi between the Ganges and Yamuna rivers. The spark was a conflict over the grease provided for the soldiers' ammunition. Suspected of being animal grease, this offended both Hindus and Muslims with taboos governing contact with cows and pigs. A group of soldiers who refused to touch the cartridges were court martialled and imprisoned. The rebellion that ensued was bloody, spreading across the Ganges Valley to other regiments and civilians. A large rebel force made for the capital at Delhi where they hailed as their leader the unsuspecting Bahadur Shah II, Mughal emperor and a poet not a fighter. When the British finally regained control in early 1858, they killed thousands of Indians in revenge. Emperor Bahadur Shah and his wives were removed from their palace to permanent exile in Burma, ending the reign of the Mughals after more than 300 years. Several of their sons were executed. Ratios of Indian to European soldiers within the army were adjusted. The British government stopped hiding behind the East India Company, wound it up, and began direct rule in India.[40]

Atrocities on both sides were not forgotten. The British erected memorials in the decade that followed: one at a water well in Cawnpore surmounted by an angel to remember the 400 people massacred one night at Bibighar, their bodies having been thrown into a well. Another, the Mutiny Memorial, was placed in Delhi on the Yamuna River, commemorating the British and the 'enemy' who died; later to be renamed by the post-independence Indian government in the 1970s: Ajitgarh or 'place of the unvanquished'.[41] There were post-mortems on the loyalty of regiments and Indian state rulers; more killings, demotions and promotions. Those who had remained loyal to the British Crown were rewarded.

In this world of suddenly revealed enmities, it was important to know who your friends were. The city state of Benares (Varanasi) was a place of refuge for the British on the Ganges. An ancient and revered city for the Hindus, the earthly home of Lord Shiva, it was also a major commercial centre and producer of silks. Few could resist its charms; Ghalib (Mirza Asadullah Khan), poet at the Muslim Mughal court, once declared he should have settled down there as a pilgrim on its riverbanks, 'so that I could wash the contamination of existence away from myself and like a drop be one with the river'.[42] The British elite could also enjoy this place, from the safety of the Maharajah's palace. The Maharajah of Benares, Ishwari Prasad Narayan Singh, had kept his state out of the fray during the rebellion, though situated within the rebel territory of the Nawab of Awadh.[43]

The Maharajah of Benares provided a home from home for the British who returned there again and again. When they weren't busy governing, the British were looking for something to do, whether as army officers boar-hunting in the shallows of the Ganges or amateur painters water-colouring the beauties of the Indian landscape. A photograph from 1912 shows a large group of women and men sitting on a boat in their Sunday best, midstream in the Ganges at Benares, spectating as a small group of Hindu Indians burned their dead on the riverbank. Many colonials remained as mystified, disapproving and fascinated by what they witnessed in India in the autumn of the empire as those of their grandparents' generation. On 6 March 1910, Joan Kennard – wife of an English army officer and a total product of the empire: born in Bengal and died in Cairo – wrote to her father from the safety of a mosquito net in the guest house of the Maharajah of Benares. It was the eve of Lord Shiva's birthday, and she and her companions had been that day to see the crowds in the Golden Temple. Peering through holes in the temple wall, she noticed that the Hindus 'worshipped chiefly the god Ganesh, an image of a man with an elephant's head, and also the wooden image of the Sacred Bull, painted red'. She was appalled to see 'those poor people worshipping these horrible images', though reassured that '[t]o the high-class Hindus, they are merely emblematical'. The next day she was going back for more 'in the Maharajahs barge to see the people come to bathe'.[44]

Indian-British official relations were a complex brew in which it wasn't easy to separate individual ingredients: nationalism, religious differences, racial animosity, class tensions; exacerbating issues could spring up anywhere. Even in Benares. When in 1891 a riot broke out in the city, it was over water pipes. British engineers were in town installing a new water supply, as they were right across the formal and informal empire: from Alexandria to Montevideo. Everyone was drawn into the effort to halt the water installation in Benares: leading Hindu citizens and the poor were protesting; so were Muslim weavers. Local butchers went on strike. Cholera was present in the town and the authorities might have expected a clamour for clean water. But a grain shortage was also creating anxiety, and the waterworks were to be paid for by those same people of the town through a brand new and very British tax: municipal water rates. Installing new supplies meant shutting down traditional – and free – water wells, condemned as public health risks by British engineers and sanitarians following a well-trodden path on the model of cities back at home.[45]

In addition, the engineers and builders were considered to be behaving carelessly around a nearby temple. When the trouble started, the rioters attacked equipment for the new works, then the street lights, telegraph booth and railway station – the whole package of modern urban improvements – with surgical accuracy.[46] Objections and delays to new waterworks and reservoirs were repeated across towns from India to Burma, making it difficult to deliver the benefits of modernity to the people of India or the promised dividends to the shareholders at home.

The turn of the twentieth century was a time of increasing polarisation in India. Nationalist consciousness was becoming politically mobilised as seen in the work of the Indian National Congress, founded in 1885. It had also gained a radical, terrorist wing. Sporadic attacks on officials of the colonial machinery were to become common, so too organised conspiracies and plots. This was happening across the country – from Uttar Pradesh in the north to Southern India. But government officials thought they had a real problem in Bengal – a region with a history of rebellion.

The Partition of Bengal Presidency in 1905 was meant to make things easier. As British officials explained, Bengal was simply too big and difficult to administer. They divided the region into one district of Eastern Bengal and Assam (creating a Muslim majority) and another district of Western Bengal, Bihar and Orissa. Bengali Hindus were numerous in Western Bengal but a minority in this new district. This partition also ignored Bengali regional identities. As the policy created more trouble than it was worth, it was reversed, but such problems were reignited on a much larger scale in the partition of South Asia in the 1940s. Bengal was reunited in 1911 but British officials were left with a simmering sense of an ungovernable region. The East India Sedition Committee of 1918, which doggedly reported on the activities, lifestyles and reading matter of revolutionaries (Garibaldi, *Indian Sociology* and the *Bhagavad Gita*), pointed especially to the many mouths of the Ganges delta in Eastern Bengal.[47] This was a place of complex hierarchies, of rich and poor, farmers, moneylenders, schoolteachers, fishing communities and small traders, of Muslims and Hindus. But one thing that united it all was the impossibility of policing the district. The terrain problem and the political problem were as one in the mangrove forests of the Sundarbans, that suspected refuge of revolutionaries, petty criminals and the Bengal Tiger.

In 1917, Lord Curzon, former Viceroy of India, sponsored a scheme for Indian self-government within the British Empire. The need for change was obvious, even to Curzon – the poster boy for colonial India with his pith helmet and dead tigers – and yet he could not imagine life without India and its great octopus of money-making schemes. He had summed up in 1904 India's great and continuing value:

> . . . if you desire to defend any of your extreme out-posts or coaling stations of the Empire, Aden, Mauritius, Singapore, Hong-Kong, even Tien-stin or Shan-hai-kwan, it is to the Indian Army that you turn . . . It is with India coolie labour that you exploit the plantations . . . of Demerara and Natal; with Indian trained officers that you irrigate and dam the Nile; with Indian forest officers that you tap the resources of Central Africa and Siam; with Indian surveyors that you explore all the hidden places of the earth.[48]

In this vision, all rivers, seas, canals and irrigation schemes of the empire were connected. The Ganges, in its guise as the great trading river, was the perfect imperial highway. It was those other more unruly waters of the delta and the unpredictable real people that complicated things. The next forty years saw Indians continuing to wear away at this edifice of imperial interconnectedness. The waterways of the Ganges remained crucial threads in this journey to independence and in the complexities of South Asia in the post-independence years.

9
Dividing the Waters

'We are all in the same boat. We must sink or swim together. Government cannot but treat us all alike.'

Dadabhai Naoroji, 'Ninth Congress – Lahore – 1893'[1]

This was the Indian nationalist Dadabhai Naoroji speaking in 1890s Lahore – in today's Pakistan – about the need for harmony between Indians of all faiths. In the event, of course, Indians did not swim together but were divided in the hasty carve-up of India into Muslim-majority Pakistan and Hindu-majority India of 1947. The Ganges went to India; the Indus to Pakistan, with its Sutlej tributary forming part of the western boundary.[2] East Bengal became first East Pakistan then independent Bangladesh in 1971; the silty veins of Bengal province now separated its people. 'I want Brahmaputra as much as I want Subarnarekha,' wrote the exiled Bangladeshi poet Taslima Nasrin in 1994.[3] These two rivers – the Brahmaputra, flowing through Bangladesh, and India's Subarnarekha, which enters the sea south of Calcutta – remind us that Partition divided the waters as well as the land. This chapter is about the way rivers are divided by values and by territory. It looks first at rivers caught up in Partition. Secondly it explores differing perceptions of the value of rivers and asks what happened to the Ganges' numinous waters in this fractured post-colonial world.

The Indus River was once a defining feature of India: for outsiders its fluid border and everything east of the Indus was one place.[4] The Indus Valley was home to India's earliest settlements: the Indus Civilisation – with its still un-deciphered scripts on seals – is estimated to date from around 9,000 years ago, declining for reasons that are not clear a few hundred years before the cities of the Ganges plain began to emerge around 3,200 years ago.[5] Sindhu, the Sanskrit term for the Indus, gave its name to both Hinduism and to the subcontinent of India.[6] Babur, founder of India's Mughal Empire, declared as he passed through this new land on his conquest tour starting in Kabul in the 1520s: 'Once the water of Sind is crossed, everything is in the Hindūstān way . . . land, water, tree, rock, people and horde, opinion and custom.'[7] But Babur was a newcomer. Long-standing contacts with Islamic Central Asian neighbours, and conquests from Islamic Arab Caliphates and later Mongols, meant that however mobile and intermixed the people of India were, the Indus River far over to the west was somehow set apart.

The emergence of a fragmented South Asia, divided between Pakistan and India, mirrored in some ways the dissolution of empires along the Danube River. The end of empire brought new nation states more easily built around sameness than difference. By the 1940s when India's colonial years finally seemed to be coming to an end, the representatives of its 400 million people had to decide what the future nation should look like.[8] Two very different Indian nationalists were to lead the two new nations. Muhammad Ali Jinnah (1876–1948) of the Muslim League would become Pakistan's first Governor General, and the (Hindu) secularist Jawaharlal Nehru (1889–1964) became India's first prime minister for the Congress Party. Early in 1940, Jinnah outlined his 'Two Nations Theory', proposing irreconcilable differences between Muslims and Hindus. As he put it:

> Notwithstanding a thousand years of close contact, nationalities, which are divergent today as ever, cannot at any time be expected to transform themselves into one nation merely by means of subjecting them to a democratic constitution. . . . The Hindus and Muslims belong to two different religions, philosophies, social customs, literatures. . . . Musulmans are a nation according to any definition of a nation, and they must

> have their homelands, their territory, and their State.[9]

While very different groups and classes of people had been living alongside each other for centuries, religious difference was a potential fault line.

Those who wanted multi-faith co-existence in India's post-independence future lost the argument to those moving towards partition of the subcontinent on lines reflecting its two major faiths. The impossible task of drawing suitable boundary lines was given to the British lawyer Cyril Radcliffe, '[h]aving never set eyes on this land he was called to partition', as immortalised in W.H. Auden's 1966 poem. Radcliffe pored over maps, reports and out-of-date census figures, holed up in the Viceroy's hill-station in East Punjab from where he was sent news of the latest backroom deals.[10]

The Radcliffe Lines established what aspired to be a Hindu-majority India and a Muslim-majority West Pakistan – centred on the Indus River – with an annex in East Bengal called East Pakistan. Boundary lines were to follow the principle of a faith majority within specific regions, even though most regions were to varying extents intermixed. East Bengal's war of secession with West Pakistan later created the independent state of Bangladesh in 1971. When Partition came at midnight on 14 August 1947, millions had already taken to the roads and railways looking for safety across borders. In the panic and violence, perhaps half a million people died and millions more were exiled for ever.[11]

Rivers were caught up in the politics of Partition from the start. Shared rivers now crossed boundaries. Rivers that were now claimed as national rivers turned out to water other lands. River basins re-engineered in the colonial era with the whole of the subcontinent in mind had to be replanned. As a geographer noted at the time of Partition, although rivers are often used as boundaries, they don't do the job all that well. They are effective, 'natural' boundaries only if they flow:

> ... through a deep rock-walled canyon ... with a fairly constant volume of water, without shifts of course, with few

> crossing-places, and useless for navigation or rafting, irrigation or hydro-electric power.[12]

Nor are most borders created from scratch. Many are created by armies grabbing as much useful territory as possible then establishing a defensive line, which may happen to be a river. Partitioning a country in such a way as to minimise conflict between neighbours required a fair balance of resources, land and water supplies, using the hand of cards dealt by nature and history. In 1940s India, this was carried out with unseemly haste in the few weeks allocated to Radcliffe. It took the British government longer to design the 'new town' of Milton Keynes than independent India.[13]

With Partition decided it was clear that India would have an east/west partition to reflect the majority Muslim population of the Indus River region. But the Indus was tied by many threads to the waters and lands to its east. Like the Ganges, the Indus River flows from snowmelt high in the Tibetan Himalayas with the headwaters of some of its tributaries in India. From here it heads to the Indian zone of the disputed region of Kashmir – a region so geopolitically sensitive that Pakistan and India are still on permanent high alert around a 'line of control'.[14] From here the river flows south-west down to the Arabian Sea at Karachi, with the Thar Desert to its east.

At a time when river basins were starting to be treated as integrated wholes for water management, the Indus River basin, 430,000 square miles in size, was split between Pakistan and India.[15] A line had to be drawn through the prime agricultural region of the Punjab, or 'land of five rivers', that flowed from the east and into the Indus system: the Jhelum, Chenab, Ravi and Sutlej rivers.[16] The easternmost rivers of the Punjab, the Ravi and the Sutlej would eventually form part of the India/Pakistan boundary. In the late nineteenth century, the Punjab was extensively developed for raising grain and cotton cash crops in a series of so-called 'canal colonies': a web of canals created by the British authorities for irrigation in this dry but fertile land. The Punjab region under the British had a Latin motto: *crescat e fluviis* (strength from the waters).[17] Farmers had been encouraged to settle here, especially those from Sikh communities. As of the 1940s, two main grain crops were grown each year: sowing the spring-harvested Rabi crops (especially wheat) and the autumn-harvested Kharif crops (especially rice). Two-thirds of irrigated farmland across India was in the Indus River basin.[18] Both India and Pakistan had reasons to be worried about what would happen next.

The British agricultural policy left a strong Sikh population in this canal zone. Sikh representatives in the Punjab, wanting to be included within India, lobbied for India's western border along the Chenab River and cited 700 holy sites located in affected regions. India's Congress Party supported this claim to the Chenab, though it flowed through a Muslim majority region. The Sikhs lost their holy site of Nankana Sahib, birthplace of Sikhism's founder Guru Nanak (1469–1539), which went to Pakistan's Punjab Province.[19] But they retained the city of Amritsar between the Ravi River and Beas River (a tributary of the Sutlej), a city allocated to India, with its Golden Temple mirrored in the water of the Amrit Sarovar.[20]

The water question dragged on beyond Partition. India was concerned for its economic prospects should it lose its eastern agricultural land and water supplies. But with its access to some of the canals watering Pakistan's territory, it had power. Amid tensions in 1948, India showed that it was prepared to use its power, as the upstream party, by cutting the water supply on some of the canals temporarily. Pakistan claimed rights to the water on the basis of 'historical usage'. But in its defence India invoked a dubious and short-lived ruling, the Harmon Doctrine, relating to an 1890s dispute on the Rio Grande: the United States–Mexico border river. Here, the states of Colorado and New Mexico had been taking so much water from the Rio Grande that at times it was running dry for hundreds of miles, leaving nothing for the frontier towns of El Paso in Texas or the 300-year-old town Ciudad Juárez in Mexico. Here, according to the Mexican consul in 1894, farmers 'were unable to raise any Indian corn, vegetables, or grapes, and . . . even the fruit trees began to wither'.[21] The US Attorney General, Judson Harmon, had declared there to be no limit on the water the United States could take from the river because: 'The fundamental principle of international law is the absolute sovereignty of every nation, as against all others, within its own territory.'[22] As the American government pondered its future with Canada, situated upstream on its own rivers and lakes, the doctrine was ultimately revoked.[23]

Pakistan wanted to appeal to the newly formed International Court of Justice, but the Indian government resisted this as an internal matter. Nehru considered possibilities for a TVA-style Indus Valley Authority, which would find echoes in planning for Indian basins such as the Damodar Valley. But it was Eugene Black of the World Bank who eventually brokered a deal. The Indus Water Treaty (1960) allotted to Pakistan the water of the Indus and its two neighbouring tributaries: the Jhelum which flows south-west into the Indus, and the Chenab. India was allocated the waters of the easterly tributaries: the Ravi and the Sutlej.[24]

To the east, there were also difficult issues. The region of Bengal in the Sundarbans with a mixed Muslim/Hindu population was the second line of Partition. In a vote in the Bengal Legislative Assembly in 1947 on the partition of Bengal, majority Hindu districts in the Assembly voted in favour of Partition. The majority Muslim districts voted against. Muslims represented around a 55 per cent majority in Bengal and already had the potential to shape the future of the region through the existing Bengal assembly.[25] But Partition won the day. After lobbying by representative groups and regions, Cyril Radcliffe drew a line south to north through the Ganges-Brahmaputra-Meghna delta and the Sundarbans.[26]

The Sundarbans is home to a vast variety of nature's wildlife – home to more than 200 species of birds and well over 300 species of fish.[27] The waters of the delta are mixed: some are marine salty water, some are a brackish mixture of seawater and freshwater from upstream flows. The fish that come and go from the delta choose their route through the waters. The longnosed stargazer (*Ichthyscopus lebeck*) and moontail bullseye (*Priacanthus hamrur*) swim only in marine waters. The Indian river shad (*Gudusia chapra*) occupies the freshwater and brackish water higher up the delta streams. The rainbow sardine (*Dussumieria acuta*), also known as the common sprat, flows through all waters, as does the amphibious mudskipper (*Periophthalmus barbarus*), as happy on the land as in the water or its muddy banks.[28]

The Radcliffe line in the prodigious Sundarbans began where the waters flow into the Bay of Bengal and ran upstream through the middle (thalweg) of the Ichhamati River.[29] To the west of this river border was Calcutta (and the 24 Parganas district), which went to India. East of the Radcliffe line went to East Pakistan. The line then followed a convoluted path northward, eventually allocating most of the lucrative tea regions of Darjeeling and Jalpaiguri to West Bengal (India). This winding path also ensured that the Indian port of Calcutta controlled the Hooghly River on which it was situated (a distributary of the Ganges). This involved many compromises of the majority-faith principle, including the allocation of the Muslim majority district of Murshidabad to India.[30]

The mutating delta rivers made particularly bad borders. The Mathabhanga, forming part of the border, was monsoon fed: sometimes it was dry and at other times flooded. It had also already changed course by the time the Radcliffe line was drawn up.[31] The Ichhamati River forming the southernmost border changed course almost immediately after Partition. The everchanging life of the delta and its floodplains meant that sandy islands, or *chars*, could spontaneously form in the middle of the streams, sometimes big enough for whole villages to settle on them; the islands could just as easily disappear. The land here 'is demonstrably alive', wrote Amitav Ghosh in *The Great Derangement* (2016).[32]

For those people living, farming, fishing and trading along the rivers the uncertainties of these borders had frequent devastating consequences, as Joya Chatterji has shown. They could be found at any given moment to be on the wrong side of an imaginary line, at a time of acute animosity, vigilantism and punitive border policing.[33] The sprats could weave their way back and forth across the rivers, the mudskippers skuttle over the silty banks, and the mangrove whistlers fly from tree to tree, but the people could not.

Relations between India and Pakistan were also very tense in the east of the subcontinent. The Ganges was reborn in 1947 as the national river of independent India, from its source in the Himalayan province of Uttarakhand down to the sea.[34] The complexities of riparian rights only gradually became apparent. When in 1960 the Indian government wanted to dilute the great load of silt the Ganges carried into the shipping channels and reduce the heavy dredging demands, it devised a project called the Farakka Barrage. This would increase the amount of Ganges water already flowing into the Bhagirathi and Hooghly rivers, to aid the port of Calcutta. The problem was that while some Ganges water did naturally flow south into the Bhagirathi (and then the Hooghly), much of the river's flow continued in a south-easterly direction and into the Padma River of East Pakistan. Only prolonged protests from East Pakistan and then Bangladesh from 1971 brought an acknowledgement from India that the Ganges is an international river, subject to international treaties. India and Bangladesh are still working on how to share the fifty-three other rivers that connect their territories.[35]

Then there was East Pakistan, led by a national government in West Pakistan that was trying to impose its will from over a thousand miles away. The imposition of Urdu as the official language in 1948 was a bad omen in a Bengali-speaking land. From the Bengali Language Movement protests of the early 1950s onwards, this was a time of government by violent suppression, culminating in East Pakistan's invasion of its Bengali territory in 1971. The subsequent Bangladesh War of Independence ended in the creation of the state of Bangladesh in December 1971. Rivers were at the heart of Bengali poetry from these years, with images of killings, sacrifice and hopes for a future redemption: 'and when the need arises / we shall offer a river of our blood', Sikandar Abu Jafar wrote in 'This Struggle Will Go On'.[36]

Both elemental and mercurial, these rivers symbolized innate connections to the land and also an intangible faith in re-birth in the midst of oppression. In a poem dedicated 'To the Mother of a Martyr', Shaheedulla Qaiser fused the music of the sons and daughters of Bangla Desh, singing 'a common song', with the 'storm' of their resistance. This 'river of music / was flooded with blood', he wrote, and 'our songs became birds / and flew away'.[37] But one day the children of these birds and songs would return as a gathering storm on the river, and into the arms of the mother.

In 'The Blood Bank', Humayun Azaad invoked an image of the martyred people of Bengal, both young and old, donating their blood to the soil for the future of the country. As their blood sank into the earth, 'though the river may dry and the sea disappear', it was stored up for a future time. The lost blood and waters would rise again:

> from this same blood
> shall emerge a new river,
> a fresh garland of nature . . .[38]

In this final section, we turn to the impact of Partition and independence on ideas about the value of the waters of the Ganges. Now that India could shape its own future, how would it use its rivers and other natural resources? Within independent India, what kind of river should the Ganges be? From the start during the time of the first premier, Jawaharlal Nehru, the government was committed to a secular India, with modern approaches to water supply and management of rivers and other natural resources.[39] The commitment to modern economic development was maintained in the face of a rising environmental consciousness both within India and globally. At the first UN Conference for the Environment in Stockholm, Sweden, in 1972, speakers from developing countries from Egypt to China demanded the right to shape their own futures, and not be held back by the environmental concerns of already industrialised nations. Most famously, India's prime minister, Indira Gandhi, asked, 'Are not poverty and need the greatest polluters?'[40]

The Ganges River is complex from an environmental point of view. The Ganges has 'two bodies', as Sudipta Sen has put it: the spiritual and the physical.[41] Its highly polluted nature remains a paradox, set against its symbolic status as a purifying force. When India's current prime minister, Narendra Modi of the Hindu nationalist Bharatiya Janata Party, makes intermittent statements about pollution, and its impact on religious festivals such as Durga Puja and Kumbh Mela on the Ganges, he treads carefully due to popular sensitivities about the sacred river.[42] This dual nature of the river results in a much wider – and puzzling to outsiders – set of perceptions of purity than for those informed by sanitary or ecological approaches to river health, as determined by high levels of dissolved oxygen or the presence of 'indicator species'.[43]

The tension between sacred and instrumental/scientific views of rivers may also be found in relation to water supply, also sourced in nature but converted, like Tseqaye Gabre-Medhin's poem 'Nile', into 'miserable billions of petty cubic yards'.[44] Indian officials in the 1940s took charge of the piped-water networks built under British supervision from the nineteenth century on an industrialised European model.[45] An article written by a Delhi water engineer suggests some tensions between, on the one hand, piped networks that provide essential water supplies, and on the other hand, India's historical constellation of stepwells, tube wells and water tanks that had been largely ignored by British colonists. In 1982, the Delhi water engineer Colonel Brij Lal Verma called for his city to become 'a region of lakes once again'. Why not revive the old water tanks of the Delhi Sultanate and the old Mughal wells sunk into rock, where you could still see the water spring out? In addition, the city's existing piped-water network was breeding injustice, Verma suggested. The people of 'Lutyens Delhi' (the former colonial capital from 1911) were getting 90 gallons each per day, whereas people in the poor district of Shahdara received only 3 gallons a day. Meanwhile all the sewage and pollution of the city was flowing into the 'super drain': the 'sacred Yamuna' River.[46]

Tensions and contradictions between shared values were to emerge in many settings on the waters and rivers of independent India. Conflicts arose at the same time over the impacts of development on the natural world and people's lives. Contradictions within shared values found expression in the Indian government's development projects in the lower Himalayas, which came to be seen by some as degrading natural environments and eroding the livelihoods of the people living near the source of the holy Bhagirathi River. In the 1970s a local protest movement – Chipko, the original 'tree huggers' – became known globally.[47] Groups of local people wanted to halt the felling of trees for commercial forestry in the Uttarakhand region of the Himalayas. One of the impacts of deforestation was thought to be increased flooding downstream in the monsoon season. A flood in 1970 saw 100 square kilometres of the Alaknanda Valley under water, including the Ganga irrigation canal in Uttar Pradesh. The protestors pledged to hug the trees even as they were being felled (Chipko meaning 'to embrace'). These forest protests were also to take the form of hunger strikes and public readings of the *Bhagavad Gita* ('As It Is'). Eventually, the Indian government backed down in 1980.[48] As the historian Ramachandra Guha put it: 'Faced with a popular movement which originated in the watershed of the holy Ganga, used techniques of non-violence and was led by Gandhians, the state has been hoist with its own petard.'[49] Before long, though, the government was back with a raft of hydroelectric dam proposals for the upper Ganges watershed, including the Tehri Dam on the Bhagirathi River. Local people once again rose up to defend their rivers and resist displacement, but the dam went ahead.[50] Today, every river has its activists, from Save the Ganga to the Save Narmada Movement.[51]

One species has emerged as a global symbol of the precariousness of the life of the river: the river dolphins that make their way without sight using ultrasound through the silty, turbid waters of South Asia, South America and China (until its extinction).[52] Equally, the river dolphin represents how nature can be valued even as it is being destroyed. They are well known to be among the first casualties of pollution, dams and barrages on the Ganges and other rivers. The Ganges river dolphin (*Platanista gangetica*), named the 'National Aquatic Animal of India' in 2010, is today confined to the upstream waters of the eastern Himalayas and no longer to be found in the Ganges delta.[53] The *bhulan* of the Indus River (*Platanista gangetica minor*) – the National Mammal of Pakistan – is also struggling. Scarcer than the Ganges river dolphin, the *bhulan* inhabits the Beas River and the lower Indus, but here six barrages divide the *bhulan* into six separate populations.[54] The official value of this river species, as we will see later in the case of the Yangtze river dolphin, has little bearing on its safety.

New ways of trying to protect rivers are always emerging. Recent years have seen the development of an 'eco-centric' approach to rivers that transcends their human instrumental uses. Can we try to 'think like a river'? There have been calls for a global forum to allow a 'Parliament of Rivers'. And there is the movement to create 'legal personhood' for rivers and other natural entities, which can be seen taking root from South America to Lake Erie in North America and the River Ouse in England.[55] Two cases were brought before the Uttarakhand courts in 2017 to try to establish legal protection for the rivers and the wider ecology of the Ganges watershed. The first case claimed both the Ganga and Yamuna rivers as 'legal persons' with rights. The Uttarakhand court agreed that the state was neglecting its duties on behalf of the rivers and that they should be handed over to a protective body (such as the Ganga Management Board), acting as a substitute parent (on the principle of *parens patriae*). The second case focused on environmental hazards in the Himalayan region of Uttarakhand, including climate change, arguing that there 'is a grave threat to the very existence of Glaciers, Air, Rivers, rivulets, streams, Water Bodies including Meadows and Dales'. Again the court found that the state was failing in its duties.[56] The state of Uttarakhand and the government of India opposed these cases, however, and they were overturned. One question raised was who would be legally responsible for river flooding? Another problem arises from the close identification between the river as a Hindu entity and its legal personhood. How could this work in a pluralistic environment for those who are not Hindu? For the legal scholar Bushra Quasmi, a scientific approach is needed: 'the . . .

ecology and biodiversity of the country are in a shambles despite the fact that rivers and nature are culturally regarded as maternal figures'.[57]

Rivers, because they are so complex, do not make straightforward dividing lines. They invite competing claims and perceptions.

River 4: Thames

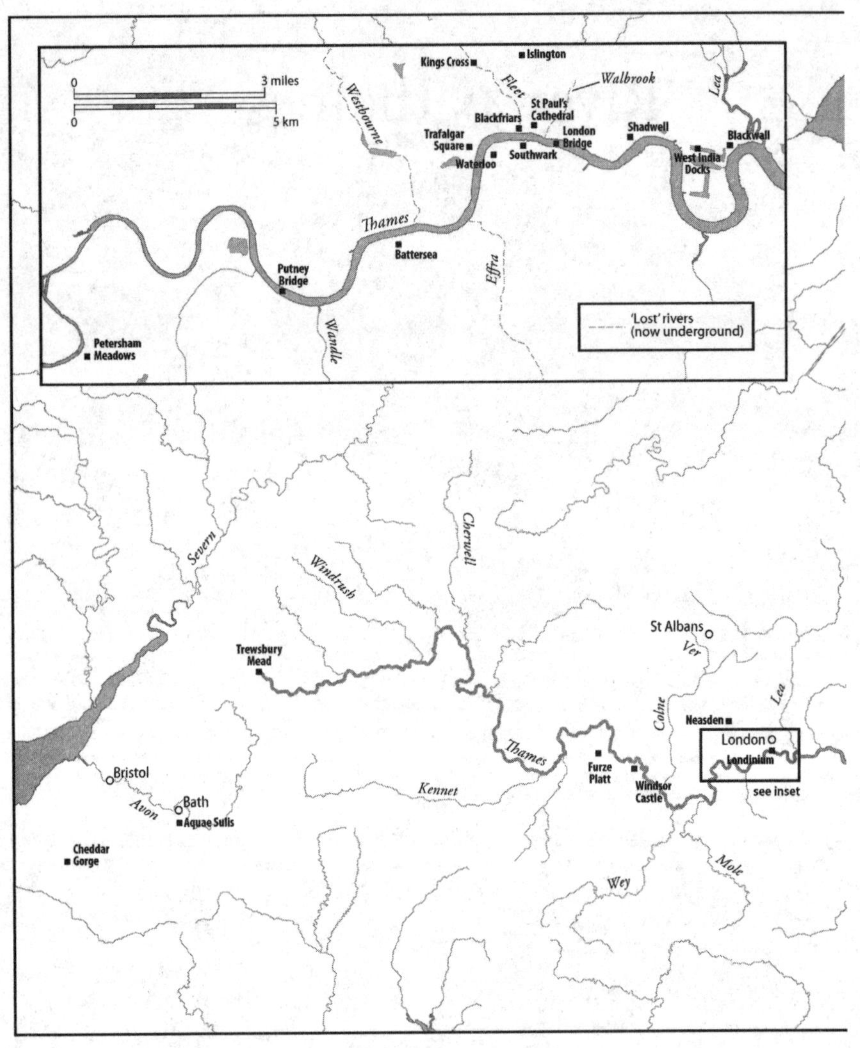

Kings Cross
Islington
0
3 miles
0
5 km
Westbourne
Fleet
Walbrook
Lea
St Paul's Cathedral
Blackfriars
London Bridge
Shadwell
Blackwall
Trafalgar Square
Waterloo
Southwark
West India Docks
Thames
Battersea
Putney Bridge
Effra
Wandle
Petersham Meadows
'Lost' rivers (now underground)
Severn
Windrush
Cherwell
St Albans
Ver
Trewsbury Mead
Colne
Lea
Neasden
London
Londinium
Thames
Furze Platt
Windsor Castle
see inset
Bristol
Bath
Aquae Sulis
Avon
Kennet
Cheddar Gorge
Mole
Wey

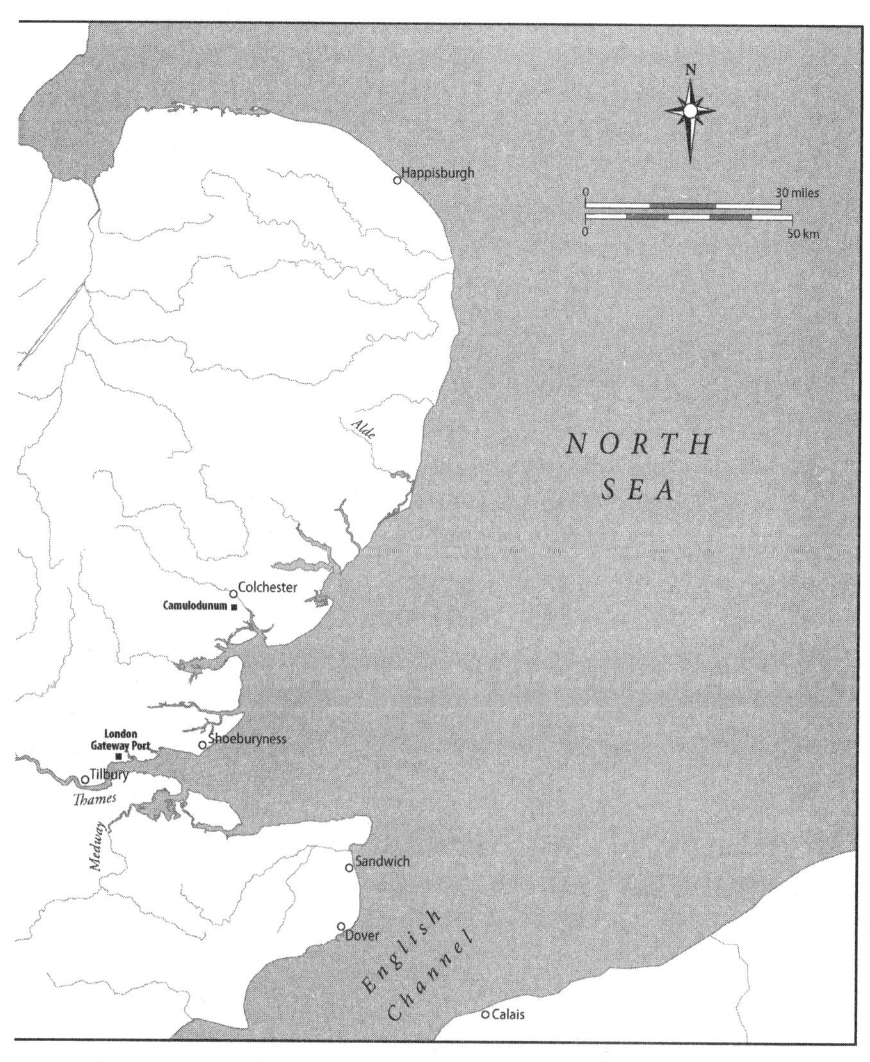

N
Happisburgh
0
30 miles
0
50 km
Alde
NORTH
SEA
Colchester
Camulodunum
London
Gateway Port
Shoeburyness
Tilbury
Thames
Medway
Sandwich
Dover
English
Channel
Calais

10
Birth of a River

> 'With respect to the name, it is derived directly from that by which it was known in the time of Julius Caesar, *Tameses*, which, as well as its Anglo-Saxon representative, *Temese*, is sufficiently near the modern *Thames* to be considered as identical with it. Lhwyd, the learned Welsh scholar, believes it to be identical also with the Taf – the name of several rivers in Wales. But there are other English rivers bearing names almost the same.'
>
> Mr and Mrs S.C. Hall, *The Book of the Thames* (1859)[1]

In the company of the six other rivers here, the Thames is a minnow among dolphins and whales. At only 215 miles long, it is less than 14 per cent of the next one up in length: the Ganges at 1,557 miles. The Thames River basin would fit 132 times into the combined Ganges-Brahmaputra-Meghna river basins.[2] But size, as they say, isn't everything. A great deal of history is packed into this small stream, though much of it in recent centuries is not as glorious as it seemed in the era of the imperial river. This chapter is about the genesis of this history. It begins with the birth of the River Thames itself and considers a longer history of the island up to the time when the Romans made their mark on the Thames banks at the edge of their known world.

The Thames River flows from its bubbling groundwater source in a Gloucestershire field east towards London and out into the North Sea between the counties of Essex and Kent. But it has travelled many paths over time. Brooding shifts of tectonic plates, massive fluctuations in global temperatures, and the rising and falling of the seas mean river channels have been carved out, re-routed and drowned. The continents have been shuffled round the globe by a drunken jigsaw player. Pieces of the British Isles – or Atlantic archipelago – have been fused with and broken loose from successive continents over time – before settling (for now) at the western extremity of Eurasia. This has been while slowly drifting northwards over millions of years to their present position between 50° N and 60° N.[3] All land, rivers and coastlines are just the latest incarnation of this perpetual change.

This prehistory is still in the ground. The London Clay that today sticks to spades in city gardens and swells and contracts beneath its housing stock is the deposit of a once semi-tropical coastline from perhaps 57 million years ago. Around 500 fossil species have been found in this dull 'mudstone': bay trees and cinnamon berries, dogwood and mangrove, and the *Nypa* palm that today flourishes in the Sundarbans of the Ganges.[4] The Thames region began gradually morphing towards its current shape while also being lifted out of the sea around 50 million years ago; a process perhaps connected to the grinding plates that over to the east were helping to build up the Alps.[5]

The ghosts of submerged forests still haunt the Thames foreshore, where the tides now rise and fall. Those digging new docks at Blackwall in the seventeenth century for the Thames 'East India' fleet found 'perfect trees over-covered with earth' at a depth of 12 feet underground. Nuts harvested from these subterranean treasures were proudly displayed by the dock-owner to his dinner guest the diarist Samuel Pepys, along with a yew tree that had been lifted out of the silty ground with the 'very ivy . . . taken up whole about it'.[6] Signs of early Thames-side people also emerged in this period as London was becoming more intensively developed. Just a few years later in the 1670s an ancient flint tool, a hand-axe, was spotted in the bed of the River Fleet at King's Cross, near an old well named Black Mary's. The apothecary John Conyers was part of a team culverting – covering up – a section of this Thames tributary. Lying inexplicably beside the flint tool was an elephant's tusk and other remains.[7] Conyer's friend, one John Bagford, writing about the world's first published report of a hand-axe, tried to explain this. The flint could be a weapon, he said. But the elephant tusk: though 'some will have it to have layn there ever since the Universal Deluge', he thought that more likely it was one of the war elephants brought over by the Romans under Claudius, 'killed in some Fight by a Britain'.[8] The Bible provided the limits of known time. Only recently, a leading churchman had pinned the moment of the world's creation down to 4004 BCE, using just the Bible and maths. By today's calculations, this is out by 4.5 billion years. The King's Cross hand-axe itself is thought to date back to 350,000 BCE.[9]

So who were the people and other creatures who left behind these relics beside the ancient Thames? We know they weren't modern humans. *Homo sapiens* didn't arrive in Britain until maybe 40,000 years ago.[10] There is no shortage of artefacts left behind. At a single site on an ancient flood terrace of the Thames in Surrey, over 1,600 stone hand-axes have been found including Europe's largest hand-axe: the so-called 'Furze Platt Giant', at around 32 centimetres long, 7.5 pounds in weight, and dating to around 300,000 years ago.[11] But there are few human remains to go on. Three fragments of what became known as the 'Swanscombe Woman' were found in gravel beside the Thames estuary in Kent between the 1930s and 1950s, along with the remains of lions and monkeys that lived in the trees along the riverside. Thought to be *Homo neanderthalensis*, the woman lived perhaps 400,000 years ago, during an interglacial period preceding those that produced the King's Cross and Furze Platt axes. Many thousands of hand tools were recovered from this same spot on the Kent riverside. But there is little to tell us who crafted them. Swanscombe Woman is one of only two human remains found in the whole of Britain from this long 'Lower Palaeolithic' period (2.58 million to 300,000 years ago).[12]

The Thames was also at the heart of a longer human story in Britain that has recently been extended backwards in time by nearly half a million years. The evidence is not bones or stones but shapes in the ground. One day in 2013 on a rainy beach in

East Anglia a set of preserved footprints was found, belonging to a group of adult humans and children who may have lived up to 900,000 years ago. These are the oldest preserved footprints outside of Africa, thought to be those of *Homo antecessor* ('pioneer man').[13] Strangely these too are Thames-side remains, though they were discovered on the coast of Norfolk at Happisburgh. This spot has been identified as the muddy estuary bed of the 'proto-Thames', when the river still flowed from London to East Anglia and beyond.[14] Along with the footprints are the remains of pike and sea sturgeon that used to swim in its waters, of frogs or toads, of field vole, and an ancient Southern Mammoth that once loomed over them. There was also the giant beaver (*Trogontherium cuvieri*), much larger than the Eurasian beaver, that once gnawed its way along riverbanks from one end of the continent to another, from the proto-Thames to the Yangtze, but became globally extinct by perhaps 40,000 years ago.[15]

How did the Thames get from East Anglia to its current route? Several prolonged Ice Ages separate the people of the Happisburgh Thames-side and the site of today's river. The game-changer for the Thames was the Anglian glaciation which covered much, though not all, of Britain and helped to turn Britain into an island. About 450,000 years ago a huge lake had built up in front of the advancing ice in today's southern North Sea, pressing against the chalk ridge that still connected Dover and Calais. At some point around this time the pressure burst through the chalk land ridge, creating the conditions for the Channel River to be flooded by rising seas. The English Channel (or French La Manche) was born from this.[16] As the winter kingdom of this same Anglian ice sheet crept southwards, halting around 450,000 years ago on the outskirts of today's north and east London, the course of the Thames was gradually edged towards its current position. This new site was where 50,000 years later (during the warm 'Hoxne' interglacial) Swanscombe Woman lived on its southern banks.[17] So, people have been living along the banks of the Thames on and (frequently) off for at least 900,000 years.

During this time there have been some very different creatures living in its waters. In the 1920s, when builders were digging the foundations of a new insurance building in Trafalgar Square, they found 30 feet deep in the sand and gravel the remains of European pond terrapins and *hippopotamus amphibius* that had lived and died in the wide, balmy 'Mediterranean' Thames of around 120,000 years ago.[18] This warm Ipswichian interglacial period (around 130,000 to 115,000 years ago) is thought to have been a time without humans in Britain. Everyone had left long ago for a Southern European refuge to escape the bitterly cold temperatures of the preceding late 'Wolstonian' Ice Age.[19] But for many thousands of years in this period, eastern Britain was connected to mainland Europe by the region known as Doggerland or 'Rhine-Thames Land': a once thriving and now lost world perhaps 60,000–70,000 square kilometres in size. Spearheads and hand-axes, hyena bones and mammoth tusks have been pulled from deep beneath the waves by fishing trawlers and dredgers.[20] Before the end of the last glacial period, 20,000 years ago when sea levels were still very low, the waters of the Rhine and Meuse rivers flowed westwards across Doggerland and met the Thames near its outer estuary. Here their combined waters journeyed southwards into the 'Channel River' and continued west through a British/French landscape, now replaced by the straits of Dover.[21]

As the ice melted from around 14,000 years ago, both Doggerland and the Thames/Rhine confluence slowly drowned beneath the waves of the North Sea, leaving the shallows of Dogger Bank as a relic. From around 6,000 BCE, future journeys between Britain and the rest of its continent must have been by boat and the non-human fauna now stayed put on the island, leaving just the birds and fishes to go their own ways.[22] The British Isles today are just those parts that happened to have remained above sea level, after the great pool of glacial meltwater stabilised. It was not until about 11,500 years ago that there is evidence of more continuous occupation, by different groups of people, across perhaps 500 generations.[23]

On the Thames it was a long time before a city evolved, though the river indicates plenty of action and long-distance cultural/trading relationships. The Thames River has been found to contain one of Europe's highest concentrations of prehistoric weapons.[24] The Thames was both a battleground, as a border between tribes and kingdoms, and also potentially a sacred river for some. Rivers, like springs, lakes and bogs – deep into the distant past – are considered by archaeologists as 'liminal places' between the seen and unseen worlds.[25] A bronze shield pulled out of the river at Battersea (south-west London) dates perhaps to the second century BCE. An Iron Age helmet in copper alloy, complete with horns, was found near Waterloo Bridge, dating from around 150–50 BCE. Both are decorated in the La Tène style (named after a site at Lake Neuchâtel, Switzerland), with its swirling and mutating animal forms also found in continental Europe from around 450 BCE.[26]

Britain was already in a global orbit of sorts before the Romans arrived. Amber worked into jewellery in Britain somehow journeyed all the way to Mycenae into the graves of elite families who died 3,500 years ago.[27] But as Roman influence moved westwards along the Rhine, the Romans were able to start dominating Britain's trade with continental Europe. Corn, cattle and animal skins were exported from Britain into the Roman Empire along with metals, slaves and hunting dogs. When Julius Caesar invaded south-east Britain in 55 and 54 BCE, he left behind some intimidated trading partners and pliable rulers.[28]

When the Romans eventually came to stay during the reign of Claudius in 43 CE, breaching this island 'fortress built by nature' had proved quite easy, albeit with 40,000 soldiers.[29] If his route took him across the Thames River (probably without the elephants that later writers mentioned), Claudius didn't linger there but headed for Colchester (Camulodunum) for a victory parade. A triumphal arch commissioned to celebrate this event back in Rome – mounted on top of the Aqua Virgo aqueduct – bore the names of possibly eleven client 'kings' of Britain, but it is sadly now lost.[30] By this point there may have been over thirty tribal areas in Iron Age Britain. Some of them were already quite Romanised, such as the Atrabates south of the Thames and, north of the river, the Catuvellauni. Featured in Shakespeare's *Cymbeline*, this group had settled in Colchester on the River Colne from where they dominated Britain's trade across the North Sea via the River Rhine in the years before the Roman invasion. It was partly to protect threats in Britain to this lucrative trade that Claudius's forces crossed the Channel.[31]

Britain marked the end of Rome's westward expansion and the end of the known world. Beyond this lay the Atlantic – or Oceanus, the 'encircling ocean' – which not even the Romans could penetrate. As one imperial writer put it (allowing licence for unconquered Ireland): 'Is there any thing else remaining behind, to which the power and ambition of Man can extend, beyond the Ocean, what is there more than Britain?'[32] Neither London nor Britons had an origin myth to match those of Rome – the fratricidal twins Romulus and Remus raised by wolves, who according to legend, founded the city many centuries before. As the Roman politician and historian Tacitus (c. 56–c. 120 CE) said: 'Who the first inhabitants of Britannia were, whether natives or immigrants, remains obscure, as one would expect when dealing with barbarians.'[33] Tacitus also noted with what alacrity British elites adopted Roman ways with their 'assembly-rooms, bathing establishments and smart dinner parties. In their inexperience the Britons called it civilization when it was really all part of their servitude'.[34] There was nothing on the Thames to impress the Romans in the way that the Nile had impressed them. No temples, obelisks or pharaohs with their daily interactions with the sky god. There are some signs of cultural fusion, but much about the interaction between Romans and Britons remains obscure. In the city of Bath in south-west England, by contrast, a major temple complex was created around a thermal spring dedicated to the Celtic-Roman goddess Sulis Minerva, including hundreds of Celtic offerings.[35] When a new London Bridge was being built many centuries later in the 1830s, those working on its foundations in the riverbed came across thousands of Roman coins. (This is the same bridge that now stands on a reservoir of the Colorado River in the Arizona desert.) Archaeologists consider that these coins were probably offerings, thrown into the water from the Roman-era London Bridge that sat around 30 metres downstream.[36] But to what gods they were offered and by whom is unknown.

The Romans brought about widespread but not universal cultural change, especially in urban settlements. Using Latin in official communications with their subject people, they also Latinised the names of places and rivers they encountered, including that of Londinium's river, which they called Thamesis.[37] The Britons seem to have known the river as Tamesis or Tamesa but the exact origin and meaning of this are also unknown. Some believe, as Peter Ackroyd says in *Thames: Sacred River* (2008), that this river for Celtic-speaking people meant 'dark' waters.[38]

By the time the Romans arrived on the Thames they were well-equipped to know where to put down roots. Londinium was built on the river's lowest fordable point and here they built the first London Bridge. This was a good defensive site, situated on solid north-bank river terraces between two hills: today's Ludgate Hill in the west and Cornhill in the east. The Thames here was probably tidal as it is today but also shallower, broader, and with more shoals and islands on the riverside. Drinking water was plentiful. Wells, often simple affairs reusing timber from wine barrels made from Alpine fir trees, were sunk into the water-logged sands and gravels that lay beneath the city above the impermeable London Clay.[39]

At its height, Londinium had all the infrastructure of any self-respecting Roman city, with its Forum, temples, bathhouses and public baths, mosaic floors, craft workshops and kilns. At the prow of Ludgate Hill, where St Paul's Cathedral sits today, there is a possible (disputed) site of a Roman temple. Beneath today's Guildhall an amphitheatre once stood where the City of London Corporation meets today. Built in 70 CE and rebuilt in the early second century, it had gated spaces for the animals and was large enough to accommodate 6,000 people to enjoy the spectacle. Such facilities linked life across the empire, from the Danube at Aquincum (Budapest) to Alexandria in Egypt.[40]

Near the riverside on the northern bank were temples, public baths, workshops and housing. The Walbrook River and its tributaries flowed southwards entering the Thames through two streams.[41] At this confluence were timber waterfronts and from the late third century a defensive wall. South of the river was far more porous, with islands, tidal creeks, fish traps and mudflats. A Museum of London map recreating its landscape shows Southwark as a kind of peninsula between Borough Channel in the west and Guy's Channel in the east. But it also shows a thriving world of markets, palace buildings, warehouses and quarries. Already parts of London's riverside were being 'reclaimed'[42] from the water, both in Southwark and on the north bank. Excavations in the Temple of Mithras on the Walbrook River show that some of this stream had been filled in by refuse to support foundations for the Temple.

This was not just a city of brick, stone and timber. Plant remains unearthed by archaeologists tell us there were grassy wetlands within as well as beyond the city walls. Seeds of rushes, sedges, lesser spearwort and buttercups still lie in the ground today, in the foundations of the Roman city.[43] A pellet left by a barn owl who once took up residence in the city's Basilica contained the remains of a mole and field voles from the city's nocturnal hunting ground.[44] The Thames foreshore was a stopping-off point for migratory birds on ancient flyways, like the black-crowned night heron and the handsome crested northern lapwing (*Vanellus vanellus*), whose remains have been found at a Roman-era site at London Wall, and were also discovered both in the wetlands of the ancient Nile and on their temple walls where lapwings seem to have represented people subjugated under Egyptian rule. Ninety-four species of birds have been identified from Roman Britain. Remains from Roman-era London include the raven and carrion crow, song thrush and white-tailed eagle.[45] In a Roman cemetery at St Clare Street (north of today's Tower of London) a square pit has been discovered with a timber box and below it the remains of a grey heron, several small rodents, and more than a hundred common frogs. It isn't clear whether these creatures were part of a ritual offering or a hoard created by the grey heron itself.[46]

A strong military presence was required throughout the Roman occupation. Conquest was one thing but permanently quelling the tribes across Britain was another.[47] The major rebellion of this period in 60–61 CE, led by Boudica, queen of the East Anglian Iceni tribe, saw Colchester, Londinium and Verulamium (St Albans), the territory of the Catuvellauni tribe, burnt to the ground and many killed. In London the Iceni left a charred crust beneath today's city. And recent evidence shows that they also crossed London Bridge and set the southern suburb alight.[48] The internal security of Rome's occupation depended on a network of military roads and fortified cities across their territory. At Scotland's undefeated border, second-century defensive walls were brilliantly chosen by the occupiers to cross the island at its narrowest points with estuaries at each end: Hadrian's Wall linked the Solway Firth to the River Tyne; that of Antoninus Pius linked the Clyde to the Firth of Forth.[49] They did this without the aid of Google Maps. Within London, sporadic signs of turbulence can be found in the waters and gravel pits of the Roman City, including a single bronze arm, perhaps of Emperor Nero, thrown into a Roman pond possibly in the year 70 CE, two years after his death. At London Bridge in 1907, a bronze head of Emperor Hadrian, who visited London in 122 CE, was pulled from the river.[50]

Rome proved resilient to internal rebellions. After Boudica's destruction (and defeat), Londinium's major rebuilding started almost straight away. A new fortress recently found near today's Fenchurch Street is dated to the year 63, along with a hammer and pickaxe dropped by builders 2,000 years ago. There were new quays on the riverside, new roads, buildings, and water wells already underway by this time. An elaborate well with 'bucket-chain' dating to this year – and recently discovered near London's Guildhall – could haul up enough water to supply thousands of Londoners.[51]

Rome pulled the Thames into its mythical orbit, leaving the traces of its own imperial journey through Greece, Persia, North Africa and Europe embedded in the riverbanks. There are a thousand clues to a time when London's river was in the grip of the

Roman Empire: a monumental arch with figures of Hercules and Minerva, stone images of 'mother goddesses', a screen with the seven Graeco-Roman gods of the days of the week. The Walbrook River has yielded a river god, a figure of Venus, and a temple of Mithras dating to 240 CE. The cult of Mithras the bull-slayer, a secretive male-only affair, is thought to have distant origins in a Persian cult and to have spread westwards with the Roman army along the Danube and Rhine. Mithraic objects from the Walbrook temple foundations include figures of Serapis – god of the fertility and the harvest – and the so-called Danubian Riders, closely connected with the Mithraic cult: always twin figures side by side, on horseback.[52] But in this fast-moving polytheistic world within a century the temple was re-dedicated; this time to Bacchus, Graeco-Roman god of fertility and wine.[53] Also found, south of the Thames, in the grave of a young woman who died early in the second century were decorated lamps bearing the image of Anubis: the jackal-headed Egyptian god who oversaw the passage of the dead to the underworld.[54] And from a first-century quarry in Bow Churchyard is a rare glass cameo from the Graeco-Roman world, depicting the demi-god Hercules with his male companion Iolaos, both naked but for their headwear.[55]

All this was to fade. By the late fourth century, the once supremely confident Roman military was being outdone on all sides. By 402, Roman coins stopped being imported, meaning that neither army nor officials would get paid, and the Roman government machine in Britain was gradually abandoned. The year 410 CE, when Rome was sacked by Alaric the Visigoth, is seen as marking the final year of Roman rule in Britain. Trade continued to flow along the usual channels for a time.[56] Imperial power departed, as the Eastern Empire rose at Byzantium (Istanbul), though Rome wasn't to forget Britain altogether. Late in the next century they were back with their bishops and Bibles.[57]

The decline of the Roman world is also embedded in the ground on the banks of the Thames: once-valuable monuments were torn down and reused for river walls in the unstable years of the late fourth century.[58] It is tempting to see the treasure of metal kitchenware – jugs, ladles, a trivet – found recently at the bottom of a Late Roman well by the Walbrook River (today's Drapers' Gardens) as a hoard hurriedly concealed in an increasingly unsafe city.[59] But like those in rivers, bogs and streams, deposits in water wells are seen by archaeologists as more likely to be the focus of acts of ritual and propitiation, than hiding places.

When the Roman army abandoned Britain, it became a destination for incursions and migrations by Saxons, Angles, Jutes and Vikings from across the North Sea.[60] London's river port moved around a mile upstream to Lundenwic, to today's Strand and Covent Garden. The walled city of Londinium itself was largely forgotten for perhaps around 450 years, abandoned to songbirds and the croaking of frogs along the Walbrook.[61] A barge sunk at the mouth of the River Fleet at Blackfriars with its cargo of Kentish Ragstone – the stone used for London's late second-century Roman wall – is a reminder of something that started during the Roman occupation.[62] The great haulage of stuff to this city on the Thames had begun, and would continue: stone, timber, metals, cement, plastic bottles, sweet wrappers. London today is estimated to weigh around 6 billion tons.[63] Shanghai isn't the only city that is sinking.

11
Shadows of an Imperial River

'. . . all our Creekes seeke to one River, all our Rivers run to one Port, all our Ports joyne to one Towne, all our Townes make but one Citty, and all our Citties but Suburbes to one vast, unweldy, and disorderlie Babell of buildings, which the worlde calls London.'

Thomas Milles (1608)[1]

This was Thomas Milles, a customs officer on the Kent coast under Elizabeth I and James I, complaining about a trade monopoly that was favouring London's port. Milles doesn't seem to have done badly himself. Not all rivers did flow to London, of course. Most were flowing at this point with utter indifference to it, but this perfectly worded peevishness has lived on. London merchants in the early 1600s were ambitious for trade and power. This was successfully achieved over the next 300 years. The city spread its shadow across Britain and also, more remarkably, over distant lands, 'ghost acres' and rivers of the world. Between the sixteenth and early twentieth centuries, success on the Thames was reflected in the way it pulled in other places and other waterways as shadow rivers. All major rivers have their shadows, which they dominate and depend on, their trading routes and their hinterlands.

With the expansion of sea empires and rising international trade, rivers too became increasingly interconnected. This chapter looks at the changing role of the River Thames and the impacts of its role as an imperial highway. How did the Thames evolve to match its new status, and how did this change the city on its banks? We end in the early twentieth century as the global centre of gravity started to shift and the Thames itself was about to become overshadowed by other lands and rivers.

Any self-respecting imperial river needed river gods to match, as we have seen on the Nile and Danube. And on the Thames from the late Elizabethan age there was a shift in representations of the Thames as the river accumulated symbols of wealth and status like a rising star. The Thames was already a stage-set for royal palaces on its banks from Windsor to Greenwich, and it was given a fulsome place in Edmund Spenser's neoclassical epic *The Faerie Queen* (1590s), which celebrated the English Queen Elizabeth and Tudor England. Here the marriage of the Thames, 'the louely Bridegroome', and his bride the Medway River, featured an impressive A-List of wedding guests. All the Thames' tributaries came of course: its vassals, from the 'chaulky Kenet' and 'morish Cole' to the 'wanton Lee, that oft doth loose his way'. All 'the famous riuers' of the globe were also there, from the primal river with perhaps the garden of Eden – 'the fertile Nile, which creatures new doth frame', to 'Faire Ister' and 'Deepe Indus', 'Great Ganges, and immortall Euphrates', 'Swift Rhene, and Alpheus immaculate'.[2] South American rivers also showed up, more recently discovered but already enveloped in myth:

> Rich Oranochy, though but knowen late;
> And that huge Riuer, which doth beare his name
> Of warlike Amazons, which doe possesse the same.[3]

Another poem, 'Cooper's Hill', written by the Royalist poet John Denham from a vista overlooking Windsor Castle, reflects ambitions for the Thames' eminence on the world's stage:

> Nor are his Blessings to his banks confin'd,
> But free and common as the Sea or Wind;
> . . .
> So that to us no thing, no place is strange,
> While his fair bosom is the world's exchange.[4]

Written a decade before the 'Fountain of the Four Rivers' (1651) was installed in Rome, glorifying the papacy and Habsburgs among the world's rivers, the Thames was quietly being inserted into this ideological world. Denham's poem did not just add the Thames to the pantheon of river gods; it was, he wrote, 'the most lov'd of all the Oceans sons'. The Thames had acquired a firm sense of purpose by the late eighteenth century. 'Commerce, or the Triumph of the Thames' celebrated Britain's naval supremacy as part of a series of images by the Irish artist James Barry charting *The Progress of Human Knowledge* for the Royal Society of Arts in the 1790s. This shows the Thames, a semi-recumbent god being borne over the waves in what can only be described as a slipper bath, supported by a crowded scene of sea nymphs, navigational instruments and explorers: Francis Drake, Walter Raleigh and James Cook. Presenting their bounty to the god are figures representing the four known continents of Asia, Africa, Europe and America. Other versions of this image were also produced soon after its first appearance with the lines from 'Cooper's Hill' (quoted above) now also inserted. The 'fair bosom' of the Thames was now 'the world's exchange'.[5]

London was also acquiring three-dimensional river gods modelled on the Roman Tiber and other classical rivers, around the same time. The reclining Thames river gods created by the sculptors John Bacon (1780s) and Raffaelle Monti (1850s) still lie on the Thames riverside today. Even the Thames' industrialised tributary, the River Lea, got its own deity, designed by Joseph Theakston (1811), now located at the former East London Waterworks in the Lea Valley.[6] Londoners didn't believe in these gods any more than the Romans in Egypt believed in Nilus with his sixteen cherubs. What they all worshipped was the horn of plenty, overflowing with natural wealth, whether this was attached to the Nile, Danube, Rhine, Scheldt or any other river.

But the Thames was not just a triumphant highway for the engines of its imperial trade. Over time it absorbed heat and pollution into its waters, becoming a hazard to its own citizens. Industrial development and environmental degradation already went hand in hand. London had always been a combustible city.[7] It wasn't just the timber houses; everything was combustible. By the early 1600s, many thousands of tons of coal a year were being shipped from the 'coaly Tyne' River at Newcastle and down along the east coast to London.[8] On the eve of the Great Fire in 1666, London was home to a population of about 400,000 souls lining the river from Whitechapel in the east to Westminster. Many of these were warmed and fed by the stoves of thousands of hearths, each one of which was individually taxed to raise money for the Crown. Most of the houses had hearths burning wood, faggots or coal. There were sixty-eight hearths in Pudding Lane alone, where the fire began. And the home of Thomas Farriner, baker to King Charles II, had five fireplaces in addition to the notorious oven where a faggot was allowed to stay alight on the September night while the household one by one fell asleep, and where the housemaid was to become the first of six casualties.[9] The riverside city was also packed with flammable and explosive materials from across the world: from the barrels of tar in ship-chandlers' shops to the saltpetre (potassium nitrate) for gunpowder stored in East India Company warehouses along the river. The fire burned out of control for three nights and two days and across 373 acres on the river's north bank, destroying the homes of 100,000 people. Iron bells melted in church towers and crashed to the ground while the stone walls burned around them. Coal would still be glowing in City basements two months after the fire.[10] Samuel Pepys, the diarist and naval administrator, took to a boat on the river on the first night and watched the City burn: 'all over the Thames,' he wrote, 'with one's face in the wind, you were almost burned with a shower of firedrops'.[11]

After the fire, it was coal that came to the City's aid. Tax on this solid fuel brought into the City contributed to the reconstruction of public buildings, including the fifty-one new City churches rebuilt by architects Christopher Wren and Nicholas Hawksmoor, with St Paul's Cathedral completed in 1711. For these churches, stone was shipped from quarries all over Britain and northern France. White limestone from the Isle of Portland on England's south coast, Kentish ragstone from the lower estuary, and Caen stone from Normandy was moved along rivers and coastal routes before being unloaded onto low barges able to pass under London Bridge to continue the journey upstream to St Paul's Wharf. Here a single contractor, one John Slyford, monopolised this lucrative last leg of the journey and carted the stones up from the riverside to the top of Ludgate Hill at the cathedral steps. In the end, the transport cost more than the stone.[12] The panorama of the riverside City was now studded with Portland Stone church buildings: their limestone walls composed of Jurassic seabeds, complete with fossilised oyster shells and shrimp burrows from 150 million years earlier, their altars all facing downstream and east towards Jerusalem.[13]

The city on the Thames was growing. As new domes and spires traced the skyline of the old City, it was also a boom time in suburbs to the west. By 1700, London's population was ten times more than in 1500; 10 per cent of England's population was living there.[14] And as the population increased, so did the volume of discarded materials that found their way into the Thames and its waterways. Some of the Thames tributaries were already by this time covered over as the 'lost rivers' of London. The Walbrook – the key tributary of Roman London – for example was flowing underground into the Thames by 1500. But the lower reach of the River Fleet, flowing into the Thames just west of the old Roman wall, had a resurgence in the 1670s after the Great Fire. Christopher Wren and Robert Hooke were busy turning the lower Fleet River into a canal, embanked with new wharves and with new bridges across the waterway – around the same time that the apothecary John Conyer, while working on the Fleet, found his intriguing stone axe in the riverbed upstream at King's Cross. The Fleet wharves, it seems, didn't flourish but some of this aspirational spirit was captured in a Canaletto-style moment of glory in Samuel Scott's painting of around 1750. Here the Fleet makes a triumphal entrance into the River Thames as it passes under the Bridewell Footbridge, with sailing barges and decorous rowing boats on a rippling Thames surface of clear blue waves in the foreground.[15] This moment was fleeting and possibly only ever imaginary. The Fleet River was to revert to its traditional function as a drain for refuse, slops, broken clay pipes and dead animals.[16]

London's port river had started to become linked by an extensive canal system to the industrialising Midlands, and by trade to the port cities of Britain's west coast: the Severn, Mersey and Clyde.[17] The Thames ships setting out for gold, silver, spices, tobacco, furs, cotton, opium, palm oil, and people to enslave, took British vessels along the coasts and later into the river basins of other lands. For a while it was fair to say that 'all our Rivers run to one port'. Globally rivers, like the web of international finance, became increasingly interconnected during these years.

As Britain's reach expanded it did what all imperial powers had done before and collected bounty to grace its capital city. The British Museum opened in 1759 with Hans Sloane's collection at its core; an eclectic mix of Egyptian antiquities and botanicals – all fringe benefits of Britain's activities overseas. When British and Ottoman forces beat the French in the Battle of the Nile in 1798, Britain (George III) took ownership of French archaeological booty under the 1801 Treaty of Alexandria, including the Rosetta Stone. The first arrivals of Egyptian antiquities back at the British Museum were so heavy that the floor of the building couldn't take the weight. When a dedicated Egyptian Sculpture Gallery was installed, these were followed by a procession of mummies, scarab beetles, stone heads, palm columns, and figures of the Nile flood god Hapi.[18]

London's urban expansion was underpinned by Britain's growing prosperity in international trade and, later, its industries. Trading companies staked their claims across the globe in the seventeenth century, closely competing with the Netherlands, France and other European nations, as played out on the Ganges. London merchants had an early advantage over other British cities with their proximity to the court. Royal monopolies provided exclusive rights to English trade within certain territories to players such as the Levant Company in Ottoman territories, the Muscovy Company, Hudson's Bay Company and East India

Company.[19] Between 1600 and 1833 the East India Company sent out around 4,600 ships from the Thames, increasing from around eight a year in 1720 to forty-two each year by 1800.[20] The Hudson's Bay Company was given rights for fur trading and exploration in 1670. Twelve years before the Frenchman René-Robert Cavelier, Sieur de La Salle, claimed the entire Mississippi River basin, King Charles II established a similarly expansive claim in granting a monopoly to the whole of the Hudson Bay drainage: 40 per cent of today's Canada, including 'all those Seas, Streights, Bays, Rivers, Lakes, Creeks, and Sounds . . .'[21] In the non-human animal world, the rodent dam-builders were to suffer most. The Eurasian beaver is thought to have become extinct on the rivers of the British Isles somewhere between the late 1500s and late 1700s, probably through over-hunting and the expansion of agriculture. Beavers, nature's 'ecosystem engineers', were inconvenient for farmers who had their own land-management plans.[22] But they were perfect for hats. And so from the late 1660s, two or three ships set off each year from the Thames for Hudson Bay to bring back furs of the North American beaver (*Castor canadensis*), hunted and traded by the Algonquin-speaking Assiniboin, Chipewyan, Cree and Dakota.[23]

The London-based Royal African Company (RAC) was granted an enviable charter from Charles II in 1663 'for ever hereafter' (though in fact terminated in 1698). The RAC set out to find gold on the Gambia River in West Africa, but soon settled instead for trading in people, drawing the River Thames into this Atlantic triangle. The RAC was to gain three-quarters of the Atlantic slave trade by 1683, overtaking the Netherlands, France and Portugal. And, in the fifty years between 1672 and the 1720s, it transported 150,000 people from the west coast of Africa.[24] This trade in enslaved people sank deep into the fabric of British culture in a way that is hard today to comprehend. Following a British military victory over France and Spain, the Treaty of Utrecht in 1713 transferred Spain's *Asiento des Negros* (slave-trading contract) to a newly formed British South Sea Company, allowing them to supply 4,000 enslaved people each year to Spain's New World ports, with the support of the RAC.[25] There is no sign of this dark underbelly in the beautiful *Utrecht Te Deum* and *Jubilate* first performed that year in the rebuilt St Paul's Cathedral, composed by George Frideric Handel, himself a shareholder in these trading companies, along with his chief patrons.[26]

London's port had a natural disadvantage for an Atlantic coast trade in competition with the rivers of Britain's west coast and this became more apparent when the monopoly rights of the Royal African Company were revoked by King William III in 1698. Located several miles upstream on the wrong coast, it was overtaken in the slave trade by the so-called 'outports': first by Bristol on the Severn and then by Liverpool where great stone docks started to line the Mersey. Liverpool's shipping interests, concerned for their supply chain to Lancashire's textile mills, remained closely tied to the slave-grown cotton from states in the American South for the duration of the American Civil War (1861–5). The disruption of the American cotton supply made it all the more important that Britain turn to other lands and rivers for its cotton supplies, in the Ganges region, the Nile, the Niger; wherever it could be grown for the right price. Glasgow on the River Clyde specialised in slave-grown tobacco while its port river was augmented in the 1760s by the Forth–Clyde shipping canal flowing 39 miles to the Firth of Forth along the line of the old Roman wall of Antoninus Pius.[27]

The price at home of this economic growth was paid for by ordinary people in the rapidly expanding cities of the nineteenth century. Urban expansion outstripped any capacity to deal with the disease that poverty and overcrowding bred in Britain's major industrial cities. People began to live far too close both to each other and to their rivers, as sewage and water sources became intermingled. Manchester and Liverpool, though the beneficiaries of the economic boom, were also the 'shock cities' of industrialisation, with the highest mortality rates in Britain, matched by industrialising cities elsewhere: the German cities of Munich on the River Isar, Hamburg on the Elbe, and Breslau on the Oder (Poland, then eastern Germany).[28]

Rivers were particularly hit by the two water-borne diseases of the era. Typhoid fever was the biggest killer and endemic (always present) but the new disease of cholera created more fear. Cholera arrived out of the blue in the 1830s, then went away and returned in unpredictable waves. It may have been spread by increased European trading activities on the Ganges (where cholera was endemic), as some thought at the time.[29] When it first appeared in Britain in autumn 1831 in the coastal city of Sunderland on the River Wear, local shipowners and merchants gathered to rebuff claims that they had imported this so-called 'Asiatic Cholera' from the port of Hamburg. Local physicians confirmed that the local outbreak was only the familiar 'English cholera' and 'not contagious'. In fact, the epidemic went on to kill 32,000 people in Britain by the following year. Three more outbreaks followed from the late 1840s, incurring many more deaths.[30]

Wherever cholera came from, it was the new piped water technologies of the nineteenth-century industrialising cities that spread it. One of the striking features of the Thames during the nineteenth century is how it became a stream dreaded for its hazards alongside its status as an imperial highway. The sewers of London had been built for rainwater – to channel this into the Thames and its tributaries. The real problems started in 1815 when water closets (flushable lavatories) began being plumbed into these rainwater sewers, creating a direct link between sewage and drinking water. Cholera hit low-lying Thames-side areas particularly hard, such as Southwark in south London where some residents would collect water direct from the river. But many suspected that cholera was caused by the 'miasma' (or bad air) rising from the Thames. In the 1853–4 outbreak that killed over 20,000 people, over half of all fatalities occurred in London.[31]

As no one knew what caused the disease in the years before the cholera bacillus was discovered in the 1880s, the recommended precautions veered wildly from lime-washing walls to the avoidance of vice.[32] But as the River Thames also seemed directly implicated, legislation from the 1850s stated that the water supply must be filtered and could not be sourced from the river within five miles of St Paul's Cathedral. The now famous parish water pump in Soho, taken out of action by the physician John Snow during the 1854 outbreak, effectively demonstrated that water was a deadly source, but uncertainty remained. Customers of East London Waterworks constituted the majority of those killed in London (around 5,500 people) in Britain's final wave of cholera in 1866. Here it became clear that officials of the company had supplied water from an illegal unfiltered source fed by the River Lea, a Thames tributary and at that time a strangely coloured industrial drain.[33]

Critics and satirical periodicals such as *Punch* magazine drove home the degraded and deadly nature of the Thames during these years, and the political negligence of those responsible for its conservation. Images of the Thames river god, now domesticated as Old Father Thames, showed him still ripped but ancient with his long locks dripping with the filth and effluvia of the city. The Great Stink on the Thames in the summer of 1858 was just the most widely publicised sensory moment highlighting the 'filth diseases' then raging on the Thames and other British rivers. The most famous smell in British history occurred on the foreshore right outside the Houses of Parliament, where hydrogen sulphide from sewage and other foul-smelling substances had built up on the foreshore. This seems to have finally created the political will to spend public money. The Thames was spoken of as a shame at the heart of the empire.[34]

The key thing was to expel London's sewage from the city. This was achieved by engineer Joseph Bazalgette's scheme in the 1860s. Diverting the sewers before they reached the Thames, this re-routed the city's human waste via two great 'intercepting sewers' running parallel to the river to pumping stations downstream, from where the waste was released into the lower river and became someone else's problem.[35] Improving the London Thames meant reducing many of its tributaries to the status of common sewers. These tributaries in London – the Walbrook and Westbourne, Falcon's Brook and the Fleet, among others – now became actively connected to Bazalgette's sewage system, sent underground as Combined Storm Overflows. These 'lost rivers' still flush out sewage as well as rainwater into the Thames today during heavy rainfall – increasingly often nowadays – a situation that the 15.5-mile Thames Tideway Tunnel, or 'Super Sewer', recently opened, aims to bring to an end.[36] The River Fleet, for which Christopher Wren had such high hopes, now entered the river as a tunnel beneath Blackfriars Bridge.[37]

While the engineers were at it, the Thames River itself became narrowed drastically to accommodate the sewers and a new Underground system – a level of 'encroachment' that today would be unthinkable. London gained 52 acres of land. Granite river embankments fit for an empire went up along the north and south riverbanks. The obelisk Cleopatra's Needle – an 1819 gift from Egypt's Mehmed Ali Pasha – arrived in London fifty years later, just in time to cap the embankment project off in 1878. Although perhaps more significant than this misnamed stray from Heliopolis in the 1450s BCE was the ring of miniature obelisks and posts that went up to help pay for it all. London's 'Coal and Wine Duties' were allocated to fund its new sewers, the Thames Embankment and several river bridges, just as those duties had come to the rescue after the Great Fire.[38] The Duty Posts installed round London in the mid-nineteenth century left traders entering the capital in no doubt of its taxation boundary, whether arriving by canal or railway, by turnpike road or woodland track, or for those arriving by sea, at Yantlet Creek in the Thames outer estuary.[39]

The pulling of resources into London was accompanied by the expulsion of all the stuff the capital did not want, including its sewage – dumped downstream near Beckton where it was to create the conditions for the *Princess Alice* leisure boat disaster in the 1870s.[40] Some 640 people died, as much from poisoning, many people thought, as from drowning. Sewage dumped in the river was moved progressively downstream – right up to the 1990s when (treated) sewage deposits in the North Sea were finally discontinued. But this did not solve all the pollution problems of the London Thames, as we shall see; from the late nineteenth century the river was steadily declining towards biological death or total deoxygenation.[41] Throughout this time, the lower estuary served as a kind of ecological hinterland for the capital: the place where its refuse too was conveyed downstream by contractors and dumped as 'land-fill' on the low-lying riverside marshes of Essex and Kent. Fishermen in the late nineteenth century persistently complained that the rubbish frequently wasn't reaching the banks but was simply being thrown over the side of the refuse lighters under cover of darkness, destroying their fishing grounds. An Inspector of Fisheries in 1888 described just some of the items he had seen hauled up in fishermen's nets, suggesting our throwaway society is not completely new:

> . . . boots and shoes; hats, caps, and bonnets, . . . scrap iron; cocoa-nut matting . . .; coal-scuttles and kettles: pots and pans; . . . gridirons and fire-guards; bones; cane chair-seats; cabbage stalks; oil cans and iron drums; sardine, meat and milk tins; . . . brickbats and chimney-pots . . .[42]

By the end of the First World War, Britain's formal empire covered one-quarter of the world.[43] Being on the winning side provided a new lease of life for its overseas ambitions, even if there was a new power emerging across the Atlantic. Plans for development from the Danube to the Ganges, Niger, Nile, Yangtze and other rivers went ahead. Confidence was still high and London's river retained its imperial flavour well into the twentieth century. 'Londoners,' said Thomas Wiles of the Port of London Authority in 1929, 'should make obeisance to Father Thames who had made their city the greatest city in the world.'[44] The port and its wharves lining the river continued to suck in nature from across the globe: sea sponges, elephants for London Zoo, ivory, tea leaves, wine from Oporto, shells, aloe plants for medicines conveyed in the skins of monkeys, ostrich feathers from South African farms, still in fashion – just about – for ladies' hats. The biggest fur auction in the world was opened by the Hudson's Bay Company at Beaver House in the City at this time.[45] A variety of small marine creatures also arrived, uninvited. The zebra mussel (*Dreissena polymorpha*), riding in on timber from the Volga River, was first spotted in Surrey Commercial Docks in 1824, then spread through London's water networks. In 1912, 90 tons of mussels were cleared from a single Thames water main. Suckered onto the hulls of ships came the tube-worm (*Ficopomatus enigmaticus*), first recorded in London docks in 1922. Chinese mitten crabs, travelling in style in the ballast tanks of ships, were first sighted in the Thames in 1935 and have now spread across the world's rivers and lake systems. Trials to see whether the mitten crab is a delicacy that people might pay to eat have so far proved inconclusive.[46]

The Thames was becoming T.S. Eliot's river of 'oil and tar'. In his Houndsditch home in the 1880s, Marcus Samuels morphed from a maker of fancy goods and shell-covered trinkets into a major shipper of oil products and (as Viscount Bearsted) he would later build the Thames's first oil refinery at Shell Haven on the Essex coast in 1916.[47] Other British traders were also investing in this increasingly important fuel, through the Russian Oil Company. The banks of the Thames became host to the storage facilities of both the Russian Oil Company and Rockefeller's Standard Oil – headquartered at Cleveland by the southern shore of Lake Erie – facilities that hunkered precariously side by side in storage tanks on the reclaimed Thames-side marshes at Purfleet. The tidal Thames became a stage for explosions from the Isle of Dogs to the North Sea, with noxious gases building up in the ill-ventilated holds of vessels, and petroleum seeping from wooden barrels. The wreck of the ketch the *Maria Lee* that now lies on the riverbed in Long Reach, upstream from Queen Elizabeth Bridge, went down as a fireball of petrol, naphtha and linseed oil at dawn after a night of thunder and lightning on the river in June 1873. This was one of countless disasters on the Thames, some of them taking the bodies of crewmen and boys with them. One winter night in 1897 a conflagration began at the Russian (Baku) Oil Company's stores in Purfleet, and spread to Standard Oil next door. 'The blazing oil' was reported to be 'running in veritable rivers of fire down towards' the Thames. In thick fog the race was on to stop the blaze reaching the largest gunpowder store in England, situated improbably nearby.[48]

The Thames at the heart of Britain's coal empire would in time give way to trade routes radiating out from the empires of oil. In 1883 the British journalist Charles Marvin leant over a new stone embankment at Baku in Azerbaijan on the shore of the Caspian Sea. Watching the 'water splashing against its base', Marvin saw a vision of the future in which Baku, the oil-rich 'region of eternal fire', overtook the British capital on the Thames. This water, he wrote, was 'stretching in never ending ripples all the way from one embankment to the other, from Baku Bay to the River Thames'. Soon Black Sea steamers that now burned British coal would be using Baku oil, he said, like those travelling from the Caspian Sea up the Volga and Neva rivers towards St Petersburg and the Baltic Sea.[49]

The next century saw life on the Thames reshaped by Britain's changing role in the wider world.

12
Thames Gateway

> **Crow Stone (The).** – An obelisk on the Essex bank, about a mile westward of Southend, marks the limit of the jurisdiction of the Thames Conservancy; an imaginary line being drawn across the river here to Yantlet Creek in Kent.
>
> Charles Dickens Jr, *Dickens's Dictionary of the Thames, From Its Source to the Nore* (1885)[1]

Something interesting has been happening on the banks of the River Thames in recent years. Mudlarks who dig for treasures in the foreshore are used to unearthing clay pipes, old coins, and keys to doors that went missing a long time ago. But a couple of decades ago they started to report objects that seemed to be of Indian origin. This was happening so often that the Museum of London became involved. What were they to make of this? The Museum consulted with the representatives of London's Hindu communities, who helped to explain what the objects were, when they were made, and who they represented: Vishnu, Shiva and Hanuman, the monkey god from the *Ramayana* epic. How they ended up in the river was a different matter. Archaeologists speculated that the Thames had become a 'proxy' for the River Ganges. Far from their ancestral rivers, had Hindu British Indians started to place votive offerings in the nearest river? The Hindu community leaders consulted at the time didn't think so. Some of the deities didn't belong in a river: Vishnu, for example. For some, the symbolic powers of the Ganges cannot be transplanted elsewhere. They are rooted in the riverbed, waters and banks of the Ganges watershed in northern India. As a Hindu Forum of Great Britain representative put it in 2005, 'the Ganges . . . is specifically associated with many important events in the lives of Lord Krishna and Lord Rama'. More likely, people were disposing of their broken ritual objects in water, according to the usual custom.[2]

The Thames has always offered up objects from distant cultures: the La Tène-era Battersea Shield or Saxon-Norman sword found in the Thames at Putney, coins found under ancient posts in the foreshore near the 'lost river' Effra.[3] But when the objects are so closely tied up with recent imperial relations, potential misinterpretation is more fraught. Science can identify and date sunken artefacts from the past with increasing accuracy. It is not so easy to identify the spirit in which they ended up in the river.

Sometimes, the meaning is quite obvious. When the 1959 drought caused the Welsh Harp reservoir on the Thames's Brent tributary to dry out, it revealed a small orgy of crime. There on the dry bed in the late summer were three prised-open safes, a motorbike last seen four years earlier, and a ladies handbag reported stolen that January, though mysteriously still containing six £1 notes – £100 in today's money.[4]

This chapter is about the Thames as a gateway, for people, migration, goods, and 'gateways to other worlds'.[5] It looks at how the river has been shaped by changes in Britain's relationship to the world since the decline of its empire, and how the inward flows of people, beliefs and ideas, and technology and capital, have transformed the Thames and its riverside.

Part of the mythology of the Thames in its imperial years was of the river as a stage for the outward flow of the English, sailing out on the ebb tide to explore the world: from the brooding wait in the Thames estuary that begins the journey to the Congo in Joseph Conrad's *Heart of Darkness* (1901) to Charles Dickens's Mormons in the emigrant ship 'down by the docks' in 'Bound for the Great Salt Lake' (1863), or the ten million or so other people who left the British Isles for the United States, Canada, Australia, New Zealand and South Africa in the century after 1815. More difficult to handle was the inward flow or flood tide. Who should be allowed in? Could they pay their way? The Thames has been transformed by 'comers and goers' since the beginning of human history.[6]

What of the Hindu artefacts in the Thames? The picture has changed over time as ceremonies have become more public and integrated in the life of the river. Hindu priests have blessed the Thames, changing its nature as a sacred river.[7] One day at Putney Bridge on the Thames in the summer of 1970, followers of Lord Swaminarayan (1781–1830) gathered on the banks at the ceremony in which a sacred image or murti of Harikrishna Maharaj was lowered into the river to purify it for future acts of worship.[8] London's Shree Swaminarayan Temple was set up in a former Baptist temple that same year, while a poster announced: 'India's ancient wisdom can assist the west's current spiritual confusion.'[9] No water body is too humble for purification. At FantaSeas Water Park in London's Lea Valley in the 1990s, swimmers witnessed the spiritual leader 'spraying the crowd with sanctified water from the swimming pool'.[10] Swaminarayan followers went on to build in London the largest Hindu temple outside of India as of the 1990s.[11] After the death of the spiritual leader Pramukh Swami Maharaj, his ashes were scattered across the Gondali River in India's west coast state of Gujarat, the Ganges and other 'holy rivers of India', as well as the Thames, Niagara Falls and Jinja (near the source of the White Nile). On the Hudson River in New Jersey, home to four Swaminarayan temples, the Swami's ashes were emptied over the side of a shining white motor cruiser on a sunny afternoon in September 2017, 'sanctifying the waters of the Hudson as well as the hearts of all those who were present', as worshippers on the shore and jet-skiers in the river looked on.[12]

Several Hindu groups have become rooted on the Thames, adding to its dense layers of mythology. Also at Putney Bridge, Bengali Londoners have celebrated the autumn festival of Durga Puja, the many-armed goddess riding a lion in a ritual triumph of good over evil. Bamboo, jute and rice straw were imported from India in 2006, coated with cow dung and mud from the Ganges to purify the materials. The Thames too had to be made ready with the Ganges water. As one of the organisers told a press team, the 'Thames is not mentioned in any of the ancient Hindu scriptures', so soon 'you will see a small ceremony . . . we will use Ganges water to purify the Thames so that Mother Durga can be floated away in the holy water'.[13] Hindu organisations in West London have established a festival for the elephant god Lord Ganesh (Ganeshotsav), alongside the Thames Landscape Strategy conservation group.[14] Other British rivers are also being transformed. Today there is a platform for Hindus and Sikhs to scatter the ashes of their dead on the Aire River in the heart of Leeds. 'It will be a sort of Holy Ganges in Bradford,' said the president of the Hindu Cultural Society of Bradford said of the Aire (upstream) back in 2002.[15]

A second gateway is represented by a famous image by William Rainey called 'Aliens Arriving at Irongate Stairs' (1901), showing the arrival of Jewish refugee families from Eastern Europe at St Katherine's Dock, with a large steamship in the background, their baggage around them on the riverside, and a mother breastfeeding her baby in the foreground. The arrival of those in flight from pogroms and persecution in Russia, Latvia and Lithuania, as well as Romanian 'fusgeyers' (wayfarers) at St Katherine's Dock, brought new Jewish communities to London's Whitechapel district, a short walk away. Between 1851 and 1900, the city's Jewish population rose from 20,000 to around 144,000, transforming the East End, as the Huguenot refugees had done on the same riverside streets 200 years earlier.[16] These new arrivals brought synagogues, tailors, kosher butchers and steam baths. In response, significant numbers were drawn to the anti-semitic British Brothers' League, organised against 'destitute foreigners'. A League meeting in London's East End in 1902 called on the government to stem 'the alien flood'. One Liberal MP declared that London was 'not the dustbin of Austria and Russia' and proposed that a sign be fixed 'at the mouth of the Thames' with the words 'No rubbish to be shot [thrown] here'.[17]

Instead of a signpost, legislation began to be introduced that amounted to the same thing. The Aliens Act of 1905 restricted the entry of 'alien steerage passengers' (those with the cheapest tickets), people who had failed a medical inspection at Gravesend (also related to ticket prices), and those unable to prove they could support themselves. Cabin passengers and those with prepaid tickets to other destinations beyond Britain were free to enter.[18]

The spring of 1919 saw a wave of violent attacks and 'race riots' in port cities across Britain's east and west coasts, from London to Hull and Cardiff to Glasgow. Port workers and sailors of South Asian, West African, North African and Chinese origin were targeted by white Britons resentful about competition for jobs, housing and other benefits, even though many had only months before been serving together in the war effort. Several people died including former merchant seaman Charles Wotten, born in Bermuda, who was chased into the water at Queen's Dock on the Mersey at Liverpool and killed, aged twenty-four. When the violence subsided, the government concluded that non-white dockland populations should be 'repatriated'. Perhaps 3,000 non-white seamen were deported to the Caribbean, West Africa and the Gulf of Aden.[19] More aliens acts followed and a few years later, the Coloured and Alien Seaman Order of 1925 was the first legislation to refer specifically to race, restricting employment and residency rights, and requiring documentation to prove British status.[20]

So drawbridges were being raised, but the power was not all flowing in one direction. One of the hubs for people coming and going on the Thames in the nineteenth and early twentieth century was a brick edifice in Shadwell called the Strangers' Home for Asiatics, Africans and South Sea Islanders, a charity set up in 1856. This was classic Victorian philanthropy: well-intentioned, attractive to rich donors and, in its conviction about Britain's exemplary place in the world, delusional. It aimed to help foreign sailors in the docks who found themselves stranded, homeless and cold over the winter months or when the shipping trade was slow. It offered food, board and Christian instruction.[21]

In 1863 the firm of Cama & Cama Ltd threw down a gauntlet into this complacent world, offering the sum of £4,000 to the charity – well over £400,000 today.[22] The Bombay merchants K.R.

Cama and M.H. Cama were part of a London community of Indian Parsis of the ancient Persian Zoroastrian faith.[23] But they had one condition. The Home must remove its first rule: to offer 'protection and aid, with Christian instruction, to such natives occasionally resident in this country'. This proposal was received with great indignation by the charity and refused. '[N]ot a single complaint has been heard,' its secretary assured the firm.[24] The incident was still rankling sufficiently for the correspondence to be reproduced in full ten years later in the Home's publication *The Asiatic in England*, alongside a list of wealthy South Asian donors loyal to their vision: from the Maharaja of Jeypore to the Parsi merchant Cowasjee Jehanghier.[25] But members of the Bombay merchant class who were critical of British imperialist values would become an important part of the London scene, from Dadabhai Naoroji, who helped establish the Indian National Congress in 1885, and later became Britain's first South Asian member of parliament, to Bhikaiji Rustom Cama (daughter-in-law of K.R. Cama) – aka Madame Cama and 'Mother of Indian Revolution' – who was prevented from re-entering India by the British government until just before her death in 1936.[26]

The Strangers' Home continued to be a refuge for sailors and a target for protests in the years before it closed in 1937. In 1919 rioters came looking for outsiders to attack in the Shadwell building. But the Home was also a magnet for people agitating for overseas sailors' rights in the face of increasing restrictions on entry and residence in Britain at this time. In the 1920s the Home barred one Nathalal Jagivan Upadhyaya when they discovered him recruiting residents for his Communist Indian Seamen's Union (1925). Upadhyaya – also known as Paddy – moved on to Liverpool, forming the Liverpool Indian Association, and went about the Mersey docks with Communist leaflets tucked into his Bible.[27] Interwar London was a centre for political agitation of all kinds, including Pan-African and anti-imperialist organisations such as the League of Coloured Peoples, International African Service Bureau and the Colonial Seamen's Association, who represented South Asian, Arab, Chinese and black seamen.[28]

Fluctuating government policies continued to shape life on the Thames dockside. Following the Second World War, the new Labour government decided that more workers were needed to power Britain's economy, particularly for the public transport system and new National Health Service. In May 1948 HMT *Empire Windrush* embarked from Kingston in Jamaica with over a thousand passengers bound for the Thames port of Tilbury in Essex. A former Nazi troopship, the vessel had been renamed after the bucolic River Windrush, a Thames tributary. British Pathé newsreels from the time suggested a warm welcome at the docks. But behind the scenes, as the ship was still awaiting departure, Prime Minister Clement Atlee was hurriedly consulting on whether the ship could be re-routed to East Africa, even though his own party's policies had prompted the journey. The *Windrush* arrived as the 1948 Nationality Bill was working its way through Parliament but this legislation went on to confer citizenship on all subjects of Britain and its empire. This wasn't the first or the last such voyage. Others came via Liverpool and Southampton ports, or by air. But it symbolised the optimism of those arriving in Britain from the Caribbean, South Asia and other parts of Britain's empire in the 1940s, and suggests the continuing power of the Thames to tell a national story.[29] By contrast, the 1962 Commonwealth Immigrants Act and later measures set out to put the genie back in the bottle, creating different citizenship rights for living and working in Britain for non-white, 'New Commonwealth' citizens. In recent years, since the notorious 'hostile environment' initiated by the Home Office in 2012 and legislation in 2014 under the Coalition government began withdrawing existing rights and deporting those long-settled in Britain, the term 'Windrush Generation' has stuck like a broken promise.[30]

During these decades from the 1960s, goods continued to flow into London's docks. But the port had been utterly transformed by the changing global economy and geopolitical landscape, and by the arrival of shipping containers, invented in 1950s America.[31] Once deep-water container ships and oil tankers became the norm, the size of vessels was limited only by the dimensions of the world's two most important artificial waterways: the Suez Canal and the Panama Canal. Inner-city, upstream docks were no good for this kind of transport. From the 1970s, Thames shipping saw cascading liquidations and mass lay-offs. Like other upstream docks all over the world, the inner-city Port of London began to be dismantled, its once powerful unionised labour force of dockers and stevedores, lightermen and tally clerks, replaced by giant machines in lower estuary ports, with miniature teams of crane operators and forklift truck drivers. During an almighty struggle to keep the docklands open for business or reused as community 'waterspace', the port began a temporary return to nature. Wildflowers appeared in the cracks between untrodden cobbles and bricks. The Royal Docks were home to twelve species of butterflies in the mid-1980s, with partridges, stonechats and the occasional flash of a kingfisher across the ship-less waters of Poplar and Blackwall. Gradually but, it turned out, unstoppably, the 'East London skyscraper cluster' Canary Wharf arose on the site of the former docklands: now home to Morgan Stanley, Barclays and the Hong Kong Shanghai Banking Corporation, among others.[32]

But Britain's glorious trading history was not entirely forgotten. Because totems of the past were retained in waterfront regeneration schemes – a warehouse and Victorian crane here, a whiskery statesman and slave trader there – port cities became cultural battlegrounds in a world of very conflicting views on Britain's past and the role of its lucrative river trades. When the Thames's West India Docks, built in 1802 for slave-grown goods from the Caribbean, gained a heritage quarter in the 1990s, the statue of Robert Milligan, owner of a Jamaican sugar plantation and a driving force behind the docks, was brought out of mothballs.[33] With his bronze cut-away coat, tight breeches and buckled shoes, he was placed by the Canary Wharf estate in front of what would become the Museum of London Docklands, itself a former slave-grown sugar warehouse. And the museum did its best to 'curate' its Robert Milligan problem.

When African-American George Floyd was killed by police in the city of Minneapolis on 25 May 2020, his death reverberated round the world through the Black Lives Matter movement. Rivers were closely drawn into the protests that followed. Why did so many remnants of the imperial and slave-trading past retain such a presence in public spaces and waterfronts? Statues toppled across the world. On 10 June, at the Minnesota state capital in St Paul facing the city of Minneapolis across the Mississippi, a bronze statue of Christopher Columbus was pulled to the ground by members of the Bad River Band of Lake Superior Chippewa. This statue was on Native American land, they said, and the Dakota people should decide what happened next. Three days later, at the mouth of the Mississippi in New Orleans, the bust of John McDonogh, landlord, philanthropist and slave-owner, was pulled from its pedestal near City Hall, and hauled into the river.[34]

Protests also spread across port cities in the United Kingdom. When Bristol's port relocated to the Severn estuary, its old upstream docks had been transformed into a cultural quarter. Here, on a 'culverted' section of the River Frome, stood the solitary figure of Edward Colston, a seventeenth-century 'merchant venturer' once known for his charity works but now also notorious for his role in the London-based slave-trading Royal African Society. On 7 June 2020 a crowd of people dragged Colston from his pedestal and threw him into Bristol harbour. Here he lay in the murky silt for five days before being raised by council frogmen. His defaced statue now lies on its side on display at the M Shed exhibition space in the former docklands, perhaps one of the speediest transitions from active monument to disgraced riverbed to heritage item.[35] Meanwhile in Edinburgh, protesters called for the first Viscount Melville – a 'gradualist' in the slave-trade abolition debate – to be pulled from his high plinth in St Andrew's Square and thrown into the Firth of Forth. On 9 June 2020 the Museum of London Docklands issued a series of tweets distancing themselves from the statue of Robert Milligan on their doorstep. As this was clearly catching, the statue was boarded up by Canary Wharf authorities later that day then removed, before Milligan too ended up in the water.[36]

The River Thames today remains a crucial gateway for Britain's economy, and it demonstrates how the world's power structures are still reflected in its rivers. Ships continue to transport the vast majority of Britain's global trade (around 90 per cent). London lost its place as the key international port to Rotterdam in 1955 and has continued to tumble through the ranks. But most goods still enter Britain through the Thames ports. After 125 years, the Port of London Authority remains the Thames's harbour authority, overseeing navigation on the tidal river up to the freshwater boundary at Teddington Lock in West London. Its Latin motto *Floreat Imperii Portus* (May the Port of Empire Flourish) has been quietly dropped and the Port's dominion over the London docklands is also long gone.[37]

Britain's capital once flowed into every corner of the globe through investments in ports, water supply and railways, and from Shanghai on the Yangtze to Montevideo on the Rio de la Plata. Today, the flow is decidedly reversed. The ports of the River Thames, the docklands real estate, and the very water of the Thames River basin itself (Thames Water plc) are all owned by foreign investors. Canary Wharf was bought for £2.6 billion in 2015 by the Qatar royal family investment wing and Canadian multi-national Brookfield.[38] London Gateway, the major Thames port, was built by DP World (the Dubai government) on the site of the former Shell oil refinery. Although DP World were blocked by the American government as a potential security risk when they bought port operations at New Orleans and New York in 2006, London Gateway was approved in Britain one year later. At the time of writing, DP World 'handles 10 per cent of world trade' and operates a triangle of gateways across the North Sea from the Thames estuary to the Rhine and Scheldt (Rotterdam and Antwerp World Gateways).[39] The consequences of the flow of oil wealth have fulfilled and outstripped the prophecy of Charles Marvin looking into the water in Baku, 'region of eternal fire'.

This brings us to our final gateway. The Thames is not just a highway but a 215-mile-long river corridor and ecosystem. We saw how the Thames as an imperial and industrial river in the nineteenth century led to a steady decline towards total de-oxygenation of the river, choked by sewage, industrial effluents, and later warm 'cooling water' expelled from power stations. It was declared 'biologically dead' by 1957. In 1954 the Port of London's River Purification Officer noted that in the summer months at high tide the temperature of the water was reaching almost 70°F, which put the Thames 'in the same category as the Amazon or Zambezi River'. During this time, pollution formed a 'plug' in central London. Between 1920 and the 1950s there were no fish in the tidal River Thames for the 40-mile stretch between Richmond in west London and the port of Tilbury, downstream in Essex. Mysteriously, only the European eel was able to survive and had the river to itself.[40]

Another iconic Thames migrant, the Atlantic salmon (*Salmo salar*), started to leave the river long ago, its numbers dropping dramatically in the late nineteenth century, even in the freshwater river. Among many efforts to preserve it, the Thames Angling Preservation Society released 48,000 salmon into the river near Hampton Court in Surrey in the 1860s, but none were ever seen again. In the early 1900s the Thames Salmon Association introduced thousands of young 'Danube salmon' (*Hucho hucho*) into the Thames in Oxfordshire; many were said to be spotted but none were caught. And there was an arrangement put in place by the angling society between Teddington and Kingston that would today alarm the most old-school of fisheries managers. Sunk onto the riverbed were a pair of 'iron waggons', seven punts (flat-bottomed boats used by wildfowlers), a load of rusting gas lamps, and 450 wooden stakes driven into the riverbed. This was a desperate bid to preserve fish stocks by preventing the use of large nets along the river.[41] But this didn't work either. The Atlantic salmon needs clean, cold water and wasn't likely to come back.

The official clean-up of the Thames of the 1960s and 1970s overseen by the Port Authority and London government bodies was genuinely effective. Ailing sewage systems were repaired; the treated sewage was dumped ever further downstream in the estuary 'deeps' so that it became the North Sea's problem, no longer that of the Thames. This was probably helped by the departure of the polluting ships from the Thames stream in London. Fish have returned to the river in the decades since the 1970s. According to a recent report by the Zoological Society of London, 115 species of fish have been reliably identified in the tidal Thames.[42] Until the recent escalation of sewage spills and fish deaths, this was a success story even though set against a backdrop of gradually increasing river temperatures and rising sea levels.

Like all rivers, the Thames isn't just a river corridor, but a whole water world, connected to other rivers and ecosystems and to all the activities on the Thames: the storm-sewer overflows, the Thames Bubblers that oxygenate the river, the mudlarks and the commuter hydrofoils. It includes pintail ducks digging for tubifex worms on the foreshore at low tide, the mallards slicing up the water's surface, the seagulls on the refuse lighters, the sedge-warblers in the reeds of Thames-side marshes, their lives linked to the rainfall in distant wetlands, the East Atlantic Flyway overhead. It also includes canals, filter beds and reservoirs now connected to the Thames and its streams, and the European eels that travel 6,000 kilometres from their birthplace in the Sargasso Sea to live upstream in the fresh water and when ready turn back home to the sea to spawn, travelling unseen on rain-swelled and moonless stormy nights. It includes the rising seas and the Thames Barrier. It includes tidal flaps where tributaries meet the Thames to defend against flooding, which also block out the eels, and the 'eel passes' now being installed to let them through.[43] It includes Eurasian beavers, hunted to extinction hundreds of years ago and now being reintroduced into Thames tributaries and other British rivers.

River 5: Mississippi

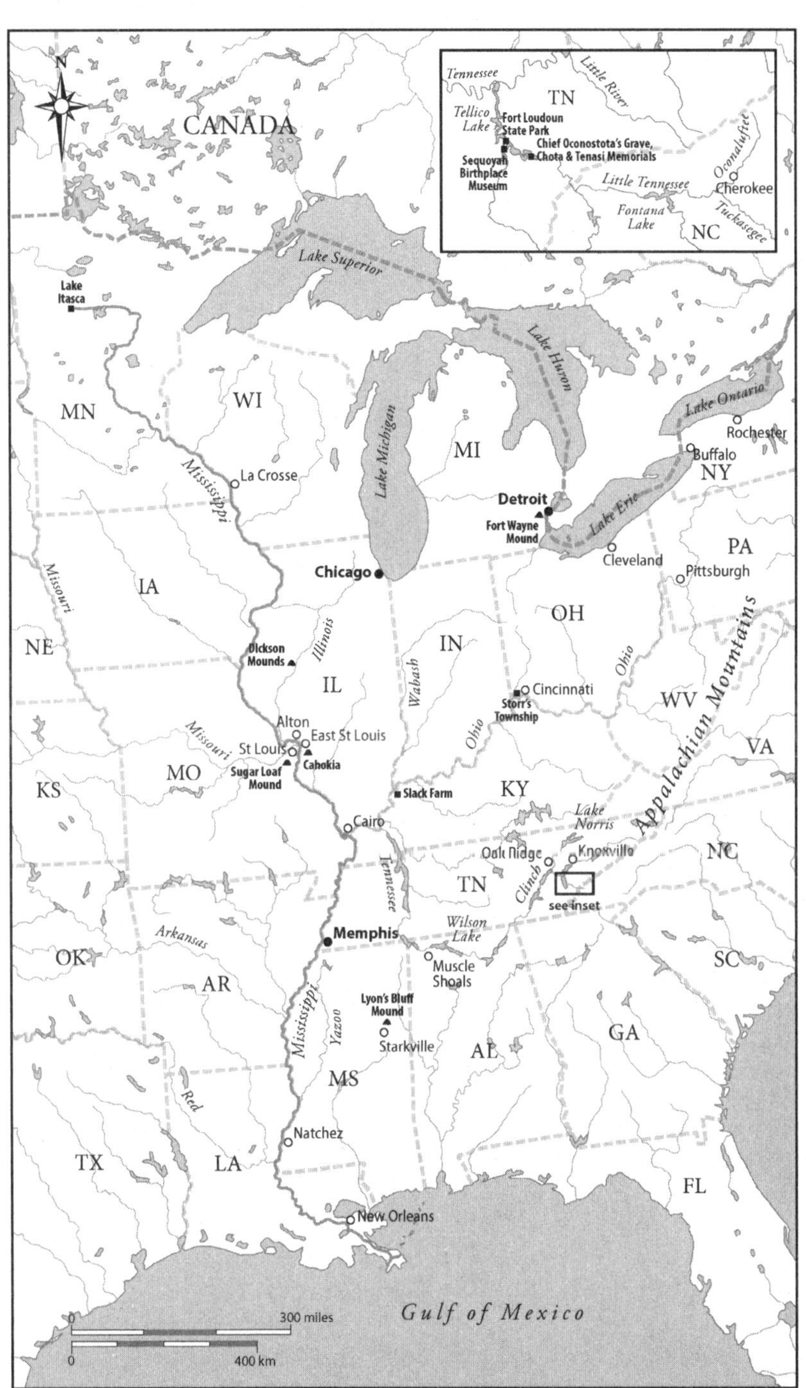

Tennessee
Little River
TN
Tellico Lake
Fort Loudoun State Park
Chief Oconostota's Grave, Chota & Tenasi Memorials
Sequoyah Birthplace Museum
Little Tennessee
Oconaluftee
Cherokee
Fontana Lake
Tuckasegee
NC
N
CANADA
Lake Superior
Lake Itasca
Lake Huron
Lake Ontario
Rochester
Buffalo
NY
MN
WI
MI
Lake Michigan
Mississippi
La Crosse
Detroit
Fort Wayne Mound
Lake Erie
Cleveland
PA
Pittsburgh
Missouri
IA
Chicago
OH
NE
Dickson Mounds
Illinois
IN
Appalachian Mountains
Ohio
IL
Wabash
Cincinnati
Storr's Township
WV
Alton
East St Louis
Missouri
St Louis
Cahokia
Ohio
VA
Sugar Loaf Mound
MO
KS
Slack Farm
KY
Lake Norris
Cairo
Oak Ridge
Knoxville
NC
Tennessee
TN
Clinch
see inset
Arkansas
Wilson Lake
Memphis
OK
Muscle Shoals
SC
AR
Lyon's Bluff Mound
Mississippi
Yazoo
Starkville
AL
GA
MS
Red
Natchez
TX
LA
FL
New Orleans
Gulf of Mexico
0
300 miles
0
400 km

13
Disappearances?

ni-u′-thi-bthi, an eddy; the whirling motion of water; the vortex.
ni-u-thi′-xa-xa, the shallows of a river where the water rushes noisily over the rocks.
ni-u′-tho^{n}-da, an island. [. . .]
niu′-thu-btha-ge, placid water.
ni-u′-thu-ga, the channel.
ni u′-thu-ga-ṭo^{n}—ni, water; **u-thu-ga-ṭo^{n}**, with which to dip: a dipper.
ni′-u-thu-zhu, a pitcher; glass water pitcher.
Ni-u ṭo^{n}-ga, Big water, the Osage name for the Mississippi River.

Francis La Flesche, *A Dictionary of the Osage Language* (1932)[1]

In 1680, a French ex-Jesuit turned trader in buffalo skins, René-Robert Cavelier de La Salle, set off with his men from the early settlement of Montreal along the canoe routes of the Great Lakes. After many setbacks, leaving Lake Michigan in the south-west he crossed into the Mississippi watershed via the Chicago Portage – where the canoes were carried over land by a route already trodden by Native Americans, Jesuits and French Canadian *coureurs de bois* (runners of the woods). From the Mississippi headwaters they made their way south downstream. La Salle's mission was to map the Mississippi, plus inevitably he hoped to find a route west to China.[2] Other Frenchmen had journeyed this way before. La Salle's achievement was to press on beyond the Ohio River until he reached the Mississippi delta.

A contemporary map commissioned by a French abbot shows the river as a fairly straight line from near today's Canadian border as far as its confluence with the Ohio River. Between this confluence and Spanish-named coastal inlets on the Gulf of Mexico lay a blank. The land to the west of the river is marked *Terres Inconnues* (unknown lands) and down the west bank is written *La Louisiane* in honour of Louis XIV.[3] At times, the river party were helped by Native Americans on the banks; at other times they were met with hostility. Sometimes the fog was so dense they had no idea what lay beyond.

When La Salle arrived in the delta on 9 April 1682 he performed a ceremony to lay claim to the whole Mississippi watershed. The terms were highly reminiscent of those used just a few years before in the English Hudson Bay Company claim to 40 per cent of today's Canada. On behalf of France, La Salle claimed 'the seas, harbors, ports, bays, adjacent straits, and all the nations, people, provinces, cities, towns, villages, mines, minerals, fisheries, streams and rivers', and all 'along the River Colbert, or Mississippi, and rivers which discharge themselves therein, from its source' to 'its mouth at the sea'.[4]

All this – his proclamation was reassuring on this point – had the full 'consent' of specific named tribes along the river. La Salle returned to the Gulf coast a few years later to establish a colony but was killed by a bullet to his head from one of his own men in 1687.[5] Despite this unedifying beginning, the European takeover of the Mississippi would change things forever. The Mississippi River basin became a focus for strategic alliances with Native American tribes and a bargaining chip between distant powers.

In the centuries that followed, there were some dramatic turnarounds. When the French suffered a military defeat at the hands of Britain in 1763, they were obliged to cede to the victors their land east of the Mississippi up to the Appalachians, beyond which lay the thirteen Atlantic-facing British sugar and tobacco colonies. The port of New Orleans and land to the west of the river was ceded to the Spanish.[6] This converted the imperial watershed into a boundary line along the Mississippi itself. British defeat in the

American Revolutionary War (1776–83) transferred land east of the Mississippi (and south of Canada) to the new republic. When Spain made to return the western Mississippi bank to Napoleonic France, Thomas Jefferson bolted into action and initiated the Louisiana Purchase, paying $15 million for the land west of the Mississippi – known and unknown – from New Orleans to the Canadian border, an area that turned out to be 530,000 square miles.[7]

To establish what had been acquired, captains Meriwether Lewis and William Clark were dispatched westwards. Travelling via the Missouri River, they portaged across the Rocky Mountains – and over the Continental Divide from where all streams and rivers begin to flow west into the Pacific Ocean – and down into the Columbia River basin eventually reaching its estuary at the Pacific Ocean, laying down a trail for the westward expansion of Euro-Americans. Their starting point from St Louis at the Missouri-Mississippi confluence would become the 'gateway to the West'.[8] Also leaving St Louis around the same time in a 70-foot keel boat was army captain Zebulon Pike, sent upstream by Jefferson to find the Mississippi headwaters and to signal the change of ownership on the Mississippi River. Switching to smaller boats at Prairie du Chien, Pike's party eventually reached the fast-flowing, braided upper river of the Grand Rapids, Minnesota; in snowfall reaching Sangsue Lake: named for the plentiful bloodsuckers that filled the water (now Leech Lake). Pike took this to be the source of the Mississippi (rather than the actual source of Lake Itasca to the west). At a British camp nearby, Pike hoisted the American flag with fifteen stars, one for each state of the young republic (the thirteen colonies plus Vermont and Kentucky). A group of Native Americans (probably Ojibwe) aimed their weapons at the flag, 'broke the iron pin to which it was fastened, and brought it to the ground'.[9]

The Mississippi River system is an elemental force of nature but like all major rivers it is woven at every turn into human history. This chapter explores how this great spine of river has been shaped and reinvented by very different groups of people living along its banks and tributaries. Throughout, the river has acted as an anchor for memories of the past: a fixed line of cable connecting the living to the dead, though one that sends out intermittent and sometimes puzzling signals.

The Mississippi rises in Lake Itasca, Minnesota, in the northern United States and flows southwards for 2,350 miles, forming state borders as it goes. Along its west bank are Iowa, Missouri and Arkansas. Its east bank lines the states of Wisconsin, Illinois, Tennessee and Mississippi. Southern Louisiana spans both sides of the river delta as it enters the Gulf of Mexico. Its Algonkian, or indigenous, name means 'great river', though its common translation as 'Father of Waters' captures the river's nature as the conduit for a vast network of streams.[10] The multiple headwater streams from the north-west appear on maps like the branches of a tree blown by the east wind. The river's main tributaries flow towards the spine of the Mississippi from Montana and headwaters in Alberta, Canada, in the north-west (Missouri River), from streams as far away as New York State in the north-east (Ohio River), from Colorado in the west (Arkansas River), and from the east coast state of Virginia (Tennessee River). Just below Cairo, Illinois – mirroring the Nile, that other great north-south river – the Mississippi is joined by the Ohio River and takes on its iconic width, over a mile wide in places, before forming a slow-moving 'crow's foot' delta. The waters of the Ohio, the most capacious and volatile, are a source of the region's frequent floods in the lower Mississippi.[11] The Mississippi watershed is separated from the drainage area to its north by a ridge known as the Laurentian Divide, or to the local Ojibwe people as the *Mesabi*: the 'sleeping giant'.[12] This watershed drains most of the United States.

The Mississippi River is ancient. At least 250 million years ago in the time of the super-continent Pangea, the eastern seaboard of South America still rested in the crook of coastal West Africa, and to the north both were fused above to North American Laurasia. Mystifyingly, geologists today can already discern in these early days signs of a proto-Mississippi River between the proto-Ouachita mountains in the west and the Appalachians in the east.[13] The upper river valley assumed its present form and southbound route through glaciation and flows of melting ice at the end of the last (Wisconsian) Ice Age, lasting from around 35,000 to 10,000 years ago. Its tributaries are said to have moved into roughly their current position about 8,000 years ago.[14]

But in human terms the Mississippi is the youngest of the seven rivers in this book. No one older than *Homo Sapiens Sapiens* has been found anywhere in the Americas. No *Denisovans* or *Neanderthals.* Just a single puzzling and controversial mastodon, 130,000-year-old bones with possible signs of human butchery, found in Southern California in 2017.[15] Most research suggests that humans first entered the Americas from around 20,000 years ago in three main waves across the cold tundra of Beringia, a temporary land bridge perhaps 1,000 miles from top to bottom before the seas rose with the melting ice. This land bridge stretched between the Lena River in north-east Russia and Canada's Mackenzie River today, which flow north into the Arctic Ocean.[16] Some of these early mammoth hunters stayed in the Arctic north; others moved south along coastal routes and later into the interior.

When Europeans first arrived and settled on the Mississippi between the 1500s and 1700s, they saw a great series of mounds along the banks of the river, its tributaries and confluences. There were up to 10,000 of these earthen mounds along the Ohio River alone. Some were up to 30 metres high and the largest covered more than 50,000 square metres.[17]

The cities of St Louis (Missouri) and East St Louis (Illinois) face each other across the Mississippi just south of the confluence of the Mississippi and Missouri rivers: a region known as the American Bottom and home to thousands of mounds. On the eastern Illinois riverside is the once huge settlement of Cahokia, which at its height had more than 100 mounds and perhaps over 20,000 people. Despite intensive archaeology at the site, many questions remain about the place, its sudden rise around 1050 CE and decline a century or so later.[18] Historians in recent decades have been at pains to debunk the myth of the 'vanishing Indian' and to demonstrate the complex ongoing relationships between Native Americans and the Europeans who arrived on their land. Recent research at Cahokia, for example, has shown that still in the early eighteenth century around 1,700 Cahokians were living by the mounds at Horseshoe Lake, far outnumbering the small French population of missionaries and colonists. A mixture of epidemic diseases carried by Europeans and warfare between indigenous groups may have contributed to a decline in the Cahokian population that followed over the next fifty years.[19]

These mound-builders, now known as the Mississippians, were part of a long line of pottery makers and copper artists going back thousands of years, with trading routes stretching from Mesoamerica to the Great Lakes. This so-called Mississippian stage was only the latest in a series of cultural phases currently understood, from the Paleo-Indian, possibly dating from 12,000 years ago, to the Archaic (perhaps 10,000 years ago) and the Woodland (3,000 years ago).[20] For reasons that are unclear, the Mississippian mound culture went into decline in the 1400s; possibly an effect of changing climate – droughts and colder winters – or warfare, or both.[21]

The scale and sophistication of the mounds came to be a thing of wonder. The largest, Monk's Mound, is thought to have been a hundred foot high, with a base covering 15 acres – greater than that of the Great Pyramid of Giza, though smaller in height.[22] Some were funerary mounds; others were home to densely populated cities. Over time wild speculations were to grow among European settlers about who could have built these structures. Were they a 'lost race'? Surely whoever created them would have had a culture to match the pyramid-builders of Egypt? Theories of a lost race began to be rebuffed from the 1870s, with a massive ethnology report produced by Cyrus Thomas. This concluded that the mound-builders were the ancestors of the very same people the Europeans of the time were still displacing.[23] Today over fifty mounds remain, including the famous Monk's Mound, the grass-covered terraced earthwork that still evokes its former glory as a great dark silhouette at sunrise and sunset.[24]

The mystery of this 'lost race' persisted into the twentieth century.[25] At a farm just north of the confluence of the Spoon River and Illinois River in the 1920s, chiropractor Don Dickson started digging up the mounds on his Illinois property. Discovering human remains, he kept going until he had uncovered nearly 250 skeletons. Over the top of these, he built a private museum, advertising the 'greatest display of stone age man in the world'.[26] The shelves of august American institutions also began to fill up with the remains of disinterred Native Americans over the twentieth century. But the treatment of the Native American dead became a hotly contested political issue, with collective action against such disinterment.

A notorious case at a Kentucky Farm in 1987, near the confluence of the Ohio and Wabash rivers, helped pave the way to legislation, having been fought out in American courts by Native American activists from the 1960s and 1970s. Here a group of 'pot hunters' took out a lease on Slack Farm, a site containing a Native American burial ground on its property and a nearby mound; they dug up the graves of over 600 people, many dating back to the early 1400s.[27] Despite protests and nationwide coverage, there were insufficient grounds for prosecution. Even so, the Chief of the Onondaga Nation, Leon Shenandoah, and members of the American Indian Movement were able to take possession of the bones through a 'friend of the deceased' claim. Within three years, the Native American Graves Protection and Repatriation Act 1990 strengthened Native American claims and the threads between the living and the dead. This stated that for 'any Native American human remains or funerary objects, excavated or discovered on Federal or tribal land after enactment of this Act, the lineal descendants shall have the right of possession', or failing that, those with 'the closest cultural affiliation to those items'.[28]

The museum at 'Dickson Mounds', by now around seventy years old and in the hands of the state of Illinois, was one of the first tests of the Act.[29] In response to mounting pressure to close down, the then Illinois Governor, James R. Thompson, denied any links between its human remains and living people. These Mississippian mounds belonged to a people 'unique to the culture of Illinois,' who could not 'be traced to any tribe of Indians in our country today'.[30] Archaeologists had confirmed that 'no direct blood link was established by the protesting Native Americans'. Thompson's successor was obliged to back down in the face of what the *Chicago Tribune* in 1991 called 'out-of-state special interest groups'. When the display was shut, the dead were ceremoniously covered up in situ beneath a limestone vault. Campaigner Michael Haney of the United Indian Nations (from Oklahoma) declared: 'We rejoice that our ancestors will now be treated with respect.'[31]

In St Louis, once known as 'Mound City', in the 260 years since its founding by French fur traders, all but one of the mounds have disappeared – beneath the concrete path of urban progress, or reshaped as levees for flood defences.[32] Only Sugarloaf Mound remains, dating from the Mississippian or perhaps the Woodland period. Part of this mound was bought in the 1920s as private property and a small house built near its summit, which perhaps saved it from further development. By the time the property came up for sale in 2009, extensive research had been carried out, through oral traditions, migration stories and archive documents, to establish those with strong historic links to the mounds of the region. Sugarloaf Mound was bought by the Osage Nation of Oklahoma, part of the Dhegiha-speaking Sioux, originally from the Ohio River.[33] The process of 'repatriation' of the mounds, burial grounds and human remains is ongoing along the river. Between 1990 and 2021 the remains of 83,000 people were restored to Native American Nations, though at least 116,000 remained on the shelves of cultural institutions. In 2021 the Mississippi state archives transferred the remains of over 400 people removed in earlier excavations to members of the Chickasaw Nation of Oklahoma. These were placed in muslin bags and reburied in the Mississippi region where the Chickasaw traced their historic homeland. 'These are our grandmothers, grandfathers, aunts, uncles and cousins from long ago,' declared their representative Amber Hood.[34]

For past cultures of the Mississippi region, there was no early written script such as Sanskrit to fix oral traditions forever to revered riverside sites, as on the Ganges. There were no steles or stone tombs, as on the Nile, connecting named rulers to their gods. The sacred past of the Mississippi region has been a matter of oral traditions, human memory and thousands of stories – now joined by written texts, legal cases, historic preservation officers and websites – reflecting the sometimes shared and sometimes competing histories of the people who have occupied its multiverse of sacred streams.

Repatriation policies are a bridge back in time across countless dislocations. How did the pieces get so scrambled in the first place? Amid all the displacement, coercion and unequal land treaties that followed the Louisiana Purchase, one moment stands out: the Indian Removal Act of 1830. Signed by President Andrew Jackson, this Act formalised the Mississippi River into a boundary for the expulsion of Native Americans from the fertile lands east of the river, or, as the legislation put it: 'An Act to provide for an exchange of lands with the Indians residing in any of the states or territories, and for their removal west of the river Mississippi.'[35] Native Americans in their thousands were coerced to exchange their land for new land west of the Mississippi in what became known as 'Indian Territory', west of Arkansas. This was later reduced and recreated as the state of Oklahoma. Many of those who didn't go willingly faced deadly forced removals. Around fifty tribal nations moved to this Territory over the next decades, though others adopted evasive strategies.[36]

The next section turns to another feature of dislocation, this time brought about by modern development in the Mississippi River basin. The colonisation of the American continent is ongoing, one dam, mine, pipeline and drained swamp at a time. An 'empire of rivers' is what environmental historian Donald Worster calls American irrigation policies in the arid west.[37] Navajo people on the Colorado River are still fighting the US Bureau of Reclamation for a just allocation of water from the 1960s Glen Canyon Dam built on their land. In the Mississippi River basin, post-war dams built by the US Army Corps of Engineers along the Missouri River took over thousands of acres of Sioux land in the Dakotas.[38] Waterways have been crucial to America's modernisation: draining wetlands, damming rivers and converting the braided and flood-prone Mississippi into a navigable highway. Today an annual 500 million tons of cargo float down the river each year, including corn and soybeans produced on farms in Iowa and other parts of the Midwest: 60 per cent of all US grain exports.[39] In this new world, the American government and its water wizards – the Board of Reclamation, US Army Corps of Engineers and Tennessee Valley Authority – had a shared vision of what a river was for. They could turn wetlands into cities, and dry land into lakes.

The Tennessee Valley Authority (TVA) was a flagship economic development project to bring prosperity to the American South established in 1933. Federally funded under Franklin D. Roosevelt's New Deal, its remit was to harness power on the streams of the Tennessee River which flowed west into the Mississippi.[40] Hydro-electric dams and artificial lakes would create electricity, control flooding and store water for farming. We will come back to this in Chapter 15 in a global context. But not everyone shared this vision of the economic development of the rivers of the watershed.

For some, the TVA was a 'Big Government' northern import. And its dams threatened both the living and the dead. As Donald Davidson, conservative and Tennessee river historian, put it in the 1940s:

> Hearth Fires would be extinguished . . . as old as the Republic itself. Old landmarks would vanish; old graveyards would be obliterated; the ancient mounds of the Indian, which had resisted both the plow of the farmer and the pick of the curiosity seeker would go under the water. There would be tears . . . and lawsuits.[41]

The TVA's Lake Norris on the Clinch and Powell rivers (opened in 1936) provided some evidence for this, displacing over 3,000 families in once-prosperous cotton-belt communities. A planned national cemetery to gather in all the dead of the drowned land had met with fierce opposition, so instead thousands of bodies were moved to new graveyards beside new churches, with TVA labourers carrying out the grim work. Only thirteen people elected to leave their dead beneath the water of Lake Norris in the first round of work.[42]

Increasingly these displacements raised the question of who and what rivers were for. A TVA project on the Tellico River in the 1960s brought both the rights of Native American communities and also the natural worlds of rivers into the frame. The plan was to dam the Tellico River where it joined the Little Tennessee River. The 'Little T', or '135 miles of Appalachian Mountain glory' as the NGO American Rivers calls it, rises in the mountains of Georgia and flows north into the Tennessee River at Lenoir City.[43] The TVA saw this fast-running stream as prime hydro country. But members of the local Cherokee community saw their ancestral land and water under threat. Part of the problem was what the TVA's archaeological teams were bringing to the surface. Past and present collided as the TVA explored the lands they prepared to drown, as happened on the Aswan Dam in Egypt. The more the TVA unearthed, the more significant the land became to the Cherokee, reconnecting them to their past.[44]

Evidence emerged of occupation along the Little Tennessee River going back to the Woodland and Archaic periods, thousands of years before. Key sites, artefacts and the remains of Cherokee forebears were located. One of those disinterred was Chief Oconostota (c. 1710–83), identified by his spectacles, in a burial at Chota.[45] Once the 'mother town' for the Overhill Cherokee, Chota had been destroyed after siding with the British in the American Revolutionary War. Soon afterwards, Cherokee land began to be ceded to American settlers. The Indian Removal Act 1830 followed. Some Cherokee were forced to cross the river, including along the infamous 'trail of tears'. Among those who managed to remain in the east, some went upstream to North Carolina's Little Tennessee region.[46]

The Native American fight against the Tellico dam project was launched under the American Indian Religious Freedom Act of 1978. This protected 'access to sites, use and possession of sacred objects, and the freedom to worship through ceremonials and traditional rites'.[47] But proving what was sacred was far from easy.

The Cherokee were not a single unit with a shared memory of the region. On one side were the Eastern Band of Cherokee who had remained in the Tennessee region. Headquartered at the North Carolina town of Cherokee on the banks of the Oconaluftee River, they were allied with the United Keetoowah Band of Cherokee Indians resident in Oklahoma.[48] The case was brought in the name of medicine man Ammoneta Sequoyah and other named allies. For the Cherokee opposition, it was vital to show that their spiritual connection to the waters of Tellico and Little Tennessee was not dead. Then seventy-eight years of age, Sequoyah had spent his youth in the land around Chota and still went back there to collect herbs for his practice.[49] 'If this land is flooded and these sacred places are destroyed, the knowledge and beliefs of my people who are in the ground will be destroyed,' he said.[50]

On the other side, the TVA had a valuable asset west of the Mississippi in Ross Swimmer: lawyer and head of the Oklahoma-based Cherokee Nation. Swimmer's affidavit for the dam-builders made it difficult to pin down who really spoke for the Cherokee. 'The village sites in the lower Little Tennessee River are important to the cultural history of the Cherokee Nation,' Swimmer declared, 'but are not a part of its religion.'[51] The judge agreed – 'the plaintiffs are now claiming that the entire Valley is sacred' – and found in the TVA's favour.[52]

Despite the lost case, the sense of these rivers as sacred only expanded with the rise of environmentalism in the 1960s and 1970s, which brought with it the idea of 'endangered species' – identifiable by scientists, protected in law, and easier to defend than more intangible claims of spiritual and cultural value.

One day in 1973 an ecology professor from the University of Tennessee noticed an unfamiliar fish in the upper Tennessee River. This turned out to be a small member of the perch family, which he named the snail darter (*Percina tanasi*) for its rapid, darting motions across the rocks and gravel of the clear riverbed and its favoured diet of freshwater snails. Its only spawning ground seemed to be the 12 miles of the Little T planned for destruction in the dam zone. University lawyers took the TVA to court citing the Endangered Species Act passed that year.[53] This small fish held up construction for years – a soulmate to the eelgrass-eating dark-bellied brent-goose far away on the Thames River that helped delay the Port of London's planned Maplin sea/airport/oil terminal long enough for the 1973 fuel crisis to kill it off.[54] In the American case, the Supreme Court upheld Tennessee Valley Authority v. Hill 1978, but it was overridden by the bigger and beefier Energy and Water Development Appropriation Act 1980, signed into law by President Jimmy Carter. The snail darter has lived on, however, and after successful reintroductions into local rivers was off the endangered species list by 2021.[55]

The 14,000-acre Tellico Lake was completed in 1979, along with 20,000 acres of land for 'economic development'.[56] Among the drowned sites were three Mississippian mounds and the once-thriving river port of Morganton. The body of the bespectacled Chief Oconostota was laid to rest once again above the shoreline of the new Tellico Lake.[57] Near the sunken 'mother towns', signs commemorated the Cherokee past, though not, as critics pointed out, the Cherokee people who still lived nearby.[58]

The political climate has changed. The TVA estate as of 2009 contained around 600,000 acres of drowned land, half as much again of land, and 11,000 historical and archaeological sites from the Appalachians to the eastern bank of the Mississippi. The TVA today has an environmental remit and tries to balance their hydro mission with ecological stewardship. Their website lists twenty-three 'federally recognized tribes', from Oklahoma to Virginia, as 'stakeholders' with 'a cultural and historical interest in the Tennessee Valley'.[59] But across the Mississippi and rivers globally, intractable conflicts remain. Hydroelectric dams have caused massive disruption and displacement across rivers globally.

Alliances between indigenous and environmental activists are part of a wider patten of resistance to the degradation of rivers and environmental injustice. One August evening in 2021, at Solway, Minnesota, near the headwaters of the Mississippi, a group of activists and 'water protectors' were arrested for conducting a healing ceremony for the river in protest at the proposed replacement for the Enbridge Line 3 tar sands pipeline from Alberta – an operation with a history of severe oil spills in the upper Mississippi. As she was arrested, Nancy Beaulieu of the Minnesota Chippewa Tribe said:

> Today we are here to assert our treaty rights, our inherent rights to protect the water and all that is sacred. Line 3 violates the 1855, 1854, and 1863 treaties, and all treaties downstream where people rely on Mississippi. We are calling on the Biden administration to end the continued genocide, honor the treaties, and Stop Line 3.[60]

Downstream at the Gulf of Mexico, the United Houma Nation and other groups in Southern Louisiana have been opposing plans for the Bayou Bridge Pipeline: the 'black snake' that begins at the controversial Standing Rock site in North Dakota and now had a planned extension from Texas to the St James Parish in the Mississippi delta.[61] This oil pipeline brought more hazards to a delta region already home to polluting industries and a degraded ecosystem in the face of rising seas. Amid protests, arrests and on-going legal cases, the project was approved by the US Army Corps of Engineers and completed in 2019.[62] The pipeline activist Cherri Foytlin of the Indigenous Environmental Network brought past and present inequalities together in a 2017 statement about the affected communities:

> How is that any different from the horrors that . . . their ancestors lived through from slavery? . . . We have whole groups, Isle de Jean Charles, Choctaw Biloxi Chitimacha . . . being moved. They're the first climate refugees here in south Louisiana . . .. How is that different from being moved off your land through a trail of tears? We're strong together now and we have an understanding of that. And in some of that trauma that we have in our genes is also resistance that we have in our genes.[63]

14
Sold Down the River

> 'Though slavery is thought, by some, to be mild in Missouri, when compared with the cotton, sugar and rice growing states, yet no part of our slave-holding country is more noted for the barbarity of its inhabitants than St. Louis.'
>
> William Wells Brown, *Narrative of William W. Brown, A Fugitive Slave. Written by Himself* (1849)[1]

This was William Wells Brown, born into slavery in Kentucky around 1814, looking back on his life at St Louis, the inland port at the confluence of the Mississippi and Missouri rivers. Wells Brown had worked on steamboats, as a waiter and to assist in the forced transport of people for sale down the river. In 1808 the abolition of the US foreign slave trade on the West African coast had reduced the supply of slaves into North America at a time when demand for cotton was booming.[2] And so a domestic slave trade had developed. Slave owners on the cotton plantations of the Deep South states of Alabama and Georgia purchased slaves from owners in the Upper South and former tobacco colonies in Virginia. This re-selling and transport of those already enslaved, separating them from their families, became known as the Second Middle Passage.[3]

'Slave droving' developed along the roads, waterways and, later, railroads of the region. The Mississippi River and its main arteries proved vital both to this internal trade and to the export of slave-grown goods. The main inland ports for the slave transfers were St Louis (Missouri), Natchez (Mississippi), Memphis (Tennessee) and Louisville (Kentucky). New Orleans on the Gulf coast – as the furthest point from the free states – was dreaded as a 'place of no return'.[4] This chapter tells the story of the Mississippi rivers as both a place of enslavement and a means of escape for those who successfully crossed over them into freedom. And it looks at how the rivers themselves became symbols of supremacy, possession and freedom.

The political map of North America is formed in part by liquid borders. Rivers separated early British colonies, such as Delaware and New Jersey. Over half of the US/Canadian boundary line runs along rivers and lakes.[5] To the south, the US-Mexican boundary lies midstream along the Rio Grande for around two-thirds of its length, though as temperatures climb today the Rio Grande is drying out, becoming less a border river and more a series of unreliable lakes. Each year the heat of the summer exposes long stretches of dry bed, where stranded carp lie with tails curled up in the sand like dead fortune-teller fish, prey to coyotes and carrion birds.[6] Lizards and rattlesnakes come and go as they please across the desiccated hollow. Over time the Mississippi also began to shape state boundaries along its length from north to south, and its tributaries the Missouri and Ohio did the same.[7] As a result, these rivers also helped forge the grid that expanded across the growing republic, marking out degrees of freedom and unfreedom for African Americans in the era of slavery.

The Mississippi became a conduit for slavery only gradually. The thirteen English colonies that started on America's Atlantic coast used the Royal African Company to transport enslaved West Africans for their tobacco fields, indigo crops and rice-growing in the cypress-tree swamps of South Carolina.[8] Over in the Mississippi region, the French Crown entrusted Louisiana's trade and political matters to a series of monopoly joint-stock companies. A map of the territory dated 1720 shows that it was at that time in the hands of the Mississippi Company, then being run by a Scottish economist John Law, a kind of eighteenth-century Bernie Madoff confidently offering disastrous financial advice to the French Crown. On the Mississippi Company's coat of arms, water flows through a pipe-like horn of plenty beneath a crown and the heraldic French *fleur-de-lys*, with a Native American on either side.[9] The Mississippi Company and the British South Sea Company, by that time importing enslaved people to Spanish and British colonies in the Americas, proved to be speculative bubbles that burst in 1720, but the slave transportation continued. By 1731, over 5,500 West Africans had been transported to Louisiana, around two-thirds of them captured and traded from agriculturalist communities around the Senegal and Gambia rivers, and nearly a third from the region west of the Niger delta.[10] This escalated when Spain acquired the Louisiana territory west of the Mississippi following a French defeat in 1763; the Spanish were more actively interested in developing slave-grown tobacco plantations, transporting people from Benin and the Central African Congo region. It is estimated that around 15,000 enslaved Africans were shipped to Louisiana during the years of Spanish rule.[11]

After the American victory in the Revolutionary War of 1783, in which British rule was ended in the east coast colonies, the US also formalised their possession of the so-called North-West Territory: this would become the Midwestern states of Ohio, Indiana, Illinois, and in the north, Michigan, Wisconsin and Minnesota, where the Mississippi begins. By the 1790s the western fringe along the Mississippi was only a 'paper levee' for those Americans who decided to settle on its Spanish western bank.[12] But for the moment the Spanish retained the land west of the Mississippi and the port of New Orleans.

When in 1792 Napoleonic France had issued the 'Scheldt decree' on rivers as a common asset, the American President and lawyer Thomas Jefferson had energetically endorsed this and applied it to the Port of New Orleans, without irony, though slave-trading would only intensify when America gained full access to the port. 'What sentiment is written in deeper characters,' he asked, 'than that the Ocean is free to all men, and the Rivers to all their inhabitants? Is there a man, savage or civilized, unbiassed by habit, who does not feel and attest this truth?'[13] This defence of free navigation was followed by the Treaty of San Lorenzo with Spain, allowing the United States rights to trade along the Mississippi to

New Orleans. But when around 1800 the Spanish made to hand over Louisiana and 'the Floridas' (south-east of the Mississippi) to France, Jefferson was in no doubt about the grave economic threat. As he wrote to his ambassador in Paris in 1802:

> . . . there is on the globe one single spot, the possessor of which is our natural & habitual enemy. [I]t is New Orleans, through which the produce of three eighths of our territory must pass to market, and from it's [sic] fertility it will ere long yield more than half of our whole produce and contain more than half our inhabitants.[14]

Six months later, a Spanish official shut the port of New Orleans to American vessels. Ships arriving laden with flour and cotton from river ports upstream were barred from docking and American farmers threatened to take the port by force.[15] When Jefferson made an offer of $15 million to buy the territory, Napoleon accepted, perhaps glad of some good news while at war with almost everybody from the British in the North Sea to the Haitian rebel army in the Caribbean. The Louisiana Purchase (1803) transferred to the United States the port of New Orleans and territory of Louisiana, almost doubling its size.

This expansion came not a moment too soon for the republic. The late eighteenth and nineteenth centuries saw the decline of the old tobacco regions, and a westward shift in search of fresh soils in Kentucky, Tennessee and later Ohio, then across the Mississippi River into Missouri. But tobacco was to be superseded by King Cotton. By the 1790s, the cotton gin (engine) was revolutionising the processing of cotton, removing cotton seeds from cotton fibres mechanically. The machine allowed up to 50 pounds a day to be processed by a single person. But the cotton gin was also an insatiable eater of land. The cotton belt spread across the rich soils of the deep south: through South Carolina and Georgia, into Alabama and Mississippi, and on to Arkansas, Louisiana, Tennessee and Texas, transforming the populations, landscapes and lives of those in the Mississippi region.[16] These were the lands cleared of Native American communities, replaced by European farmers growing cotton with an enslaved African labour force. Around 388,000 Africans were transported across the Atlantic into the United States in total, by one estimate.[17]

Nearly 114 million acres of land had already been cleared in the United States even before the Swamp Lands Act of 1849–50 allowed states to take possession of swamps and drain them for agriculture and settlements. The sound of metal hammering away at wood echoed through ancient cypress forests, and of 'thunder' as gigantic trunks fell to the ground. The swamps were cleared and drained by the same enslaved labourers who would later work on the fields that replaced them. The cypress timber was sold to Midwestern lumber traders, to meet demand for shipbuilding, construction, and to fire up domestic hearths and the voracious engines of steam vessels on the region's rivers and coasts.[18]

Annual cotton production increased from 1.5 million pounds in 1790 to 2,275 million pounds by the eve of the Civil War in the late 1850s: destined especially for the textile mills of the northern United States and Lancashire, England. Cotton constituted up to 40 per cent of Britain's exports, by the end of that decade, with 88 per cent of its raw cotton supply sourced from enslaved labour in the US.[19] These years saw massive shifts in land ownership and agricultural patterns, and a grid of freedom and unfreedom started to spread across the continent.

The impact, or possibly, the purpose of ending the import trade in slaves in 1808 was to raise the value of existing enslaved labourers. This helped those colonies, such as Virginia, with exhausted tobacco plantations and a need to reduce their enslaved labour force. In the years after 1808, something like 66,000 people are estimated to have been forcibly transported from the upper south and south-east colonies to the cotton regions of the South via the internal slave trade.[20]

The South became the place of slavery and in theory freedom for the enslaved lay in the North. The founding legislators who had drawn up the Northwest Ordinance of 1787 had envisaged a zone of freedom in the new American territory north of the

Ohio River, the eastern tributary of the Mississippi.[21] The North Star – the bright supergiant of Ursa Minor, 4,000 million million miles above the North Pole – was both a fixed navigation point and a symbol of freedom.[22] Those escaping slavery needed to keep heading north, often travelling by night to evade detection, though clouds overhead and forked paths full of risk often obscured the way. Some made the journey alone, some via the Underground Railroad, the improvised network of river crossings, land routes, safe houses and railways, that led north and north-east to the free states and Canada. *The North Star* was the name of the anti-slavery weekly published in 1840s Rochester, New York State, by Frederick Douglass (1818–1895), the celebrated journalist, activist and public speaker, who had escaped north from slavery in Maryland to Pennsylvania in the late 1830s.[23] But the free North was a complicated place. Those escaping slavery had to keep moving across many rivers and many gradations of threat even in the North.[24]

Despite the Northwest Ordinance, the northern boundary of the Ohio River was blurred from the start. An agreement in Congress to maintain a balance between slave-holding states and free states had led to the 'Missouri Compromise', by which Missouri was admitted to the Union as a slave-holding state even though most of the state lay further north than the Ohio River because Maine had recently joined as a free state. The Compromise also established that there was otherwise to be no slavery in the Louisiana Territory north of 36° 30′ latitude. But this line too was eroded by the Kansas-Nebraska Act of 1854, which permitted slavery where it was demanded by a voting majority.[25] The other pervasive barrier to freedom for journeys north was a series of Fugitive Slave laws, the first contained in a clause of the Northwest Ordinance which allowed those who had escaped across state lines to be returned to their masters – strengthened by further legislation up to 1850.[26]

The Ohio River, forming the southern border of the free states of Illinois, Indiana and Ohio, has sometimes been called a second River Jordan – a crossing point to freedom. But neither the passage north across the Ohio River nor crossing the Mississippi from Missouri into Illinois could guarantee freedom.[27] For those making the crossing, there was no knowing what lay on the other side. One night in May 1855 a group of nine enslaved people gathered by the Mississippi bank on the dark northern edge of St Louis, Missouri, and crossed the river at a narrow point – only to be met on the Illinois bank by men with guns. Five of their party were recaptured. One of the abolitionists travelling with them was shot. Mary Meachum, a freed woman of colour, widow of a prominent St Louis Baptist minister and member of the Underground Railway, was tried for her role in the escape but eventually released. One of those recaptured, a woman called Esther, was separated from her children and sold down the river. Four people escaped.[28]

Thick ice that gathered on the Ohio River in cold winters made this one of the famous routes north on the Underground Railway.[29] In January 1856, Margaret Garner managed to cross the frozen Ohio by night from the Kentucky shore with her husband and family and a group of others. Stopping in a black household in Storr's Township, across Mill Creek from Cincinnati, good fortune was not with them. Before they could go any further, a US marshal and his men caught up with them. When apprehended, Margaret Garner stabbed her young daughter Mary and had to be restrained from killing her other children to prevent their capture. This tale of fathomless desperation later inspired Toni Morrison's 1987 Pulitzer Prize-winning novel *Beloved*. But it was also a famous case at the time. Margaret Garner was tried successfully, not for murder but under Fugitive Slave law. Split up from her husband, she and her children were sent downstream on the Mississippi – her daughter Cilla being killed in a collision en route – and then sold by their owner at New Orleans.[30]

Working on the riverboats potentially allowed more leeway.[31] Steamboats began plying their trade across this grid in the decade after the Louisiana Purchase. The first of these in the Mississippi region, the *New Orleans*, left its Pittsburgh shipyard in October 1811 and travelled down the Ohio River at a speed of perhaps 8 miles per hour, allowing for stops. Turning south into the Mississippi river at what later became Cairo, it reached New Orleans in early January 1812.[32] Steamships would become engines of the economy as much as the cotton gin and slave labour, their furnaces consuming timber from the forests of the American Bottom. They too needed their labourers. Perhaps as many as 20,000 black workers, both free and enslaved, were engaged on Mississippi steam vessels in the years before the Civil War.[33]

The principle of free navigation along the Mississippi rivers, preserved in the Northwest Ordinance, meant that vessels carrying enslaved people were free to navigate along the rivers of ostensibly free states. And vessels from free states could likewise navigate through slave-owning states. Where states were divided (arguably) by river boundaries, state lines ran along the *thalweg*: the midpoint of the main navigation channel.[34] Steamers moving from landing to landing along the rivers traversed back and forth across these liquid boundaries. So, the escape of boat hands was a known risk for slave owners and ships' captains. Cases became frequent in the courts. In one such case, legal action was taken even before an offence had been committed. In 1845 courts heard the case of Henry Hoppess, travelling nervously east along the Ohio River on a journey from Arkansas to Virginia, with his enslaved labourer, named Watson. At Cincinnati in the free state of Ohio, Hoppess had reluctantly moored for the night. The next morning, he woke to find Watson already up and 'leaning . . . against a post at the landing', with intentions that were never divulged. In order to forestall any attempt by Watson to claim his freedom, Hoppess took him to court. Taking Watson's side was Portman Chase, an Ohio lawyer who came to specialise in such cases. It was Chase's contention that riparian law was on Watson's side. Hoppess had willingly moored on the northern bank. State boundaries were effective from midstream on the principle of the *thalweg* and this overrode the Fugitive Slave Act. So Watson was not in fact a fugitive under the south-bank Kentucky laws, but free under Ohio law. The argument was lost, however, to principles of free navigation and cooperation between states. Hoppess won his case and established his claim over Watson.[35]

Another court case concerned twenty-four-year-old Celeste, enslaved but working as a steamboat chambermaid while her pay was transferred to her master back on shore. This was not uncommon. Of the eighty-five women registered as chambermaids on boats moored in St Louis in 1850, forty-one were free black women and twenty-two were enslaved.[36] Celeste had accepted instructions from her St Louis master to confine her work on the rivers to the Mississippi below St Louis and the rivers to the west. Instead in 1855 she had found work on the *Reindeer*, trading eastwards along the Ohio River. One day, when docked at Alton, Illinois, it became clear to the ship's captain that Celeste had abandoned her chambermaid post and, indeed, the boat. All that remained to her master was to sue the owner of the *Reindeer* for $1,000, which he successfully achieved. Celeste herself was never seen again by her pursuers. Because these river passages between territories became increasingly legally precarious for slave owners and navigators, some slave-owning states such as Missouri, Louisiana and Mississippi passed laws barring even free black passengers or steamboat workers from alighting on their shores. The nominally free riverside state of Illinois also had prohibitions against free black people entering the state.[37]

William Wells Brown's journey from slavery on the steamships to freedom in the 1830s was to become famous. Brown was born in 1814 in Lexington, Kentucky, on a farm where the master grew tobacco and hemp, among other trades: one of seven children born to his enslaved mother, Elizabeth, each by a different father. William's father, a white man named George Higgins, was related to his master but seems to have played no further part in William's life, and William rejected his given name as a young man. His family was later fractured through sales to different masters.[38] His time in slavery involved work in the fields but more often he was hired out by his master in the city or on the water: as a waiter, a printer's mate, and a steward. Hired for a year to a Mr Walker on the *Enterprise* steamship, William was engaged in the work of picking up and transporting 'droves' of enslaved people bound for sale in New Orleans. Finding out during this time that his sister, also Elizabeth, had been sold to a new master and was awaiting her departure downstream to Natchez, William determined to escape and take his mother with him. From the north of St Louis he took a skiff one evening and with her crossed over to Alton, Illinois. Keeping to the woods by day, they travelled at night heading for Canada, 'having no guide but the NORTH STAR'.[39] Just as they were starting to think they were on their way, on the tenth day they were stopped by three slave-catchers on horseback, carrying a handbill offering a $200 reward. On being returned to St Louis, Elizabeth's punishment was to be sold south. She said goodbye to her son on a boat, chained to another woman, bound with fifty others for New Orleans.[40]

William's next escape attempt was successful, although he was in agony about the family he left behind. By 1833, now aged twenty, he was working in the household of a couple named the Prices, who owned a steamship: the *Chester*, advertising for cargo to transport along the rivers of the Mississippi. Collecting freight that winter destined for Cincinnati, they would need to journey up the Ohio River. The Prices took care to elicit reassurances of loyalty from their boat-hand before proceeding up the free side of the *thalweg*, while William made his own plans. On the morning of New Year's Day 1834, as the *Chester* unloaded its freight at an Ohio river port, he picked up some cargo and went ashore. Unnoticed, William swiftly abandoned his burden and disappeared from the riverside into the woods. Travelling through frozen woodland by night, again he followed the North Star, until forced by hunger to put his faith in a passing Quaker with his wife and their horse and wagon. This elderly Wells Brown and his wife fed and helped William on his way; William also carried away the old man's name.[41] The next leg of William Wells Brown's journey ended in freedom at the town of Cleveland on Lake Erie's southern shore. Here, he hired himself out as a free boat-hand on a Lake Erie steamship, becoming for a time a link in the Underground Railroad helping fugitives towards Buffalo, Detroit and Canada.[42]

William Wells Brown was on a five-year stay in England by the time of the passage of the Fugitive Slave Act in 1849–50. England was safer than the United States; as Brown said in a speech in 1854, 'there are no free States in the United States of America'.[43] Slave catchers operated as far north as Buffalo in upstate New York. The long arm of Fugitive Slave law reached even Quakerish Boston from where Brown's friends, a husband and wife called the Crafts, had to flee into free if chilly and unwelcoming Maritime Canada and from there to England.[44] Brown himself delivered lectures across the British Isles, sometimes with the aid of a great panorama that he had commissioned – sadly now lost – showing the Mississippi, St Louis and various episodes from his life.[45] Brown had the satisfaction of sending his 1847 autobiography to certain Southern slaveowners 'with whom I was acquainted'. His final master, Enoch Price, was among these and subsequently offered to relinquish his claim to Brown in return for $325 from the Boston Anti-Slavery Society; his freedom was later purchased by members of the Quaker abolitionist Richardson family, who had also purchased the freedom of Frederick Douglass.[46] It seems fitting that Brown would also publish a novel *Clotel* (1853), inspired by the double standards of Thomas Jefferson: a fictional account of the children that Jefferson fathered with Sally Hemings, his enslaved housekeeper. Brown lived in later life as an activist for anti-slavery, temperance and other good works in the Massachusetts town of Chelsea, facing Boston across the Mystic River, and he died in his family home in 1884.[47]

The rivers in this chapter had two natures: both lines of enslavement and crossing places to freedom on the other side. Ultimately, this complex grid with rivers sliced down the middle by thalwegs collapsed as the country descended into civil war. The dividing lines of race continued of course into the next century, with borders across buses, steamboats, drinking fountains, schools and workplaces.[48]

Rivers are both fixed in space and can also migrate in spirit from place to place, as we saw with the Ganges. For the white settlers who arrived in the late eighteenth and early nineteenth centuries, this landscape of a great north/south river with its flooded banks, riverside mounds and deltaic swamps was a new Egypt. The nineteenth-century place-names reflect this association: from Memphis, Thebes and Alexandria, to the Little Egypt region in

Southern Illinois, with Cairo at its southern base, where the Ohio River flows into the mighty Mississippi.[49] St Louis itself – established in the 1760s at the confluence of the Missouri-Mississippi – was named after the thirteenth-century King Louis IX, who had led the Seventh Crusade to regain the Holy Land from Muslim hands, narrowly escaping with his life during a raid on Egypt in June 1249 when his forces had been held up by the Nile flood.[50]

For the enslaved people of this region, the Mississippi was not Nilotic Egypt but the Jordan River, evoking both bondage and liberation. The Jordan has proved very versatile, its symbolism mutating across the globe. In the Old Testament, the exodus of the people of Israel from enslavement in Egypt was sealed when they crossed the Jordan into the Promised Land of Canaan.[51] For Christians of the Western Church, the baptism of Jesus in the Jordan by his cousin John is re-enacted in the font of water at baptism. In the Eastern Church, the Jordan is there in every icy plunge each January at Epiphany, from the Sava River in Serbia to the Mississippi at Minneapolis-St Paul.

The Jordan river, flowing north to south through the Sea of Galilee and the Dead Sea, forms a boundary line for the Kingdom of Jordan to the east, and to the west, the West Bank territories of Palestine, the state of Israel and the city of Jerusalem, sacred to all three Abrahamic religions. The apparent clarity of water borders adds force to the slogan 'From the river to the sea', which has become a global rallying cry for Palestinian liberation amid the bombing of Gaza.[52]

The Christian message itself has symbolised bondage as well as freedom. As William Wells Brown put it, 'A more praying, preaching, psalm-singing people cannot be found than the slaveholders at the south.'[53] But Christian faith could just as easily be about liberation. Christians flocking to take part in mass baptisms in early twentieth-century Zambia unsettled the colonial officials of Northern Rhodesia. As one put it: 'Every river became Jordan.' The Jordan crossing to the promised land has symbolised resistance and liberation in the worship and songs of African-American Baptist churches.[54]

Rivers of the imagination can act as a metaphor for collective memory and a portal across time and space. The 1921 poem 'The Negro Speaks of Rivers' by the black Missouri-born poet Langston Hughes evoked a sense of collective memory in a way that anticipated Pan-African poetry of later decades:

> I've known rivers:
> I've known rivers ancient as the world and older than the
> flow of human blood in human veins.
>
> My soul has grown deep like the rivers.
>
> I bathed in the Euphrates when dawns were young.
> I built my hut near the Congo and it lulled me to sleep.
> I looked upon the Nile and raised the pyramids above it.
> I heard the singing of the Mississippi when Abe Lincoln went
> down to New Orleans, and I've seen its muddy bosom
> turn all golden in the sunset.[55]

In the next chapter we look at how the United States in the post-war world took its mission to tame the rivers of the Mississippi basin – above all the streams of the famous Tennessee – and exported it as an emblem of a different kind of global freedom.

15
Globalising the River Basin

'. . . there is a body of interdependent and unified interests and values, all collected in one hydrographic basin . . .'

John Wesley Powell, 'Institutions for the Arid Lands', 1890[1]

The Tennessee Valley Authority (TVA) was, as we have seen, a new way of approaching rivers. Encompassing the whole river basin as a zone for integrated planning, it aimed to leave behind the small-scale and piecemeal ways of the past. Its headquarters were in Knoxville on the Tennessee River, the 650-mile-long tributary of the Ohio River.[2] But the TVA was never just about the Tennessee Valley. It was to prove hugely influential across the world, spawning a generation of river authorities with grand schemes for hydro-electricity, agricultural irrigation, flood defences and trans-national water sharing. By the 1960s, its influence was felt from the Jordan Valley to the Mekong River basin, from South America to India and the Danube.

A report produced by the TVA in 1953, during the Korean War, showed a map of the world with lines radiating out from Knoxville to link it with thirty-six countries across the globe. A quote from US Supreme Court Judge William O. Douglas prefaced the report:

> It may come as a surprise to many Americans that their Tennessee Valley Authority program is not only well known to countless Asiatics, even in the remotest reaches of that continent, but has come to mean to them a symbol of a hopeful new way of life for themselves and their children.[3]

In this chapter we look at the expansion and legacy of this globalised model for how to handle a river – the moment when the mega-dam went global. This was both a vision for water engineering as a project for international cooperation and an arm of expansionist US foreign policy.

Hydro-electricity needs water, height and a lot of concrete. The dam collects the water upstream; this then drops from a height to move turbines that generate electricity. The electrical current flows through cables into a power grid. The potential to create electricity by damming mountainous rivers had been proved in Europe in the 1870s on the Isar, the Danube's Bavarian tributary, and, with a Social Democratic twist of 'electricity for all', in the work of Canada's Ontario Hydro Board (1906).[4] Early hydro plants in the United States were on the Fox River which flows into Lake Michigan and, unsurprisingly, at Niagara Falls, where as much as 6 million cubic feet of water per minute – mostly 'fossil water' from the last Ice Age – cascades up to 188 feet on a gorge between Lake Erie and Lake Ontario.[5] Hydroelectric dams were appearing across the world by 1900.

Looming over the TVA like jockish older brothers were the US Army Corp of Engineers (formed in 1802), responsible for countless navigation and flood-control projects, and the US Bureau of Reclamation (1902) – builders of Hoover and Glen Canyon dams from the 1930s to 60s on the Colorado River which harnessed water for development in the west.[6] These agencies competed with the TVA for funding and projects. All three are still going today. Although they came to adopt similar integrated approaches to rivers, and also worked overseas, neither the US Army Corp of Engineers nor the US Bureau of Reclamation had the charisma of the TVA.

With Illinois-born David Lilienthal as its passionate missionary from 1933 to the end of the Second World War, the TVA managed to imbue this gigantic and dislocating technology with an appealing ideological vision for better lives and communities.[7] It promised that watersheds would pull together and river-valley communities would spring into life. Interest in the idea of rivers as part of wider drainage basins or 'watersheds' goes back at least to the 1700s.[8] But in the late nineteenth century a large-scale 'river basin' approach to managing rivers and water supply began to emerge. The geologist and famous chronicler of the Colorado River, John Wesley Powell (1834–1902), wanted to create a new kind of community politics, calling for 'watershed democracy'. The TVA had distant echoes of this vision in the way it promised to harness river basins to provide people with a better life and bring 'grassroots democracy'[9] to the people of the Tennessee Valley, though the nature of the democratic process on offer was never very explicit.

As Franklin D. Roosevelt put it: 'we are conducting a social experiment that is the first of its kind in the world . . . covering a convenient geographical area . . . the watershed of a great river'.[10] The agricultural South was almost as depressed in the 1930s as it was booming in the 1830s, suffering from soil degradation and infestation by the boll weevil – a Mexican beetle that had contributed to a collapse of the cotton trade. Lilienthal's vision was clear: electricity would restore the lost prosperity of the southern cotton belt by awakening its slumbering rivers. The TVA promised new lifestyles and opportunities. Electricity meant 'freedom from drudgery, a symbol of a new way of living' for the housewife and the farmer. Cutting the dependence of industry on coal and steam power would 'help us to eliminate the sweatshop and the slum'.[11]

This was part of a wider project for the expansion of trade in the whole Mississippi region, in whatever form this took. Connected waterways and improved navigation channels, said Lilienthal in 1938, could enhance the capacity of the Mississippi for global exports. By 1938 pianos and coin-operated pianolas manufactured in LaCrosse, Wisconsin, were steaming south to the Mexican Gulf, through the Panama Canal and up the Californian coast. Rubber from plantations in Liberia and the Far East now flowed to a brand-new production plant in Memphis to make Firestone Tires. On the Mississippi River by 1939 they already had everything they needed to build a car: the tyres; the steel plants and Ford factory at St Louis; Shell Petroleum and Socony Vacuum Oil at Minneapolis and St Paul. The same giants of the fossil-fuel industry were to be found on riversides across the globe by this time. Ford and Shell were also on the shores of the Thames; Ford was staking out land on the banks of the Huangpu River, the Yangtze's coastal port outlet. Socony Vacuum Oil (later part of Standard Oil-Mobil) had operations on the banks of the Nile at Cairo and was working in the Yangtze delta.[12] In theory, exporting the TVA's knowhow might bring some of America's economic magic to other nations, but exports were also part of this vision, from selling expertise to finding ways into foreign markets.

The TVA was from the start a strange mixture of homespun wisdom and global ambition. It was about people-power but also about weapons. Its origins were in defence. Soon after the entry of America into the First World War in 1917, a hydroelectric dam was begun at Muscle Shoals, Alabama, on the Tennessee River, to power the domestic manufacture of nitrates for arms. Like other river sections that were treacherous for navigation, the rapids at Muscle Shoals had been tackled first with canals then submerged by a hydroelectric dam and lake. Built by the US Army Corps of Engineers, the Wilson Dam wasn't completed until 1924. It became for a while a white elephant until its transfer to TVA as its first major asset when it was put to work in fertiliser production. During the Second World War, a universe away from shiny new all-electric kitchens and the sound of trickling streams, the TVA put its shoulder to creating electricity for two wartime industries: aluminium and the atom bomb.

The secret facility at Oak Ridge, a small, racially segregated industrial town nearly 60,000 acres in size, was built from scratch in 1942/43 on the Clinch River in the foothills of the western Appalachians, west of Knoxville and just downstream from the TVA's Norris Dam on the Clinch. Oak Ridge was one of three major installations for the Manhattan Project, along with Hanford on the Columbia River in Washington state and its headquarters at Los Alamos in the New Mexico desert. The Hiroshima bomb, with materials from Oak Ridge, was dropped on 6 August 1945 on the coastal city of Hiroshima on the island of Honshu, with estimates suggesting at least 140,000 dying that year. Three days later a bomb with plutonium from the Hanford site was dropped on the city of Nagasaki, killing at least 74,000 people. Japan's surrender was signed on 2 September on board the USS *Missouri* in Tokyo Bay.[13] Lilienthal went on to lead the Atomic Energy Commission, while half the electricity produced by the TVA was consumed by atomic energy production in the 1950s.[14]

Despite these patriotic activities, the TVA was never embraced by advocates of private energy. Roosevelt died in office a month before the German surrender in May 1945. None of the post-war presidents, from Roosevelt's successor Harry Truman to Lyndon Johnson in the 1960s, shared his vision for the TVA. The former actor and later US president Ronald Reagan used his platform as the face of the General Electric Company in the 1960s to criticise the big-state TVA, which was, he complained, as 'sacred as motherhood'.[15] There was to be no duplicate for the TVA outside of the Tennessee Valley within the United States. Plans to create river-valley authorities on the Missouri and Columbia rivers came to nothing. Instead multi-purpose river-basin projects on a more modest scale were undertaken by agencies including the US Army Corps of Engineers and US Bureau of Reclamation.[16] But if the TVA was beleaguered at home, beyond America's borders it became a powerful tool for foreign policy, attempting to shape the post-war world through modernisation programmes, exports of American technology, know-how and financial aid to favoured partners. The TVA, President Eisenhower considered, was 'For Export Only'. Helping other nations to develop economically through the magic of hydro-electricity was, as Lilienthal's 1944 bestseller argued, *Democracy on the March*.[17] The TVA's missionary approach, first pursued in its own backyard in the agrarian South, could now go forth into the wider world.

One of the first international schemes appeared in *Palestine, Land of Promise* (1944) by US soil expert Walter C. Lowdermilk, written during the years of Holocaust. A Jordan Valley Authority would supply water and electricity to Palestine, then under British authority but promised as 'a national home for the Jewish people' since 1917. Lowdermilk's faith in irrigation and re-education pre-figured other TVA exports. And people could be relocated like piped water. Palestinian Jews and Arabs would benefit equally from development, he argued, but '[i]f individual Arabs found that they disliked living in an industrialized land, they could easily settle in the great alluvial plain of the Tigris and Euphrates Valley'. While some of Lowdermilk's plans were realised, conflicts over water allocations exacerbate tensions in this region to this day.[18]

The United States aimed to reach into every crevice of the globe after the Second World War in its ceaseless pursuit of resources, markets and political influence, looking for rivers to dam and nation states to mould in its own image. Riding this wave, Lilienthal set up a new private Development & Resources Corporation in 1955, though he remained known as 'Mr TVA'.[19] Proposals for the TVA-style river management started popping up with the bubbly optimism of Coca-Cola all over the post-war world, offering affluence and global harmony. Well-tamed river valleys, *Democracy on the March* promised, brought not just national prosperity but also peace across borders. Nations had no more reason to be jealous of each other, Lilienthal claimed, than the state of Ohio had to fear the success of Alabama. Some 1,800 overseas visitors were said to have come to the TVA in the year 1951 from among a tally of sixty countries up to that date, though when the world came to Knoxville, special arrangements had to be made for black visitors because of its Jim Crow workplaces.[20]

Within two years of the Hiroshima and Nagasaki bombings, TVA officials were in Japan advising the post-war government how to manage its rivers. They didn't go in alone, because from 1945 to 1952 Japan was under US military occupation. But the TVA marketing approach here was very similar to that pursued elsewhere. A Japanese translation of Lilienthal's *Democracy on the March* published in 1949 sold 10,000 copies in its first year. The idea above all was to help bolster Japan's 'indigenous resources' for energy.[21] The country's lack of coal or oil – and the United States withholding its oil exports from a militarily aggressive Japan – had contributed to the attack on the US Pacific Fleet at Pearl Harbor in December 1941. The US government funded visits from Japanese officials to the Tennessee Valley in the early 1950s. Japanese observers were well aware of the role of the TVA's Oak Ridge facility in the development of the atom bomb.[22] But a diplomatic silence must have been observed in these years. Lilienthal noted in the 1953 edition of his *Democracy on the March*, despite his recent work leading the US Atomic Energy Commission, 'in none of the countries I visited was there evidenced the slightest interest in the atom'. '[N]or', he said, 'did anyone seem to think of their visitor in these terms.' All people wanted to talk about the world over, he said, was the TVA. 'History may well record . . . that it is in its highly symbolic value "in a thousand valleys" beyond the seas that TVA has rendered its greatest service in safeguarding and nurturing freedom in the world.'[23] This was a different kind of freedom than that of the happy housewife in her all-electric hydro kitchen. Lilienthal also noted that most of the TVA's electricity now went towards the creation of a nuclear arsenal against the USSR.

When the American occupation ended in 1951–2, the Japanese passion for all things Tennessee waned. The Kitakami Valley Authority on Honshu island ended up with separate agencies for irrigation, flood control and electricity: a far cry from the TVA's holistic model.[24] But there was no stopping the dams, which spread like knotweed along Japan's mountainous rivers. By 2000, Japan was in the top four countries worldwide in possession of 'large dams' – with over 2,600 (5.6 per cent of dams, globally), outpaced only by China (with a massive 46 per cent), the United States (nearly 14 per cent) and India (9 per cent). Even so, hydro-power as of 2023 generated less than 9 per cent of electricity in Japan, which is still largely reliant on imported fossil fuels: Middle Eastern oil and natural gas, and coal from Australia and elsewhere.[25]

The more serious the threat from Communism in a region, the more the American government wanted to dam its rivers. In 1949, President Truman made it clear to Lilienthal that he wanted a TVA in the Yangtze River Valley and on the Danube.[26] On the post-war Danube, in the narrow window between the end of the war and the Soviet takeover, an American geographer in 1947 argued that the river's 315,000-square-mile river basin, with its 80 million people, was an 'almost ideal regional unit for . . . an authority similar to the TVA'. Might it even 'bring a modicum of peace and prosperity to one of the stormiest corners of our planet'?[27] But the USSR had control of the lower Danube and planned their own dams on the river. A proposed hydro-plant at the Iron Gate – shared between Yugoslavia (now Serbia) and Soviet Romania in the 1960s – looked capable of providing more electricity than the Columbia River's Grand Coulee and Bonneville dams combined.[28] The USSR had already also swooped in like a falcon on the ailing Anglo-US-Egyptian Aswan High Dam project and carried it off.

In post-war China, things initially developed further than on the Danube. With its eyes on a Yangtze Valley Authority, the US war propaganda wing provided translations of *Democracy on the March* to Nationalist China (1928–49) led by Chiang Kai-shek. Morrison Knudsen, the engineering firm responsible for the Hoover Dam, were working on plans to dam the Yangtze River when the Chinese Communist Party defeated the Nationalist Government in 1949.[29] Chairman Mao Zedong took over the Three Gorges Dam project and placed it in a different but perhaps no more mythical bubble, as we see in chapter 20.

The vagueness of what was meant by the words 'Tennessee' and 'TVA' in a global context made it easy to adapt to any circumstance in which they might advance American influence through water projects. In south-east Asia, President Johnson in the 1950s wanted 'to turn the Mekong into a Tennessee Valley' through a series of dams to benefit the people of Cambodia, Laos, Thailand and South Vietnam, and keep out the Communists.[30] The Mekong, like the Yangtze and Yellow rivers, rises in the great Tibetan Plateau – the Sanjiangyuan ('source of three rivers') region – and flows south-eastwards, forming borders between Myanmar and Laos, Laos and Thailand, down through Cambodia's capital city of Phnom Penh and on into Vietnam, where it finally enters the South China Sea just to the west of the coastal city of Ho Chi Minh (on the Saigon River).[31] American dollars and Bureau of Reclamation officials were pouring into the Mekong River basin even as American bombs were dropping on North Vietnam in 1973. Only when Communists in North Vietnam decisively defeated the South in 1975 did the United States withdraw from the Mekong Committee.[32]

American water engineers were also found in Iran and Afghanistan. Here too, even when water projects were seen through to completion, the result did not provide the hoped-for social glue within or between nations. The dam may have been built but the TVA vision was discarded. The work of Lilienthal's Development and Resources Corporation in Iran, funded by the World Bank, resulted in one of the largest dams in the world, opened in 1963. The Mohammad Reza Shah Pahlavi dam on the Dez River, rising in the Zagros Mountains and flowing into the Karun River and then south into the Persian Gulf, was part of a modernisation drive by the aforementioned last Shah of Iran (1919–1980). When he was deposed in 1979, it was renamed the Dez Dam and the United States had no further involvement.[33]

In the 1950s in Southern Afghanistan, a series of dams was built for a TVA-style Helmand and Arghandab Valley Authority by the US Bureau of Reclamation and the firm Morrison Knudsen. US Aid and other agencies provided funding. A 'Little America' was planned to bloom in the irrigated desert.[34] A UN report in 1961 listed some of the anticipated benefits: 'educational institutions, sanitation and public health centres, modern housing, resettlement, particularly for the nomadic tribes, cottage and small industries [. . .] to raise the levels of living of the people in general'.[35] There was instead a series of unfortunate incidents. The nomadic people of the Helmand Valley were resettled. This did not create the orderly community of wheat farmers the development agencies hoped for. When it turned out that bigger fields and another resettlement would be needed, some of those affected resisted relocation with guns.[36] Failed monsoons and drought in the early 1970s caused by El Niño – the unpredictable warming of air over the Pacific Ocean – undermined the high-yield 'Green Revolution' grain that had been provided by the aid agencies. Deserts spread in some areas. In others the soil became waterlogged.

In the Shamalan district, it was said, the water table was so high that homes and mosques were sinking into the ground.[37]

When American funders began to pull out of Afghanistan in the 1970s, the region was able to fall back on aid it had been accepting all along from the USSR. Pro-Soviet factions took over in 1978, though resisted by the Mujaheddin (later supported by the United States), and the USSR invaded in 1979. The dry climate and saline soil, it transpired, provided perfect conditions not for wheat and cottage industries but for the opium poppy. In 2000 a UN agency estimated that 39 per cent of the world's heroin supply was issuing from the Helmand Valley.[38] Pashtun clans from the Helmand Valley that formed the core of the Taliban took the capital city of Kabul in 1996, and retained the city of Kandahar as their base on the east bank of the Arghandab River. To provide electricity for Kandahar, they finished off the Kajakai Dam that had been left incomplete by the departing Americans, with the opium crop providing the funding. When the United States invaded Afghanistan in 2001 they took care to bomb the dam. But because of constant fluctuations in American policy towards Afghanistan, its approach to this structure soon changed again. Within a few years, US Aid was again flowing into the province for US/Afghan collaboration on the Kajakai Dam.[39]

Dams provide a focus for selling expertise and materials, and for diplomacy and political influence, but they are an uncertain investment in the future. The world proved much more difficult to predict and control. The global TVA was an ideology-packed dream that was taken up, discarded and modified at will, both by the Americans and by their clients. Only the dams remained. The gigantic infrastructure and cost of dams invite grandiose justifications for the benefits they bring. This is a feature shared by all dam projects regardless of their ideological window dressing.

The Dnieper Dam built and completed (1925–32) under Stalin's leadership was central to the Soviet Union's plans for industrial development.[40] As Leon Trotsky said of the Dnieper River when in charge of electrification in 1926, shortly before his removal from this post:

> . . . the Dnieper runs its course through the wealthiest industrial land; and it is wasting the prodigious weight of its pressure, playing over age-old rapids and waiting until we harness its stream, curb it with dams, and compel it to give lights to cities, to drive factories, and to enrich ploughland. We shall compel it![41]

The tone was different but the general message is recognisable from the Mississippi River basin. The dam there has been seen as providing a 'mirror image' of the Wilson Dam on the Tennessee River.[42] The same engineer, Colonel Hugh Cooper, oversaw work on both dams. He was the former chief engineer of the Muscle Shoals Wilson Dam project – the TVA's first acquisition – also for a dam on the Mississippi at Keokuk, Iowa, and at Canada's Horseshoe Falls at Niagara.

For the Dnieper Dam, Cooper and his American colleagues were given spacious accommodation, with American food shipped via the port of Odesa. The turbines were provided by the General Electric Company and indeed the Dnieper Dam has been seen as contributing to a détente between the USA and USSR in the decade after the Russian Revolution of 1917, which may have provided some encouragement for further dam diplomacy.[43] There was no talk of river basins here. A 1970s promotional brochure on Soviet Ukraine called the dam 'a component of the Soviet Union's single national economic complex'.[44] There is a chequered history to Russia's own relationship to this dam: blown up in 1941 in the face of advancing German forces, rebuilt in the 1940s, and today still in Ukrainian hands – just about – it is subject to missile and drone attacks by Russia.[45] The re-engineered river itself is a neutral blank space for states to do what they like.

Today the TVA continues to promote its twin international mission of economic development for the Tennessee and wider Mississippi – it is a 'global valley' with a car industry 'nipping hard on the heels of Detroit' – and a 'classroom for the world'.[46] Its website feels older and wiser than its messages from the 1950s. Looking back at the mid-century TVA it is easy to see how simplistic its stated mission was and how deluded its prophecies were for a peaceful future through international cooperation on rivers. It is also striking how vague and instrumental the idea of Tennessee and the TVA became on a global stage in the post-war world. Is it fair to rescue these hydrological empire-builders from what the historian E.P. Thompson once called 'the enormous condescension of posterity': the national and international policymakers, engineers, financiers and lawyers?[47] In the early days many negative consequences of dams were unanticipated: the silted-up dams, species wiped out by degraded ecosystems, blocking of migratory species, silt that doesn't reach the delta, the economic prosperity that did not trickle down after all. Some negative consequences, such as the mass displacement of people, were fully apparent from the start. And the ecological downsides are now also evident.

The German writer Karl Wittfogel famously claimed in the 1950s that the hydrological projects of ancient regimes in China and Egypt were the essence of authoritarian state-building and control of the populace: the mark of an 'oriental despotism' which he saw mirrored in the USSR and China in his time.[48] Time has proved that there is nothing specifically oriental about these gigantic projects, though an element of despotism may be part of the dam-building and what we might now call the decision-making process. Despite the TVA rhetoric on the world stage, it is one of the defining features of large dams that they do not display obvious signs of democracy: early consultation, meaningful participation of all those affected, a genuine consideration of alternatives. Dams have been cited as the very essence of 'thinking like a state' or 'development from above'. Geographer Bill Adams has called for a 'river industry, not a dams industry' that takes account of the 'floodplain people'.[49]

Dams, like rivers elsewhere in this book, share the same quality in many contexts – of reflecting dreams and grandiose ambitions as if they were living entities, whether in the name of Democracy or 'the Good of Soviet Man' or Sustainability.[50] The International Hydropower Association in 2024 considered that the electrical capacity currently generated needs to be doubled to meet the

Paris Agreement targets for achieving net-zero carbon emissions by 2050. Today, over two-thirds of the world's major rivers are already dammed along their course. Many rivers can no longer be relied on to reach the sea.[51]

Some 80 million people globally have been internally displaced by dam-building, by one recent estimate – often people who have then moved out of view and out of history.[52] Today history is repeating itself as modernisation and resource extraction move restlessly from river to river. Globalised networks of resistance have developed to stand up to the global dam movement, often a coalition of indigenous and environmental activists, opposing the damming and pollution of rivers, mining operations, and internal displacement of people.[53] When the World Hydropower Congress met in Paris in conjunction with UNESCO in 2019 – its theme 'The Power of Water in a Sustainable, Interconnected World' – it faced a protest from 250 civil-society groups. Spearheaded by the (Latin American) Interamerican Association for Environmental Defense (AIDA), they range from groups such as the Pakistan Fisherfolk Forum, to the Bangladesh Poribesh Andolon, the African Law Foundation of Nigeria, and the Indigenous Environmental Network (USA), who we saw in chapter 13.[54] This activism is a different kind of march of democracy from the technocratic and opaque world of river engineering.

River 6: Niger

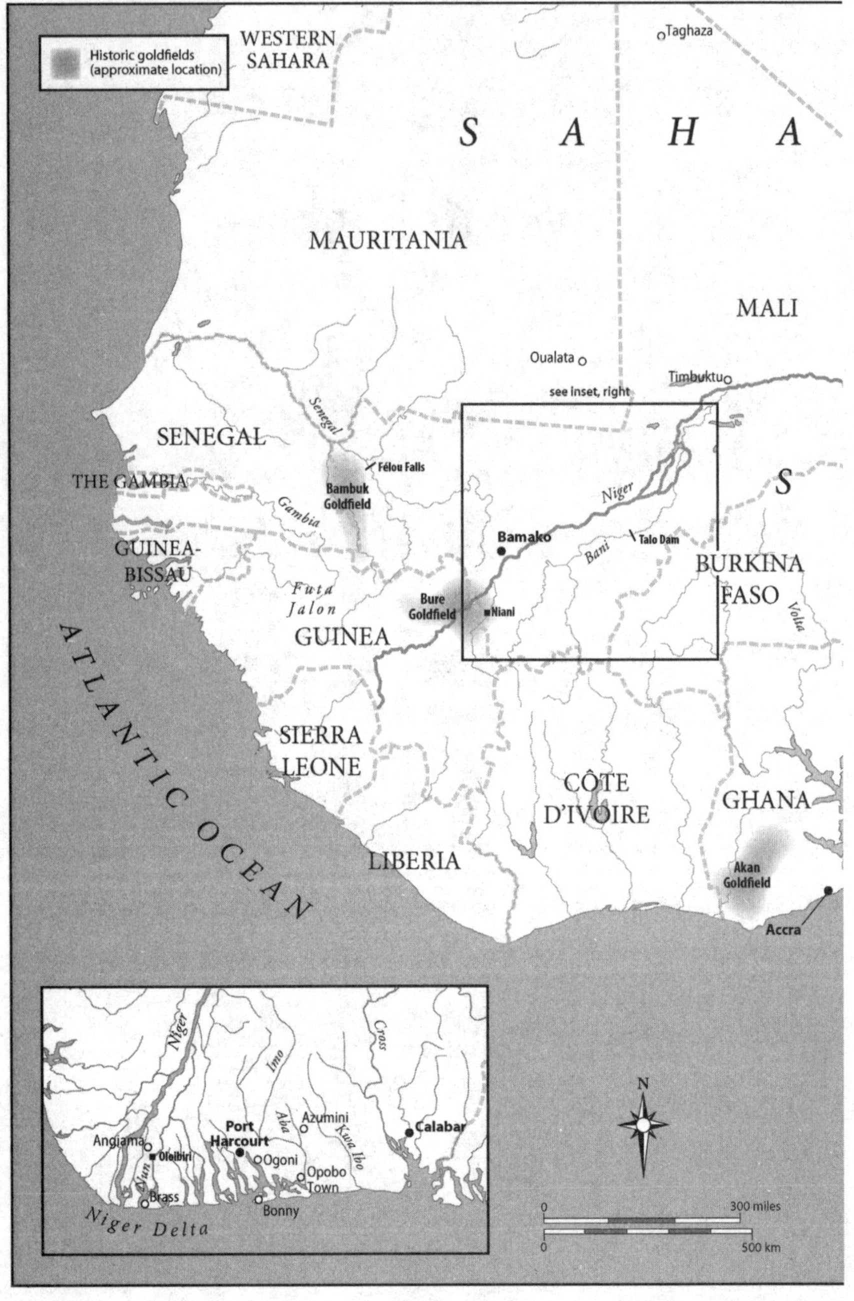

Historic goldfields (approximate location)
WESTERN SAHARA
Taghaza
S A H A
MAURITANIA
MALI
Oualata
Timbuktu
see inset, right
Senegal
SENEGAL
Félou Falls
Bambuk Goldfield
THE GAMBIA
Gambia
Niger
Bamako
Talo Dam
Bani
GUINEA-BISSAU
BURKINA FASO
Futa Jalon
Bure Goldfield
Niani
GUINEA
Volta
ATLANTIC OCEAN
SIERRA LEONE
CÔTE D'IVOIRE
GHANA
LIBERIA
Akan Goldfield
Accra
Niger
Imo
Cross
Aba
Azumini
Kwa Ibo
Calabar
Angiama
Oloibiri
Port Harcourt
Ogoni
Nun
Opobo Town
Brass
Bonny
Niger Delta
N
0
300 miles
0
500 km

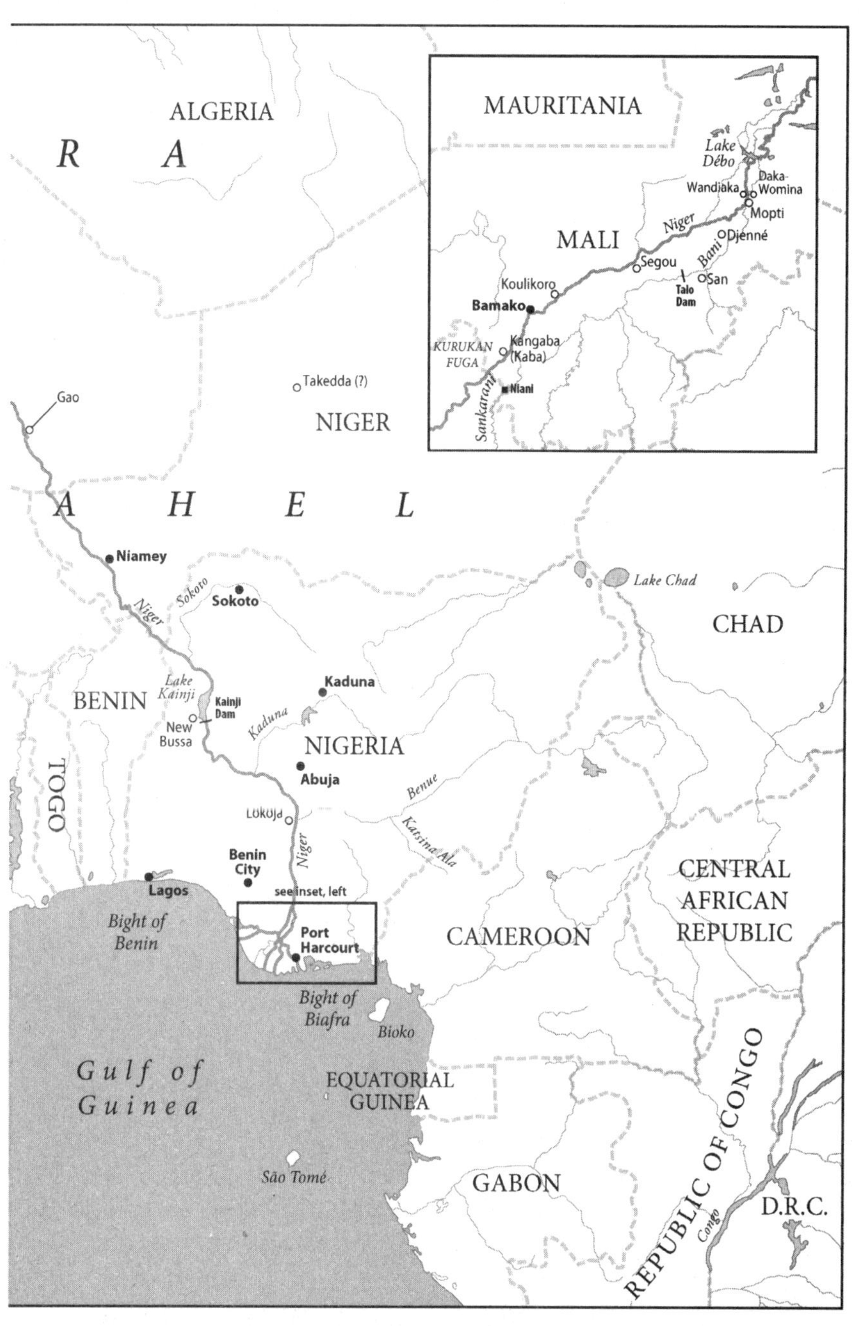

ALGERIA
R A
MAURITANIA
Lake Débo
Daka-Womina
Wandiaka
Mopti
Niger
MALI
Djenné
Bani
Segou
San
Talo Dam
Koulikoro
Bamako
KURUKAN FUGA
Kangaba (Kaba)
Niani
Sankarani
Takedda (?)
Gao
NIGER
A H E L
Niamey
Lake Chad
Sokoto
Sokoto
Niger
CHAD
Lake Kainji
Kainji Dam
Kaduna
BENIN
New Bussa
Kaduna
NIGERIA
TOGO
Abuja
Benue
Lokoja
Katsina Ala
Benin City
Niger
CENTRAL AFRICAN REPUBLIC
Lagos
see inset, left
Bight of Benin
Port Harcourt
CAMEROON
Bight of Biafra
Bioko
Gulf of Guinea
EQUATORIAL GUINEA
REPUBLIC OF CONGO
São Tomé
GABON
D.R.C.
Congo

16

River at the Crossroads

> 'For the riuer Niger together with the water which falleth from certaine mountaines doth so moisten their grounds, that no places can be deuised to be more fruitful . . . .'
>
> *The History and Description of Africa of Leo Africanus*, trans. John Pory (1600)[1]

This chapter tells the story of the upper Niger and its great Inner Delta as a river at the crossroads between the Sahara and towns and cities of the Sahel and West Africa. This crossroads was the source of the region's great wealth during the time of its medieval empires and also a source of conflict and competition for control of its trade routes, fertile streams and floodplains. Its location has shaped the history of the upper Niger region, but like all rivers the upper Niger has a barely imaginable prehistory long before any kind of humans arrived. The upper Niger hasn't always been a watery crossroads at the base of a desert. Both the wider region and the Niger's own path from source to sea have been subject to wild fluctuations of climate. This chapter looks at the rise of the crossroads and the history that followed.

Around 250 million years ago a great expanse of water – the Tethys Sea – formed between the two supercontinents of Gondwana in the south and Laurasia in the north. Slowly the supercontinents broke up and the African and Indian plates collided with Eurasia, creating the great mountain ranges of the Alps in the west and the Himalayas in the east. During the warm Eocene years, from around 56 million years ago, when sea levels were high, ocean washed across north and west Africa where the desert and inner delta now lie. The sand and salt mines of the Sahara Desert are a legacy of this time. Stretching round Africa's shorter Eocene coastline was an ecosystem of woven roots in this 'golden age of mangroves'.[2]

From eleven to seven million years ago, in a drying climate the seas retreated, leaving the Mediterranean as the liquid remnant of Tethys. Perhaps seven million years ago great sand dunes started to form in the Sahara. Changes in the tilt of the turning Earth since this time continued to pull the Sahara region between extremes of wet to dry. The most recent rainy (pluvial) phase, from around 15,000 to 5,000 years ago, produced a web of river valleys, lakes and seasonal streams whose palaeo-channels are still carved into the desert floor. Some of these, like the long-gone Tilemsi River, used to flow south into the Niger River. Remains of cattle and hippopotami found in the desert sands come from this time of the Green Sahara; from the same pluvial phase that produced the rock art of the once verdant Qurta region east of the Nile.[3] The people and non-human creatures living in the Sahara either migrated or adapted to wildly changing conditions ranging from rainy to utterly arid.

A proto-Niger River itself is estimated to have formed around 29 to 34 million years ago. It is impossible, though, to say which of the many streams of this river over its long gestation is the true Niger. Scholars have been slowly unravelling the ancient pathways of Africa's rivers, both the connections that used to weave them together, and their role as equally corridors and barriers. Specialists in 'hydrochory' look at how different organisms – from fish to human populations – are shaped by rivers as 'ecological corridors'. Many of the rivers of North-West Africa were once interconnected. So at times of greater rainfall, the Niger River has been variously linked to the Senegal River and to the basin of Lake Chad (around 12,000 to 8,000 years ago), while the Chad was once connected to the Nile River. These ancient shared corridors saw Nilo-Sudanian fish swimming freely between channels of rivers that are now separate. Species such as the Kafue pike (*Hepsetus odoe*) or the electric catfish (*Malapterurus electricus*), a night fisher that lurks among rocks and roots ready to stun its prey, are relics of this past.[4] Likewise, some endemic species found in very particular places are evidence of long-standing river barriers. Over its long evolution, the Niger has slowly created 'biogeographic barriers' for a great variety of species: sending members of single species that lived along its banks their separate ways to form new species of frogs, shrews and primates. Two species of tree snakes have recently been identified that were probably once a single species but diverged somewhere in the Miocene-Pliocene period (between 5.3 and 2.6 million years ago) with the formation of the Niger's coastal delta. This left *Toxicodryas pulverulenta* to the west of the delta, and to the east *Toxicodryas adamanteus*, though both species are becoming hard to find in the delta's shrinking forest habitats.[5]

As the climate continued to mutate, so did the waters of the Niger, discovering new pathways over time. During the most recent glacial period, around 18,000 years ago, sand dunes formed around today's city of Timbuktu, blocking the north-easterly path of the western Niger. Then during the last pluvial phase somewhere around 8,000 to 10,000 years ago, the swelling western Niger River – still blocked by dunes in the north-east – was diverted southwards to form the Great Bend. Around today's city of Niamey, it joined the headwaters of an eastern Niger River becoming one river which journeyed southwards towards the sea. The Niger River is thought to have assumed its present course, along with its Benue tributary, around 6,500 to 5,000 years ago, as the Sahara and Sahel were drying out.[6] This was the slow birth of the Niger with two deltas and the crossroads at the base of the desert.

The Niger today goes by many names along its course. The Tuareg nomadic herders of the upper Niger and inland delta region have long called it *egerou n-igereou*, or 'river of rivers'.[7] Today it rises in the Futa Jalon highlands of northern Guinea in the west: the region's 'water tower' and source also of the Gambia and Senegal rivers. But whereas those rivers flow north-west into the Atlantic Ocean, the Niger River begins an epic 2,600-mile journey away from the sea, north-east through the Sahel and the many channels of the inland Niger delta along the southern fringe of the Sahara Desert. The rains that fall in the mountains from May to September reach the inland delta by October, transforming the dry basin into a huge wetland system of streams, ponds and seasonal lakes around 264 miles in length. Here the Niger slows almost to a halt, losing around two-thirds of its water into the surrounding wetlands and releasing its silt so that it emerges almost clear at the delta's end. Then the river curves expansively at the Niger's Great Bend and heads south-east, gradually reaching the Gulf of Guinea in the Atlantic Ocean through a delta of forests and mangroves. The Niger is shorter than both the Nile and the Congo, but its massive river basin spans over 500,000 square miles across nine countries in West and Central Africa, from arid Burkina Faso to Nigeria's rain-soaked delta.[8]

No one understood the full course of the Niger for many thousands of years. Written accounts in traveller's tales referred to the Niger as the same river as the Nile. Ibn Battuta, visiting the inner delta in the mid-1300s, thought the Niger continued eastwards from there until it reached Dongola (today's Sudan) and flowed north to the Nile cataracts and Aswan. The first written reference to the name 'Niger' is thought to have occurred two centuries later in the writings of the sixteenth-century Andalusian diplomat and traveller, Leo Africanus (al-Hasan ibn Muhammad al-Wazzan).[9]

Towns of the upper Niger region were important centres of regional trade as well as long-distance trans-Saharan trade probably in the first millennium CE. A cache of over fifty hippopotamus tusks has been found at Gao on the Niger in layers dating from the mid-800s to the late 900s CE, specifically the canines and incisors of the hippo's lower jaw, used for delicate ivory carvings. The town of Djenné, home of the famous mosque, also has deep roots. Situated on a stream leading to the Bani River, itself a southern tributary that meets the Niger at the town of Mopti, its earlier incarnation as Jenne-jeno may have been a regional centre already from the third century BCE and a well-developed town by 850 CE.[10]

Timbuktu is situated 15 kilometres north of the Niger River at the northern tip of the upside down 'V' of the Niger at the base of the Sahara, a key to its legendary status in this region. During the wetter centuries of the late first millennia CE up to the 1600s in this region there were probably seasonal and permanent ponds and streams here, with a channel linking Timbuktu to the Niger. A stream flowing from the 'pool of Kabara', Timbuktu's port, at times linked the city to the Niger River at Korioume. An area of Timbuktu today is still known as Badjindé, a Songhai word for 'stream of the Hippos', probably recalling the Badjindé ponds of Timbuktu that dried up with the arrival of arid conditions in the seventeenth century.[11] Timbuktu has various origin stories. According to one nineteenth-century account, it was established as a seasonal camp around 1100 CE at the site of a water well overseen by an old woman. But Timbuktu has a much longer history than this. Archaeology suggests settlement in this area from at least 2,000 BCE, indicated by *tells*, or mounds, formed over the centuries from mud-brick buildings. Archaeology at Dia-Shoma near today's Dia suggests an early well-populated settlement in the region in the ninth century BCE: a place of fishers, pastoralists and farmers, as well as iron smelting and terracotta pottery. A still deeper human past is likely to lie still buried under the sands for now. The whole region at the base of the Sahara, like the desert to the north, is subject to the constant encroachment of windblown sand, a process known as 'ensablement', burying the deeper history. When the Sankoré Mosque in Timbuktu was restored in the 1990s, sixty trucks of sand were removed from the site.[12]

Why was this upper Niger region so strategically important? As a wetland and river at the base of the desert, it provided a natural intermediate zone for the long-distance trans-Saharan trade between North Africa's coast, the desert and sub-Saharan Africa. During the time of the great medieval empires the cities of the upper Niger and Inner Niger Delta sat at the intersection of major trading routes for salt, gold and slaves. This was the source of the region's fabled wealth. Traders in charge of the Saharan routes brought salt from deposits laid down millions of years earlier by disappearing seas and drying out lakes. Essential for preserving food, salt was also exchanged for gold, slaves and copper. Everyone knew where the salt came from, but the location of the goldfields, near the headwaters of the Niger and Gambia rivers, and in the Senegal and Volta River basins, was for a long time a closely guarded secret. The only way to access the gold was via the middlemen in touch with those controlling the mines, where it was extracted from exposed rockfaces and alluvial sources in the rivers.[13]

The trans-Saharan journey too was a major undertaking that required local cooperation and expertise. Birds can cross the Sahara Desert in a single flight, but humans with their clipped wings need staging posts. The blank landscape of the Sahara to the untrained eye and its sheer size – 3,000 kilometres from north to south and 5,000 kilometres across – made this a treacherous journey. A valuable cache of copper bars, textiles and cowrie shells found buried in the Mauritanian desert in the 1960s may have belonged to travellers who came unstuck there somewhere around the eleventh to thirteenth century, but their stories have been lost forever.[14]

Water and the knowledge of local guides were the two keys to survival. A journey across the Sahara in the 1350s was described by Ibn Battuta. A Moroccan *qadi* (travelling judge) of Libyan descent, Ibn Battuta was a prodigious traveller through Africa, the Black Sea region, India and East Asia (possibly), and also a prolific diarist. His *Travels*, or *Riḥlah*, have left eyewitness accounts of his journeys and encounters with rulers, including his appointment in Delhi in the time of Muḥammad ibn Tughluq. Ibn Battuta visited the legendary imperial court of Mali, after the death of the famous Mansa Musa during the reign of his brother Sulaiman. Ibn Battuta's account of his journey from the Moroccan coast to the banks of the Niger provided a vivid account of a typical journey, one of the three main routes.[15]

Setting out in February from Marrakesh, Ibn Battuta travelled south to the Moroccan town of Sijilmasa, 'a very beautiful city' where the desert began. Here he bought camels and enough fodder for four months. The dromedary Arabian camel (one hump), which first arrived in North Africa around the first century CE, drinks prodigious quantities of water and can then travel without liquids and carry great weights for several weeks – up to a month in extremes. Travelling in a group, after twenty-five days Ibn Battuta arrived at the oasis village of Taghaza, its houses and mosques built from walls of salt blocks and its roofs made of camel skin: a place of 'no attractions' and no escape from the flies, according to him. Even the water tasted of salt. But gold dust came in great quantities to this bleak place, brought by 'the Blacks' from south of the desert, to be exchanged for blocks of salt. From here Ibn Battuta's party moved south to Tasarahla, which was furnished with a groundwater well. This was, he said, where 'caravans . . . stop for three days to rest, and to repair and fill their waterskins and sew on to them coarse bags to protect them from the wind'. They sent a guide ahead to fetch fresh water and a welcome party. Two months after leaving Sijilmasa, the whole party arrived and spent over a month at the trading city of Iwalatan (today's Oualata), which Ibn Battuta called 'the first district of the country of the Blacks'. From here it was a journey of ten to fifteen days to the Niger River.[16]

Other travellers help to fill in this picture of the final stages of the salt/gold exchange across the desert, tales of entrepôts, merchants, and arduous upstream journeys undertaken by slaves. A story from a traveller named Valentim Fernandes relays the situation as he understood it from travellers at the end of the fifteenth century: Timbuktu, he said, was the 'entrepot for all the gold that is exchanged, to the east as well as the west, for salt. . . . There the camel and its salt, together, is sold for one hundred mithqals . . .' For the unsuspecting camels, their work was done: they were killed and eaten. The salt was put onto boats at Timbuktu. From here, it was said, these:

> . . . boats are then hauled by ropes up the river for fourteen days, to a town called Gyni [Jenne/Djenné] in the kingdom of Melly [Mali].

According to this account, the traders from the gold mines came here, and were of

> a particular race called the Vngaros [Wangara], who are red or brown. In fact, no one else is allowed to approach the mines save those of this race, to the exclusion of others, because they are regarded as very worthy of confidence. Other people, whether white or black, are not able to go there.

At Djenné, the Wangara merchants, it was said, 'consign a hundred or two hundred black slaves, or more, to carry the salt on their heads from Gyni to the gold mines, and from there to bring back the gold'.[17]

Across the expanse of sand between north and south, east and west, flowed goods, slaves and conquerors, and also ideas. The upper Niger River was also a crossing point for faiths. It was here that Islam is thought to have first reached West Africa in the eighth century. The river and region were pulled towards a cardinal point as mosques went up in the region's riverside towns, each with its Mihrab orientated east towards Mecca. Most famous of all, the Great Mosque in the town of Djenné, made from mud bricks, is said to have been built by the city's first Muslim ruler, King Koi Konboro, in the 1200s.[18]

This upper Niger region was also a crossing point between the 'white' people of North Africa and the 'black' people of the Sahel, and a centre for the slave trade. When Ibn Battutah travelled to this 'country of the Blacks', he noted that northern merchants were treated with some disdain by their black customers. But it was from here that black sub-Saharan Africans were trafficked, procured through raids and wars of conquest. The enslaved were everywhere in the Niger region too: used for status, for household service, and for hard labour. Near Takadda in the Sahara was a copper mine where the houses were red and water metallic, and enslaved men and women dug out the copper and smelted it into rods. The rods were used as currency to buy meat, millet, wheat, butter, firewood, and more people to work as slaves.[19]

The upper Niger region and inland delta became the site of three famed empires, moving successively from west to east: the empire of Ghana, the Mali Empire and the Songhay Empire. Each gained wealth and power from their strategic position between the goldfields of West Africa and the salt traders of the Sahara Desert who connected them to North Africa and the Mediterranean world from Arabic Spain to Egypt and beyond. The first, the formidable Soninke Empire of Ghana, held sway along the Senegal and Gambia rivers from around the eighth to eleventh centuries before its defeat by the Soso people. The second, the Malian Empire, was founded in the thirteenth century by Sundiata Keita after a decisive victory over the Soso. According to tradition, in 1235 Sundiata summoned both supporters and the vanquished to the plain of Kurukan Fuga near Kangaba (Kaba) where the Sankarani River joins the Niger, delivering the famous Manden Charter, laying down rules for his kingdom.[20]

The centre of gravity shifted along the river over time, within and between empires. During the reign of Sundiata Keita, the Mali Empire seems to have been focused in the region between the Niger and Sankarani rivers.[21] One oral tradition identified Niani on the Sankarani River (today a village in Guinea) as both Sundiata's capital and the centre of the regional world. As a *griot*'s (keeper of oral history and tradition, singer and musician) account conveyed by Guinean historian D.T. Niane put it:

> . . . If you want salt, go to Niani, for Niani is the camping place of the Sahel caravans. If you want gold, go to Niani, for Bouré, Bambougou and Wagadou work for Niani. If you want fine cloth, go to Niani, for the Mecca road passes by Niani.

The produce of the animal kingdom was also gathered here, and the might and muscle of the empire.

> If you want fish, go to Niani, for it is there that the fishermen of Maouti and Djenné come to sell their catches. If you want meat, go to Niani, the country of the great hunters, and the

> land of the ox and the sheep. If you want to see an army, go to Niani, for it [is] there that the united forces of Mali are to be found.[22]

It was in this Sankarani tributary that Sundiata Keita is reputed to have died. And here too, according to tradition, he transformed himself into a hippopotamus. The name 'Mali' itself, according to Niane, derives from the word for 'hippopotamus' in the regional Mandingo language.[23]

Sundiata remains an iconic figure in Mali, but in the following century a successor was to achieve global fame. Mansa Musa (c. 1270–c. 1337), ruler of the Mali Empire, stood out on the rivers of the fourteenth-century world. It was he who took the empire to its greatest extent, stretching along the north-western arc of the Niger River from today's Guinea through the Inner Niger Delta, including the trading centres of Djenné and Timbuktu, continuing eastwards towards Gao on the Niger Bend, where the river turns southwards. Reputed to be the richest of kings, Mansa Musa's streams were thought to run with gold. The wealth of this region was brought to global fame by the *hajj* or pilgrimage of Mansa Musa in the 1320s. With 80,000 attendants and 500 camels, this was a moving panorama of devotion, wealth and style. Stopping in Cairo – still a *hajj* hub city today – Mansa Musa swapped anecdotes with the Mamluk caliph about raiders on their doorsteps. His largesse and distribution of gold, it is said, caused 20 per cent inflation in the region by the time he left the shores of the Nile.[24] On his return from Mecca the emperor embarked on a building spree employing the Granada-based poet-architect Abu Ishaq Al-Sahili (1290–1346) in the cities of Niani and Timbuktu, including for (perhaps) construction of the Djingareyber mosque which still stands today. It is said that in a single day Mansa Musa handed Al-Sahili 4,000 mithqals of gold. One hundred mithqals are roughly equivalent to 425 grams, so this was around 17 kilograms of gold. At the time of writing, a single kilogram of gold at the UK Royal Mint costs just over £75,000.[25]

As his fame spread, Mansa Musa began to appear on maps created for European courts. One map above all fixed the king's image in European eyes and has ever since: a magical cartoon moment. The *Catalan Atlas* by Abraham Cresques, a Jewish Majorcan cartographer, was presented to the Spanish King of Aragon in 1375. It beautifully laid out the principal features and rulers of lands around the Mediterranean Sea. In it Mansa Musa is shown seated on a throne with a golden sceptre in one hand, a huge gold coin in the other, and on his head a golden crown. Next to him is the town of Timbuktu and a text: 'This black Lord is called Musse Melly and is the sovereign of the land of the negroes of Gineva [Guinea]. This king is the richest and noblest of all these lands due to the abundance of gold that is extracted from his lands.' The map was both a representation of the known world and a ragbag of fables and travellers' tales. You could locate the places where the women were half fish, an island where there were 'two summers and three winters', and a city entirely 'deserted due to snakes'. The emperor's throne is shown suspended over what was considered to be the 'Western Nile': a lake and river seemingly flowing to the headwaters of the Nile in the east. The map borrowed features used by earlier cartographers such as turreted elephants signifying Africa and the Nile River, and flowing from two southern streams that are flanked by green parrots. Mansa Musa was already dead by the time this map was created, but powerful men lived forever here.[26]

In time, the Mali Empire gave way to the third medieval empire: the Songhay Empire in the fourteenth and fifteenth centuries, centred on the city of Gao downstream on the Niger Bend. The Songhay took Timbuktu in 1468 and turned the city into a centre of Islamic scholarship and worship, until new conquerors arrived from Morocco in 1591, and others followed.[27]

While Cresques's 1370s map showed the Niger's imperial highpoint, it also contained a clue to a later arrival in West Africa and on the Niger River. It shows a small vessel bearing Majorcan sailors in the year 1346 just off the West African coast, searching for the Rio d'Oro (River of Gold): outsiders looking for gold. The European pursuit of West African gold from this time would launch countless sea and river voyages, all hoping to cut out the inconvenient middlemen of the gold trade. During the time of the Portuguese King Henry 'the Navigator' in the mid-1400s, perhaps two-thirds of all metals entering Europe each year were arriving via the Saharan caravan trade. It was during his reign that the Portuguese conquered the navigational problems of the treacherous Cape Bojador which allowed their ships to round Africa's southern Cape of Good Hope in the late 1400s. In the 1430s, some of Henry's sailors navigated part of the way up what they too called the Rio de Oro. Finding no gold, they made do instead with pelts and oil from some unlucky seals they met on the estuary banks.[28]

But the rivers would not open up to the Portuguese. Those navigating the Gambia River a few years later were met by formidable attacks from war canoes. Waterways also provided their own natural barriers to navigation as they did on the Nile's cataracts and the Danube's Iron Gates. The rapids of the unstoppable Congo (or Zaïre) River blocked passage to the interior. On the Senegal River, the men of Portugal's King John II (r. 1481–95) were under orders to lay explosives at the Felou Rapids, but to little effect. Ultimately Europeans did not manage to find the goldfields during these centuries and settled instead for a coastal trade in people.[29] The Iberian trade would develop to transport enslaved Africans across the Atlantic to the Americas in the sixteenth century.

Some historians consider that the rise of Atlantic trade sparked the decline of Mediterranean trade and with it the golden era of the upper Niger River. The flooding of precious metals into Europe following Spain's American conquests in the 1500s altered the international significance of West African gold. But gold remained a powerful symbol of Europe's trade in West Africa. The golden Guinea coin of the Royal African Company (RAC) in the reign of the English King Charles II (r. 1660–85) bore the image of an African elephant and castle to suggest its origins. Although, like other European trading companies in the region, the RAC's principal business was not gold but human trafficking. By the

1720s the company had transported nearly 150,000 Africans to the Americas.[30]

The crossroads in the Sahel remained a crucial site in the region, a centre for trade in gold, salt, grain and cattle, and a place for rival empire-builders. If its days of great wealth were behind it, Timbuktu maintained its place at the crossroads while its fame only spread as Europeans arrived. In the 1890s, when the upper Niger region had become part of imperial French Sudan, the French journalist Félix Dubois described Timbuktu as 'a temporary dépôt, situated between the borders of the desert and the copiously watered valleys of the south'. The Arabic scholar Abd al-Rahman al-Sadi around the same time called the city 'a haunt of saints and ascetics, and a meeting place of caravans and boats'.[31]

When this part of French Sudan gained independence in 1960, Mali was the name selected for its new nation state. Since Malian independence the Inner Delta has remained a crossing point of ancient traditions and modernity, of neo-colonialism and nationalism, and of rival versions of faith – from Islam infused with water spirits, to Sufism, to fundamentalist Jihadi movements aligned with economic and political grievances. The mosques of the inner delta and upper Niger have come to symbolise the power struggles of the region over time. The thirteenth-century Great Mosque at Djenné was destroyed by the fundamentalist Seku Ahmadu (r. 1818–43), by stopping its gutters, according to oral histories, and allowing rain to gather on its muddy roof. When the French arrived they paid homage to the past glories of the region, including the rebuilding in 1906–7 of Djenné's Great Mosque that still stands today, designed by a local mason. Today this mosque is one of Mali's icons of its ancient glory – a UNESCO World Heritage Site and recently restructured with funding from the Aga Kahn Foundation. Each spring the whole structure is replastered with mud (banco) from the Bano riverbank mixed with sand, rice husks, cow dung and river water. In 2016 Sufi tombs in a mosque in Timbuktu were vandalised by members of the Ansar Dine, part of a wider conflict across the delta and Mali region.[32] This place remains crossroads for faiths and political conflict.

But for all these metaphors of crossroads, the significance of this upper Niger region as a literal cross-roads for the trans-Saharan trade has altered today. The salt trade continues, but navigable streams and watering holes have lost some of their status in the era of international airports and desert toll roads. And as we shall see in chapter 18, the wetlands of the upper Niger itself are also changing, through both anthropogenic global warming and human re-engineering of the river itself.

17
Oil Rivers

> 'After April 5, 1873, the King of Opobo shall allow no trading establishment or hulk in or off Opobo Town, or any trading vessel to come higher up the river than the white man's beach opposite Hippopotamus Creek.'
>
> British Treaty with Opobo (1873)[1]

On the morning of 19 September 1887, King JaJa of Opobo (1821–1891) stepped aboard the British gunboat HMS *Goshawk*, anchored in a river in the Niger delta. A group of his followers stood watchfully on the sand. King JaJa had received an urgent invitation from Harry Johnston, Acting Consul for the Protectorate of Oil Rivers, to discuss the way in which rivers in the eastern Niger Delta were being blocked against British merchants. Johnston had made it clear that if King Jaja did not attend, he would be deemed guilty and liable to 'punishment' of an unspecified nature. If he did attend, the consul gave 'my word that you will be free to come and go'. As it was, no sooner had JaJa arrived at the meeting place – the riverside 'factory' of a Liverpool trader – than the guns of the *Goshawk* were swung round to face his followers on the shore. Johnston announced that the king must now proceed to Accra (Ghana) and submit to a trial. He had an hour to choose whether to go quietly or be tried as 'a common malefactor', leaving the court a 'ruined man, for ever cut off from your people and your children'.[2] Choosing the trial, JaJa was in fact never to see his people again anyway. With Patience, one of his wives, and some attendants he boarded the *Goshawk* and was conveyed to

Accra where, with a Nigerian defence solicitor, he was tried at a Navy court.[3]

This is one version of the story, largely taken from William Neville Geary, a colonial official in the Gold Coast (Ghana) and later practising lawyer in Lagos. In another account of that morning, the first-hand testimony of Acting Consul Henry Johnston himself – recollecting his by now much criticised actions in the 1920s – King Jaja arrived at the beach 'with many canoes and an armed escort of seven hundred warriors, each with a Snider rifle'. He had been told of the trial right there on the beach, whereupon he 'assented and went quietly' onto the *Goshawk*. Along the coastal journey west to Accra, JaJa would 'sit by my side . . . and amuse himself by looking over my sketch book,' Johnston recalled.[4]

Either way, King Jaja faced a trial which centred on alleged treaty breaches. Did JaJa exceed his territory as King of the Opobo people when he barred the way on the Imo River, 25 miles upstream from Opobo? Who placed the 'boom' along Azumena creek that left space for JaJa's canoes while blocking British vessels? Had JaJa made an agreement or 'oath of ju ju' with neighbouring territories not to trade with white men? Found guilty of breaking the terms of an 1884 Treaty and blocking access to trade on the rivers, the King of Opobo was sentenced to deportation for at least five years. He was to receive an annual payment of around £800 and retain his property at home.[5] This was allowed to stand, even though everyone up to the British prime minister, Lord Salisbury, knew it was effectively a kidnap.

King JaJa was offered a choice of distant exile within Britain's overseas territories, including the island of St Helena many miles off the coast of Africa (where Napoleon had died). He selected the island of St Vincent in the Caribbean Sea. Here he became ill and was moved to Barbados. After numerous appeals, JaJa was eventually pardoned and allowed to return home in the summer of 1891. But he died on the journey at the Canary Islands, under conditions of some secrecy, and was buried there. In the following year his body was exhumed and reburied with ceremony at JaJa's palace in Opobo. This building, a prefabricated three-storey structure that the king had ordered from Liverpool, still stands in Opobo today. Nearby is a statue erected in 1907 by 'his European friends, his relations, chiefs and connections'. He holds a staff in his right hand and in his left an emblem of an oil-palm. By 1961, the year after Nigerian independence, the memorial had been updated with the addition of a sign: 'He was the First African Ruler to Oppose British Imperialism in West Africa. Defending the course of the Independence of His Country, He was Kidnapped by British Imperialists and Died in Harness in 1891 in Tenerife.'[6]

This is just one example of the struggles for power on the Niger River and delta distributaries in the nineteenth century. Britain's ceaseless quest for ghost acres of natural resources beyond its own windy shores saw it convert slave-trading interests to 'legitimate trade' in the delta's oil-palm products. By the early nineteenth century, Europeans had been trading along the West African coast for 400 years. But they had made little headway in the interior, though the slave trade had pulled increasing numbers of people – both traders and the enslaved – from inland regions to the coastal delta. Despite disastrous early British expeditions along the Niger River, persistence paid off, supported by steam, rifles and naval power. But as the British government tried to secure access to resources and trade, it became steadily drawn in to efforts to control the rivers of the Niger Delta. What started with trade ended with a need to try to dominate the whole territory. This is a story of bribery, slavery, kidnapping, and armed monopolies on the Niger River and of creeping micro-management.

King JaJa of Opobo encapsulated many of the problems that the European powers faced from the start. How to access the resources of the African interior and manage the coastal middlemen? The Opobo king was a divisive figure – with a strong following in his home territory but hated by those he had cut out of the palm-oil trade, especially his powerful Bonny rivals. He also represented the most successful resistance to British attempts to set the terms of trade in his land. Sold into slavery in Bonny on the delta coast, from his native Igboland as a child, he had worked his way to freedom and headship of a trading house. He gradually expanded his fiefdom and founded a new kingdom on the Opobo River, between the Bonny River in the west and the Cross River to the east. From here, through a combination of political skill and armed force, he cut out his former Bonny associates in the palm-oil trade and built a new monopoly around the Opobo and Imo rivers.[7]

The raft of agreements with the British that JaJa was alleged at the trial to have broken was matched by those that he and other delta traders themselves had earlier drawn up for British merchants and officials.[8] Back in 1873, when JaJa still had the upper hand, a treaty he drew up had obliged Britain to recognise him as King of the Opobo and respect his territorial boundaries, as the treaty clause at the head of this chapter suggests. The British were not to attempt to establish any trading centre in Opobo Town. In 1882, JaJa told British authorities of the territory he had annexed around the Qua Eboe River: 'My first and last words are that the country belongs to me and I do not want white traders . . . there. Anyone who wants to trade . . . with me,' he declared, could come to the port of Opobo.[9]

Acting-Consul Johnston later recalled JaJa as 'little more than a puppet'. The real action was between the Liverpool traders wanting 'free trade' along the rivers and Glasgow merchants seeking a monopoly through their trade with JaJa. The Gold Coast official Geary, by contrast, considered that the king had been 'drowned in a Liver*pool*': a cartel to lower the prices paid for palm oil. Puppet or puppet-master, there was no denying the tangle that still bound together river traders on the two Atlantic coasts of Britain and Africa. For Acting-Consul Johnston, his own actions had 'ended the tyranny of the "middle man" which had been the great obstacle to a wide development of trade in the vast Niger Delta for a hundred years'.[10]

A dramatic U-turn in 1807 had seen Britain abolish its trade in enslaved Africans and recreate itself with astonishing speed into a crusading anti-slavery nation, with its squadrons cruising the West African coastline to apprehend slaving ships and develop 'legitimate trade'. The 1841 Niger Expedition typified this aspiration: the brainchild of Thomas Fowell 'Elephant' Buxton, seen until recently on the British £5 note along with Elizabeth Fry and her Quakers. Buxton was a leading anti-slavery campaigner and prodigious supporter of good works, from Bible societies to the Aborigines' Protection Society and of this new effort: the Society for the Extinction of the Slave Trade and for the Civilisation of Africa. The idea was to use the ground nut and other crops as the cradle of agriculture, Christianity and civilisation, and to access a wondrous list of natural resources available for commerce. The expedition set off from Britain's south coast for the Niger delta in spring 1841: three steamboats packed full of dreams. There were naval officers, scientists, missionaries, and – for the officers only – crates of bottled beer from Buxton's own Truman Hanbury Buxton brewery. But almost immediately on arriving in the delta, members of the expedition started dying, mostly from fever. Out of 159 people, 55 had died by the time the party arrived home in 1842.[11]

The principal 'legitimate trade' to emerge from these years was in fact the oil palm. This didn't need model farms and missionaries but grew prodigiously in wild groves in the Niger Delta. Oil extracted from the fruit pulp of the oil palm (*Elaeis guineensis*) could be used extensively as a lubricant for machinery, and its value only increased in the 1850s when the Crimean War stopped the flow of Russian tallow (animal fats) to Britain. Oil palm was also used increasingly for soap.[12] Today the everyday lives of millions of consumers across the world are still tied to this crop: from Palmolive to donuts to peanut butter.

But the European struggle to access and control the oil-palm trade or any commodity was long in the making and required charting the rivers of the interior, to which there was strong resistance. Explorers trying to trace the course of the Niger made enough headway to send news of the natural bounty of the Niger region, whetting the appetites of officials back home, but the cost to them could be high. The Niger River's great length and uncharted waters left openings for things to go badly wrong. These river journeys saw small groups of suspect white foreigners confined to boats moving like sitting ducks through territory and political landscapes of which they understood very little. In 1806 the Scottish explorer Mungo Park was shadowed along the Niger's upper and middle course, avoiding injury as far as the great Bussa Rapids that now lie beneath Kainji Dam and Lake Kainji. But here his progress was halted; he and his men died in an attack from the riverbank. Another Scot, Alexander Gordon Laing, commissioned by the army to trace the course of the Niger, set out for the Inner Delta via the desert, accompanied by two West African boatbuilders. In Timbuktu, he ignored instructions to go no further from the city's overlord, Ahmadu, and was killed just a few days after leaving the city. The British Lander brothers successfully traced the Niger's lower course during a perilous journey in the summer of 1830. They had explored the middle Niger between Bussa and Yelwa, before continuing south and eventually entering the Nun River in the delta, which discharged into the Atlantic Ocean. But when Richard Lander returned four years later, hoping to open up some inland trade, his luck ran out. He met his death on that same Nun River at Angiama, one of the so-called 'hostile villages' whose riverbanks were armed by men ready to fire on intruders, with the connivance, some thought, of rival British coastal traders.[13]

Steam vessels gradually changed the power dynamics on the Niger and other rivers, as they became faster and fully armoured over time. The world's first ocean-going iron steamship was commissioned in the early 1830s by Macgregor Laird of the Cammell Laird shipyard on the River Mersey in England for the purpose of his own navigation of the Niger. The Scottish Miller Brothers' steamer – the *Sultan of Socotoo* – was armed in the 1870s with heavy guns and 'iron screens for protection of those on board' as they tried to establish delta trading stations on the Qua Eboe River, though they were still forced to leave by King JaJa and others. In the next decade the Miller Brothers were among the chosen few who came to trade amicably with the Opobo ruler.[14]

Rivers of West Africa had long been ensnared in European rivalries. This came to a head with the late nineteenth-century 'Scramble for Africa', when European powers carved out tracts of land and water. To instil some order and hierarchy into this process, the West Africa Conference met in Berlin in 1884–5 under Bismarck, the same powerbroker who had reshaped the Danube River in the previous decade. While existing spheres of influence were formalised, there was also a new player on the scene. A massive territory in the region of Central Africa's Congo River was acquired by King Leopold II of Belgium, later notorious for the brutality of forced-labour regimes on his Congo rubber plantations. Numerous bronze statues of this king across Belgium have been targeted in protests since May 2020 and have begun to be removed from plinths by the authorities. Fittingly, the first removal was in the port city of Antwerp on the Scheldt estuary, which by the start of the twentieth century was importing 5.8 million kilos of rubber per year through forced labour in the Congo.[15]

Conference negotiations over rights to West African rivers started out with enthusiastic references to Napoleonic-era riparian rights, thrashed out in the Rhine Commission and its godchild: the European Danube Commission. A key difference here, however, was pointed out by a British official: where those European rivers 'ran through the well-defined territories of civilized States', the Congo and Niger were neither fully charted nor considered to be civilised.[16] In this scenario European colonisation of the riverside land was a precondition for allocating river rights. The absence of any African representatives among the fourteen states present is a striking feature of this conference.[17]

Just as when US President Thomas Jefferson had spoken passionately of natural rights to navigation at the Mississippi port of New Orleans, in his mind's eye were white men, their vessels and their cargo – here no mechanism was considered necessary to represent the rights of existing rulers, kings, emirates, or any kind of riparian community along the Niger or other West African rivers.[18] The Danube Riverain Commission of the 1850s had provided a precedent of sorts for this omission: the Ottomans and Austro-Hungarians on the Danube were presumed to speak for their 'vassal states', even though nationalism was bubbling up all along the river. The West Africa Conference magnified this model of suppressed autonomy across West Africa's rivers. Russia still resented the Danube Commission created after their defeat in the Crimean War. Count Vladimir Kapnist spoke of the 'evil tendency to enlarge and generalize' the Danube acts as 'doctrines of international law'.[19] Portugal wasn't on-message, either. Its claim to full sovereignty on the mouth of the Congo was rejected. In fact, nor was Britain, but it still gained control of the Niger Delta. There was no call for shared riparian rights here, their official claimed: they were not 'one of many Powers', but the sole '*Niger Power*'.[20] Britain's so-called 'Oil Rivers Protectorate' was established that same year (1885) and the Royal Niger Company acquired monopoly trading rights and the status of a miniature government on similar lines as the discredited East India Company.[21] International riparian commissions were forgotten.

Britain, in fact, was not the sole European power on the Niger River. It had to share the river in the end with France, which claimed its northern stretches within a great swathe of sub-Saharan West Africa known as French Sudan by the late nineteenth century. A boundary was grudgingly agreed at the point on the Niger where today three nation states meet above the river's confluence with the Sokoto tributary. South of the line went to Britain (today's Nigeria); east and north of the line to France (today's state of Niger and beyond). Benin, west of the river, was raided and annexed by Britain in 1897, the source of the contested 'Benin Bronzes' that still sit in London's British Museum and other institutions.[22]

Announcing the birth of colonies and river rights on the world's stage was one thing. Taking effective control of their waters and riverbanks was another. This brings us back to JaJa of Opobo. A powerful king had become an anomaly in a British protectorate by the 1880s, and his removal was an important victory for the colonisers. But their difficulties along the Niger's creeks and rivers did not end there. In 1889, two years after JaJa's defeat, there was still a boom positioned across the Azumena creek. The river system itself seemed to be against outsiders. In the dry season, passage along shallow creeks was slowed by labyrinthine root systems, mud and fallen trees. The monsoon from March to October made navigation easier, but there were tales of vessels becoming stuck and vulnerable at other times.[23] Colonial reports from this period describe the battle against the waters and winged insects that brought deadly malaria. Suspect water sources – shallow and stagnant rivers, ponds and lakes – could be 'oiled' with paraffin or crude oil, as the female malarial mosquito (genus *Anopheles*) will not lay eggs on 'oiled' water. But there was also relentless clearance, dredging and 'sudd-cutting' along rivers and through swamps and forests.[24] The key tasks, as one official saw it in 1908, were to build roads and railways, 'extend native footpaths', and 'clear the numerous rivers in the country and make them suitable for launch [steam] and canoe traffic'.[25] As in the inconvenient swamps of the Mississippi and south-eastern United States, imperial expansion, wetland drainage and bottomland forest clearing went hand in hand. Things escalated, as they had in India. To access the resources of the Niger River, the British in Nigeria became drawn into a dense thicket of their own creation: an all-encompassing world of regulations, taxation, telegraph poles, railway tracks, maps, theodolites, dredgers, steam launches, jetties, verandas, killings, and the policing of everyday life.

To make all this effort worth it, the riverside had to be made useful for trade and cash crops. But resistance came from all directions. Even the local Delta Church was considered a place of rebellion, with its charismatic preacher Garrick Braide arrested twice for sedition. Its congregation was reported to be 'hostile to all exotic influence, whether European or native'. That they refused all alcoholic spirits was also suspect – a tactic for 'dealing a blow to European trade' and the colonial treasury, considered the British Governor Sir Frederick Lugard in the 1920s.[26]

There were also the Munshi (or Tivi) people, occupying several thousand square miles of land south of the Niger's eastern tributary, the Benue – *Ifi u tamen*, or 'the big river'. This soil was perfect for the British Cotton Growing Association, if only the Munshi had not already been successfully growing cotton here. This land was also the colonists' proposed route for telegraph lines and railway tracks, but the Munshi were reported to be 'defying authority in the dense forest and undergrowth' and preventing all useful traffic on the Benue River. They kept this up for decades, raining poisonous arrows on Niger Company canoes, burning storehouses and killing officials.[27] Only by the 1930s were Munshi chiefs finally worn down by British forces. Their people were said to be paying their taxes; some were now working on the railway which ran through their land on a 500-mile journey from the delta town of Port Harcourt north to Kaduna.

Trouble also rumbled on in the palm-oil trade, like the 'Women's War' that broke out in the delta in 1929 over rumours of a new oil-palm tax. Traditionally women did the labour-intensive work of extracting oil from the inner kernel of the oil-palm fruit, and were not directly taxed by the British unlike the men who extracted the palm oil itself. Tax increases would mean eroding the already small profits of women's work. News of the tax rise was met with a wave of protests among the Ngwa women of the eastern Niger delta. In some places they boycotted traders; in others they attacked company offices and storehouses, cars and trains. At one office in the town of Opobo a group of women compelled the officials to sit down at their typewriters and list their demands, which showed that the problems went well beyond oil-palm tax. These included no increased tax, no warrant chiefs, no more fees charged for putting on plays, and an end to arrests for prostitution. The British response to the protests was fierce: over a three-day period their army fired shots into crowds of women at Opobo and elsewhere, leaving over fifty women dead and many injured.[28] At the subsequent Aba Commission inquiry into what had gone wrong, some women invited to speak argued that they should be exempt from the taxman. They were, after all, part of nature's life-cycle. Four witnesses, Ikonnia, Nwanyeruwa, Nwugo Enyidie and Enyidia, put it this way:

> Women are subject to men, and any such levy should be on men and not on women . . . We women are like trees which bear fruit. You should tell us the reason why women who bear seeds should be counted.

In the end, some curbs were placed on the arbitrary powers of local warrant chiefs, but much remained as before. The rumoured tax, however, was not imposed.[29]

Britain's reach progressively expanded up the Niger River. The 'Oil Rivers' state gave way to the Niger Coast Protectorate which then bought out the Royal Niger Company in 1900. At this point the colonies of Southern and Northern Nigeria were created, which later united with the colony of Lagos to form Nigeria in 1914. Major concessions were granted to the palm-oil giant Lever Brothers across the lower Niger and Congo regions by the 1920s. The flagship Lever products, Sunlight Soap and Stork Margarine, demonstrate the glamour of the commodity fetish, transforming the brutalities of this ecological hinterland into cheerful staples in the home market.[30]

From the 1920s, however, there was also a more systematic resistance to British rule, as Nigerian nationalism became a party-political force.[31] The interests of the British state remained tied to the Niger River in the decades that followed as it searched for a different kind of oil deep beneath the delta. But this was mirrored by transnational independence movements within Nigeria and across the colonised world of Africa and Asia. Rivers remained the silty highways of closely guarded protectorates but also provided a vault to different worlds with the old colonial boundaries swept away. As in 'The Negro Speaks of Rivers', Langston Hughes's 1921 poem, these streams of water helped to reach across time and space. 'The Black Eagle Awakes' by the Ghanaian poet Kofi Awooner imagined a Pan-African world with rivers as staging posts for anti-colonial victories across the continent, in a 1965 volume published by the same Afro-Asian Writers' Bureau who the following year met with Mao in China at the time of his famous Yangtze swim. Here the poem's protagonists cross over the Nile River and make for the Niger, where their 'enemy had fled before us'. Reaching the shores of the Congo in the one-time Belgian colony, they find the enemy once more assembled. But also there are the heroes of Pan-African resistance: the Congolese Patrice Lumumba and Ghanaian Kwame Nkrumah.

Then Lumumba pointed his spear at them
The spear Nkrumah gave him
And they fled like geese before a storm.[32]

In the next chapter we look at what happened on the Niger River when the European colonists had 'fled like geese'.

18

Who Are the Masters Now?

> 'The Keita of Mande divided the fishing rights in the river into the three areas related to the three section of *faro tyn* . . . The Somono of Kaba were the *dyi tigi*, "masters of the water" . . . from Kaba to Koulikoro. Those of Segou had the same rights from Koulikoro to Mopti. The Bozo were given the area from Mopti to Lake Debo.'
>
> Germaine Dieterlen, 'The Mande Creation Myth' (1957)[1]

This was the French anthropologist Germaine Dieterlen, observing the social organisation, creation stories and rituals governing life on the river that she found in 1950s French West Africa. Her team that year studied the Inner Niger Delta which had – and still has – its own 'Masters of the River', including the Bozo and in north-west Nigeria the Sorko people. The researchers focused on the area around Kangaba (or Kaba), about 60 miles upstream from the city of Bamako, which was to become Mali's capital by the end of the decade. Traditional rights and rules relating to different stretches of rivers, lakes and ponds featured prominently in the oral traditions they recorded, connected – like the Masters of the Waters – to the *Faro* or 'spirit of the River Niger' and to sacred places along the river (*Faro tyn*).[2]

In the early 2000s the World Bank in Washington DC commissioned a 'vision for sustainable management' of the Niger River basin. This report provided a detailed overview of the river system and its 'stakeholders' beyond the wildest dreams of nineteenth-century explorers. Here the '"Maître des Eaux" (Master of the Waters) who determined what was to be done on the river, and where and how it was to be done' were noted under 'Historical Use', then seen no more.[3] But one of the most important functions served by these masters, in dividing up and sharing fishing rights, has not lost its significance.

This chapter explores the challenge of sharing the bounty of the Niger River in the decades since independence. The mid-twentieth century was a time of great change for the waters of the Niger. In the world of post-independence nation states, water bodies and neighbourly relations on the Niger River have been rearranged, like moving staircases in *Harry Potter*, creating unanticipated outcomes as well as new winners and losers. The transformations across the Niger in the colonial and post-colonial years created new masters while not fully killing off the old ones. New nation states brought new boundaries on the river. At the same time, rivers were becoming harnessed to large-scale industrial technologies that brought together larger groups of people, with potential to share the benefits such as year-round irrigation, double harvests and hydro-electricity, but also the power to create larger-scale hazards and conflicts of interest. In this region too these post-war years brought a new vision of rivers as part of their wider river basins or watersheds. This recognised that interventions in one part of a watershed – upstream headwaters, tributaries or groundwater – can create knock-on effects in other parts.

Both rivers and their watersheds are a unifying as well as divisive force, a feature of all rivers in this book throughout their histories. The rivers bring together 'involuntary neighbours' and rivals. And like many 'common pool resources', they highlight the problem of human (and non-human) co-existence and how to share benefits and risks. Sometimes this public sharing of natural resources has been understood as a 'tragedy of the commons'. In this scenario, as conceived by the American ecologist Garret Hardin in the 1960s, there is a piece of common land where many individuals come to graze their cattle. Each person wants their cattle to graze to the full. No one notices or feels personally responsible as the common becomes patchy and threadbare until it is too late: the common is over-grazed and useless to everyone. The same principle applies, the argument goes, with over-use of water, over-fishing, pollution or chopping down forest trees: anything where there is free access but limited supply. If the common were privately owned, Hardin argued, the owner would be motivated to act as a responsible guardian of the land. The image of the 'tragedy of the commons' has remained influential for its evocative identification of a genuine problem – how to manage common resources – but also much criticised for its private-sector solution, ignoring how woefully bad private owners have often proved as stewards of natural resources.[4]

The chapter asks how co-existence between neighbours (voluntary or involuntary) in the Niger region has fared in the new era. Who are the masters now? It looks at six features of the Niger watershed that demonstrate in different forms the challenge of sharing water resources: the international river basin of the Niger; the Inner Niger Delta; an artificial lake and hydroelectric dam in the middle Niger; the oil-rich coastal delta; a proposed dam in the Guinea headwaters of the river; and the Inner Niger Delta as 'a floodplain of global importance'.[5]

First: how was the vast region of the Niger River basin recalibrated as the colonial authorities relinquished their power? When independence was won across much of Africa and Asia in the late 1950s and 1960s, the Niger's river basin became home to nine nation states: Guinea, Côte d'Ivoire, Mali, Burkina Faso, Niger, Chad, Nigeria, Benin and Cameroon. Independence for this region meant doing justice to visions of a free world but also dealing with everyday realities of water management and resource-sharing. There were changes straight away. Treaties signed in Niger's riverside capital of Niamey in the early 1960s abolished the nineteenth-century arrangements agreed at the Berlin West Africa Conference, and established some principles for international collaboration among the nations of the river basin (aka 'riparian states'). These spawned different governance bodies over time, including the Niger Dams Authority (1962), the Niger River Commission (1963–80), and from 1980 the Niger Basin Authority.[6] A 1964 treaty demonstrated a commitment to be good neighbours, promising to 'maintain liaison between the riparian States' and make the best use of resources across the basin. Article 12 for example laid down:

> They undertake . . . to abstain from carrying out on the portion of the River, its tributaries and sub-tributaries subject to their jurisdiction any works likely to pollute the waters, or any modification likely to affect biological characteristics of its fauna and flora, without adequate . . . prior consultation with, the [River Niger] Commission.'[7]

What room was there for Masters of Water and other traditions in this new world? The chapter explores how ideals of sharing have fared over time.

This brings us to our second water body, back in the Inner Niger Delta (or Macina). At over 16,000 square miles in size (accounts vary), the prodigious fertility of this wetland sustains around two million fishers and farmers, growing millet, sorghum and maize, floating rice on the floodplains. Hugely important for Mali's rice production, 60 per cent of its cattle-grazing takes place here during the dry season, and it is the source of 80 per cent of the country's fish yield. Almost 250 fish species have been recorded, including *mannogo*, its famous catfish. Some are endemic, found only here in the inner delta and upper Niger River. Others are Nilo-Sudanian species and those found along many rivers of West Africa. Also here are aquatic manatees in the water channels, crocodiles basking on muddy shores, and hippopotami powering through corridors of floating grass in the *bourgou* fields. There are 350 species of birds, from the over-wintering Caspian tern to the black crowned crane, with its radiant fan of golden feathers. The Inner Niger Delta brings together fishers, farmers and pastoralist herders all dependent on its waters, often with conflicting needs.[8]

This Inner Delta is also the domain of the Masters of the Water, whose authority can be traced back at least to the 1200s. In chapter 16 we saw that according to tradition, following a great victory Sundiata Keita, founder of the Mali Empire, summoned his supporters and the vanquished to the plain of Kurukan Fuga where he delivered what has become famous as the Manden Charter. This laid down rules for his kingdom and is remembered today in annual ceremonies in nearby Kangaba. The Charter overall reads like an effective, if rigid, ideal model for social harmony and good neighbourly relations. Among many versions of this story relayed by the *griots*, the Guinean historian Djibril Tamsir Niane was the first to bring it to international attention from the 1960s. The Charter, said Niane in a 1997 account, embodied 'social and political norms that still in part govern the Mande peoples'. The Charter identified seven groups, among them the hereditary 'marabout clans . . . the five guardians of the faith' whose family names were given, the '"quiver-bearing" freedmen', the clans of '*griots*, shoemakers, smiths and weavers', and the last of the seven: 'The Somono and Bozo boatmen were proclaimed "masters of the water".' In this way, says Niane, 'Sundiata "divided up the world", with each knowing his rights and duties.'[9]

This Manden Charter is one of several features of 'intangible heritage' submitted to UNESCO by the government of Mali in recent decades, a process some see as a 'heritagization of Mali's past'.[10] There is no mention of 'masters of the waters' in the UNESCO submission, which highlights instead 'blacksmiths and most of all, griots'.[11] The epic of Sundiata is the source of the singer Rokia Traore's recent 'Dream mandé – Djata' or 'Damou (Dream)' performance piece. Griots, singers and musicians – masters of the twenty-one-stringed kora, or harp – are today among Mali's most successful exports.[12] Other aspects of the Niger's past remembered as heritage include *Faro*, or spirit of the Niger River, embodied in a fountain at the women's museum (Muso Kunda) in Mali's capital of Bamako.[13]

The water spirits of the Niger region are not simply in the past. They are alive, for example, at the sacred pond in the town of San, where the Sanké Mon – the fishing festival that takes place each year – is overseen by a hereditary Priest of the Water Spirits. Like the sacred pond, which is silting up, these traditions are increasingly fragile. The traditional Masters of the Water (called *Djitigui* in Mali's Bambara language) also live on. Along stretches of the Niger today they still coordinate the activities of local fishers across the seasons, alongside municipal and central government.[14] But they too are under threat from change.

A 2010 study looked at traditional roles in fishing at villages north of the confluence of the Niger and Bani tributaries at the busy riverside market town of Mopti. At the village of Daka-Womina are the migratory Bozo fishers, who 'follow the fish' through the shallows of the floodplain. They see themselves as the original people of the Inner Niger Delta and the '"the only real fishermen"'. The neighbouring village of Wandiaka (or Wandiakia) is home to the Somono and others who trace their lineage back to the Mali Empire of the 1200s and 1300s. They are not in direct competition with the neighbouring villagers as they do not 'follow the fish', and instead use nets in the main river channels for their catch. Their Master of the Water operates a motorised ferry service. Both villages see pressures from all sides, according to the authors: caught 'between water spirits and market forces'. The climate is changing, thought to be getting drier. Cash payments are squeezing out traditional fishing practices. Outsiders are now fishing in their waters without observing local customs. 'Today,' a fisherman of Wandiaka lamented, 'everybody can become Somono.'[15]

For the third water body we need to journey downstream to the grasslands of Nigeria. Here in the Borgu region of the middle Niger is the great water planet of Lake Kainji, around 500 square miles in size. The lake and dam were a nation-building project that also embodied rival versions of nationhood. The dam was built to provide hydro-electricity for the new Nigeria and store water for crop irrigation all year round. It drowned the ancient rapids at Bussa, several riverside towns and most of Foge Island. It took eighteen months to cut down over 5 million trees on the island. When the Niger swelled with monsoon rains in August 1968 the first water was released into the lake. With it came the fish, heading for cover among drowned tree stumps and bushes in the shallow waters of the island. Backed up behind the 25,000 tons of steel and 250,000 tons of cement that is Kainji (Bussa)

Dam, the lake became a glorious sub-tropical fish tank, part natural/part machine, home to over a hundred fish species, from the Nilo-Sudanian electric aba aba (*Gymnarchus niloticus*) to the wormjawed mormyrid. By the 1970s, the lake's annual fishing yield was estimated at over 10,000 tonnes.[16]

But despite these prodigious fish stocks, over-fishing on the lake has depleted the catch over time. Competing for fish stocks across the lake are those long settled in the region, traditional migrant fishers, but also newcomers, small-scale fishers and professionals with huge nets. Lake Kainji is the essence of a 'common pool' with competing interests. 'Past failures mean that resources have remained open access', a 2003 study of Lake Kainji noted: 'This may cause the fisherfolk to believe that the exploitation of fish is a right to be enjoyed by all.'[17] Limitations on fishing would make for more 'sustainable resource management'. Efforts to banish destructive fishing gear, including *seine* nets – like large, weighted badminton nets – by traditional authorities ranging from the Emirate Councils to the *Sarkin Ruwa* (village heads for fishing), have been only partially successful. Some fishers consider traditional authorities to be irrelevant.[18] As stocks deplete, mesh sizes reduce, trapping juvenile fish that will never mature and reproduce.

From early on, in fact, great political turbulence lay under the smooth surface of Lake Kainji. Investigations into the dam began under British rule in the early 1950s and unlike the Aswan dam project on the Nile, this continued through Nigerian independence in 1960, funded by the US-led International Bank for Reconstruction and Development: along with the World Bank, responsible for countless development infrastructure projects.[19] By the 1960s, Lake Kainji and Kainji dam became a symbol for the new state of Nigeria. Its first prime minister, Sir Abubakar Tafawa Balewa, was involved from an early stage, travelling twice to the United States to learn from the TVA at New Orleans, St Louis and their headquarters at Knoxville. Tennessee of the 1930s and Nigeria were a lot alike, Balewa suggested in 1961, referring to 'underdeveloped' rivers, depleted forests and soils, and malaria.[20] As he laid the foundation stone for Kainji dam in 1964, Balewa spoke of the benefits 'to all the people of our federation and it is one of the projects I am sure is going to make a greater unity in this country'.[21]

Despite this rhetoric, the dam always represented clashing visions of nationhood. From the start some were more concerned about those whose land was drowned beneath the lake. Some 50,000 people were moved from their homes and land; among them the 'island dwellers' (Gungawa of Foge Island), the Sarkawa or Sorko ('Masters of the River' in the Songhay dialect), and the Borgu people, resettled in new villages and towns by the lake.[22] A Borgu scholar Salihu Mohammed Niworu recently claimed that the promised electricity, decent housing and fertile land did not materialise for his people displaced by the dam. The Borgu are 'a nation', he said, 'whose heritage, monuments and productive assets were forfeited for the realization of [this] national project'.[23]

But at the level of Nigeria's national, federal government, the lake has proved a rhetorical device and powerful symbol of unity that belies sharp political differences and rivalries. Sir Abubakar Tafawa Balewa was dead by the time the dam and lake were complete. Two coups in quick succession in 1966 saw Balewa and other leaders assassinated, and a new military regime installed in Nigeria's capital of Abuja. The show went on, though. When the Kainji dam was opened in 1969, General Yakubu 'Jack' Gowon – Head of the Federal Nigerian State – echoed the words of his predecessor for this project that promised the nation many thousands of kilowatts of electricity:[24]

> . . . the successful completion of this project on schedule presents not only the laying of a foundation stone for the modernization of our nation, it is also symbolic of a breakthrough in our consciousness of what can be done for the development of our country.[25]

When Gowon delivered this foundational moment for the nation, the people of the eastern Niger Delta had already seceded from federal Nigeria, declaring the independent state of Biafra in 1967.

For two years Nigeria had been mired in a deadly civil war.[26] The unifying promise of hydro-electricity on the middle Niger was undermined by another energy project downstream.

This brings us to the fourth water body: the oil-rich coastal Niger Delta. If you look at a map of the world, you can see that the west coast of Africa fits like a puzzle piece into the east coast of South America. Somewhere between 115 million and 100 million years ago when dinosaurs still roamed the earth, the two continents were slowly torn apart as the continent of Gondwana gradually splintered. As the continent fragments drifted away from each other, an Atlantic river started to flow between the two coasts, much later swelling into an ocean. Nigeria's coastal delta – a web of estuary streams spun out of the lower Niger – is part of the so-called Benue Trough that formed around this time. Here over millions of years, during the time of the Eocene (around 56 to 34 million years ago), marine organisms and ancient plants lived and died, and settled into the sediment of the delta bed. They remained there like forgotten, humble plankton for about 50 million years as they slowly transformed into a viscous, jet black, carbon-rich subterranean ooze. Then one day in the twentieth century they were rebranded as the 'Tertiary Niger Delta (Akata-Agbada) Petroleum System'[27] and became part of a new cycle of life and death. The discovery and exploitation of crude oil here has led to over half a century of conflict.

The roots of the Biafra war were complex, but oil was a key issue. In January 1956 the Dutch/British company Shell-BP discovered commercial quantities of oil 12,000 feet below the delta creek community of Oloibiri, Bayelsa, and the colonial UK government claimed ownership of mineral resources and granted its rights to Shell-BP. Crude oil began to be pumped and piped to a refinery built at Port Harcourt. Following Nigeria's transformation from colony to independence in 1960, Shell-BP retained oil rights. By the start of the Biafran war in 1967, 580,000 barrels a day were being pumped from the delta, 84 per cent of this by Shell-BP. This met 10 per cent of Britain's oil needs at the time, a figure that increased when the Suez Canal oil highway closed later that year with the Six Day (Arab-Israeli) War. Central to the Biafra secession and ensuing war was the unjust distribution of benefits from this great source of wealth. While the crude oil derived in the eastern delta (in Biafra), its revenues were flowing elsewhere. The rejection of the so-called 'derivation principle' (the idea that the region from which a resource derives should receive a proportionate benefit) has been a divisive force ever since. By the time Biafra was forced to surrender in January 1970, tens of thousands of people had died in the delta from bombing and starvation. Arms on the federal government side included 'marauding MIG-17s and Ilyushin-28 bombers, supplied . . . by the Russians and flown by Egyptian pilots,' according to *Time Magazine* in 1970, though the UK Labour Government was also under sustained scrutiny for its continued provision of arms to Gowon's regime during the war.[28]

As well as an unequal distribution of the benefits of delta oil, the hazards have also been unevenly distributed. The coastal delta is a perfect example of why the idea of the tragedy of the commons, with its solution of private ownership, is not very helpful. Both private companies and government officials have failed to contain the risks of drilling in this coveted subterranean pool and its network of pipelines. The oil-producing areas of the Niger Delta have been ecologically devastated. The oilfields have destroyed both farmland and the life of the rivers, polluting water supplies and the air that people breathe, causing sickness and high infant-mortality rates. Successive Nigerian governments and private corporations have sustained a battle of wills with delta communities and with the ecosystem of the delta itself. Campaigns against the conditions included the 1990s activism of the Federation of Ogoni Women's Association to get Shell to 'leave oil in the soil'. This decade also saw the execution of activist Ken Saro-Wiwa and eight others from the Movement for the Survival of Ogoni People in 1995. Shell left Ogoniland in 1993. They ceased operations in the western delta in 2006 because of attacks on installations and now focus on offshore drilling in the region, though other oil companies operating in the delta were producing two million barrels daily as of 2022.[29] Sabotage by activists in the region was recently estimated to lose one-third of the pumped supplies, which also ends up in the delta bed. This activism is also framed by some in secessionist terms. As a Niger Delta Avengers representative declared in 2016: 'It's better that the country divides so that we all go where we belong.'[30]

Following multiple lawsuits against Shell, including a successful case brought by the Bodo Creek community in Ogoniland, the company began a clean-up operation in 2017.[31] But the creeks and mangroves of Ogoniland have been slow to show signs of new life. On Bodo Creek (*Numuu tekuru*) in the eastern delta, a sign warns people: 'Polluted water – Do Not Drink, or Swim Here.'[32] The streams lie empty of water, with blackened stumps for trees, cooking pots glazed in crude oil sticking out of the stream beds alongside rotting fishing boats abandoned long ago. 'All we see is oil in the forest,' said fisher and farmer Pelepre Newton in 2019. 'No more periwinkles to pick. No more crabs at the river. What is happening to our creeks?'[33]

For the fifth water body we need to retrace our steps back to the headwaters of the Niger River. The planned Fomi Dam in Guinea's Futa Jalon mountains, on the Niandan River upstream of its confluence with the Niger, constitutes a potential threat to the wetlands of the Inner Niger Delta itself. Plans for the dam have crossed many desks over the years, in the spirit of international collaboration first announced in the 1960s. Guinea has collaborated with Mali and other riparian states, the transboundary Niger Basin Authority and the World Bank, to assess the dam's economic and environmental impacts. The proposed dam promises hydroelectric power for several countries within the Niger basin and beyond, from Senegal to Sierra Leone. Its second function is to provide year-round irrigation for Mali's agriculture. Back in the 1930s when the Sahel and Upper Niger region were part of French Sudan, the French colonial authorities created the Office du Niger. This was both an irrigated zone and administrative unit, established in 1932 as a vast social and technical experiment to bring the fertile delta land under the plough to grow cotton and rice, irrigated by a series of dams.[34] Located over 1,300 square kilometres along the region upstream of Mopti, this also aimed to transform the inhabitants into settled farmers on a European model. The rice would feed those working in the peanut-oil industry in Senegal; the cotton would be shipped to France for the textile industry. Although the plans were not fully realised the Office du Niger remains today as the 'rice bowl' of West Africa, an area of paddy rice, potatoes, corn and fish farms which produces 52 per cent of Mali's rice output. The Fomi Dam has the potential to expand Mali's irrigated Office du Niger several times over, with all-year-round water supply replacing the seasonal flows from the highlands.[35] The environmental impacts of these proposals are still being thrashed out.

In 2017 the government of Guinea suddenly announced an imminent start on the Fomi Dam with a Chinese firm, taking many of its partners by surprise, including the government of Mali and the Niger Basin Authority. This Chinese plan has gone quiet in recent years. One view is that the international environmental scrutiny has put off Chinese interests, though there are rumours of other players, including Russia and Egypt. The benefits and hazards of the Fomi scheme are sharply divided. An African Union publication in 2023 called the dam project 'the best alternative for sustainable development in the Upper Niger, a guarantee of safeguarding the natural resources of the river basin'. By contrast, a report the same year from the Alliance for Global Water Adaptation spells out grim scenarios for a dried-out inland delta, including a 'complete collapse of the ecosystem' and the livelihoods of the two million people dependent upon it.[36]

This brings us to the sixth and final feature of the Niger waters: the status of the Inner Niger Delta as 'a floodplain of global importance'.[37] In this interconnected world of nature, the Niger is not only the concern of its nine 'riparian states'. Like the Danube biosphere, embedded in a multilayered tissue of environmental observers from the EU to ornithological NGOs, the Inner Niger Delta is closely watched. As an internationally important hotspot for biodiversity, the delta embodies a tension that has split the globe since the first international environmental conference. In Stockholm in 1972 the representatives of less economically developed countries stood up – one by one, from China to Egypt – to insist that their right to develop their own nation was equal to that of the industrialised world.

The inner delta is one of the largest wetlands (out of a total of around 2,500) on the global list kept by the Ramsar Convention on Wetlands.[38] A host of international environmental bodies and reports are currently focused on the Inner Niger Delta and its threatened status, among them Wetlands International, the Water, Peace and Security (WPS) Partnership, and the World Wildlife Fund (WWF). Because major wetlands are innately transboundary, they present a challenge to national sovereignty. Some of them literally cross national borders. But they are also crucial to international flyways: the rivers in the sky that carry migrating species of birds across the globe.

These flyways have evolved over many millennia. Some bar-headed geese (*Anser indicus*) spend their winters in the Ganges wetlands at Haridwar, then in the spring they set off across the Himalayas to breed at China's Bande Lake, at the headwaters of the Yangtze River. One theory about this amazing bird, able to ascend the thin air of peaks rising over 26,000 feet, is that both the goose and the Himalayan mountain range evolved together over millions of years. As the mountains grew higher, the lung capacity of the geese adapted. Do they belong to China or to India? An electronic tracker placed on a Montagu's harrier in 2016 traced all the stages in its journey between chalk downland in the Severn river basin and the Inner Niger Delta.[39] One study has found that the extent of the Inner Niger Delta's seasonal floodwaters, where wetland birds spend their winters, is directly linked to the size of breeding populations of sand martins and sedge-warblers in the UK, of purple herons in the Netherlands and of the black-crowned night-heron in France. In 2023 the United Kingdom applied for the East Atlantic Flyway, which links England's remaining east coast wetlands northwards to the Arctic and southwards to South Africa, to be added to UNESCO's list of Natural World Heritage Sites.[40] The fragile state of the Thames and other industrialised estuary ecosystems shows how depleted wetlands can become.

There is no one set of masters of the Niger's waters. They are all in flux. At a national level, the Sahel region is being rearranged through a series of recent coups in Chad, Guinea, Mali and Niger. French interests and responsibilities have been driven out in the name of national sovereignty, though often with the support of other foreign states. Russian flags were waving on the streets of Mali's capital city Bamako on the banks of the Niger following the 2020 military coup.[41] The governments of the riparian states, the oil companies, dam-builders, the Niger basin organisations, Office du Niger, World Bank and foreign states are all part of this mix; so too are the 130 million people of its river basin, activists of the coastal delta, Masters of the Water, international law courts and environmental NGOs.[42] All of these will continue to play a part in the unequal struggles to shape the future of this great water commons of the Niger River.

River 7: Yangtze

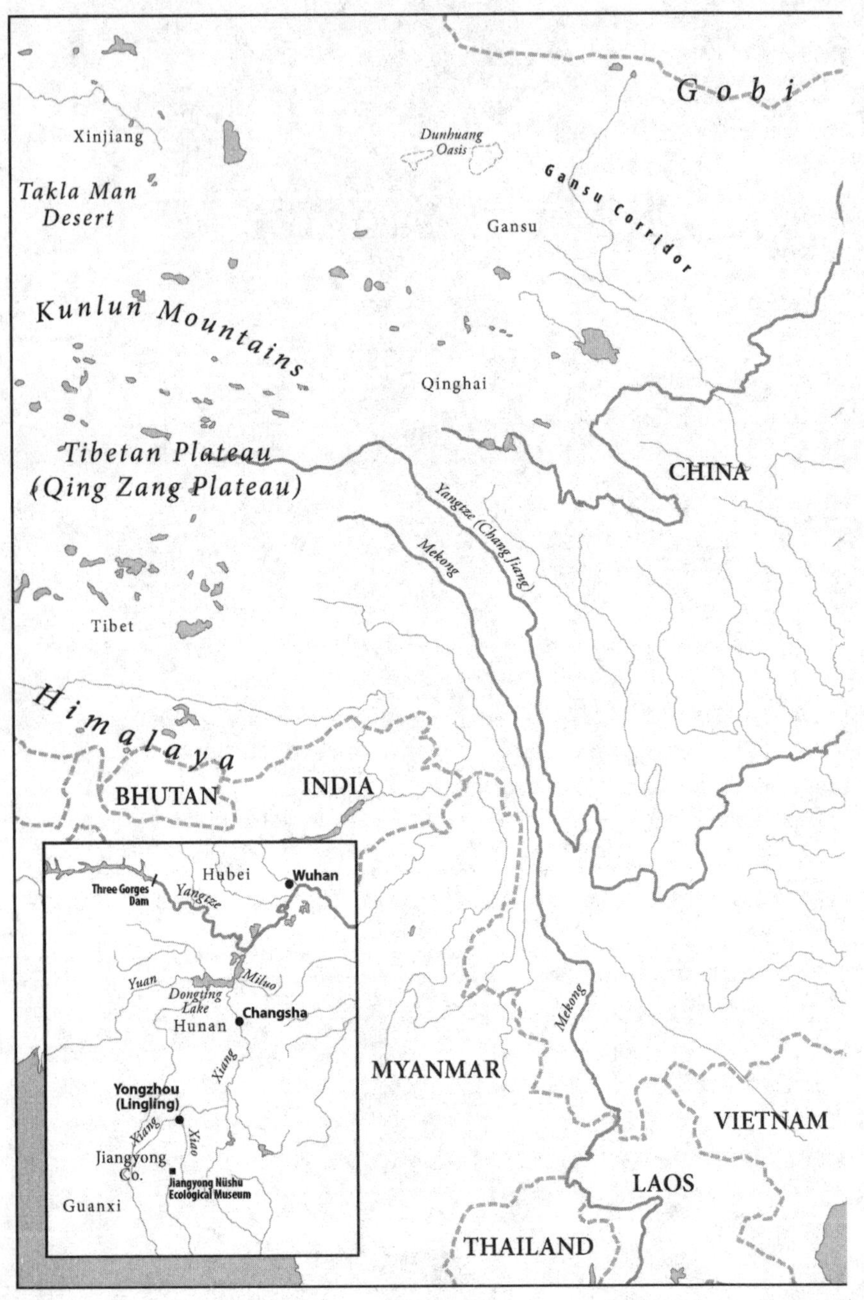
Gobi
Xinjiang
Dunhuang Oasis
Takla Man Desert
Gansu Corridor
Gansu
Kunlun Mountains
Qinghai
Tibetan Plateau (Qing Zang Plateau)
CHINA
Yangtze (Chang Jiang)
Mekong
Tibet
Himalaya
BHUTAN
INDIA
Hubei
Wuhan
Three Gorges Dam
Yangtze
Yuan
Miluo
Dongting Lake
Changsha
Hunan
Xiang
Yongzhou (Lingling)
Xiang
Xiao
Jiangyong Co.
Jiangyong Nüshu Ecological Museum
Guanxi
MYANMAR
Mekong
VIETNAM
LAOS
THAILAND

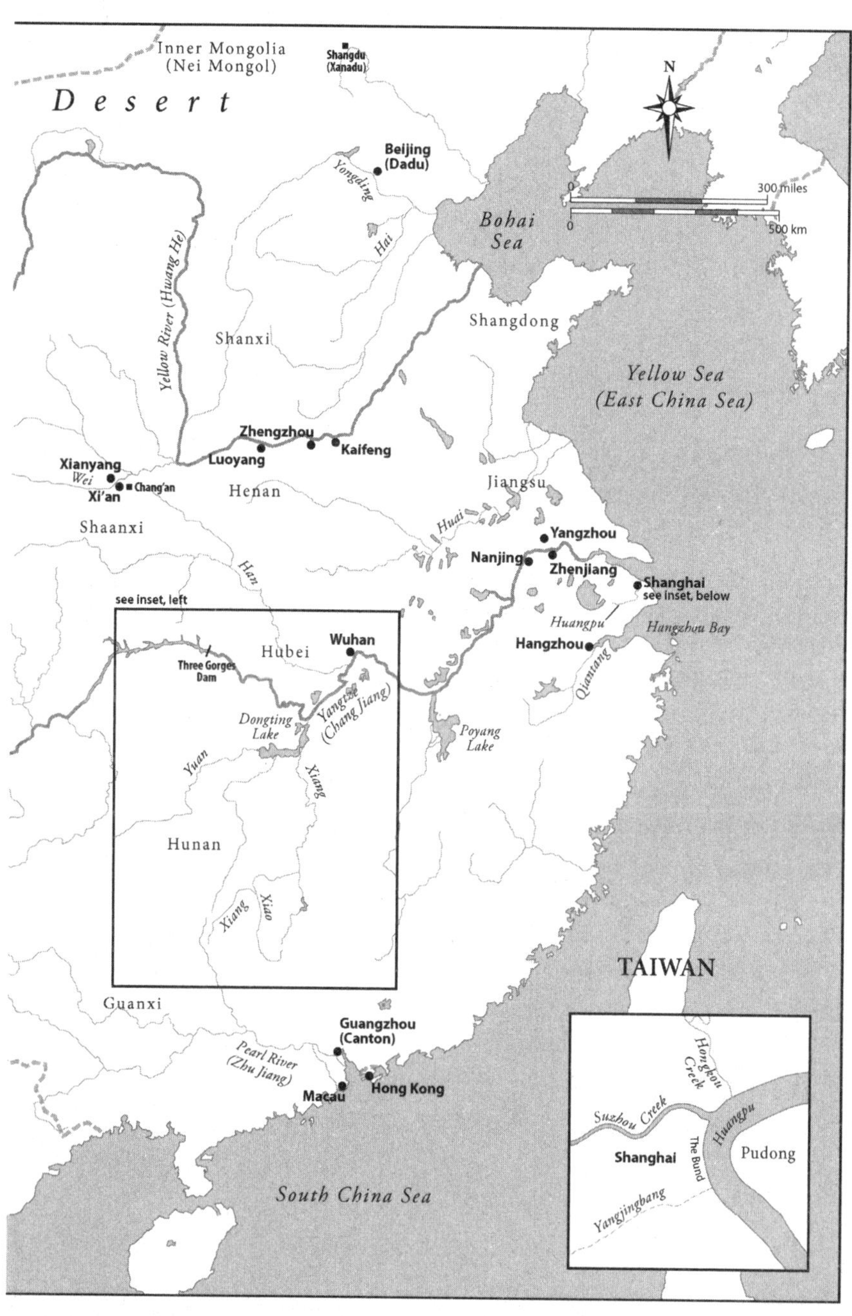

Inner Mongolia
(Nei Mongol)
Shangdu
(Xanadu)
Desert
N
Beijing
(Dadu)
Yongding
0
300 miles
0
500 km
Bohai
Sea
Hai
Yellow River (Hwang He)
Shanxi
Shangdong
Yellow Sea
(East China Sea)
Zhengzhou
Luoyang
Kaifeng
Xianyang
Wei
Chang'an
Xi'an
Henan
Jiangsu
Shaanxi
Huai
Yangzhou
Nanjing
Zhenjiang
Han
Shanghai
see inset, below
see inset, left
Huangpu
Hangzhou Bay
Wuhan
Hubei
Hangzhou
Three Gorges
Dam
Qiantang
Dongting
Lake
Yangtze
(Chang Jiang)
Poyang
Lake
Yuan
Xiang
Hunan
Xiang
Xiao
TAIWAN
Guanxi
Guangzhou
(Canton)
Pearl River
(Zhu Jiang)
Hong Kong
Macau
South China Sea
Hongkou
Creek
Suzhou Creek
Huangpu
Shanghai
The Bund
Pudong
Yangjingbang

19
Grand Canal

> 'Here are collected large quantities of corn and rice; and there is a passage by water to the city of Kambalu [Dadu/Beijing] and the court of the khan; grain from this place forms a considerable part of the provision required by his court. The monarch made this communication by digging long and deep canals from one river to another, and from lake to lake, so that a large ship may pass through.'
>
> *The Travels of Marco Polo* (1298)[1]

The Yangtze River, or Chang Jiang, meaning 'long river', flows for 3,900 miles: the third-longest of the world's rivers. It rises on the Tibetan Plateau at the eastern end of the Himalayan mountains where bar-tailed geese gather on the wetlands around Bande Lake. This plateau – the 'Roof of the World' – is also the source of the Yellow and Mekong rivers. From here, the Yangtze and Yellow rivers both set off on an easterly course but then take very different paths to the sea. Far to the north of the Yangtze, the Yellow River (Huang He) follows a wandering course. It crosses the plateau just south of the China/Mongolia border, collecting great volumes of sediment, then zigzags to the south and east across the North China Plain into the East China (or Yellow) Sea (named, like the river, after its load of loess, or yellow glacial silt). The Yangtze today isn't where it started out. For a long time, it flowed southwards and into the South China Sea. But the same tectonic forces that created the Himalayas from around 50 million years ago – the crash of the Indian subcontinent into Eurasia – redirected the Yangtze's southward curving channel so that it turned north-east through the Lower Yangtze Plain. Today the river empties into the East China Sea around 14 miles north of today's Shanghai.[2]

These two great rivers co-existed separately for a very long time. The earliest Chinese settlements evolved on the Yellow River where it flowed through the North China Plain. It was here that the imperial courts of the first dynasties were situated, in cities such as Kaifeng, Luoyang, Chang'an (Xi'an) and, later, Beijing. Enduring threats of invasion from the north ensured that this Yellow River region remained the heartland for imperial rule. But an expanding imperial China could not have been built on a single river system. Gradually its roots began to reach down deeper and deeper across the lands to its south. The rainy, warm and fertile Yangtze River Valley to the south was a prize sufficiently motivating to launch the digging of millions of tons of earth and laying of stone, and hundreds of thousands of forced labourers marshalled over many centuries. In warm periods, this zone supported citrus trees and two rice crops a year.[3] With both these great rivers flowing west to east, the Grand Canal made good the lack of north-south communications.

The Grand Canal was an unparalleled building project that evolved from around the fifth century BCE to the 1400s CE. That is, from a century or so before the time of the famous First Emperor Qin up to the Ming Dynasty. It was until recently the longest canal in the world, reaching well over 1,000 miles, with many sections that are still in use or have had new segments bolted on since the 1960s. The Grand Canal wasn't a single canal but like an expensive Meccano set that took a very long time to build. Cutting channels between rivers and lakes, and across plains and mountains, new links were added over time to existing canals to meet changing strategic priorities. Capitals moved, new trading routes opened and old routes silted up, their commercial hubs left to fend for themselves. This chapter is the story of the Grand Canal as the navigable arms of the Yangtze River for over 2,000 years.

What powered everything, above all, was rice. Millet was a staple grain in the north. But from the mid-700s rice produced in the Yangtze Valley and regions south of the river increasingly became a staple for the people and to feed the imperial court. Through this 'tribute grain' transport, or *Caoyun* system, imperial rulers were able to feed the court and army, with surplus rice shipped to the capital as a tax or tribute from agricultural regions. Canal-side granaries were added over time to provide reserves in times of famine, war and popular rebellions.[4]

Rice cultivation had been carried out in the Yangtze Valley at least since 5000 BCE. This was a highly labour-intensive process undertaken, as far as history records, by corvée labourers (doing compulsory and unpaid work). Water buffaloes may have been used from the time of the Shang Dynasty (c. 1500–c. 1050 BCE), pulling ploughs to prepare the land for sowing. Methods of rice production varied over time and according to region. Especially in sub-tropical regions such as south of the Yangtze River, the monsoon rains fed the rice crops. Irrigation might be possible, using supplies from rivers and the Grand Canal where water levels allowed, though the grain transport was the priority. By the time of the Song Dynasty in the twelfth century CE, scrolls show a technologically advanced and well-honed process for rice irrigation and production. In one image, men are sowing a rice field with bare feet and their leggings hitched up. In another, the fields are flooded and drained using mechanical pumps. In a neighbouring field, seedlings are being transplanted to paddy fields to allow another round of seeds to be sown.[5]

Grain remained the priority cargo of the canals for over 2,000 years. Over time silk, salt, iron, also subject to a royal monopoly, and other goods came to be loaded onto the canal boats. Salt and iron became integrated into the *Caoyun* system itself, and the Grand Canal boosted established trading centres, such as Yangzhou – city of salt – where the canal meets the Yangtze, and south of the river the city of Suzhou, a centre of silk manufacture and trade.[6]

The earliest canals of the system probably served military functions, begun in the 480s BCE during the time of the Eastern Zhou Dynasty (c. 771–256 BCE), based at Luoyang on the Yellow River.

The Hangou Canal may have been the first to connect the Yangtze to the Huai River to its north as far back as the 480s BCE. This was around the same time in which, far to the west, the Persian King Darius I (r. 522–486 BCE) was consolidating power on the Nile with his canal linking that river to the Red Sea.[7] But where the Red Sea Canal was intermittent and died out with changes in ruling elites, the Grand Canal was perpetuated over thousands of years despite all the political crises.

The origins of the grain tribute on what became the Grand Canal are attributed to the short-lived but unforgotten Qin Dynasty (221–206 BCE). Qin Shi Huangdi, the boy king who named himself First Emperor, had an unsurpassed sense of his own destiny. It was his stronghold, in the state of Qin (or Chin), that gave its name not just to a new dynasty but in time to the whole territory of China. It was Emperor Qin who commissioned an 8,000-strong army of terracotta soldiers to accompany him in death, with chariots drawn by life-sized horses. He conquered neighbouring states, tore down their walls and built his own instead along the northern frontier, initiating the Great Wall of China. Defeated leading families were forced to come and live in his capital. Efforts to exert imperial control found expression in everything from standardising the written script, weights and measures to canal-building.[8] In this early period there is unlikely to have been extensive transport of grain from the Yangtze Valley itself. Canal-side granaries brought tribute grain to Qin's capital at Xianyang on the banks of the Wei River, a tributary of the Yellow River. To aid conquest in the far south, Qin commissioned the Lingqu Canal for his military campaign against the Baiyue people in the Lingnan region in 214 BCE. This new water route, 36 kilometres long, connected the Xiang River, a right-bank tributary of the Yangtze, to the Li River which flows south through the Pearl River basin. This canal also doubled as a grain-transport and water-control system. All being well, it was now possible in principle to convey goods via water from the Yellow River all the way down to China's south coast, though only the most costly and desirable items warranted this royal road: from feathers to rhinoceros horns.[9]

It was in the time of the Sui Dynasty (581–618 CE) that the Yangtze was truly integrated into the Grand Canal complex. This engineering project too went hand in hand with conquest. The Sui, based at Luoyang on the Yellow River, fought their way south to the Yangtze River, wrecking the city of Nanjing on the lower Yangtze on their way. In time-honoured fashion, they uprooted the conquered nobles and transplanted them to the Sui's northern capital, where they could be watched. This also aimed to end the role of Nanjing as the power-base-in-exile for the descendants of the Qin Dynasty who had decamped here when they lost power in the north in the 300s CE. By this time, however, the Yangtze Valley itself had begun its slow rise to prominence as a rice producer, capable of feeding populations far beyond its watershed. In order to secure the riches of the Yangtze Valley, the first Sui emperor Wen Di (r. 581–604 CE) ordered canals to be rebuilt between Luoyang in the north-east and the city of Yangzhou on the banks of the Yangtze.[10]

The second Sui emperor, Yang Di (r. 604–17/18), was also a committed canal builder and understood the importance of publicising his mastery of this vast network and the marvellous life along its banks. Scrolls from his reign show him inspecting his works in a great flotilla that stretched for 65 miles along the canal.[11] One image reproduced later (gouache on silk) shows an array of imperial vessels with sails unfurled; some are dragon boats, with the ornate heads of dragons cutting through the water. On the canal banks are men on horseback with colourful standards on tall poles, and others in groups pulling the vessels by rope. Everywhere there is a general air of anxiety to please. An eighteenth-century collection of the images notes that Emperor Yang Di:

> . . . had such a large quantity of magnificent boats built for his use that they occupied twenty leagues in length. When they proceeded, both sides of the river had to be lined by horsemen, to whom the neighbouring towns were obliged to provide the best they could find.[12]

With the Sui completion of the Jiangnan Canal (meaning 'south of the river'), canal routes now reached south from the Yangtze River to the city of Hangzhou on the Qiantang River, which flows into Hangzhou Bay. The new Yongji Canal provisioned Sui forces in the north. At this point in the seventh century, the Grand Canal may be seen as complete, or at least a completed gestalt. In all, it connected five major river basins.[13]

The Grand Canal was a complex but highly effective system when in good repair and at its height. The grain ships (*cao fang*), during the time of the Ming, for example (1368–1644), were shallow-bottomed sailing barges to match the regulation maximum depths of the canals. They were fitted with sails, though on the Grand Canal these were rarely used due to the abundance of bridges and locks. Here instead the vessels were propelled by 'poling' – a man was positioned on a ledge fixed to each side of the vessel with a pole to punt the vessel along the canal bed; on the towpaths there were 'trackers' with ropes to haul the barges. The barges were equipped with sleeping quarters, granaries, and holds to store goods for private trade by the boatmen. A great variety of timber was used for different parts of the vessel – the hull, the masts for sails, the 'poling' ledge – from the wood of the local Nanmu tree, to the chestnut, cedar, elm, the Chinese fir and Japanese emperor oak.[14]

The technical challenges were vast and intricate, involving emperors, astronomers, landowners, peasants with local knowledge, hydraulic engineers, and thousands of forced labourers. Ingenious solutions were found for forging the necessary routes between the economic and political centres, establishing interconnections across rivers and lakes, ensuring water depths, and managing the varied terrain. The world's first pound lock – maintaining a uniform water level across steep gradients – is thought to date from the Song Dynasty (960–1279 CE) by a transport commissioner in the Grand Canal city of Huai-yin, north of the Yangtze, where grain-tax vessels coming to grief on the slipways were being targeted for theft. Ancient patches made from willow, bamboo and stone fixed breaches in embankments torn apart during storms and floods across the centuries.[15]

Over time the Grand Canal became a semi-naturalised part of eastern China's land and waterscapes, both the working sections and the abandoned, silted-up ghost-ways. Nature was used to support the engineering works, as rulers and officials saw to it that trees were planted to stabilise the banks: the elm and locust tree, the Chinese willow in the north and the weeping willow in the warm south.[16] As one Yuan Dynasty instruction to local officials put it:

> . . . plant elm or willow or locust trees around the cities, along the Grand Canal, near the courier stations and shops, according to local climate . . . [T]he trees are to be planted at the beginning of spring, and are sure to survive.[17]

Grasses and bog plants like the Common Bulrush, Three-Leaf Arrowhead and Manchurian Wild Rice flourished on the water's edge.

Whole worlds evolved along these routes: cities, market towns and villages; shops, bridges, inland customs houses, imposing ceremonial gates and towers; lock-keepers' dwellings and towpaths; granaries and guard-posts; stelae showing water levels; shrines dedicated to water gods and goddesses, to pray for good weather and safety on the boats; sacred iron bulls and Temples of the Dragon King. Communities took root along the canal-sides. When in 1963 during the time of Chairman Mao, a single stretch of canal was rebuilt (the Han Zhuang), thirty-nine villages were lost displacing 1,400 households and 108 family tombs.[18] But this was the story of the Grand Canal throughout its history, as new rulers and dynasties selected new power bases and their hinterlands.

The arrival of Kublai Khan (r. 1260–94), founder of the Yuan Dynasty in China, reshaped the Grand Canal. Kublai was the grandson of the unbreakable Genghis Khan (r. 1206–27), whose nomadic Mongolian horsemen had conquered the entire Silk Road across Central Asia, and taken Beijing in 1215. Their legendary power was felt from the rivers of China to the Danube in the west. Under Genghis Khan, they had spread across the Caspian and Black Sea, briefly as far as Poland and Hungary in the mid-thirteenth century, with their heirs staying on in Russia as the so-called Golden Horde, dominating the north coast of the Black Sea and lower Danube River into the early fourteenth century. It has been said that a virgin carrying gold across the 3,700-mile journey from the Yellow River to the Danube Delta at this time would be quite safe with an endorsement from the Great Khans, though there were no female Marco Polos or Ibn Battutas, virgins or otherwise, to tell the tale. Having inherited Northern China as part of the Mongolian conquest of the east, Kublai Khan was the first ruler to base his capital at Beijing (Dadu) and built Xanadu (Shangdu), his legendary summer palace north of the city on the Mongolian steppe.[19] But before he could truly claim his inheritance Kublai Khan had to vanquish the Southern Song, who ruled from their capital at Hangzhou at the southern terminus of the Grand Canal.

And between Kublai Khan and the Southern Song lay the Yangtze River. Sometimes during this era called 'the Great Wall', the river helped to protect the Hangzhou rulers from northern invaders. But the river didn't prove a match for Kublai Khan's forces, who are said to have arrived at the river with 1,000 ships, siege equipment, and a multitude of horsemen, foot soldiers and sailors. They worked their way down the Han River, a major Yangtze tributary on the northern bank, and picked off the cities along the way. In 1276 they took the stronghold of Yangzhou.[20] According to a contemporary account, one snowy winter's night in January, a commander (A-chu):

> . . . saw from a distance a very much exposed sandbar along the southern bank. A-chu, embarking in a ship, pointed [it] out to the generals and had [them] hasten . . . directly to this sandbar with the horses to follow on boats. . . . A-chu bearing the brunt of the attack, engaged in reckless and bloody combat in midstream.

The Song general was taken and many died on the river. A thousand ships were said to be captured. When they reached the south bank of the Yangtze:

> A-chu with . . . several tens of men, after climbing up the bank and fighting on foot were dispersed and reunited in their ranks several times. The southern army, being blocked by the River, was not able to press upon us. Then, constructing a 'floating bridge', we crossed in formation.[21]

Once the fighting was over, Kublai Khan initiated a reorientation of the Grand Canal system, bypassing the ancient capitals on the Yellow River to achieve a more direct north-south route between his new capital in Beijing in the north and the Yangtze Valley. He commissioned numerous works to improve the inland waterways. The Huitong Canal, completed in 1289, revived and re-routed sections of the network, providing shorter journeys. Old northern sections in the Tonghui Canal were extended to the emperor's capital in Beijing by 1293.[22]

It was in the time of Kublai Khan in the late thirteenth century that the Venetian traveller Marco Polo visited China, describing cities that he passed through along the Grand Canal, such as Suzhou, 'a large and very splendid city', west of today's Shanghai. The people here, said Marco Polo:

> . . . live by trade and crafts and weave large quantities of silk fabric to make into clothes. Its merchants are rich and powerful. . . . I give you my word that in this city there are no fewer than 6,000 stone bridges under which one or two galleys could easily pass.

In the mountains near the city, he assured his readers, 'rhubarb and ginger grow very profusely'.[23]

The Yangtze, which Marco Polo seems to have seen from the city of Zhenzhou (today's Yizheng, Jiangsu Province), he declared to be 'the greatest river in the world'. In this city alone there were 15,000 ships on the river. It was in places:

> ten miles wide, . . . ; it is more than 120 days' journey in length. Countless rivers flow into it from every direction, all of them navigable and each enlarging and swelling it in turn.

Such was the extent of the Yangtze and so numerous were its cities that

> 'the number of boats that sail it, and the quantity and value of their precious wares, exceeds that of all the rivers of Christendom put together, and all the seas to boot.

Salt was the most important commodity shipped along the river, loaded in Zhenzhou onto boats, and from there conveyed 'to all the regions bordering the river as well as further upcountry, leaving the main river and sailing up its tributaries to supply all the surrounding districts'. Iron was also transported on the outward journey and on the way back downstream 'charcoal, hemp and many other articles that are supplied to the regions near the seashore'.[24]

Marco Polo's tales of his visits to China and its fabulous wealth, like the stories of Mansa Musa on the Niger, filtered through to the world map by the Majorcan Abraham Cresques in the next century. They are also thought to have fed the ambitions of Europeans to find a sea route to China. On commission from the Spanish Crown, Columbus was searching for a sea passage to China and the Spice Islands in the Pacific Ocean when he set out west across the Atlantic in 1492, though when he made landfall five weeks later, it was not of course Ming China.[25]

Despite all this fame and power, Kublai Khan could not fully conquer his rivers and waterways, which were always subject to unpredictable forces of nature. In the Grand Canal, he struggled to get the water levels right. Heavy siltation of the channels and persistent low water flows disrupted the passage of the grain tribute boats, so that the payment of officials could not be guaranteed. Even Kublai Khan's famous summer palace at Xanadu suffered from famine when the transport system failed. For this reason, during much of the Yuan Dynasty coastal routes were favoured for the grain boats, sometimes using the services of pirates, sometimes having to evade them. While repair and building work on the canal system was underway, Kublai Khan's sailors were redirected to the task of protecting the coastal trade.[26] Rulers used the canal system to extend and consolidate their power. But, like the Pharaohs of Ancient Egypt with their Nilometers and propitiation of the Nile gods, China's rulers were expected to ensure that the grain kept flowing along this great taxation system and its artificial waterways. But if the Nile River was difficult to control, the waterways of China's empire were a challenge of a different magnitude.

The other indispensable part of an emperor's job in this land was to keep people safe from flooding. From the time of the earliest 'sage-kings', such as the Great Yu, the mythical flood emperor, an ability to control floods was a sign that the emperor was aligned with Heaven. But the tumultuous Yellow River was forever undermining the rulers. This volatile, flood-prone river built up the level of the riverbed with its heavy silt load of loess as it flowed through the North China Plain. Often its water levels were higher than its riverbanks and the protective dykes (embankments or levees) which needed continual maintenance. A painting of the Yellow River by Ma Yuen from the Southern Song period, round the turn of the thirteenth century CE, shows this watercourse with great rolling waves like an ocean. Very frequently breaching its banks, it periodically changed course altogether with deadly effects, as happened for example in the Northern Song period in 1048, again in the late Yuan Dynasty of the mid-fourteenth century, and in the 1850s.[27]

The effects were not confined to the Yellow River, where natural river systems and canals were interlinked. Before its re-routing northwards to roughly its present position in the 1850s, the Yellow River and Huai River intersected for several centuries at Lake

Hongze, from where they flowed as one to the sea. This lake was itself connected (as today) by a series of lakes and rivers that flow south into the Yangtze. In particularly bad conditions, floodwaters could reach down to this southern region.[28] The more interconnected the system, the more things there were to go wrong. There was no simple correlation between floods and rebellion, but in times of economic and political difficulty it was less likely that essential maintenance works would be carried out. Floods and rebellions were more likely to follow in such circumstances. And rebellion could get in the way of routine maintenance.

Kublai Khan's Yuan Dynasty was quite short-lived (c. 1271–1368). As their influence waned both within China and beyond, they faced increasing peasant rebellions. One of these was to give birth to the Ming Dynasty. In April 1344 the rain in the Yellow River region fell continuously for twenty days until eventually the swelling river spilled over its banks and shifted course altogether. River water flooded into the channels of the Grand Canal and breached its defences. Some say the peasant rebellions of the late Yuan Dynasty were fuelled in part by the grievances of the huge labour force on the waterways, 150,000 strong, compelled to mend the breaches in the Yellow River and Grand Canal after the 1344 flood. Among the many dead from the floods, famine and sickness that followed, were the parents of Zhu Yuanzhang, orphaned at the age of sixteen.[29] Zhu Yuanzhang joined and eventually rose to the leadership of the Red Turbans rebels, fusing religious zeal with political grievance. He was to lead a successful attack on Nanjing (aka Chinling) on the south bank of the Yangtze in the 1350s. It was here in the Yangtze region that resistance to the Ming forces had been most fierce. From this base they later took Beijing as the last of the Yuan rulers disappeared into Mongolia. Zhu Yuanzhang would become Emperor Taizu (r. 1368–98) – also known as Hongwu – first ruler of the Ming Dynasty.[30]

The Ming Dynasty (1368–1644) was the first to base its capital at Nanjing as the heart of a unified China, though the capital would move back to Beijing as the most secure imperial base, after the death of Hongwu. His eventual successor was the ruthless Emperor

Yongle (r. 1402–24), who gained power by burning his younger rival to death (allegedly) alongside his family in the imperial palace. But wickedness is no barrier to effective canal management, and Yongle is remembered for successful restorations of the Huitong Canal and other canal sections, fixing the silted-up and battered links to Beijing. When new work on the Grand Canal was complete in 1422, supplies of grain reaching Beijing had almost doubled from six years earlier.[31]

The Yuan and Ming dynasties were prosperous times for those in charge of silk and cotton production in the Yangtze Delta. Traders from within China, as well as from Japan, the Netherlands and Spain, were circling China's coastline, while Portugal had managed in the 1550s to establish a European base at Macau on the South China Sea coast, west of the Pearl estuary (Zhujiang). Despite imperial attempts to restrict foreign trade, silver was pouring into the empire to acquire its silk and porcelain. From the 1600s, elite European consumers bought imported tea from China along with the China teapots they brewed it in. Domestic craftsmen obsessively tried to reproduce the secret porcelain process. Potters such as Josiah Wedgwood based in Britain's industrial heartland – also increasingly linked by canals by the eighteenth century – created a lucrative niche with designs that represented idealised life in imperial China, such as the famous 'Willow Pattern'.[32]

When the heyday of the Ming too had passed, it wasn't Europeans who brought them down, but a fresh group of invaders from the north. In the 1640s China was invaded by forces from Manchuria, north-east of China, ushering in the Qing Dynasty (1644–1912). The Qing also selected Beijing as their capital. They crushed resistance in the Yangtze Valley and sealed this with a massacre of Ming supporters and other helpless bystanders in the city of Yangzhou, sending a clear message to the rest of the empire.[33] At the same time, great pains were taken to demonstrate imperial authority on the Grand Canal. The second Qing Emperor Kangxi (r. 1661–1722) is particularly remembered for his conventional imperial tours along the canal system of this conquered kingdom. This was no ministerial visit to a pie factory but a lavish affair that had to be properly publicised throughout the empire. For his second canal tour, Kangxi commissioned a set of twelve scrolls, totalling 200 metres in length. 'The Yellow River and the Grand Canal are intimately connected to the livelihood of the people', he let it be known: 'I care about them dearly . . .'[34] The scrolls showed the emperor and his entourage engaged in a series of set pieces: visiting a scene of drought in Pizhou; observing the flooding of the Yellow and Huai rivers; inspecting a dike, with the Yellow River rolling away in the background. They commemorated Kangxi's journey of 1689 from Beijing to Shaoxing, below Hangzhou, at the very base of the Grand Canal. The seventh scroll in this tour shows the part of the journey from Wuxi down to Suzhou to its south-east. This shows a rich waterside world of canals, bridges, inland customs offices, shop counters, rice fields, mules, ponds shared by water buffalo and ducks, and at the Suzhou end, the Chang Gate and the house of the Silk Commissioner who hosted the emperor during his stay in the city.[35]

China continued to prosper economically into the early nineteenth century under the Qing Dynasty, but imperial powers began to fade. Perhaps the time of the fourth Emperor Qianlong (r. 1736–96) saw the last age of imperial affluence and control. The Grand Canal tours remained an important symbol of this. Between 1751 and 1784 Emperor Qianglong undertook six ceremonial tours at a cost of 20 million ounces of silver, commissioning a record of the first tour in twenty-six handscrolls by the artist Su Yang. The tour in 1784 along the southern Grand Canal was to be his last, and no others followed from subsequent emperors. When British emissaries arrived in China in the 1810s they considered they were witnessing a fading dynasty. The grand buildings along the ceremonial canal route were falling into disrepair, though Britain's increasingly confident industrial power was still then a long way from overtaking China.[36] In 1750 the output of cloth in the Lower Yangtze region was comparable with that of industrialising Britain in 1800. And in 1815, China still had the biggest economy in the world.[37] When British traders came calling, they didn't really have anything that the Chinese authorities wanted.

Britain adopted an aggressive commercial strategy, therefore, which saw them arrive in the Yangtze estuary in the 1840s, bringing with them an entirely different set of priorities and trade strategies. China was the key market for East India Company opium grown in the Ganges region, as we have seen. Against Qing wishes, sales by the East India Company of Indian opium began to rise and the balance of trade began to tip in Britain's favour. So when at this time Chinese officials seized British opium from a warehouse in the port of Canton (Guangzhou) on the Pearl River, Britain declared war. In July 1842 they blockaded the city of Zhenjiang on the south bank of the Yangtze River where it intersects with the Grand Canal. That year's tribute of grain boats had already set off but the blockade threatened to paralyse all further canal trade in this crucial grain region and this brought the Qing emperor to terms. British victory in the Opium Wars of 1839–42 forced the Qing authorities to allow imports of Indian opium, which proved an effective gateway drug to access China's ports and markets. The Treaty of Nanjing (1842) handed a series of so-called Treaty Ports to the British, including Hong Kong on the South China Sea, and Shanghai in the Yangtze Delta with a concession to develop a port.[38]

More trouble came to the people of China in the late Qing years when another major peasant rebellion and violent conflict broke out in 1850 that would claim millions of lives. The Taiping Heavenly Kingdom rejected the Manchu Qing, considered still 'foreign' with their pigtails and shaven heads at the front (queue). The men cut off their pigtails – a symbol of their servitude – and let their hair grow out. Gathering up armies of men and women, the willing and unwilling, the 'long-hair rebels' spread down the Yangtze Valley, set up headquarters at Nanjing and dominated the city and lower Yangtze region for the next fifteen years.[39] Amid this turbulence, the waterways were also rebelling. The Yellow River is thought to have been many metres above the surrounding riverside land. Following a series of floods, in 1855 it changed course altogether once again, veering 200 miles to the north beyond Shangdong Province – taking over the course of the

Daqing River – and flowed into the Bohai Gulf (as it does today).[40] Creating great hardship this unravelled the threads of the Grand Canal in the Yangtze region and the grain tribute system had to be diverted via coastal routes.

The canals observed from British gunboats during the Taiping Rebellion of the 1850s and 1860s were strewn with bodies. But for foreign powers, the fracturing of Chinese authority was an opportunity. Further opium battles in the 1850s secured more concessions and ports, though in the 1860s Britain pivoted to provide assistance in the Qing's fight against the Heavenly Kingdom. For this effort General Charles 'Chinese' Gordon was drafted in: a true servant of the British Empire, redeployed to China from hated desk-jobs on the lower Danube and the Russian-Ottoman border – and later to die at the hands of another group of rebels on the Nile at Khartoum. Looting carried out by British troops at Beijing's Summer Palace, like the later removal of artefacts around the time of the Boxer Rebellion, continues to complicate Chinese-British relations to this day.[41]

The Grand Canal was not to fully recover from the disasters of these years. Nor did the pre-eminent Grand Canal cities in the Yangtze such as Suzhou and Yangzhou, while the coastal city of Shanghai on the Yangtze estuary began its transformation into a playground for international capital. The grain tribute system on the Grand Canal was abandoned altogether in 1901/02 soon after a major revolt against foreign interests arose in Northern China: the Boxer Rebellion (1900). The flat-bottomed barges still navigated the canals southwards, carrying coal from northern mines. Grain boats for private trade continued to sail along the Grand Canal and connected waterways in Shanghai, by now a major city, many under the control of regionally affiliated bandits, such as the Green and Red Gangs. By the time the Qing Dynasty was deposed in 1911 and replaced by the Republic of China (1912–49), those with responsibility for the upkeep of the Grand Canal were struggling with multiple foreign powers on their doorstep.[42]

For many centuries, China's Grand Canal was a model for the rest of the world. Industrialising countries such as Britain created an extensive canal network to transport coal and other heavy loads between the late seventeenth century and 1800. But nothing approached the sophistication or longevity of China. Pennsylvania-born Robert Fulton, author of a 1796 treatise on canal navigation, noted of the Chinese model that 'their canals have the reputation of being infinitely superior to anything of the kind in Europe'. Fulton was later to produce the world's first steamboat – which made its debut on New York's Hudson River – and he went on to ply his trade along the Mississippi, but canals were the future, not rivers. Where natural channels, he said, were prone to 'torrents, in time of rain [. . .] shoals in dry seasons, together with the current ever standing one way', it was canals or 'the channels of art, which can only effectually assist the country', though this underestimated the problem of keeping the river torrents out of the canals. The Grand Canal, as we have seen, was frequently damaged by river flooding. Meanwhile in the United States, the Chesapeake and Ohio Canal begun in the 1820s (Maryland and West Virginia) was flooded so persistently by its feeder river, the Potomac, that its commercial life didn't last more than a century.[43]

By the twentieth century the world was catching up with the Grand Canal. The emerging superpower of the United States was beginning to slice canal routes across the world to suit its geopolitical interests. In 1914 it completed the Panama Canal, finally providing easy access between the Atlantic and Pacific Oceans, just as the Suez Canal had linked the Mediterranean Sea and Indian Ocean forty-five years earlier. In the unsettled years of the Republic of China, with more devastating flooding and famine in the Yellow and Huai River regions, some in its government looked to America for expertise and money in repairing its rivers and canals. However, 'economic nationalism' in the Chinese Nationalist Government from the late 1920s may have contributed to a delay in plans for a US-backed recovery of the Grand Canal.[44]

The victory of the Chinese Communist Party over the Nationalists after the Second World War and the Chinese Civil War ensured that from 1949 any solutions to China's water problems would be dealt with domestically. In the post-war years Chairman Mao Zedong announced an array of ambitious plans for the canals and rivers of the new People's Republic of China. The Grand Canal was to become linked by a new canal section focused on China's northern coal-producing region. The four major rivers of China – the Amur-Sungari, the Yellow, the Yangtze and the Si Kiang – would be linked together by canal. The Chinese and Soviet government were to collaborate on their shared border along the Amur River. Rivers were to be harnessed to the full and their destructive powers brought under control. A water transfer scheme would carry water from the Yangtze up to the dry north; plans started afresh on a dam in the Three Gorges region of the middle Yangtze. Although these plans were slow to evolve, many of them have become a reality, like the Three Gorges Dam opened in 2003 and the massive South-to-North Water Transfer Project currently underway.[45]

The Grand Canal has continued to evolve through a mixture of grandiose planning and more modest practical achievements. Today it still occupies an important place in China's economy as well as its cultural life. New links are being added as we speak, and there has been significant re-engineering and widening along many sections in recent decades. The Beijing-Hangzhou Grand Canal (at over 1,000 miles) is today a major goods highway, with 100,000 vessels passing along it each year, carrying 260 million tons of mostly building materials annually.[46] Although it no longer holds the same place in a world now connected by canals that can cut across oceans, the model of the Grand Canal has been replicated globally. Engineered waterways create strategic routes that nature did not provide, helping to service imperial centres along their favoured geopolitical pathways.

20
The Riverfly

'Ever the river has risen and brought us the flood,
the mayfly floating on the water.
On the face of the sun its countenance gazes,
then all of a sudden nothing is there!'

The Epic of Gilgamesh, X[1]

Rivers abound with mythical and literary significance in China, as well as their physical importance for trade and infrastructure. There are said to be 45,203 rivers in China. In Chinese myth and literature, they are everywhere. Yu, its first great (though mythical) emperor, was a controller of floods on the tempestuous Yellow River, Yangtze and other waterways. This 'water kingdom' carved out over thousands of years was a driver of economic growth and change, but also a source of great cultural continuity. Ancient tales of rivers and lakes are at the heart of Chinese literary and folk traditions which have persisted over centuries: tales of murder by drowning, suicide and magical transformations; mythic dragons as creative and destructive forces on the waters; shamanistic leaps between rivers and mountains; and legends of the 'river of heaven' written on the night sky, like the tale of the Oxherd – of the constellation Aquila – and the Weaver Girl: separated stars, facing each other across the river of the Milky Way.[2] As on other rivers in this book, with their gods, water spirits or myths of progress, the waters are a blank slate and reflect back human ambitions and hopes, propitiations and memories. Even the Grand Canal became part of the world of nature and myth over time.

China seems the very essence of cultural continuity. Its script is the most ancient continuous writing system in the world. Some modern Chinese characters still retain a distant echo of ancient pictograms (signs that mimic the things they represent) found on 'oracle bones' from the time of the Shang Dynasty (1600–1050 BCE), for example the signs for woman, mountain and river. It was also the Chinese who invented paper from pulped plant fibre, perhaps as early as the second century BCE.[3]

The Yangtze is one of the rivers here with ancient written records, like the Ganges and Nile. These ancient writings can tell us about (some of) the people who lived along the rivers of the ancient world, just as it can about those on the Tigris and Euphrates in Mesopotamia (roughly today's Iraq), where writing may have begun around 3100 BCE.[4] But the Yangtze has also been a place of great change. Some seemingly timeless myths obscure these changes. This chapter looks at continuity and change in the relationship between water and myth in the Yangtze region. In the first part, rivers provide metaphors of life and death in the poetry and tales of this area. The second part looks at how the Yangtze and other rivers were reimagined for the modern age, from the time of Mao and the Communists in 1949 to our own age of efficiency and extinction. It ends with the *baiji*, the Yangtze river dolphin, as both an enduring myth and an ecological casualty.

Rivers provide an endless source of metaphor, from the origin stories of the Blue Nile to symbolic transference from one river to another, and they can add meaning to moments of life and death. When Thomas, a Native American *Menominee* chief, met Zebulon Pike on the upper Mississippi and wanted to describe the experience of allying with the British or Americans in the early 1800s, he reached for a river metaphor:

> You are now at war; how are we to know which has justice on their side? Besides, you white people are, in number, like the leaves on the trees. Should I march, with my forty warriors to the field of battle; they, with their chief, will be swallowed up, as the big water embosoms the small rivulets which run into it.[5]

Rivers, as we've seen, can also be portals to other worlds. In Jeanette Winterson's novel *Sexing the Cherry* (1989), the River Thames carries the protagonist away from 1980s London and back to the city of the seventeenth century. Stopping on Waterloo Bridge, she says:

> . . . the smells of rubber and exhaust receded. I felt I was alone on a different afternoon.
>
> I looked at my forearms resting on the wall. They were massive, like thighs, but there was no wall, just a wooden spit . . .
>
> I could see rickety vegetable boats and women arguing with one another and a regiment on horseback crossing the Thames.
>
> I had to get on to Blackfriars, there was someone waiting for me.[6]

Chinese literature teems with river metaphors. Sometimes they are wrapped in a thick shroud of myth; sometimes they are naturalistic and easily accessible. In a famous poem by Su Shi, the politician and poet exiled from the court of the Northern Song in 1066, 'First Rhyme-prose on a Red Cliff', Su and a companion are together in a boat on the Yangtze. Passing the site of a famous defeat of the Han Dynasty long ago on the river, Su's companion is struck by the inconsequentiality of human life.[7] 'And what of you and me, brother?' he says:

> Mere fishermen and woodcutters on the sandbars of the River, companions of fish and shrimp, friends of stags and deer, sailing on this boat no larger than a leaf, toasting each other with gourd flagons: like mayflies between heaven and earth, like a single grain in the vast dark sea. We lament that our lives last but a moment, envy the endlessness of this Long River.

To this, Su replies with a reassuring, if baffling, comment on constancy and change in nature:

> Master Su replied, 'Do you also know this about this River and

> the moon: "That which passes away is like this", and yet it is never gone; what waxes and wanes is like that, and yet in the end it never diminishes or increases. If we look at a situation from that which changes, then neither Heaven nor Earth has ever lasted more than a blink; if we look at it from that which does not change, then neither things nor I will ever come to an end. What is there further to envy.'[8]

A very similar image is found in the passage that opens this chapter, from the *Epic of Gilgamesh* of ancient Mesopotamia. This story, compiled long ago from many fragments found in the land between the Tigris and Euphrates rivers, contains a great primeval flood which may have fed into the Genesis myth. Here a 'sage flood hero' is talking with the wandering king Gilgamesh again about the shortness and smallness of life, though there isn't a counter-balancing image; only more of the same: 'Man is snapped off like a reed in a canebrake!'

Mayflies or riverflies (*Insecta: Ephemeroptera*) are the essence of transitory existence. They emerge one by one from a river and form a great cloud; they reproduce; the female lays her eggs in the river and then they die: sometimes just in a single day. The whole thing happens around the same time next year.[9] This is a long way from the spirit invoked on many other rivers in this book: the grandeur and permanence of the river gods of Greek, Roman and Egyptian belief, or of the Ganges or the Christian God in baptismal waters. There is no eternal life on this river, apart from the life of the river itself: just mayflies.

Rivers and the natural world provide a great stock of metaphors for human experience and emotional states. Images of bamboo suggest constancy or unfailing allegiance. Pairs of mandarin ducks are inseparable couples.[10]

In a land of destructive floods and powerful currents, rivers can convey an irresistible force. In Nüshu tales – stories retold in the 'secret script' of rural Jiangyong women in the southern Yangtze basin – river metaphors can express the irresistible path of their lives. As one says, 'Women are like willows along the river / The yellow [flood] waters push them around.'[11] Rivers are a metaphor for separation in another Nüshu script, a retelling of 'The Maiden Meng Jiang' dating back to at least the Tang Dynasty (618–907). Here Meng Jiang is separated from her husband who has been called far away to join the workforce at the Great Wall. The Maiden accompanies her husband for the first few miles until they reach a river. 'Never be like the water below the bridge,' she says, 'as it only / Flows off toward the eastern sea and never returns!' That winter, Maiden Meng Jiang travels a great distance to take clothes to her husband only to find that he is already dead, and his bones have been discarded beneath the Great Wall. So great are Meng Jiang's tears that she brings down the wall, and her husband's bones are released.[12]

Rivers also invoked the flow of historical change. In the poem 'Li Sao' ('On Encountering Trouble') by Qu Yuan (c. 339–278 BCE), another exile from the imperial court, the poet mourns lost days of beauty and wisdom, when people did not simply follow the crowd:

> Why have all the fragrant flowers of days gone by
> Now all transformed themselves into worthless mugwort.
> . . .
> Since, then, the world's way is to drift the way the tide runs,
> Who can stay the same and not change with all the rest?[13]

Qu Yuan is said to have killed himself by leaping into the Miluo River, a tributary of the Xiang River. His time of official exile is over: today a Dragon Boat Festival is held each year to mark the day of his death. The drowned poet is 'rescued' from the water in races on lakes and rivers across China. Qu Yuan and other so-called 'literati' are closely associated with a region to the south of the Yangtze that is rich in poetry and landscape painting. This was a place of banishment: a semi-barbarous southern outpost for officials who had displeased the court, forced to move from their homes and far from northern civilisation. It was also a place of great natural beauty and very different from the North China plain. Some say the mountain and river landscapes of third-century

Shan Shui poetry reflect the exiles of Han elites forced south to this new landscape following military defeat.[14]

If you follow the Xiang River from its headwaters in the south and up into Hunan Province, you pass Yongzhou at its confluence with the Xiao River, then the city of Changsha where Chairman Mao was a student, and eventually reach the confluence of the Xiang and Yuan rivers. Here you find Dongting Lake (Dongti Hu, meaning Grotto Court), a huge freshwater lake that acts as a southern tributary to the Yangtze. This also gives the province of Hunan its name: 'south of the lake' as Hubei is 'north of the lake' (and the Yangtze).[15] This river confluence and lake region has a particularly rich tradition of myth, painting and poetry. It is at the heart of the landscape tradition known as 'Eight Views of Xiao-Xiang' ('xiao' meaning 'clear and deep'). Beginning with the exiled writer and painter Song Di (c. 1015–1080 CE) in the Song Period, the landscape tradition has been widely copied and reinterpreted since, spinning timeless scenes such as 'The rain at night on the Xiaoxiang' out of banishment. Also here at Dongting Lake live the Goddesses of the Xiang River: two sisters who drowned themselves long ago out of grief for their husband, the wise, drowned King Shun, and remain to this day in a cavern beneath the water.[16] A centuries-old stone pagoda – said to ward off floods – still stands beside the lake, having somehow escaped the hammers of Mao's cultural revolution.

This brings us to the time of great change on the rivers. The victory of the Communists over the Nationalist Party of Chiang Kai-shek in 1949 brought a shock to nature. For a time, before he secured control of territory south of the Yangtze, Mao is thought to have considered the river a possible southern border for Communist China.[17] Once he held the whole territory, Chairman Mao set out to disenchant and control the waters of China. In the process he added some magical thinking of his own. Water and rivers were to be of great importance both to Mao's revolutionary modernisation drive and to his mythologising of Communist destiny.

In the People's Republic of China, 'the people' were very much a collective idea rather than an assembly of actual people. For this vision, rivers proved to be a convenient metaphor. Mao expressed his view of political rule, and the harmony necessary between people and rulers, in 1957 in terms that were like a refracted mirror of Qu Yuan's 'On Encountering Trouble' many centuries before. 'The people are like the water,' said Mao, 'and the leaders at all levels are like the swimmers. You mustn't leave the water. You must go with [the flow of] the water.'[18] In fact, 'the people' also turned out to be like Su Shi's mayfly: individually expendable but part of a bigger picture. By this point, Mao had already been on his first Yangtze swim, which would take the river metaphor to its fullest potential as propaganda.

Two practical policies were important for Mao's approach to rivers during this period. The first targeted the heavily symbolic waterscapes of China. An 'Eliminate Superstition' campaign set out to re-educate the masses with attractive technicolour posters, that rang out with messages to bury the past. In one 1965 poster produced by the Science Popularisation Press, entitled 'There is No "Dragon's Palace" or "Dragon King" under the Sea', submarine headlights shine through blue ocean water, revealing human divers, corals, starfish and water snakes. A dinosaur shows the true ancient history of the waters: not 'dragon bones', but ancient fossils revealed by science. Another poster of the same year illustrated the hydrological cycle under the headline 'Rain is no dragon's spit'. Science could predict the weather, it said, and one day may even 'control the weather': 'man-made clouds and falling rain obey the demands of the people'.[19] In practical terms, at the same time, along the Grand Canal and other waterways Mao's forces destroyed shrines to water gods and Temples of the Dragon King wherever they found them.[20]

The second policy targeted physical waters in the 'War against Nature'.[21] Mao set out to demonstrate his ability to control the waters, like any emperor who came before him. But by now rivers were being re-engineered and dammed, and canals carved into the landscape, all over the industrialising world spearheaded by the United States and the Soviet Union. The main difference in Mao's China was one of tone. The domination of nature wasn't a sad necessity but a goal to be aggressively pursued. A poster campaign drove this home in exhibitions, on hoardings and café walls. The poster artists managed to invoke classical images of landscapes at the same time as conveying the necessity to destroy them. In a poster from 1973, a classic scene of a misty chasm between high mountains, workers are roped to a cliff face with birds flying in a ravine far below, alongside the message: 'Cleave the peak, split the ridge, cut a canal into the mountain'. More positively, another poster (1972), called 'The new look of mountains and rivers', contains a classical landscape giving way to an orderly scene with a hydroelectric dam; a watercourse runs between irrigated fields lined by electricity pylons and a road along which a little red and yellow motor coach is travelling. In the far distance, smoke rises from industrial chimneys.[22]

The Yangtze River was at the heart of Mao's policy to control nature. This was particularly urgent after a flood on the Yangtze in 1954 claimed the lives of 30,000 people. It became a focal point for Maoist propaganda and policy.[23] Shortly afterwards in 1956, Mao swam the Yangtze River. He followed this up with a poem: 'Swimming'. With a similar mixture of classical imagery and ambitions for a new future, it anticipated what was to come. The poem tracks Mao's swims from a river at Changsha – the city of his youth – to the Yangtze. As he crosses over the water from Wuhan, he looks prophetically at the southern skies beyond its far shore. Already he is contemplating 'great projects' for the great river: a bridge that will connect the two banks – 'Nature's barrier becomes a throughway' – and the dam that will one day hold back the waters and drown the Three Gorges. 'These projects should not harm the goddess,' Mao reassures his people, 'but / She will certainly be surprised by the changing world.'[24]

Ten years later, on the morning of 16 July 1966 in the city of Wuhan, 5,000 people swam across the Yangtze River beneath an 'azure blue' sky. Among them were 200 children. It was the 11th Cross-Yangtze Annual Swim to celebrate Mao's 1956 swim. Later that morning the seventy-two-year-old Mao also removed his white robe and took to the water alongside his henchmen and swam across the river, or perhaps downstream. This was to become the most famous swim ever, leaving Lord Byron's swim across the Dardanelles doing doggy paddle in its wake.[25] Official photographs and posters publicised the event widely right up to the ten-year anniversary posters in 1976 a few months before Mao's death.

This was no mere swim but a 'battle against Nature', Mao said: against class domination and against American imperialism.[26] Lest any nuance be missed, the *Peking Review* described the event in detail. The 'current was swift and the rolling waves pounded the shores'. The '10,000-li long Yangtze River is torrential each wave pushing the one ahead, each wave higher than the one before. It symbolises the history of the Chinese nation and . . . the Chinese revolution'.[27] Mao's role in the international anti-colonial struggles was not forgotten. Some members of the Afro-Asian Writers' Bureau had travelled to the Yangtze, fresh from a meeting in Beijing, to watch the event from vessels on the river. Delegates from Niger to Laos sent messages to hail 'the conquest of the natural barrier of the Yangtse'. This was not just a struggle for the 700 million people of China; as a 'friend from Africa remarked: "Chairman Mao's good health and long life is the happiness of the world's oppressed people and of the people of the whole world."'[28]

The Yangtze swims took on a life of their own but were always part of Mao's wider project to master the waters. The Three Gorges Dam project – holding back the rainfall in the river – was not underway by the time of Mao's death. Work began in 1994 and its environmental consequences suggest that the war on nature has proved all too successful. We turn to some of these consequences now.

One spring afternoon in 1916 on Dongting Lake two shots rang out. Charles Hoy, son of an American missionary, out duck-hunting, had spotted a dolphin swimming at the far end of the lake and decided to shoot it. He later delivered the dolphin's head and neck to the National Museum of Natural History in Washington DC. From there, news of the freshwater river dolphin spread globally.[29]

The Yangtze river dolphin (*Lipotes vexillifer*), with its long blunt nose, is effectively blind and uses sonar to navigate turbid waters, like the river dolphins of South Asia. Its main habitats seem for a long time to have been the Qiantang River which flows into the East China Sea, south of the Yangtze, the Yangtze River itself, and the Dongting and Poyang Lakes connected to the Yangtze, which may have formed at the end of the most recent Ice Age when sea levels rose and crept upstream through the river channel and into its tributaries.[30]

The earliest reference to the Yangtze river dolphin or *baiji* (white dolphin) in literature is thought to be in *Er Ya* (or *Erya*), a kind of ancient dictionary dating back to the Han Dynasty (206 BCE–220 CE). And these freshwater dolphins have long been valued as sentinels that come to the aid of those out on the waters by anticipating oncoming storms, like the unsettled Irrawaddy dolphins of the Sundarbans before the cyclone in Amitav Ghosh's 2004 novel *The Hungry Tide*.[31] A Song-dynasty (960–1279) poem describes the transformation on the placid waves of the Yangtze River – '[t]en thousand li of glittering ripples' – when *baiji* start to rise to the surface, two-by-two. Seeing their arrival, 'diving and leaping', the men out on the river retreat hurriedly to their harbours and secure their boats before the storm breaks. 'Ah, thank you, Goddess Baiji,' they cry: 'You've saved us from a disaster, / And we'll always remember your favors.'[32]

The Yangtze river dolphin is also the Goddess Baiji in one of the Yangtze's drowning myths. As the story goes, Princess Baiji refuses to marry a man she doesn't love, who her father has chosen for her. Baiji is drowned in the Yangtze by her father, but the river comes to the rescue by transforming her into the Yangtze river dolphin.[33]

The freshwater river dolphin is an ancient species, and like other cetaceans (dolphins and whales) may have evolved long ago from even-toed ungulates; improbably from the hippopotamus, in particular. Four other river dolphins are known. In the Amazon River there is the *boto* (*Inia geoffrensis*) and in the rivers of South

America's east coast is found the *franciscana*, or La Plata dolphin (*Pontopria blainvillei*). The Ganges has the *susu* (*Platanista gangetica gangetica*) and the Indus river dolphin, or *bhulan*, has traditionally been designated a sub-species of the Ganges dolphin (*Platanista gangetica minor*), though this is changing. How these different river dolphins relate to each other and when and how they may have once been connected by seaways or rivers still puzzles biologists. Something they have long shared is their vulnerability as prey and food: hunted for meat and oil, caught by various fishing nets, rolling hooks, electro-fishing (stunning fish), or accidently by ship propellers, killed by pollution or construction work on river channels, or above all by major dams which prevent free passage for swimming. The building of the Three Gorges Dam was widely anticipated to be a major threat to the *baiji* – and so it proved.[34]

In 1992, prior to start of work on the dam, a *baiji* dolphinarium was built at the Institute of Hydrobiology in Wuhan on the Yangtze's south bank, complete with pools, a fridge big enough for one ton of fish, and a small museum. And for twenty-two years a *baiji* named Qi Qi lived here, dying in the early 2000s. In the year 2003 when the Three Gorges Dam was completed, an International Union for Conservation of Nature (IUCN) reported that *baiji* were to be found only in the middle Yangtze between Dongting and Poyang lakes. With no further sightings, the *baiji* was declared extinct in 2006. This was followed by the Chinese paddlefish and, in the wild, the Yangtze sturgeon. The Yangtze finless porpoise, a relative of *baiji*, is currently severely endangered and is being monitored at the Wuhan laboratory.[35]

A survey carried out in 2010 among Yangtze fishers suggests how quickly the river dolphin is passing out of human memory. Around 600 fishers aged twenty-two to ninety were interviewed at different points along the Yangtze, from the Three Gorges Dam to the estuary at Shanghai. When shown photographs of different Yangtze species including the *baiji* (alive and dead, swimming free and in 'captivity'), just over 60 per cent of the fishers had seen one, including most of the older fishermen who easily recognised the dolphin and many who said they had caught one. But the newer and younger fishers were less likely to have seen a *baiji* (or a paddlefish), to recognise one, or even to have heard of them. The study's authors took this as a sign of a 'shifting baseline syndrome'. This idea of the 'shifting baseline' comes from a 1995 article by fisheries expert Daniel Pauly, who argued that 'each generation of fisheries scientists accepts as a baseline the stock size and species composition that occurred at the beginning of their careers, and uses this to evaluate changes'. When younger scientists come along, they accept the new reduced baseline and a 'creeping disappearance' is the result.[36]

This tells us something about the way in which memories of the natural world change and fade over time. Fish may become scarcer or smaller, with little knowledge among new generations of their past abundance. This is happening everywhere: from the declining fish stocks landed at the riverside market at Mopti in the Inner Niger Delta since the 1960s, to the shrinking numbers of eels in the Thames – once the mainstay of eel and mash shops and gobbled up in eel-pie eating competitions – or the once-abundant endangered Danube salmon; the lake sturgeon approaching extinction in the Mississippi River and the Great Lakes; the already disappeared hippopotamus on the Egyptian Nile; the reduced swimming range of the Gangetic river dolphins. The situation has changed significantly even since the 1990s. Past baselines are taken seriously by scientists. Literature on the Yangtze River today is dominated not by poetry but by scientific reports. As I write, a Google Scholar search of 'Yangtze ecosystem' brings up 215,000 results. Far more is known about the natural world of the river than ever before. Nevertheless, one in three freshwater (river and lake) species globally is under threat of extinction.[37] The erosion of nature is continuing today less in the spirit of Mao than in shifting expectations and memories.

The legend of Princess Baiji has become synonymous with the extinction of the Yangtze dolphin, which couldn't be saved without sacrificing Yangtze River development plans. Science is providing us with new myths to weave about the decline and fall of the natural world on the rivers. One day, the Three Gorges Dam may also come to be seen as part of the natural order of things, like the ancient Grand Canal before it.

21
Sinking City

> 'The mouths of large rivers are "battlegrounds", so to speak, on which many geologic processes are actively engaged.'
>
> Gerald M. Friedman and John E. Sanders, *Principles of Sedimentology* (1978)[1]

In 1921 someone noticed that Shanghai, at the mouth of the Yangtze, was sinking. Regular monitoring began and since 1921 it has continued to sink. This seems to have been happening since at least the nineteenth century when people started to flood into this port city, and with them came the construction work. The weight of the buildings settled onto exceptionally soft ground. By the 1950s, the city was sinking at a rate of 10 centimetres per year. There was also heavy groundwater use. The more people extracted water from beneath their feet, the more the city sank. By one estimate, Shanghai is thought to have sunk over three metres since the late 1800s.[2]

This chapter is a story of Shanghai, how it started to sink and what has been done about it. And how, it asks, will Shanghai and other sinking cities fare in a world of rising sea levels, and contradictory policies. This is a dilemma faced by all estuary cities. London is sinking. So are Venice and New Orleans. The people of the Yangtze and Mississippi deltas share the additional problem of hurricanes. Pisa, on the marshland of the River Arno, has been sinking for a very long time. But even its famous Leaning Tower, built in the twelfth century, took a turn for the worse when the population of Pisa grew in the 1960s and groundwater extraction increased. Sea levels are also creeping up and have been since around 1700 – perhaps by nearly 30 centimetres over these past centuries.[3] Today global warming is intensifying this rise by melting the glaciers.

The name 'Shanghai' means 'above the sea' or 'up from the sea'. But like many coastal cities it is low-lying, only around 3 to 4 metres above sea level. The city is situated on the banks of the Huangpu River, the final tributary to flow into the Yangtze estuary and part of its southern delta.[4] Shanghai was one of the territories conceded to Britain under the Treaty of Nanjing in 1842 after the Opium Wars, and it was an obvious place for foreign powers to try to make their mark. The Yangtze River provided a highway into China's interior. The Grand Canal, in good times, linked Shanghai to cities such as Hangzhou in the south, Suzhou in the west, and Beijing in the north. It was also very well-positioned for international shipping. Close to the already established walled city of Shanghai, the British chose this place for their harbour and colonial settlement in the 1840s. The Huangpu (or Whangpoo to colonial settlers), was more sheltered from typhoons than the main Yangtze channel and, in theory, easier to keep dredged for seagoing vessels.[5]

Shanghai has also gone by the name 'Hu Tu', referring to an estuary set with bamboo fish traps. But this was no humble fishing village by the nineteenth century:[6] already it was a thriving commercial city. One estimate put the population of the city at several hundred thousand by the early 1800s. There were thriving industries including silk, salt and cotton: a major crop in the Yangtze Valley. Many families in and around Shanghai were active in spinning and weaving cotton cloth and muslin in the 1830s. But the Opium Wars brought change. More foreigners flowed into the city in the 1890s following a Japanese victory over Qing forces in this decade, with a treaty allowing foreign interests to set up industries in the city.[7] Japan, Britain, France, Germany and the United States remained a dominant presence in the city into the mid-twentieth century. Their officials and foreign merchants developed their own settlements within the city, segregated from Chinese communities.

Building a European industrial-style city had begun. Creeks and small rivers were 'reclaimed' into land like those of other developing cities, from eighteenth-century London to the lost 'floating world' of twentieth-century Tokyo. The Yangjingbang Creek that flowed by old Shanghai disappeared in the early 1900s, reclaimed to form part of Avenue Edward VII, now part of Yan'an Road.[8]

The Boxer Rebellion of 1900 against foreigners and in support of the Qing Dynasty brought only more defeat and further conditions imposed on the Qing regime. Turbulence gave way to all-out revolution and an end to the Qing Dynasty in 1911. The new Republican Government of China had to deal with a reconstituted Whangpoo Conservancy Board created the following year, now dominated by foreign interests and engineers who set about dredging the Huangpu River and harbour. The China Merchants Steam Navigation Company and its network of boathands and hardmen across Shanghai mounted direct competition against Western steamship companies.[9] Likewise, the hard-bitten European and American imperialists pursued their aims through political instability and escalating nationalist hostility.

Business was booming. Shanghai was still growing on the eve of the Second World War. All of international capital was here. As well as the Chinese textile mills, there were Japanese banks, the Hong Kong Shanghai Bank (HSBC), British American Tobacco and Standard Oil, and the titans of the foreign opium trade: Matthieson, Jardine & Co. and Sir Ellice Victor Sassoon. Foreign merchants and officials had stayed on as Japanese forces bombarded the city in 1932 and invaded Shanghai in 1937.[10]

While Shanghai grew and its people weathered tumult on the streets, there was another drama unfolding underground. Two dramas, in fact. The first was well-known: land in this coastal region was building up between the city and the East China Sea. For at least 2,000 years, port and customs facilities had complied with nature, moving eastward as necessary to follow the sea. The gradual build-up and extension of coastal land seawards – known as 'progradation' – is the opposite of coastal erosion where the sea is eating away at the land.

Progradation was the fate of the city of Pisa. This flourishing Roman coastal city of Portus Pisanus, where the Arno Delta once met the Mediterranean (Ligurian) Sea, was in the 1100s a trading centre equal with Amalfi, Genoa and Venice. But as the Arno River deposited its silt load, from around 1350 the coast gradually stole away westward, leaving Pisa stranded inland. Its place was taken by a port to the south-west on the rocky Livorno coast, bought by the city of Florence in the 1420s, which became the coastal hub for Cosimo de' Medici in the late sixteenth century. The leaning bell tower of Pisa's cathedral built in its heyday (1174) had to be corrected only a century later and continued to tilt on its marshy sponge until concrete was injected beneath the tower in the 1960s.[11]

For millions of years, silt and waves come and go along coastlines without consequence, as non-human life has adapted to changing conditions and habitats. Like coastal erosion, progradation is a problem only where there are important fixed structures and human settlements. As we have seen on the Danube and other port cities, harbour authorities wanting to maintain maritime channels for ocean-going ships need a sufficient depth of water. For Shanghai farmers, the build-up of silt in the Yangtze Delta was a bonus. They would come up the creeks and canals and with bamboo poles dredge up the silt into buckets and take it away as topsoil. But for Shanghai's international shippers and the Whangpoo Conservancy Board, the sandbars at the harbour became an obsession. The Chinese authorities on the other hand, at least according to an American missionary writing at the time, considered the sandbars 'a heaven-sent barrier intended to prevent war vessels . . . and ironclads from entering the harbour'.[12] This wedge of mud and sand was perhaps like the river boulders of the Danube's Iron Gates for the Ottomans, or the heavy chain across the Golden Horn beside the city of Byzantium: helpful but not ultimately successful at keeping out intruders.

In 1919 it was estimated that over the past nearly seventy years the land of the Yangtze Delta had moved seaward by one mile: around 25 yards per year. In the 1930s the Whangpoo Conservancy

Board acquired a new German-built suction dredger – the *Chien Si* – to work on the outer sandbar in the inter-tidal 'Fairy Flats' about 30 miles out from Shanghai, with lubrication provided by Standard Oil's Socony-Vacuum Oil Co., based on the Huangpu riverside at Pudong.[13] The gothic language of a Socony advertisement describing the dredger's job as the 'Menace Off Shanghai!' matched anything that Mao's 'war on nature' could muster, with a not very subtle anti-Chinese twist:

> No longer will the Sluggish Yangtze hold Big Ships at Bay with Coiled Ribbons of Yellow Mud . . .
>
> At each trip across the shallows, this huge, underwater 'lawn-mower' rips a gash 6 feet deep, 10 feet wide and a mile long. At the dumping ground, twenty winged flaps open, or pumps reverse, to spew the mud back upon the ocean bottom.[14]

Around eight years was the time estimated to achieve a 27-foot depth for the ships (after dredging 40 million tons), but the Whangpoo Conservancy Board ran out of time. In 1937 Japanese forces occupied Shanghai. Other foreign merchants stayed on to protect their sunk capital in an uncertain climate. An American observer noted in 1940 that although Japanese officials had done little dredging since arriving in the city, they had recently shown a more 'conciliatory' attitude to reopening the Yangtze to trade. Ultimately Japanese authorities were more interested in bombing the US Pacific Fleet at Pearl Harbor (Hawaii) in December 1941, which subsequently ended all collaboration in Shanghai.[15]

The second drama that Shanghai faced, deeper underground and less obvious at first, was that by the 1920s it was visibly sinking. The city sits on top of around 300 metres of clay, sand and silt deposited by the river, a shifting subterranean world interlaced with aquifers.[16] The challenge of building here was no secret. Civil engineers the world over discussed the problem of soft ground for the stability of construction. Mid-nineteenth-century dwellings followed existing Chinese models, bungalows or two storeys at most, with long timber 'piles' (vertical posts) driven into the mud to stabilise buildings. American Douglas Firs began to be imported to do this job, and timber from Singapore and Japan. Meanwhile, buildings got taller and taller to keep up with rising real-estate values, and ever more concrete was poured into the earth to stabilise them.[17]

Two developments in American cities had made the 'skyscraper' possible. One was the invention of steel frames for tall buildings in 1880s and 1890s Chicago on the shore of Lake Michigan. This meant that external walls no longer had to bear all the load; steel frames could be used to support the weight of buildings above twelve storeys. Skyscrapers would have been a flop if people still had to take the stairs. But everything changed with the other invention (1870s): the electric 'passenger lift', just one of many reasons why epic river rapids and gorges – icons of the landscape for millennia – have been reduced one after the other to acting as mundane electricity generators. New York's Park Row Building (1898) had no fewer than nine electric lifts for its twenty-six storeys. The city's Woolworth Building (1913) at fifty storeys was 'the first of the giant skyscrapers'. But New York City is built on ancient rock.[18]

In Shanghai during these years, innovations centred especially on 'soil mechanics' and sophisticated techniques for building the foundations for tall buildings in an effort to defy the soft ground of the Yangtze Delta. Along the Huangpu's left bank lay the river embankment and commercial hub known as the Bund, looking over the river to the industrial zone of Pudong. This Bund riverside was built on a great mass of piled concrete. In 1904 Emperor Wilhelm II sent one of his sons to lay the foundation stone for the four-storey Club Concordia (or German Club), which pioneered reinforced-concrete foundations, only for the building to be seized – like Wilhelm's throne – during the First World War. Reinforced-concrete foundations for Standard Oil's six-storey headquarters followed in 1909. The Ward Road Hospital (nine storeys), built in the 1930s by Shanghai's Public Works Department, introduced deep basements in conjunction with 'piled foundations': 40-foot-long wooden piles sunk into the soft delta ground. The tallest building in Shanghai at 77 metres (14 storeys) was for a time the Sassoon Building, built on reinforced concrete, piled foundations – and opium.[19]

This stairway to heaven was halted by the Second World War and the Civil War that ended in the birth of the People's Republic of China in 1949. In this same year, measurements must have been taken to check for subsidence against a baseline established in 1921. Reports later noted that land subsidence between 1921 and 1949 had reached 64 centimetres. By the 1960s, subsidence in Shanghai had become a talking point and Communist Party officials began to investigate its causes and extent. 'Benchmarks' round the city suggested that between 1921 and 1965 parts of the city had sunk 2.63 metres.[20] One of the causes, it was realised, was the abstraction of water from the ground.

European water companies had introduced piped water supplies to international settlements and industries in the late nineteenth century. One of these, the British Shanghai Waterworks (opened 1883), served a growing customer: a 12 per cent increase in population in Shanghai between 1921 and 1929. More significant than the company's river water supplies, private wells were also sucking up huge quantities of ground water. After the first deep water well sunk in Shanghai in 1860, hundreds more followed, dug by both industry and local farmers. Shanghai's textile industry was particularly thirsty. Cotton and other textiles need clean, soft groundwater. Iron, steel and paper industries could as easily switch to river water, but the polluted Huangpu River was not suitable for textiles.[21] As of 1921, there were fifty-two cotton mills in Shanghai (mostly Chinese and Japanese), employing over 33,000 workers. Women were being pulled in from rural areas across the Yangtze region to work in the mills. One 1920s recruitment drive in Hunan Province called for fifty women to come and work for a period of three years; in return they were promised accommodation in a purpose-built dormitory, and given a suitcase, basket and wash basin. On the eve of the Japanese invasion in 1936, sixty-five mills had a workforce of nearly 117,000. Further city development during the Communist industrialisation drive in the 1950s only increased the rate of ground subsidence. Shanghai had 6.2 million inhabitants by the first census of the people's republic in 1953, over twice the population size of Beijing. (Shanghai had over 24 million by 2017.)[22]

In 1962 a working party was established by Mao's government to consider the possible causes of the sinking. Geology became a tool of politics as well as engineering. The *Peking Review* later reported on the success of this investigation. The so-called 'skyscraper theory' – that the weight of tall buildings was compressing land surface – was rejected. Buildings generally 'stopped sinking' after around twenty years, it was found. The practice of pumping natural gas from beneath Shanghai had ceased so this couldn't be the problem. Sea levels were thought to be stable. The culprit was identified as groundwater abstraction, especially in the textile-mill districts. Some 560,000 tons of water were being extracted from beneath the city each day by 1960. Some comrades argued that groundwater abstractions should end; most thought they'd need even more water 'in line with industrial development'. Regulation of groundwater abstraction helped to slow the rate of subsidence after 1963.[23]

Engineering solutions were inseparable from politics. Engineers found that some of the groundwater could be replaced by other water sources, and there were experiments with (artificial) 'groundwater recharge'. Wells were used intensively in the hot summer when water was needed for cooling purposes. But in the winter, when demand was lower, water could be injected back into the ground to replenish aquifers.[24] As of 1966, 100 textile mills (200 wells) had joined the recharge scheme. A 1972 report in *Peking Review* announced that 'Shanghai brings surface subsidence under control'. Before 'the Great Proletarian Cultural Revolution' of 1966–71, it noted, fewer than five factories had participated in the recharge scheme, this past failure being laid at the door of former Communist Party leader and 'counter revolutionary' Liu Shao-chi (who died in prison). Similar comments appeared in the same publication about the alleged role of Liu Shao-chi in failing water projects on the Yangtze River.[25] By contrast, now 'the ground [had] not only stopped sinking but was raised 16 millimetres'. Although 'the objective law of surface subsidence' was 'far from complete', the article's technical authors stated, the assistance of their working party 'vividly tells of the superiority of the socialist system and the boundless creativeness of the masses'. Some overseas scholars agreed that this work was an example of Marxist 'dialectical materialism' in action.[26]

The results of the 1960s looked impressive, though the timing doesn't align with the Cultural Revolution; in 1965, before the purges began, groundwater use had already plummeted to 42 per cent of 1963 levels. By 1976, not only had the sinking stopped but there was a small but reassuring rebound of 3.4 centimetres. An American study noted in 1986 that Shanghai experts considered their remedies to be 'producing good results in bringing the subsidence at least to acceptable limits'.[27]

The happy ending to Shanghai's subterranean drama has been revised in the new millennium, with a series of messages issuing from Shanghai politicians and experts; some of them worrying, others reassuring and – in combination – mystifying. Belief systems, like fish stocks, have shifting baselines and there is no talk of dialectical materialism or counter-revolutionaries this time round. In a 2001 press report ('Shanghai's Sinking Under Control, Authorities Say'), Shanghai was said to be continuing to sink, but 'under control'. According to its water-resources department, subsidence had increased since 1998 and in 2000 stood at just over 1.1 centimetres a year. One centimetre per year was considered 'internationally allowable'. Aquifer recharge had continued but the old problem was back: seemingly, 'the growing number of high-rises being built and underground construction'.[28] Worst hit was Pudong, the former industrial district on the Huangpu River's right bank – now a regeneration zone and skyscraper magnet. According to one estimate, the city of Shanghai lost over 10 million yuan (1.2 million US dollars) for every sunken millimetre.[29]

A 2001 press report ('Shanghai is Sinking as Skyscrapers Make a Dent') noted that the government had powers to prevent local building projects where subsidence was found. That same month a start was announced on the (then) tallest building in Shanghai: the 333-metre Shimao International Plaza (sixty storeys, plus three underground) in central Shanghai. In 2003 *China Daily* ('Shanghai Still Sinking') declared that farmers and factories would need to halve their water consumption. The metro system would 'very probably . . . deform'.[30]

The picture is ever-changing. America's *Time Magazine* in 2012 reported that the weight of tall buildings in Shanghai was contributing 30 per cent of the subsidence problem. Four years later, the Shanghai People's Congress had passed a law to limit groundwater abstraction and prevent land subsidence, with fines of half a million yuan (77,000 US dollars). The *Shanghai Daily* ('Land Subsidence Reduced to Safe Level') announced a new exhibition: 'Geology and the Development of a City'. Subsidence was now down to a safe 0.5 centimetres.[31]

The battleground is not just in the earth and water, but between those trying to put a lid on the city and, on the other hand, architects, engineers, banks and construction firms who weave ingenious spells to stretch buildings: lighter steel frames, deeper basements, and whatever the future holds. The year 2020 brought guidelines that would 'strictly control the construction of skyscrapers': buildings over 500 metres tall would need approval from two government bodies. At the time of writing, the city's highest building is the Shanghai Tower at 632 metres, the third tallest in the world. Of its 133 storeys, five are underground.[32]

In 2015 sponge cities arrived. Concrete surfaces were out; rain gardens were in. Chinese President Xi Jinping launched targets for Shanghai, Beijing, and several other cities for sustainable urban drainage to conserve water and prevent urban flooding. By 2030, 80 per cent of all urban areas were to utilise 70 per cent of their rainwater. Landscape designers launched plans for wetland city parks, botanical walls and roadside swales for water to gather.[33] By 2017 there were reports of local-government funding problems and urban flooding has persisted.[34] Between 1960 and 2020 over 1,200 square kilometres of new land was 'reclaimed' from Shanghai's silty ground. It will take a huge amount of money and a collective iron will to reverse the impermeable city created in Shanghai and elsewhere. To protect Shanghai's coast itself, hundreds of miles of levees have been built, designed to defend against a one-in-a-thousand-years storm surge. Mechanical barriers such as those on the Rhine at Rotterdam and the Thames in London are being considered for the Huangpu. Across Hangzhou Bay, south of the Yangtze Delta, and around the islands off the east coast, over 500 kilometres of seawall have been built.[35]

Sea levels, as we know, are rising. Back in 2003 an expert from the Shanghai Institute of Geological Survey was quoted as saying that 'the current (subsidence) rate will keep the city above sea level for more than 400 years', though the subway system was under threat. Recent projections for sea-level rise range from 28 centimetres to a worst-case scenario of 2 metres by 2100.[36] Shanghai's new towers of steel and concrete have been spreading across its former mudflats in recent decades and the Three Gorges Dam today is capturing 70 per cent of the sediment that once settled and 'prograded' the Yangtze Delta, but science doesn't tell a single story here either: for those who deal in measurements much finer than centimetres and millimetres, the exact effects of this are still uncertain on the complex and dynamic coastline.[37]

Beneath the bold clarity of the skyline, the view on the ground is unclear. In this sinking, rebounding and stabilising city the benchmarks have themselves become unsteady. The days of scientific inquiry have greatly changed from cadres of geologists and party workers in regulation Mao Suits with their theodolites and elderly benchmarks round the city, to Shanghai's investment in a GPS system in the 1990s, to the latest radar (InSAR) techniques.[38] There is no knowing how high buildings will be able to climb into the sky before they reach a limit. In Shanghai and other world cities, corporate boards and engineers are still trying to find out, though sinking commercial centres and warping metro systems are serious concerns as the sea levels rise. It is just possible that the Chinese government will be capable of investing ever greater amounts of money and ingenuity into stabilising the ground, harvesting the rain, and shutting out the seas. The record of the past century in Shanghai suggests that the results will be mixed and not completely transparent.

Shanghai is only one of many coastal cities in a long-term struggle with the sea. A 1980s study found that some of the most severe cases of coastal subsidence globally existed in the United States. Top of the list was the Wilmington Oil Field region (at Long Beach in Los Angeles) – a centre of massive oil, gas and water abstraction – which had sunk 9 metres since the 1930s: almost four golf carts stacked nose to bumper. Close behind were the San Joaquin Valley (inland) and San Jose, also in California. And there were the Japanese cities of Tokyo and Osaka, Venice and London and – inland – Mexico City, though this picture is constantly changing. Today, Miami, New York-Newark and New Orleans are in the top ten globally in terms of projected financial losses from sea level rise by 2050, among other cities including the Chinese cities of Guangzhou and Tianjin, and Kolkata (Calcutta) in the Ganges delta.[39]

At the end of every major river journey lie cities and densely populated communities under threat from the sea. All the rivers in this book are losing elevation in relation to the sea. The Niger Delta is sinking; so are Alexandria and delta towns on the Nile, the Thames estuary, the deltas of the Ganges-Brahmaputra and the Mississippi. Only the Danube Delta doesn't have a major city at the river's mouth, but the Black Sea too is rising.[40]

When Hurricane Katrina devastated New Orleans in the Mississippi Delta in 2005, over 1,500 lives were lost and thousands of homes swept away. Amid it all, the 1975 Superdome football stadium stood strong. Built on more than 2,000 concrete piles, each over 40 square centimetres thick and driven 50 metres into the ground, it became a 'Refuge of Last Resort' for 30,000 people.[41] But not every building can be a Superdome. Stark disparities of race and economic resources shaped the path of the worst devastation and the capacity to escape from the oncoming storm. Some called this a 'bell in the night' for what is to come. Some places will be protected and others left to chance. In recent years members of the Biloxi-Chitimacha-Choctaw tribal community at Isle de Jean

Charles in Louisiana have had to move, as 98 per cent of their island has slipped beneath the waves since 1955.[42]

London also has been trying to manage its problems of subsidence and groundwater levels for some time now, but an issue that cannot easily be dealt with is the sinking of London and the whole of south-east England in the after-effects of glaciation. Britain is tipping downwards from Scotland in the north, still rebounding after the melt of its once-vast glaciers, towards the glacier-free south-east.[43] Something similar – called 'isostatic rebound' – is happening in New York City. Some 24,000 years ago an ice sheet a mile thick covered this North American region as far south as Albany in New York State, but it left New York City alone, today around 150 miles downstream on the Hudson River. Research published in 2023 found that New York City and its suburbs are sinking, though the numbers are quite small: from 1 to 4 millimetres a year. This is also attributed in part to the city's one million buildings, estimated to weigh 1.68 trillion pounds in total. But the research echoes earlier claims in Shanghai that subsidence from tall buildings ends after 'a year or two of construction'. Famously this city of skyscrapers is built on solid rock – 500-million-year-old Manhattan Schist and a billion-plus-year-old Fordham Gneiss – but radar reveals areas of softer ground and subsidence. Subsidence can be highly localised and the science is still evolving.[44]

The city of Venice, built on many millions of centuries-old wooden piles driven into the soft silt, now sits about 32 centimetres lower in relation to the sea level than in the early twentieth century; it is currently experimenting with injecting seawater from the Adriatic beneath the city.[45] The Indonesian government has recently taken the drastic step of turning away from its capital: the coastal city of Jakarta on the island of Java, which faces the worst subsidence problem in the world. Parts of North Jakarta were sinking by as much as 25 centimetres a year as of 2018; by 2.5 metres over the previous decade, in addition to severe air and river pollution and flooding of the city's rivers. At the time of writing, the government is building a new city from scratch: Nusantara (meaning 'outer islands' or 'archipelago') in the virgin rainforest of the south-east coast of the island of Borneo.[46]

Low-lying islands in the Pacific Ocean are even more on the front line of rising sea levels. The coastal communities all over Fiji's coastline have had to leave their ancestral homes in recent years, like the residents of Louisiana's rising seas. Residents of the state of Tuvalu – comprised of nine islands – now face having to leave altogether; they are currently investigating how to preserve their existence as a nation state when their land is under water, creating a 'digital nation' or a state that exists in the 'metaverse'.[47]

Around 11 per cent of the global population live on coasts less than 10 metres above sea level. One estimate puts the sea level on the New York coastline in 2023, the year of the *Barbie* movie, at 22 centimetres higher than in 1950, the year *All about Eve* was released. Materials made by humans were estimated in 2020 to outweigh all things that live on the earth. In total 1.1 teratonnes – all the sky-scrapers and cinemas, metro systems and trains, juggernauts and toy cars – now outweigh all living things. That means the 'global biomass': oak trees and giant sequoias, the shrinking mangroves, elephants, blue whales and plankton, black-tailed godwits from the Thames foreshore to the pygmy marmosets of the Amazon River. As the rising seas curl round this mountain of things, money may be able to protect the world's sunk capital in the richest cities and communities. As a recent debate asked, will there be 'lifeboats for the rich' in this future of fire and water?[48]

Conclusion

Time has altered the function of rivers in our lives. As transport arteries, they have been augmented and superseded: from the nineteenth-century Danube Valley Railway to the recent Rhine-Main-Danube Canal or China's Belt and Road Initiative (the '21st-century Silk Road'). Rivers have also been augmented by pipelines over the past 250 years, from water pipelines to oil and natural-gas pipelines, systems that have in many cases acquired their own complex histories of pollution and political protest. Transport routes are constantly evolving though seaborne trade remains crucial. What hasn't changed is our close dependence on rivers for water and livelihoods, from industrial farmers with their massive irrigation systems to watermelon growers on the drying riverbed of the Yamuna.

Many threats faced by rivers today are long-standing, but the scale of these problems is getting bigger. The magnificent Colorado River (which once carved out the Grand Canyon) today no longer reaches the sea, so great is the water abstraction along its route. Our ability to reshape rivers now outstrips anything possible in the pre-industrial age, though even the great dams have their precedents. The long-term effects of European colonial expansion persist. The world was watching in 2019 as the Amazon was on fire, fuelled by petrol cans under the gaze of Brazil's president. The pressure to clear the Amazon rainforest and displace its indigenous people in the interests of mining, farming and hydro-electricity continues a process set in motion when Europeans first spotted the river on 7 February 1500. The Amazon encapsulates what is best and most flawed about those of us living in rich industrial nations: our desire to work together to preserve nature or the most remote, uncontacted tribes, and our unwillingness to change lifestyles that make it necessary to rely on the Amazon as a last remaining oxygen refuge and carbon sink. When Jair Bolsonaro rejected G7 money to put out the fires, he voiced an uncomfortable truth about what Europe has done to its own forests.

Sewage is always with us, though this too has its historical rhythms. As recently as 2010 the Thames won the Thiess International Riverprize, but along with other British rivers it has been engulfed by a sewage scandal in the past few years. Some new threats have also emerged: levels of microplastic per cubic metre in the Thames are reported to have been worse over the past decade than those (in rising order) of the Rhine in Germany, the Danube in Romania, Italy's River Po and the Chicago River which flows into Lake Michigan.[1] Today, human time and geological time are being considered together more closely, as scientists and non-scientists debate the concept of the Anthropocene. Does the scale of human impacts on earth mean that we need a new name for our epoch to replace the Holocene? Contenders for a symbolic 'golden spike' to identify the start of the Anthropocene epoch have ranged from deposits trapped in the frozen waters of ice cores in Antarctica to evidence of post-war nuclear testing around a filled-in tributary of the Danube at Vienna. In 2023 Crawford Lake, a limestone sinkhole in Canada's Great Lakes region, won this dubious honour for the way it has preserved plutonium traces left by nuclear testing since 1950.[2] Others say there is no merit in a human epoch compared with the epic magnitude of geological changes. Even radioactive plutonium will degrade one day. As one academic put it: 'We are but a ripple in the river of gene flow through time.'[3]

Whatever the future is called, rivers are part of the massive changes underway: both for their role as 'organic machines' in modernisation projects across the globe and in the way they too are being fundamentally altered by global warming. As hydrological cycles across the planet are recalibrating, rainfall is being redistributed, with unprecedented flooding events here, intensifying droughts there.

Rivers remain essential to us, even if many of them will look less like rivers over time and more like canals, reservoirs, pipelines, or sewers. What is really new is the devastation we're inflicting on the climate through our intensive burning of carbon in coal, gas and oil. The Murray-Darling river system in Australia is dying in a toxic combination of over-abstraction, global warming and absolute drought. Many other, less prominent, river systems no longer provide the water needed by farmers and herders, from West Africa to the Himalayas. The future is uncertain – some say the Inner Niger Delta is getting increasingly dry, and prey to the creeping desert to its north; others that rainfall in this region is now increasing.[4]

Rivers have been governed in myriad ways over time: from the conquered rivers and forced-labour systems of flood control to recession agriculture, irrigation systems and canal-building; river commissions; river-valley authorities; 'integrated river basin management'; development funders; the environmental directives of the European Union; international diplomacy outfits such as the Ramsar Convention on Wetlands; the NGO Wetlands International or global networks of activists such as the Indigenous Environmental Network; 'water protectors' protesting against oil pipelines in the upper Mississippi; calls for rivers as 'legal persons' or calls for a Parliament of Rivers; or major projects agreed in backroom deals between corporations and states.

Water has from the earliest human settlements been tied to needs for energy – from waterwheels and mills – but rivers are harnessed for energy today as never before. And the environmental fortunes of rivers are bound up with the quest for energy as the world continues to industrialise. A battle is on between the sponsors of big infrastructure techno-fixes for 'net zero', like the hydropower industry or nuclear energy, and advocates of small-scale renewable-energy projects. This is paralleled in the flood and water conservation field between the advocates of dams for flood control and irrigation and those who want sustainable urban drainage and sponge cities.

'The future is already here,' the science-fiction writer William Gibson said, 'it's just not very evenly distributed.'[5] Rising sea levels caused by melting glaciers are sending salt water into freshwater reserves and eating into our coastlines, already displacing the first climate refugees in low-lying Pacific islands and deltas such as the Mississippi – seen as warning bells for the future. Rivers have a role in rising zoonotic diseases, such as Weil's Disease from increased flooding.[6] The river dolphins in this book are only the most iconic of the threatened and extinct species of our own time. One in three freshwater species is at risk of extinction today.

With all these threats, more people are interested in protecting rivers than ever before. Thousands of rivers – even the small tributaries – have their activist groups. There are many good news stories. In 2023 the first baby beaver for over 400 years was born in the Thames catchment on a 'rewilded' tributary of the River Lea.[7] Clear streams are luring in swimmers as never before. Though in Britain the current resurgence of a Victorian-scale sewage crisis is marring the experience, wild swimmers, like surfers on the coast, are raising the alarm. Dams are proliferating along steep river valleys, alongside pressure groups to prevent and remove the dams. There are some unlikely alliances. The Eastern Band of Cherokee Indians' recent campaign to preserve the sicklefin redhorse fish that has historically migrated to spawn high up in the Tennessee watershed has been supported by the TVA. Rivers are well recognised as part of a vast ecosystem, from the clams and crawfish of the Mississippi delta bed to the great egrets in the treetops of its swamps and the brown pelicans on the flyway overhead.[8] Rivers, like all of nature, reflect us at our best and our worst. It is up to us how we want our story to continue.

Acknowledgements

I am indebted to Adam Gauntlett for his inspired idea and all at Peters Fraser + Dunlop for their support of the project.

I am very grateful to Hélène Maloigne and to my niece, Mamie Michael, for practical assistance. I thank Katrin Hochberg for her photography, David McCutcheon for the cartography, Suzanne Fairless-Aitken for assistance with permissions, Fred Macnicol for Budapest and Charlie Christopher and Lucy Kral for the maths. The cavalry – Joseph Dobbyn, Joe Emmens, Mina Hassan, Mikail Hassan, Fatima Jafar, Anna Studsgarth, Sidra Vohra and Toby Whelton – arrived at just the right moment: thank you. Any errors that remain are all my own.

I am thankful for friends and colleagues at the University of Greenwich, past and present, who looked at drafts and offered support or expertise: Michael Talbot, Andrew Haggart, Gavin Rand and Paul Adams; Sarah Palmer and Roger Knight for the riverside collaboration that brought me here. And my thanks to the university itself for a sabbatical and funded support.

To those in my family, for multi-faceted support, I thank Dora Michael, Rex Michael, Fergus Michael and Rory Michael, Gerard Taylor and Timothy Taylor. Always, my sister Annabel Taylor. And for everything, Lisa Schmidt.

Permissions

Quotation from 'Scorpion' by Stevie Smith, from COLLECTED POEMS OF STEVIE SMITH, copyright ©1972 by Stevie Smith. Reprinted by permission of New Directions Publishing Corp.

Quotation from 'Scorpion' from Stevie Smith, reproduced in *Stevie Smith: A Selection*, ed. Hermione Lee. Reprinted with permission of Faber and Faber Ltd.

Quotation from 'Nile' by Tseqaye Gabre-Medhin from Chris Beckett and Alemu Tebeje (eds), *Songs We Learn from Trees: An Anthology of Ethiopian Amharic Poetry*. Reprinted with permission of Carcanet Press.

Quotation from *Selected Poems* by Rabindranath Tagore published by Penguin Classics. Translated by William Radice. Copyright © Rabindranath Tagore, 1985. Translation copyright © William Radice, 1985. Reprinted by permission of Penguin Books Limited.

Quotation Joan Kennard's letter from 'Letter from Joan Kennard, Grand Hotel, Darjeeling, India, to her father, John H. Oglander', 6 March 1910, Isle of Wight Record Office: OG/CC/230, by kind permission of the Isle of Wight Records Office.

Quotation from 'The Negro Speaks of Rivers' by Langston Hughes from Langston Hughes, *The Collected Works of Langston Hughes: The Poems, 1921–1940*. Reprinted with permission of David Higham Associates.

Quotation from 'The Mande Creation Myth' by Germaine Dieterlen published in *Africa: Journal of the International African Institute*, reprinted with permission of the International African Institute, School of Oriental and African Studies.

Quotation from *The Epic of Gilgamesh* by Anonymous published by Penguin Classics. Copyright © Andrew George, 1999, 2003, 2020. Reprinted by permission of Penguin Books Limited.

Quotation from 'Qian Chibi fu' ('At Red Cliffs' I), trans. Robert E. Hegel, in Robert E. Hegel, 'The Sights and Sounds of Red Cliffs: On Reading Su Shi' published in *Chinese Literature: Essays, Articles, Reviews (CLEAR)*, reprinted with kind permission of Robert E. Hegel.

Notes

Introduction

1 From Stevie Smith, 'Scorpion' [from *Scorpion and Other Poems*, 1972], reproduced in *Stevie Smith: A Selection*, ed. Hermione Lee (London: Faber and Faber, 1983), 169.
2 Igor A. Shiklomanov, 'World Fresh Water Resources', in Peter H. Gleick (ed.), *Water in Crisis: A Guide to the World's Fresh Water Resources* (New York/Oxford: Oxford University Press, 1993); cited by US Geological Survey, 'How Much Water Is There On Earth?', https://www.usgs.gov/special-topics/water-science-school/science/how-much-water-there-earth [accessed 01.03.25].
3 Marc Reisner, *Cadillac Desert: The American West and Its Disappearing Water* (New York: Viking, 1986), 13.
4 Richard White, *The Organic Machine: The Remaking of the Columbia River* (New York: Hill & Wang, 1996); Sara B. Pritchard, *Confluence: The Nature of Technology and the Remaking of the Rhône* (Cambridge, MA: Harvard University Press, 2011).
5 Lorraine Boissoneault, 'The Cuyahoga River Caught Fire at Least a Dozen Times, but No One Cared Until 1969', *Smithsonian Magazine*, 19 June 2019; Harriet Ritvo, *The Dawn of Green: Manchester, Thirlmere, and Modern Environmentalism* (Chicago, IL: University of Chicago Press, 2009); Grace Spiewak, 'Beyond Walden: What Henry David Thoreau Teaches Us About Nature and Connection', Blog, Biodiversity Heritage Library (23 July 2020). https://blog.biodiversitylibrary.org/2020/07/henry-david-thoreau.html [accessed 13.07.24].

Chapter 1: Ancient Ecosystems and the Art of Recycling

1 *The Egyptian Book of the Dead: The Papyrus of Ani in the British Museum*, trans. E.A. Wallis Budge (1895; New York: Dover Publications, 1967), 346.
2 'Amulet/god/hippopotamus' (Late Period), National Museums Scotland, A.1965.331, https://www.nms.ac.uk/explore-our-collections/collection-search-results/?item_id=299584; 'Amulet; figure', British Museum, EA24395, https://www.britishmuseum.org/collection/object/Y_EA24395

[both accessed 22.03.25].

3 'Hippopotamus' (c.1961–1878 BCE), Metropolitan Museum of Art, 17.9.1, https://www.metmuseum.org/art/collection/search/544227 [accessed 22.03.25].

4 Martin Williams, *When the Sahara Was Green: How Our Greatest Desert Came to Be* (Princeton, NJ: Princeton University Press, 2021), 40; Dirk Huyge and Salima Ikram, 'Animal Representations in the Late Palaeolithic Rock Art of Qurta', in *Desert Animals in the Eastern Sahara: Status, Economic Significance and Cultural Reflection in Antiquity: Proceedings of an Interdisciplinary ACACIA Workshop Held at the University of Cologne December 14–15, 2007*, Colloquium Africanum (Köln: Heinrich-Barth-Institut, 2009), 157–74.

5 Toby Wilkinson, 'Introduction', in Toby Wilkinson (ed.), *Writings from Ancient Egypt* (London: Penguin Books, 2016), xv.

6 Robert O. Collins, *The Nile* (New Haven: Yale University Press, 2002), 11.

7 Wilkinson (ed.), *Writings from Ancient Egypt*, 190n.

8 Morris L. Bierbrier, *Historical Dictionary of Ancient Egypt*, 2nd edn (Lanham, MD: The Scarecrow Press, 2008), 164; Elena Mahlich, 'The Appellation of the River Nile in Achaemenid Texts', *Wiener Zeitschrift für Die Kunde Des Morgenlandes* 110 (2020), 230–1.

9 Ian Shaw, *Ancient Egypt: A Very Short Introduction* (Oxford/New York: Oxford University Press, 2004), 7, 11; Riklef Kandeler and Wolfram R. Ullrich, 'Symbolism of Plants: Examples from European-Mediterranean Culture Presented with Biology and History of Art', *Journal of Experimental Botany* 60:9 (2009), 2461; J. Kipkemboi and A. A. van Dam, 'Papyrus Wetlands', in C. Finlayson et al. (eds), *The Wetland Book* (Dordrecht: Springer, 2016), 183–97.

10 Narmer Palette, The Egyptian Museum, https://egyptianmuseumcairo.eg/artefacts/narmer-palette-collection/ [accessed 22.03.25]; Shaw, *Ancient Egypt*, 1-7; 'The Royal Crowns of Egypt', Egypt Exploration Society, Blog (7 March 2019), https://www.ees.ac.uk/resource/the-royal-crowns-of-egypt.html#h_9020790371552571413696 [accessed 22.03.25].

11 Quoted in Commentary, 'Piankhi Stela', in Wilkinson (ed.), *Writings from Ancient Egypt*, 64; Shaw, *Ancient Egypt*, 1–7.

12 'Memphis and its Necropolis – the Pyramid Fields from Giza to Dahshur, Unesco World Heritage Convention', https://whc.unesco.org/en/list/86 [accessed 02.09.21]; George Hart, *The Routledge Dictionary of Egyptian Gods and Goddesses,* 2nd edn (London/New York: Routledge, 2005), 103–9.

13 Translation and discussion in Colleen Manassa, 'Defining Historical Fiction in New Kingdom Egypt', in Sarah C. Melville and Alice Louise

Slotsky (eds), *Opening the Tablet Box: Near Eastern Studies in Honor of Benjamin R. Foster* (Leiden/Boston: Brill, 2010), 247, 249–50; Colleen Manassa, *The Quarrel of Apepi and Seqenenre* (Oxford University Press, 2013), 247–53 (249); Shaw, *Ancient Egypt*, 60; Katja Goebs, 'Kingship', in Toby Wilkinson (ed.), *The Egyptian World* (London: Routledge, 2009), 287.

14 N.B. Millet, 'The Narmer Macehead and Related Objects', *Journal of the American Research Center in Egypt* 27 (1990), 53–9; Judith Bunbury et al., 'The Egyptian Nile: Human Transformation of an Ancient River', in Karl M. Wantzen (ed.), *River Culture: Life as a Dance to the Rhythm of the Waters* (UNESCO, 2023), 57, 69; Goebs, 'Kingship', 287–8; Liam McNamara, 'Ashmolean Object in Focus: The Scorpion Mace-Head', Ashmoleum Museum No. AN1896–1908 E.3632.

15 David Jeffreys, 'The Nile Valley' in Wilkinson (ed.), *Egyptian World*, 7–14; Douglas Brewer, 'Agriculture and Animal Husbandry' in Wilkinson (ed.), *Egyptian World*, 132, 135, 145.

16 John Cooper, '"We Desire to Know Which Is the True Religion": Inter-Communal Rivalry and the Verdict of the Nile in an Episode from the History of the Patriarchs of Alexandria', in Elizabeth R. O'Connell (ed.), *Egypt and Empire: The Formation of Religious Identity after Rome* (Leuven, Belgium: Peeters Publishers, 2022), 111–31; Jeffreys, 'Nile Valley', 11; Mark H. Stone, 'The Cubit: A History and Measurement Commentary', *Journal of Anthropology* (January 2014), 1.

17 William Y. Adams, 'The First Colonial Empire: Egypt in Nubia, 3200–1200 B.C.', *Comparative Studies in Society and History*, 26:1 (1984), 63.

18 Kathlyn M. Cooney, 'Labour', in Wilkinson (ed.), *The Egyptian World*, 162; R.L. Miller, 'Counting Calories in Egyptian Ration Texts', *Journal of the Economic and Social History of the Orient* 34:4 (1991), 267.

19 Cooney, 'Labour', 166–8, 173; Mark Lehner, *The Complete Pyramids* (London: Thames & Hudson, 1997), 224.

20 Dorothea Arnold, 'An Egyptian Bestiary', *The Metropolitan Museum of Art Bulletin* 52:4 (1995), 15, 30, 45, 49, 60.

21 Andrew Robinson, *Writing and Script: A Very Short Introduction* (Oxford: Oxford University Press, 2009), 131.

22 Owen Powell and Rod Fensham, 'The History and Fate of the Nubian Sandstone Aquifer Springs in the Oasis Depressions of the Western Desert, Egypt', *Hydrogeology Journal* 2 (2016), 395–406; Cooney, 'Labour', 164.

23 'Duck Cosmetic Box', The Walters Art Museum, Baltimore MD, Accession no. 71.519, https://art.thewalters.org/object/71.519/ [accessed 02.04.25];

'Apotropaic Knife' (catalogue no. 10), in Rozenn Bailleul-LeSuer (ed.), *Between Heaven and Earth: Birds in Ancient Egypt* (Chicago, IL: Oriental Institute Museum Publications/University of Chicago, 2012), 146.

24 'Donkeys and Mules', UCL Digital Egypt for Universities, University College, London, https://www.ucl.ac.uk/museums-static/digitalegypt/foodproduction/donkey.html [accessed 18.08.24].

25 Carol A. Redmount, 'The Wadi Tumilat and the "Canal of the Pharaohs"', *Journal of Near Eastern Studies* 54:2 (1995), 127–35; Thomas Hikade, 'Expeditions to the Wadi Hammamat during the New Kingdom', *The Journal of Egyptian Archaeology* 92 (2006), 153–68; Morgan E. Moroney, 'The Egyptian Road Most Taken: Mapping the Least Cost Path Routes from the Nile to the Red Sea Coast', in Rita Lucarelli, Joshua A. Roberson and Steve Vinson (eds), *Ancient Egypt, New Technology* (Leiden: Brill, 2023), 298–321.

26 John C. Darnell, 'The Deserts', in Wilkinson (ed), *The Egyptian World*, 38; Cooney, 'Labour', 166–7; Shaw, *Ancient Egypt*, 44–5.

27 Penelope Wilson, 'The Nile Delta', in Wilkinson (ed.), *Egyptian World*, 19; A.J. Shortland, 'Evaporites of the Wadi Natrun: Seasonal and Annual Variation and Its Implication for Ancient Exploitation', *Archaeometry* 46:4 (2004), 497–516; Carolyn Riccardelli, 'Egyptian Faience: Technology and Production', The Metropolitan Museum of Art (1 December 2017), https://www.metmuseum.org/toah/hd/egfc/hd_egfc.htm [accessed 22.03.25]; Scarab, British Museum, EA66503, https://www.britishmuseum.org/collection/object/Y_EA66503; Aurélia Masson, *Scarabs, Scaraboids and Amulets* (British Museum, 2018), in Alexandra Villing et al., 'Naukratis: Greeks in Egypt Project', British Museum (2004–2024), https://www.britishmuseum.org/research/projects/naukratis-greeks-egypt [accessed 22.03.24]; 'Victual Mummy and Case' (Catalogue No. 40), in Bailleul-LeSuer (ed.), *Between Heaven and Earth*, 212–13.

28 Robert J. Stern and Mohamed Gamal Abdelsalam, 'The Origin of the Great Bend of the Nile from SIR-C/X-SAR Imagery', *Science* 274:5293 (6 December 1996), 1696.

29 Adel Kelany et al., 'Granite Quarry Survey in the Aswan Region, Egypt: Shedding New Light on Ancient Quarrying', *Geological Survey of Norway Special Publication*, 12 (n.d.), 94; Gregory Phillip Gilbert, *Ancient Egyptian Sea Power and the Origin of Maritime Forces* (Canberra: Sea Power Centre of Australia, 2008), 28.

30 Gilbert, *Ancient Egyptian Sea Power*, 66–7; J.H. Breasted, *Ancient Records of Egypt, Vol 1* (Chicago: University of Chicago Press, 1906), sections 317, 324, 643–8; Hart, *Routledge Dictionary of Egyptian Gods and Goddesses*, 28, 29, 140, 164–5; Lucia Gahlin, 'Creation Myths', in Wilkinson (ed.),

Egyptian World, 305–6; Stephen Quirke, 'Sehel and Suez: Canal-Cutting and Periodisation in Ancient and Modern History', in *IBAES. Das Ereignis*, X (London: Golden House Publications, 2009), 223–4.

31 'Semna Inscription of Senusret III', in Wilkinson (ed.), *Writings from Ancient Egypt*, 186.

32 Quirke, 'Sehel and Suez', 225.

33 Commentary, 'Obelisk Inscription of Hatshepsut', in Wilkinson (ed.), *Writings from Ancient Egypt*, 191, 196n; Translation in 'Obelisk Inscription of Hatshepsut', in Wilkinson (ed.), *Writings from Ancient Egypt*, 196.

34 Brewer, 'Agriculture and Animal Husbandry', 132; Jeffreys, 'Nile Valley', 12, 21, 28n.

35 Column, British Museum, BM/Big number EA1065; Wilson, 'Nile Delta', Fig. 2.1 (map); Tobias Ullmann et al., 'Preliminary Results on the Paleo-Landscape of Tell Basta / Bubastis (Eastern Nile Delta): An Integrated Approach Combining GIS-Based Spatial Analysis, Geophysical and Archaeological Investigations', *Quaternary International* 511 (2019), 185–99.

36 'Adoption Stela of Nitiqret', in Wilkinson (ed.), *Writings from Ancient Egypt*, 213–17; Ricardo A. Caminos, 'The Nitocris Adoption Stela', *The Journal of Egyptian Archaeology* 50 (964), 71, 81, 97, 99–100; Anthony Leahy, 'The Adoption of Ankhnesneferibre at Karnak', *The Journal of Egyptian Archaeology* 82 (1996), 161–3.

37 Commentary, 'Adoption Stela of Nitiqret', in Wilkinson (ed.), *Writings from Ancient Egypt*, 212.

38 Suzanne Lynn Onstine, *The Role of the Chantress (Šm'yt) in Ancient Egypt* (Oxford: Archaeopress/Hadrian Books, 2005).

39 Commentary, 'Adoption Stela of Nitiqret', in Wilkinson (ed.), *Writings from Ancient Egypt*, 212–13.

40 Timothy Kendall, 'Egypt and Nubia', in Wilkinson (ed.), *The Egyptian World*, 412–13.

41 'Adoption Stela of Nitiqret', in Wilkinson (ed.), *Writings from Ancient Egypt*, 215; Anthony Leahy, 'The Adoption of Ankhnesneferibre at Karnak', *The Journal of Egyptian Archaeology* 82 (1996), 160–2; Nigel Strudwick, *Masterpieces of Ancient Egypt* (London: British Museum Press, 2012), 276.

42 Dodson and Hilton, *Complete Royal Families of Ancient Egypt*, 248–9.

43 Redmount, 'Wadi Tumilat and the "Canal of the Pharaohs"', 135.

44 Herodotus, *The Histories*, trans. Robin Waterfield (1998; Oxford/New York: Oxford University Press, 2008); Shaw, *Ancient Egypt*, 13.

45 Strudwick, *Masterpieces of Ancient Egypt*, 288; Dodson and Hilton, *Complete Royal Families of Ancient Egypt*, 255.

46 Ernst A. Fredricksmeyer, 'Alexander, Zeus Ammon, and the Conquest of Asia', *Transactions of the American Philological Association* 121 (1991), 199–214; Urs Mueller et al., 'Structural Preservation of the Temple of the Oracle in Siwa Oasis, Egypt', *Conservation and Management of Archaeological Sites* 5:4 (2002), 215–17.

47 Sally L.D. Katary, 'Land Tenure and Taxation', in Wilkinson (ed.), *Egyptian World*, 200.

48 Lanny Bell, 'Luxor Temple and the Cult of the Royal Ka', *Journal of Near Eastern Studies* 44:4 (1985), 254–5, 270; Edmund Richardson, 'The World's First Superhero', *BBC History Magazine* (December 2021), 21.

49 Dodson and Hilton, *Complete Royal Families of Ancient Egypt*, 258–81.

50 Shaw, *Ancient Egypt*, 154–7. Cf. Duane W. Roller, *Cleopatra: A Biography* (Oxford: Oxford University Press, 2010), 174; N. Frank Ukadike, 'Reclaiming Images of Women in Films from Africa and the Black Diaspora', *Frontiers: A Journal of Women Studies* 15:1 (1994), 102–22; Joyce Green MacDonald, 'Bodies, Race, and Performance in Derek Walcott's "A Branch of the Blue Nile"', *Theatre Journal* 57:2 (2005), 91–203; Mary Hamer, *Signs of Cleopatra: History, Politics, Representation* (London/New York: Routledge, 1993).

51 Alexander Rubel, 'What the Romans Really Meant When Using the Word "Barbarian". Some Thoughts on "Romans and Barbarians"', in Roxana-Gabriela Curcă et al. (eds), *Rome and Barbaricum* (Oxford: Archaeopress, 2020), 1–21.

52 Martina D'Alton, *The New York Obelisk, or, How Cleopatra's Needle Came to New York and What Happened When It Got Here* (New York: Metropolitan Museum of Art/Abrams, 1993), 1–7; Edward Chaney, 'Roma Britannica and the Cultural Memory of Egypt: Lord Arundel and the Obelisk of Domitian', in D. Marshall, K. Wolfe and S. Russell (eds), *Roma Britannica: Art Patronage and Cultural Exchange in Eighteenth-Century Rome* (London: British School at Rome, 2011), 148; Katharine Hoare, 'Understanding Egyptianizing Obelisks: Appropriation in Early Imperial Rome' (unpublished PhD thesis, University of Southampton, 2017), 64–5.

53 Brian Campbell, *Rivers and the Powers of Ancient Rome* (Chapel Hill, NC: The University of North Carolina Press, 2012), 154; Jeffreys, 'Nile Valley', 11; Zaraza Friedman, 'Nilometer', in Helaine Selin (ed.), *Encyclopaedia of the History of Science, Technology, and Medicine in Non-Western Cultures* (Berlin/Heidelberg/New York: Springer Verlag, 2008), 1753–60.

54 Hoare, 'Understanding Egyptianizing Obelisks', 142–4.

Chapter 2: Regime Change on the River

1 'Nile River Delta at Night', NASA Blog (20 April 2011), https://www.nasa.gov/image-article/nile-river-delta-night/ [accessed 23.12.24].

2 Quoted in Thomas Thornton, *The Present State of Turkey; Or a Description of the Political, Civil, and Religious, Constitution, Government, and Laws of the Ottoman Empire, Volume 1*, 2nd edn (London, 1809), lxxxviii–lxxxix.

3 Petra M. Sijpesteijn, 'The Arab Conquest of Egypt and the Beginning of Muslim Rule', in Roger S. Bagnall (ed.), *Egypt in the Byzantine World, 300–700* (Cambridge: Cambridge University Press, 2007), 439–43; Brewer, 'Agriculture and Animal Husbandry', 135; Hugh Kennedy, *The Caliphate: A Pelican Introduction* (London: Penguin Books, 2016), 12–13, 21.

4 Ahmad Nazmi, 'The Nile River in Muslim Geographical Sources', *Studia Arabistyczne i Islamistyczne* 12 (2004), 28.

5 Okasha N. El Daly, 'Ancient Egypt in Medieval Moslem/Arabic Writing' (unpublished PhD thesis, University College London, 2003), 37–8, 46.

6 James P. Allen, *Middle Egyptian: An Introduction to the Language and Culture of Hieroglyphs*, 2nd edn (Cambridge: Cambridge University Press, 2010), 1, 7; David Frankfurter, *Religion in Roman Egypt* (Princeton University Press, 1998), 248–9.

7 John D. Ray, *The Rosetta Stone and the Rebirth of Ancient Egypt* (Cambridge, MA: Harvard University Press, 2007), 164–70; British Museum, Rosetta Stone, donated by George III, 1802, Big Number EA24, https://www.britishmuseum.org/collection/object/Y_EA24 [accessed 02.03.25].

8 Jitse H.F. Dijkstra, 'Religious Violence in Late Antique Egypt', in Cäcilia Fluck, Gisela Helmecke and Elisabeth R. O'Connell (eds), *Egypt: Faith after the Pharaohs*, Exhibition 'One God: Abraham's Legacy on the Nile' (London: British Museum Press, 2015), 81.

9 Translated in Richard Parkinson, *Cracking Codes: The Rosetta Stone and Decipherment* (Berkeley: University of California Press, 1999), 178; Wilkinson (ed.), *Writings in Ancient Egypt*, xv; Frankfurter, *Religion in Roman Egypt*, 248–9.

10 Susan H. Auth, 'Birds in Late Antique Egypt', in Bailleul-Lesuer (ed.), *Between Heaven and Earth: Birds in Ancient Egypt*, 77; Cäcilia Fluck and Gisela Helmecke, 'Burial Practice', in Fluck, Helmecke and O'Connell (eds), *Egypt: Faith after the Pharaohs*, 235.

11 Daniel Hillel, *The Natural History of the Bible: An Environmental Exploration of the Hebrew Scriptures* (New York: Columbia University Press, 2006), 88; Mahlich, 'Appellation of the River Nile in Achaemenid Texts'; Judith Bunbury et al., 'The Egyptian Nile: Human Transformation of an Ancient River', in Karl M. Wantzen (ed.), *River Culture: Life as a Dance to*

the Rhythm of the Waters (UNESCO, 2023), 61.

12 A. Rosalie David, *The Experience of Ancient Egypt* (London/New York: Routledge, 2000), 59.

13 Peter Sheehan, 'Cairo', in Fluck, Helmecke and O'Connell (eds), *Egypt: Faith after the Pharaohs*, 142, 144–5; Sijpesteijn, 'Arab Conquest of Egypt', 448.

14 El Daly, 'Ancient Egypt in Medieval Moslem/Arabic Writing', 122; Sheehan, 'Cairo', 142, 144; Hugh Kennedy, *The Great Arab Conquests* (Philadelphia, PA: Da Capo Press, 2007), 165.

15 Sheehan, 'Cairo', 144, 146, 148; Sijpesteijn, 'Arab Conquest of Egypt', 450, 453.

16 Gillian Clark, *Late Antiquity: A Very Short Introduction* (Oxford/New York: Oxford University Press, 2011), 109; Allen, *Middle Egyptian*, 1, 7; Frankfurter, *Religion in Roman Egypt*, 248–9; Sijpesteijn, 'Arab Conquest of Egypt', 449–50.

17 Allen, *Middle Egyptian*, 1; Wilson B. Bishai, 'Coptic Lexical Influence on Egyptian Arabic', *Journal of Near Eastern Studies* 23:1 (1964), 39–47.

18 Sijpesteijn, 'Arab Conquest of Egypt', 447–8; Redmount, 'Wadi Tumilat and the "Canal of the Pharaohs"', 127–35; Henry P. Colburn, 'King Darius' Red Sea Canal', *Fezana Journal* (2021), 30.

19 Friedman, 'Nilometer', 13; Mary Kupelian, 'Festivals', in Fluck, Helmecke and O'Connell (eds), *Egypt: Faith after the Pharaohs*, 185; William Popper, *The Cairo Nilometer: Studies in Ibn Taghri Birdi's Chronicles of Egypt: I* (Berkeley, CA: University of California Press, 1951), 57–8; Bahrom Abdukhalimov, 'Aḥmad Al-Farghānī and his "Compendium of Astronomy"', *Journal of Islamic Studies* 10:2 (1999), 144–6.

20 Interior of the Nilometer, Island of Roda, Cairo (c. 1800), V&A Museum, Accession No. SD.645.

21 Kupelian, 'Festivals', 182–7; 'Muharram 2025: Sacred Month of Allah', https://www.islamic-relief.org.uk/resources/islamic-calendar/muharram/ [accessed 23.12.24].

22 Kupelian, 'Festivals', 182–7; Cooper, '"We Desire to Know Which Is the True Religion"'; Popper, *Cairo Nilometer*, 14–15; Delia Cortese, 'The Nile: Its Role in the Fortunes and Misfortunes of the Fatimid Dynasty During its Rule of Egypt (969–1171)', *History Compass* 13 (2015), 23.

23 Kupelian, 'Festivals', 185–6.

24 Kupelian, 'Festivals', 187, 266n.

25 Sijpesteijn, 'Arab Conquest of Egypt', 443.

26 'Heliopolis: The City of the Sun Reemerges', Heliopolis Project, *Nile Magazine* (August/September 2017), 17; Peter Sheehan, 'Cairo', 149.

27 Elisabeth R. O'Connell, 'Living with the Monumental Past', in Fluck,

Helmecke and O'Connell (eds), *Egypt: Faith after the Pharaohs*, 96–7.

28 Simon Sebag Montefiore, *Jerusalem: The Biography* (London: Weidenfeld & Nicolson, 2011), 214–15, 639 (map).

29 Peter Frankopan, *The Silk Roads: A New History of the World* (London/New York: Bloomsbury, 2016), 125; Thierry Bianquis, 'Autonomous Egypt from Ibn Tūlūn to Kāfūr, 868–969', in Carl F. Petry (ed.), *The Cambridge History of Egypt. Vol. 1: Islamic Egypt, 640–1517* (Cambridge: Cambridge University Press, 1998), 107, 110–11.

30 Cortese, 'Nile: Its Role in the Fortunes and Misfortunes of the Fatimid Dynasty', 20, 22, 24; Yusuf Umrethwala, 'Doing History from Below Using Geniza Documents as Evidence: A Famine in Question – the Shidda 'Uzma (c. 1062–1073)', Camedieva Blog (27 February 2023).

31 Jason Goodwin, *Lords of the Horizons: A History of the Ottoman Empire* (London: Vintage, 1999), 79–80, 86–7.

32 Alan Mikhail, 'Unleashing the Beast: Animals, Energy, and the Economy of Labor in Ottoman Egypt', *The American Historical Review* 118:2 (2013), 331–6.

33 'Stela', The Rosetta Stone, British Museum No. EA24, Curator's Note, https://www.britishmuseum.org/collection/object/Y_EA24 [accessed 23.03.25]; Andrew Middleton and Dietrich Klemm, 'The Geology of the Rosetta Stone', *The Journal of Egyptian Archaeology* 89:1 (2003), 207–16.

34 Khaled Fahmy, 'The Nation and its Deserters: Conscription in Mehmed Ali's Egypt', *International Review of Social History* 43:3 (1998), 421.

35 Quoted in Augustin Daniel Belliard, Pierre Francois Xavier Boyer and Georges Douin, *Une mission militaire française auprès de Mohamed Aly: Correspondance des généraux Belliard et Boyer* (Au Caire: Imprimerie de l'Institut français d'archéologie orientale pour la Société royale de géographie d'Egypte, 1923), 49–50. Translation by Joseph Dobbyn.

36 Mikhail, 'Unleashing the Beast', 344.

37 Mikhail, 'Unleashing the Beast', 344–6; Laura Panza and Jeffrey G. Williamson, 'Did Muhammad Ali Foster Industrialization in Early Nineteenth-Century Egypt?', *The Economic History Review* 68:1 (2015), 79–100.

38 Translated in Afaf Lutfi al-Sayyid Marsot, *Egypt in the Reign of Muhammad Ali* (Cambridge: Cambridge University Press, 1984), 151; quoted in Mikhail, 'Unleashing the Beast', 345.

39 Nathan J. Brown, 'Who Abolished Corvee Labour in Egypt and Why?', *Past & Present* 144 (1994), 116–37; 'Egypt – The Suez Canal – The Fresh Water Supply', House of Commons Debates (HC Deb), 22 June 1882, Hansard, vol. 271, cc. 43–66, https://api.parliament.uk/historic-hansard/commons/1882/jun/22/egypt-the-suez-canal-the-fresh-water [accessed 28.12.24].

40 Mary Christina Wilson, *King Abdullah, Britain and the Making of Jordan* (Cambridge: Cambridge University Press, 1990), 8; Arnold Wilson, 'The Suez Canal', *International Affairs (Royal Institute of International Affairs 1931–1939)* 18:3 (1939), 383.

41 Afaf Lutfi Al-Sayyid-Marsot, 'The British Occupation of Egypt from 1882', in Andrew N. Porter (ed.), *The Oxford History of the British Empire: Vol. III. The Nineteenth Century* (Oxford: Oxford University Press, 2009), 653–4.

42 C. Cookson-Hills, 'The Aswan Dam and Egyptian Water Control Policy, 1882–1902', *Radical History Review* 2013, 116 (2013), 59–85; James Beattie and Ruth Morgan, 'Engineering Edens on this "Rivered Earth"? A Review Article on Water Management and Hydro-Resilience in the British Empire, 1860–1940s', *Environment and History* 23:1 (2017), 46–7; Samuel Grinsell, 'Mastering the Nile? Confidence and Anxiety in D.S. George's Photographs of the First Aswan Dam, 1899–1912', *Environmental History*, 25:1 (2020), 110–33.

43 'The Great Dam at Assouan', *Illustrated London News* (13 April 1901), 6.

44 Karl Baedeker, *Egypt: Handbook for Travellers* (1908) [Electronic Version], 365–6; Captain H.G. Lyons, 'The Nile', xlvi–xlvii; 'Philae and the Assuan Dam: Total Submersion not Injurious?', *Illustrated London News* (22 June 1929), 11.

45 Friedman, 'Nilometer', 1759.

46 Frederick Eckstein, 'Cotton Growing in the Sudan', *Illustrated London News* (22 February 1930), 38.

47 Quoted in Barry Rubin, 'America and the Egyptian Revolution, 1950–1957', *Political Science Quarterly* 971 (1982), 79; Silvia Borzutzky and David Berger, 'Dammed if You Do, Dammed if You Don't: The Eisenhower Administration and the Aswan Dam', *The Middle East Journal* 64:1 (2010), 84–102; Timothy Mitchell, *Rule of Experts: Egypt, Techno-Politics, Modernity* (Berkeley: University of California Press, 2002), 43; Amy L.S. Staples, 'Seeing Diplomacy through Banker's Eyes: The World Bank, the Anglo-Iranian Oil Crisis, and the Aswan High Dam', *Diplomatic History* 26:3 (2002), 414–15.

48 'Why Was the Suez Crisis so Important?', Imperial War Museum, https://www.iwm.org.uk/history/why-was-the-suez-crisis-so-important [accessed 02.03.25].

49 Kate B Showers, 'Electrifying Africa: An Environmental History with Policy Implications', *Geografiska Annaler. Series B, Human Geography* 93:3 (2011), 200.

50 A.C. Hill, '"The Battle for Abu Simbel": Archaeology and Postcolonial Diplomacy in the UNESCO Campaign for Nubia', *Journal of Contemporary History* 56:3 (2021), 502–21.

51 Amadou-Mahtar M'Bow, 'A Single, Universal Heritage', *The Unesco Courier*, XXXIII, 2/3 (1980), 4.
52 Farah El-Akkad, '2 Years After Displacement, Scars of Loss Remain for Nubians', *Egypt Today* (25 October 2016).
53 Alan Mikhail, *The Animal in Ottoman Egypt* (Oxford/New York: Oxford University Press, 2014), 168–71; Sherif Baha el-Din, 'The Avifauna of the Egyptian Nile Valley: Changing Times', in Bailleul-LeSuer (ed.), *Between Heaven and Earth*, 125; 'Sacred Ibis', Animal Biodiversity Web, Museum of Zoology, University of Michigan, https://animaldiversity.org/accounts/Threskiornis_aethiopicus/ [accessed 17.08.24].
54 Baha el-Din, 'Avifauna', 126–7.
55 Baha el-Din, 'Avifauna', 126; Lake Nasser, Egypt. NASA Earth Observatory, https://earthobservatory.nasa.gov/images/5988/lake-nasser-egypt; 'Little Bittern', Bulgarian Society for the Protection of Birds, https://atlas.bspb.org/en/species/little-bittern/ [both accessed 17.08.24].
56 Mahmoud M. El Banna and Omran E. Frihy, 'Human-Induced Changes in the Geomorphology of the Northeastern Coast of the Nile Delta, Egypt', *Coastal Vulnerability Related to Sea-Level Rise*, 107:1 (2009), 73.

Chapter 3: Source

1 Tseqaye Gabre-Medhin, 'Nile', in Chris Beckett and Alemu Tebeje (eds), *Songs We Learn from Trees: An Anthology of Ethiopian Amharic Poetry* (Manchester: Carcanet Classics, 2020), 71–3, 278. Written in English.
2 Translations by Robin Waterfield in Herodotus, *Histories*, 2:22, 2:28; 2:34.
3 Al-Biruni paraphrased in Nazmi, 'The Nile River in Muslim Geographical Sources', 35–6.
4 John Sutcliffe and Emma Brown, 'Water Losses from the Sudd', *Hydrological Sciences Journal* 63:4 (2018), 527.
5 Sudd Wetland, South Sudan, UNESCO Tentative List, https://whc.unesco.org/en/tentativelists/6276/ [accessed 04.03.25]; Sutcliffe and Brown, 'Water Losses from the Sudd', 527.
6 Matthew P. McCartney et al., *Evaluation of Current and Future Water Resources Development in the Lake Tana Basin, Ethiopia* (Colombo: IWMI, 2010), 2–3, 18; Collins, *Nile*, 92; Hanibal Lemma et al., 'Bedload Transport Measurements in the Gilgel Abay River, Lake Tana Basin, Ethiopia', *Journal of Hydrology* 577 (2019), 3.
7 S. Uhlenbrook, Y. Mohamed and A.S. Gragne, 'Analyzing Catchment Behavior through Catchment Modeling in the Gilgel Abay, Upper Blue Nile River Basin, Ethiopia', *Hydrology and Earth System Sciences* 14:10 (2010), 2153; Collins, *Nile*, 3; Brewer, 'Agriculture and Animal Husbandry', 132.

8 L. Kirwan, 'Rome beyond the Southern Egyptian Frontier', *The Geographical Journal* 123:1 (1957), 16–17.

9 Richard Pankhurst, *The Ethiopians: A History* (Oxford/Malden, MA: Blackwell Publishers, 2001), 76–7; Peter Russell, *Prince Henry 'the Navigator': A Life* (New Haven, CT: Yale University Press, 2000), 239–41, 263; J. Devisse and S. Labib, 'Africa in Inter-Continental Relations', in D.T. Niane (ed.), *General History of Africa: Africa from the Twelfth to the Sixteenth Century, Vol. IV* (London/Berkeley, CA: UNESCO/Heinemann/University of California: 1984), 638, 664, 667–8; Víctor M. Fernández, 'Enlivening the Dying Ruins: History and Archaeology of the Jesuit Missions in Ethiopia, 1557–1632', *Culture & History Digital Journal* 2:2 (2013), 2; T. Oestigaard and A.F. Gedef, 'Gish Abay: The Source of the Blue Nile', 'Water and Society' Conference 2011, *WIT Transactions on Ecology and the Environment* 153 (2011), 28.

10 Adrian S. Wisnicki, 'Cartographical Quandaries: The Limits of Knowledge Production in Burton's and Speke's Search for the Source of the Nile', *History in Africa* 35 (2008), 455–79.

11 C.T. Beke, *Letters on the Commerce of Abessinia and Other Parts of Eastern Africa, etc.* (London, 1852), 51ff; Pankhurst, *Ethiopians*, 71–2; Nazmi, 'Nile River in Muslim Geographical Sources', 48; James McCann, 'Ethiopia, Britain, and Negotiations for the Lake Tana Dam, 1922–1935', *The International Journal of African Historical Studies* 14:4 (1981), 669–70.

12 Beke, *Letters on the Commerce of Abessinia.*

13 Michael Coogan, *The Old Testament: A Very Short Introduction* (Oxford/New York: Oxford University Press, 2008), 125; Etienne Charpentier, *How to Read the Old Testament* (New York: Crossroad, 1982), 18–20.

14 Genesis 2:10–15, *The New English Bible* (Oxford/Cambridge: Cambridge/Oxford University Presses, 1970); Yehuda T. Radday, 'The Four Rivers of Paradise', *Hebrew Studies* 23 (1982), 26; Alessandro Scafi, *Maps of Paradise* (Chicago, IL/London: The University of Chicago Press, 2013), 41.

15 The Sawley Map, England (c.1190 CE), Metropolitan Museum of Art, Blog, https://blog.metmuseum.org/penandparchment/exhibition-images/cat300r2_49e/ [accessed 04.03.25]; Scafi, *Maps of Paradise*, 91–2; Jean-Pierre Isbouts, 'Adam and Eve in Paradise', *National Geographic, Atlas of the Bible: Exploring the Holy Lands*, (2018) 13; Pankhurst, *Ethiopians*, 18.

16 Translated in Stephen N. Lambden, 'Sidra X Ibn Ḥajar al-Asqalānī (d. 853 /1449) on the Sidrat al-Muntahā', Hurgalya Publications: Centre for Shaykhī and Bābī-Bahā'ī Studies, UC Merced (last posted 9 September 2009), https://hurqalya.ucmerced.edu/node/62 [accessed 30.12.24].

17 *Marco Polo: The Travels*, trans. and ed. Nigel Cliff (London: Penguin Random House, 2016), 20, 366–7n.

18 'St. Frumentius', in Frank L. Cross and Elizabeth A. Livingstone (eds), *The Oxford Dictionary of the Christian Church* (Oxford: Oxford University Press, 2005); 'Ethiopic Versions of the Bible', in Cross and Livingstone (eds), *Oxford Dictionary of the Christian Church*; Toyin Falola, *Key Events in African History: A Reference Guide* (Westport, CT: Greenwood Publishing Group, 2002), 58–61, 68; Pankhurst, *Ethiopians*, 37.

19 Stuart Munro-Hay, 'The Rise and Fall of Aksum: Chronological Considerations', *Journal of Ethiopian Studies* 23 (1990), 47–53; Getachew Assefa, 'The Constitutional Right to Self-Determination as a Response to the "Question of Nationalities" in Ethiopia', *International Journal on Minority and Group Rights*, 25:1 (2018), 4-5.

20 Charles Poncet, *A Voyage to Aethiopia made in the Year 1698, 1699 and 1700* (1709), translated in William Foster (ed.), *The Red Sea and Adjacent Countries at the Close of the Seventeenth Century* (London: Hakluyt Society, 1949), 127; Douglas Merrey and Tadele Gebreselassie, *Promoting Improved Rainwater and Land Management in the Blue Nile (Abay) Basin of Ethiopia*, Nile BDC Technical Report – 1 (CGIAR Challenge Program on Water & Food, 2011), 31–2, 34.

21 Falola, *Key Events in African History*, 73–4; Pankhurst, *Ethiopians*, 19; Assefa, 'Constitutional Right to Self-Determination', 5–6.

22 Pankhurst, *Ethiopians*, 103, 104, 112; Fernández, 'Enlivening the Dying Ruins', 5, 7, 9, 11, 15.

23 Andreu Martinez D'alos-Mone, 'In the Company of Iyäsus: The Jesuit Mission in Ethiopia, 1557–1632' (unpublished PhD thesis, European University Institute, 2009), 222–3; Fernández, 'Enlivening the Dying Ruins', 5, 7; Pankhurst, *Ethiopians*, 103–4.

24 Joseph Ellis Duncan, *Milton's Earthly Paradise: A Historical Study of Eden* (Minneapolis, MN: University of Minnesota Press, 1972), 196; Pankhurst, *Ethiopians*, 48–9.

25 Collins, *The Nile*, 90; Simon Schama, *Landscape & Memory* (London: Fontana Press, 1998), 293, 300; Peter A. Coates, *A Story of Six Rivers: History, Culture and Ecology* (London: Reaktion Books, 2013), 9.

26 [Jerónimo Lobo], *A Voyage to Abyssinia by Father Jeronimo Lobo. Translated from the French by Samuel Johnson* (London, 1789), 135; Oestigaard and Gedef, 'Gish Abay', 28–9.

27 T.H.M. Rientjes et al., 'Changes in Land Cover, Rainfall and Stream Flow in Upper Gilgel Abbay Catchment, Blue Nile Basin – Ethiopia', *Hydrology and Earth System Sciences* 15:6 (2011), 1980; McCartney et al., *Evaluation of Current and Future Water Resources*, 2; Uhlenbrook, Mohamed and Gragne, 'Analyzing Catchment Behavior', 2153–4; A.T. Haile et al., 'Rainfall Variability over Mountainous and Adjacent Lake Areas: The

Case of Lake Tana Basin at the Source of the Blue Nile River', *Journal of Applied Meteorology and Climatology* 48 (2009), 1697.

28 Oestigaard and Gedef, 'Gish Abay', 33–4; Collins, *Nile*, 91–2.

29 C.F. Beckingham, 'Urreta and the Nine Saints of Ethiopia', in Ian Netton (ed.), *Studies in Honour of Clifford Edmund Bosworth, Volume I* (Leiden: Brill, 2000), 161–2.

30 John Milton, *Paradise Lost*, ed. Scott Elledge (1674; New York: Norton, 1975); Duncan, *Milton's Earthly Paradise*, 196–7; Evert Mordecai Clark, 'Milton's Abyssinian Paradise', *The University of Texas Studies in English* 29 (1950), 138–40, 142.

31 Milton, *Paradise Lost*, Book IV, lines 280–5.

32 Times Correspondent (Istanbul), 'Orthodox Patriarch Solemnly Ends Excommunication', *The Times* (8 December 1965), 11.

33 Pankhurst, *Ethiopians*, 106–7.

34 Niall Finneran, 'Holy Waters: Pre-Christian and Christian Water Association in Ethiopia; An Archaeological Landscape Perspective', in Terje Ostigard (ed.), *Water, Culture and Identity in the Nile Basin* (Bergen: BRIC Press, 2009), 178; Terje Oestigaard, *The Religious Nile: Water, Ritual and Society since Ancient Egypt* (London: I.B. Tauris, 2018), 76–81, 455; Dorothea McEwan, *The Story of Däräsge Maryam: The History, Buildings and Treasures of a Church Compound with a Painted Church in the Semen Mountains* (Zürich: LIT, 2013), 54–7.

35 Kupelian, 'Festivals', 185; 'Baptize', v., Etymology, in *Oxford English Dictionary* [*OED*].

36 Poncet, translated in Foster (ed.), *Red Sea and Adjacent Countries*, 129–30; Pankhurst, *Ethiopians*, 112n.

37 Pankhurst, *Ethiopians*, 147; McEwan, *Story of Däräsge Maryam*, 56.

38 Aläqa Täklä Iyäsus WaqĞera, *The Goğğam Chronicle*, trans. and ed. Girma Getahun (Oxford: British Academy/Oxford University Press, 2014), Chapter XXIX, nos. 14–15, Chapter XXX, no. 20.

39 Maqdala Collection, British Museum, https://www.britishmuseum.org/about-us/british-museum-story/contested-objects-collection/maqdala-collection [accessed 17.02.25].

40 Elizabeth Blunt, 'Ethiopia Seeks Prince's Remains', BBC News (3 June 2007), http://news.bbc.co.uk/1/hi/world/africa/6716921.stm; Maqdala Collection, British Museum; 'UK's National Army Museum to Hand Over Locks of Hair Belonging to Emperor Tewodros II of Ethiopia', Press Release, National Army Museum, https://www.nam.ac.uk/press/uks-national-army-museum-hand-over-locks-hair-belonging-emperor-tewodros-ii-ethiopia; 'Ethiopia unveils ancient obelisk', BBC News (4 September 2008), http://news.bbc.co.uk/1/hi/world/africa/7597589.

stm; Richard Pankhurst, 'An Ethiopian Hero: Tsegaye Gabre-Medhin (1936–2006)', openDemocracy (10 September 2007), https://www.opendemocracy.net/en/ethiopia_hero_3347jsp/ [all accessed 04.03.2025]; Walter Benjamin, 'The Work of Art in the Age of Mechanical Reproduction' (1935), in Hannah Arendt (ed.), *Illuminations*, trans. Harry Zohn (New York: Schocken Books, 1969), 5.

41 Pankhurst, *Ethiopians*, 1–6;. C. Gosden, *Prehistory: A Very Short Introduction*, 2nd edn (Oxford: Oxford University Press, 2018), 26–8; 'Ardipithecus ramidus', Smithsonian National Museum of Natural History, https://humanorigins.si.edu/evidence/human-fossils/species/ardipithecus-ramidus [accessed 31.12.24].

42 Gabre-Medhin, 'Nile', 71–2.

43 A.T. Zhang and V.X. Gu, 'Global Dam Tracker: A Database of More than 35,000 Dams with Location, Catchment, and Attribute Information', *Scientific Data* 10:111 (2023).

44 Cheesman, 'Lake Tana and Its Islands', 496–7; Hurst, Black and Simaika, *Nile Basin*, 6–7; McCartney et al., *Evaluation of Current and Future Water Resources Development*, 2–4.

45 Amit Ranjan, 'The Grand Ethiopian Renaissance Dam and its Discontents', LSE Blogs (28 February 2024), https://blogs.lse.ac.uk/africaatlse/2024/02/28/the-grand-ethiopian-renaissance-dam-and-its-discontents/; 'Egypt: Progress on achieving SDG 6', UN Department of Economic and Social Affairs: Sustainable Development, https://sdgs.un.org/basic-page/egypt-34124 [both accessed 04.03.25].

46 'The Sennar Dam and the Gezira Irrigation Scheme', *The Engineer* (26 September 1924), 349–50; 'Lake Tana Dam Scheme', *The Times* (14 January 1933), 9; Cheesman, 'Lake Tana and Its Islands', 489–502; R.E. Cheesman, 'The Upper Waters of the Blue Nile', *The Geographical Journal* 71:4 (1928), 358–74; R.E. Cheesman, 'Monasteries of Lake Tana', *The Times* (10 September 1934), 13; McCann, 'Ethiopia, Britain, and Negotiations'; Oestigaard and Gedef, 'Gish Abay', 31.

47 Sir William Willcocks, *From the Garden of Eden to the Crossing of the Jordan* (London: E. &. F.N. Spon, 1920), 13; Beattie and Morgan, 'Engineering Edens'.

48 Richard Bangs and Pasquale Scaturro, *Mystery of the Nile: The Epic Story of the First Descent of the World's Deadliest River* (New York: G.P. Putnam's Sons, 2005), 58–9; Collins, *Nile*, 88–92.

49 Fernández, 'Enlivening the Dying Ruins', 10.

50 Mariz Tadros, 'The Grand Egyptian Festival: Religion, Heritage and Social Cohesion', Coalition for Religious Equality and Inclusive Development (22 January 2021), https://creid.ac/blog/2021/01/22/

the-grand-egyptian-festival-religion-heritage-and-social-cohesion/; Michael Girgis, 'Epiphany: Down Memory Lane', *Watani International* (19 January 2020), https://en.wataninet.com/coptic-affairs-coptic-affairs/coptic-affairs/epiphany-down-memory-lane/31702/ [both accessed 04.03.25].

Chapter 4: Corridors and Frontiers

1 Cornelius Tacitus, 'A Treatise on the Situation, Manners, and Inhabitants of Germany', in *The Works of Tacitus: Vol. II. The Oxford Translation, Revised* (New York, 1890), 286.

2 Coates, *Story of Six Rivers*, 38–44; [Danube] River Basin, International Commission for the Protection of the Danube River (ICPDR), https://www.icpdr.org/danube-basin/danube-river-basin [accessed 16.02.25].

3 Barry Cunliffe, *Europe between the Oceans: 900 BC–AD 1000* (New Haven, CT/London: Yale University Press, 2008), 80–2; Nenad B. Miloradović, 'Lepenski Vir – The Prehistoric Energy Efficient Architecture', *REHVA Journal* 53:5 (2016), 54–9.

4 Cunliffe, *Europe between the Oceans*, vii; Felipe Fernández-Armesto, *Pathfinders: A Global History of Exploration* (Oxford: Oxford University Press, 2006), 121.

5 Cunliffe, *Europe between the Oceans*, 31–61; Eric Jones, *The European Miracle: Environments, Economies and Geopolitics in the History of Europe and Asia* (Cambridge: Cambridge University Press, 1981; 1987), 90; cf. Mark Mazower, *The Balkans: From the End of Byzantium to the Present Day* (London: Weidenfeld & Nicolson, 2000), 21–2.

6 Cunliffe, *Europe between the Oceans*, 24, 38–47.

7 Marko Serban, 'Trajan's Bridge over the Danube', *International Journal of Nautical Archaeology* 38:2 (2009), 332.

8 ICPDR, 'Danube Basin: Facts and Figures' (c. 2009), 5, https://www.icpdr.org/sites/default/files/nodes/documents/icpdr_facts_figures.pdf [accessed 25.03.25].

9 Stephen Oppenheimer, *The Origins of the British: The New Prehistory of Britain* (London: Robinson, 2007), 250; Peter Ackroyd, *Thames: Sacred River* (London: Vintage Books, 2008), 23–4.

10 J.P. Mallory and Douglas Q. Adams, *The Oxford Introduction to Proto-Indo-European and the Proto-Indo-European World* (Oxford: Oxford University Press, 2006), 6–38, 126–7, 434, 443, 447, 460–3; Terry Hoad, 'Preliminaries: Before English', in Lynda Mugglestone (ed.), *The Oxford History of English* (Oxford: Oxford University Press, 2012), Fig. 1.2.

11 Mallory and Adams, *Oxford Introduction to Proto-Indo-European*, 5.

12 Mallory and Adams, *Oxford Introduction to Proto-Indo-European*, 127, 134, 137; Duncan J. Halley, Alexander P. Saveljev and Frank Rosell, 'Population and Distribution of Beavers *Castor Fiber* and *Castor Canadensis* in Eurasia', *Mammal Review* 51:1 (2021), 1–24.

13 Mallory and Adams, *Oxford Introduction to Proto-Indo-European*, 108.

14 Emma Dench, 'Barbarian', *Oxford Classical Dictionary*; Walter Goffart, 'Rome, Constantinople, and the Barbarians', *The American Historical Review*, 86:2 (1981), 277; Campbell, *Rivers and the Powers of Ancient Rome*, 372; translation from 'VI. Panegyric of Constantine' (310), in C.E.V. Nixon and B.S. Rodgers, *In Praise of Later Roman Emperors: The Panegyrici Latini* (Berkeley/Los Angeles, CA: University of California Press, 1994), 236.

15 Christopher Kelly, *The Roman Empire: A Very Short Introduction* (Oxford/New York: Oxford University Press, 2006), 4–6.

16 Kelly, *Roman Empire*, 7–9; John Frederick Drinkwater, 'Raetia', *Oxford Classical Dictionary*; Max Cary and John Wilkes, 'Moesia', *Oxford Classical Dictionary*; Cunliffe, *Europe between the Oceans*, 380, 387.

17 Drinkwater, 'Agri Decumates', *Oxford Classical Dictionary*.

18 'XI. Genethliacus of Maximian Augustus' [c.291 CE], translated in Nixon and Rodgers, *In Praise of Later Roman Emperors*, 91.

19 *Hesiod: Theogeny, Works and Days, Testimonia*, trans. and ed. Glenn W. Most (Cambridge, MA: Harvard University Press, 2018), 31, 339; Max Cary, 'Ister', *Oxford Classical Dictionary*; Ken Dowden, 'Titan', *Oxford Classical Dictionary*; John Wilkes, 'Danuvius', *Oxford Classical Dictionary*; Anna Perdibon, *Mountains and Trees, Rivers and Springs: Animistic Beliefs and Practices in Ancient Mesopotamian Religion* (Wiesbaden: Harrassowitz Verlag, 2019), 86–133.

20 Marguerite Johnson, 'Guide to the Classics: Ovid's *Metamorphoses* and Reading Rape', The Conversation (13 September 2016), https://theconversation.com/guide-to-the-classics-ovids-metamorphoses-and-reading-rape-65316 [accessed 24.10.20]; *Ovid Metamorphoses*, trans. Ian Johnston (Vancouver Island University, 2011), Books 2, 5, 6, https://johnstoniatexts.x10host.com/ovid/ovidtofc.html [accessed 01.03.25].

21 Campbell, *Rivers and the Powers of Ancient Rome*, 154, 373.

22 Tacitus, *Agricola* and *Germania*, trans. Harold B. Mattingly, revised by J.B. Rives (London: Penguin Books, 2010), 56, 109n; D.W.R. Ridgway, 'Amber', *Oxford Classical Dictionary*; Marinella Pasquinucci, 'How Many Roads, Rivers and Seas? Amber from the Coast of North Europe to the Roman World', in P.L. Cellarosi et al. (eds), *The Amber Roads: The Ancient Cultural and Commercial Communication between the Peoples. Proceedings of the 1st International Conference on Ancient Roads, Republic*

of San Marino, April 3–4, 2014. Millenni Studi Di Archeologia Preistorica 1 (CNR Edizioni, 2016), 401, 405–6.

23 'Territorial Expansion of Rome', William R. Shepherd, *Historical Atlas 1911*, 9th edn (New York: Barnes & Noble, 1976), 34–5.

24 Ioan Cohut and Miklós Árpási, 'Ancient Uses of Geothermal Waters in the Precarpathian Area of Romania and the Pannonian Basin of Hungary', in Raffaele Cataldi, Susan F. Hodgson and John W. Lund (eds), *Stories from a Heated Earth: Our Geothermal Heritage* (Sacramento, CA: Geothermal Resources Council/International Geothermal Association, 1999), 243; Campbell, *Rivers and the Power of Ancient Rome*, 393; Branka Migotti, 'The Population of Aquae Balissae (Pannonia Superior)', *Studia Antiqua et Archaeologica* 23:1 (2017), 83–124, 246–7; Franz A.W. Schehl and John Wilkes, 'Aquincum', *Oxford Classical Dictionary.*

25 Campbell, *Rivers and the Power of Ancient Rome*, 139, 346; Simone-Antoinette Deyts, 'The Sacred Source of the Seine', *Scientific American* 225:1 (1971), 65–73; 'Coventinas Well', Historic England Research Records, Hob Uid 1013364, https://www.heritagegateway.org.uk/Gateway/Results_Single.aspx?uid=1013364&sort=4&search=all&criteria=coventina&rational=q&recordsperpage=10&resourceID=19191 [accessed 01.03.25].

26 Franz A. W. Schehl and John Frederick Drinkwater, 'Marcoman(n)I', *Oxford Classical Dictionary.*

27 Campbell, *Rivers and the Powers of Ancient Rome*, 235–9; Tony Rook, *Roman Baths in Britain*, Shire Archaeology Series 69 (Princes Risborough, Bucks: Shire Publications, 2002).

28 ROMAQ, 'The Atlas Project of Roman Aqueducts', https://romaq.org/the-project/map.html [accessed 01.03.25].

29 K. Shterev and I. Zagorchev, 'Mineral Waters and Hydrogeothermal Resources in Bulgaria', *GeoJournal* 40:4 (1996), 403; Agnieszka Tomas, 'Connecting to Public Water: The Rural Landscape and Water Supply in Lower Moesia', *Archaeologia Bulgarica* XV:2 (2011), 1–14.

30 Stephen Chappell, 'Auxiliary Regiments and New Cultural Formation in Imperial Dacia, 106–274 c.e.', *The Classical World* 104:1 (2010), 90.

31 Lynne Lancaster, 'Building Trajan's Column', *American Journal of Archaeology* 103:3 (1999), 419; Serban, 'Trajan's Bridge over the Danube', 332; Campbell, *Rivers and the Powers of Ancient Rome*, 379.

32 John M. O'Shea, 'A River Runs Through It: Landscape and the Evolution of Bronze Age Networks in the Carpathian Basin', *Journal of World Prehistory* 24:2/3 (2011), 166; Chappell, 'Auxiliary Regiments and New Cultural Formation', 90.

33 Chappell, 'Auxiliary Regiments and New Cultural Formation', 90; Mallory and Adams, *Oxford Introduction to Proto-Indo-European*, 36.

34 Cătălin Nicolae Popa, 'The Trowel as Chisel: Shaping Modern Romanian Identity through the Iron Age', in Victoria Ginn, Rebecca Enlander and Rebecca Crozier (eds), *Exploring Prehistoric Identity in Europe: Our Construct or Theirs?* (Oxford/Philadelphia: Oxbow Books, 2014), 166, 168, 170; Imola Boda, 'The Sacred Topography of Colonia Sarmizegetusa', *Acta Archaeologica Academiae Scientiarum Hungaricae* 66:2 (2015), 281–304; Csaba Szabo, 'The Cult of Mithras in Apulum: Communities and Individuals', in Livio Zerbini (ed.), *Culti e religiosità nelle province danubiane: atti del II Convegno internazionale, Ferrara 20–22 novembre 2013*, Pubblicazione del LAD, II (Convegno internazionale 'Roma e le province del Danubio' (Bologna: I libri di Emil, 2015), 407–22.

35 Translation following Petar Petrović (1969) in Lino Rossi, *Trajan's Column and the Dacian Wars* (Ithaca, NY: Cornell University Press, 1971), 32; Serban, 'Trajan's Bridge over the Danube', 332–3; Jaroslav Šašel, 'Trajan's Canal at the Iron Gate', *The Journal of Roman Studies* 63 (1973), 80–5; Coates, *Story of Six Rivers*, 55–7.

36 Ivan Tsurov, 'The Western Aqueduct for Nicopolis Ad Istrum', in Andrew Poulter (ed.), *The Transition to Late Antiquity on the Lower Danube* (Oxford: Oxbow Books, 2019), 199–220; Stephen Mitchell, John Wilkes, Nicholas Purcell and W.M. Murray, 'Nicopolis', *Oxford Classical Dictionary.*

37 Alaric Watson, *Aurelian and the Third Century* (London: Routledge, 1999), 55.

38 Judith Herrin, *Byzantium: The Surprising Life of a Medieval Empire* (London: Penguin Books, 2008), 24; Michael Kulikowski, 'Barbarians in Gaul, Usurpers in Britain', *Britannia* 31 (2000), 326–7; Walter Goffart, *Barbarian Tides: The Migration Age and the Later Roman Empire*, 73–118; Peter Heather, 'Empire and Development: The Fall of the Roman West', *History & Policy* (20 July 2006), https://www.historyandpolicy.org/policy-papers/papers/empire-and-development-the-fall-of-the-roman-west [accessed 09.06.22].

39 Frankopan, *Silk Roads*, 45–6; Michael Kulikowski, *The Tragedy of Empire: From Constantine to the Destruction of Roman Italy* (Cambridge, MA: Belknap Press, 2019).

40 Heather, 'Empire and Development'; Goffart, *Barbarian Tides*; Kulikowski, 'Barbarians in Gaul, Usurpers in Britain', 325–45; Guy Halsall, 'Germani and Germanic Migrations', in Neil Asher Silberman (ed.), *Oxford Companion to Archaeology*, 2nd edn (New York: Oxford University Press, 2012), 606–9.

41 Goffart, 'Rome, Constantinople, and the Barbarians', 287.

42 Herrin, *Byzantium*, 12, 24; Peter Heather, 'Alaric', *Oxford Classical Dictionary.*

43 Drinkwater, 'Gaul, Transalpine', *Oxford Classical Dictionary*; Cf. Kulikowski, 'Barbarians in Gaul, Usurpers in Britain'; Goffart, *Barbarian Tides*, 73–118.
44 Herrin, *Byzantium*, 24.

Chapter 5: Gods of the Transboundary River

1 The First Letter, 1 September 1555, *The Turkish Letters of Ogier Ghiselin de Busbecq, Imperial Ambassador at Constantinople 1554–1562*, trans. Edward Seymour Forster (1927) with a Foreword by Karl A. Roider (1927; Baton Rouge: Louisian State University Press, 2005), 13.
2 'The Danube Iron Gates Canal', *The Scotsman* (29 September 1896), 5; Popa, 'Trowel as Chisel', 166.
3 Dorel Bondoc (Oltenia Museum), 'Paper on Ada Kaleh', Alexis Project Association, Romania. Last modified 24 January 2011, https://web.archive.org/web/20110725000112/http://alexisphoenix.org/adakaleh.php [accessed 25.02.25].
4 'The Danube Iron Gates Canal', *The Scotsman* (29 September 1896), 5; Coates, *Story of Six Rivers*, 53–4; Martyn C. Rady, *The Habsburg Empire: A Very Short Introduction* (Oxford: Oxford University Press, 2017), 94.
5 Quoted in 'The Danube Iron Gates Canal', *The Scotsman* (29 September 1896), 5.
6 'The Danube Iron Gates Canal', *The Scotsman* (29 September 1896), 5; Brehon Somervell, 'Navigation Problems on the Danube', *The Military Engineer* 18:100 (1926), 306–7; Baths of Hercules, see Patrick Leigh Fermor, *Between the Woods and the Water* (Harmondsworth: Penguin, 1986), 210, 214, 241.
7 Richard Cavendish, 'King Alexander and Queen Draga of Serbia Assassinated', *History Today* 53:6 (2003); Mazower, *Balkans*, 102.
8 Rady, *Habsburg Empire*, 98; Lawrence Sondhaus, 'Austria-Hungary: An Inland Empire Looks to the Sea', in Christian Buchet and N.A.M. Rodger (eds), *The Sea in History – The Modern World* (Woodbridge: Boydell & Brewer, 2017), 186; Michael Howard, *The First World War: A Very Short Introduction* (Oxford/New York: Oxford University Press, 2007), Appendix 2.
9 Janet M. Hartley, *The Volga: A History of Russia's Greatest River* (New Haven, CT: Yale University Press, 2021), 5–9.
10 David Kinnersley, *Troubled Water: Rivers, Politics and Pollution* (London: Hilary Shipman Ltd., 1988), 2; 'Rival', n.2 & adj., *OED*.
11 Schama, *Landscape and Memory*, 302; Coates, *Story of Six Rivers*, 7–9; Mary Christian, 'Bernini's "Danube" and Pamphili Politics', *The Burlington Magazine* 128:998 (1986), 354.

12 Rady, *Habsburg Empire*, 2–3, 6–11, 83–4.
13 Gábor Ágoston and Bruce Masters, *Encyclopedia of the Ottoman Empire* (New York: Facts on File, 2010), 174, 613–14.
14 Michael Levey, *The World of Ottoman Art* (London: Thames & Hudson, 1975), 65.
15 Goodwin, *Lords of the Horizons*, 48, 112.
16 Busbecq translated in Goodwin, *Lords of the Horizons*, 84.
17 Goodwin, *Lords of the Horizons*, 86–7.
18 Buda, 1617, *Cities of the World* [Georg Braun and Franz Hogenberg, *Civitates Orbis Terrarum*], ed. Stephan Füssel (Köln: Taschen, 2008), 690–3; Goodman, *Lords of the Horizons*, 203–4.
19 Ágoston and Masters, *Encyclopedia of the Ottoman Empire*, 91–2.
20 *A Pocket Book for Conversation Composed after the Traveller's Companion of Madame de Genlis and Others in Six Languages. Sixth Edition Augmented and Improved* (Leipzig/London, 1833), 28.
21 *Pocket Book for Conversation*, 30, 344, 354, 356.
22 Sondhaus, 'Austria-Hungary: An Inland Empire Looks to the Sea', 180–1; cf. Bernd Kreuzer, 'The Port of Trieste and its Railway Connections in the Habsburg Monarchy: Economic Change and Infrastructure Problems, 1850–1918', *V Congreso de Historia Ferroviaria* (October 2009), 2–3, https://www.docutren.com/historiaferroviaria/PalmaMallorca2009/pdf/0208_Kreuzer.pdf; Poster, 'Société de Navigation à Vapeur du Lloyd Autrichien', Brindisi to Trieste (undated), https://commons.wikimedia.org/wiki/File:%C3%96sterreichischer_Lloyd_Trieste-Alexandria_poster.jpg [both accessed 16.02.25].
23 Gatejel, 'Overcoming the Iron Gates', 169–70; Coates, *Story of Six Rivers*, 53; Miroslav Šedivý, 'From Hostility to Cooperation? Austria, Russia and the Danubian Principalities 1829–40', *The Slavonic and East European Review* 89:4 (2011), 647–50.
24 Figes, *Crimea*, 15–17; Reid, *Borderland*, 55.
25 Reid, *Borderland*, 57–8; Robert K. Massie, *Catherine the Great: Portrait of a Woman* (London: Head of Zeus, 2012), 500–1.
26 Figes, *Crimea*, 12, 40; Gatejel, 'Overcoming the Iron Gates', 170.
27 Figes, *Crimea*, 89–92.
28 Figes, *Crimea*, 432–3.
29 Figes, *Crimea*, 185–7; Mazower, *Balkans*, 100.
30 Mazower, *Balkans*, 103.
31 Carole Fink, *Defending the Rights of Others: The Great Powers, the Jews, and International Minority Protection, 1878–1938* (Cambridge/New York: Cambridge University Press, 2004), 30–8.
32 Dana Mihăilescu, 'The Jewish Fusgeyer Migration Movement from

Early Twentieth-Century Romania as Transcultural Rhetorical Tool in US Memorial Literary Culture', *MELUS* 45:1 (2020), 139, 150; Aubrey Newman, 'The Poor Jews' Temporary Shelter: An Episode in Migration Studies', *Jewish Historical Studies* 40 (2005), 141–55.

33 Quotation from Namık Kemal, *Vatan Yahut Silistre* ('Fatherland or Silistria', 1873), ed. Kenan Akyüz (Ankara, 1960), 21, translated in Ebru Boyar, *Ottomans, Turks and the Balkans: Empire Lost, Relations Altered* (London: Tauris Academic Studies, 2007), 128; Figes, *Crimea*, 184–6.

34 Ilya Vinkovetsky, 'Strategists and Ideologues: Russians and the Making of Bulgaria's Tarnovo Constitution, 1878–1879', *The Journal of Modern History* 90:4 (2018), 752, 777; Mazower, *Balkans*, 111.

35 Yahya Kemal Beyatlı, 'Balkan'a Seyahat', *Dergâh Mecmûası* (5 Teşrin-i sani 1337) in [Beyatlı] Yahya Kemal, *Çocukluğum, Gençliğim, Siyâsî ve Edebî Hâtıralarım* (Istanbul, 1973), 146, translated in Ebru Boyar, *Ottomans, Turks and the Balkans: Empire Lost, Relations Altered* (London: Tauris Academic Studies, 2007), 128–9.

36 'Hasan Ali Yucel', *The New York Times* (27 February 1961), 27; Boyar, *Ottomans, Turks and the Balkans*, 127.

37 Stefan Dorondel, Stelu Serban and Daniel Cain, 'The Play of Islands: Emerging Borders and Danube Dynamics in Modern Southeast Europe (1830–1900)', *Environment and History* 25:4 (2019), 522, 528, 529–30.

38 Mazower, *Balkans*, 106–8.

39 *Novosti* (18 January 1914), quoted in *Collected Diplomatic Documents Relating to the Outbreak of the European War*, Cd. 7860 (London: HMSO, 1915), 475.

40 'Occupation of Ada Kaleh', *The Morning Post* (28 May 1878), 5; Rady, *Habsburg Empire*, 97.

41 Mark Mazower, 'Minorities and the League of Nations in Interwar Europe', *Daedalus* 126:2 (1997), 61.

42 'The Political Situation', *The Morning Post* (28 May 1878), 5; Mazower, *Balkans*, 102, 106.

43 Karl A. Roider, 'The Perils of Eighteenth-Century Peacemaking: Austria and the Treaty of Belgrade, 1739', *Central European History* 5:3 (1972), 195; Rady, *Habsburg Empire*, 94–7; Mazower, *Balkans*, 107.

44 *Tribuna* (26 May 1913) quoted in *Collected Diplomatic Documents Relating to the Outbreak of the European War*, 474.

45 'The Charms of Ada-Kaleh', *The Westminster Gazette* (22 May 1913), 4.

46 Mazower, *Balkans*, 108; Howard, *First World War*, 14, 24.

47 David Keys, 'Church to Mark the Real Centenary of the Start of the First World War', *The Independent* (28 July 2014).

48 From Our Special Correspondent, 'The Invasion of Belgium', *The Times*

(6 August 1914); Howard, *First World War*, 24–6; '4 August 1914: The Lead-up to Britain's Declaration of War', Imperial War Museum (IWM), Press Information, https://www.iwm.org.uk/sites/default/files/press-release/4_August_1914_Factsheet.pdf [accessed 16.02.25].

49 'Turkey and the Lausanne Treaty', *Advocate of Peace through Justice* 85:4 (1923), 149–50; Ágoston and Masters, *Encyclopedia of the Ottoman Empire*, 323–5; Robert Gerwarth and Uğur Ümit Üngör, 'The Collapse of the Ottoman and Habsburg Empires and the Brutalisation of the Successor States', *Journal of Modern European History / Zeitschrift Für Moderne Europäische Geschichte / Revue d'histoire Européenne Contemporaine* 13:2 (2015), 236; Robert Gerwarth and Erez Manela, 'The Great War as a Global War: Imperial Conflict and the Reconfiguration of World Order, 1911–1923', *Diplomatic History* 38:4 (2014), 787–8; Mazower, 'Minorities and the League of Nations in Interwar Europe', 61; Coates, *Story of Six Rivers*, 52, 54.

Chapter 6: The Case of the Undredged Delta

1 'General Treaty of Peace Between Great Britain, Austria, France, Prussia, Russia, Sardinia, and Turkey, Signed at Paris, 30th March 1856', Article XVI, in Augustus Henry Oakes and R.B. Mowat (eds), *The Great European Treaties of the Nineteenth Century* (Oxford: The Clarendon Press, 1918), 179.

2 'Etchings from the Euxine: II. The Danube and Crimea', *Fraser's Magazine for Town and Country* 50:297 (1854), 296–7.

3 'The Black Gold of Ukraine and the Most Fertile Soils in the World', Gondwana Talks, Blog (9 March 2023), https://www.gondwanatalks.com/l/the-black-gold-of-ukraine-and-the-most-fertile-soils-in-the-world [accessed 08.01.25].

4 'Russia in the Right', *The Preston Chronicle* (10 December 1853), 4.

5 Viscount Palmerston, 'Russia and the Porte – Navigation of the Danube', *HC Debates* (7 July 1853), Hansard, vol. 128, cc. 1373–5.

6 'Etchings from the Euxine', 296–7.

7 Coates, *Story of Six Rivers*, 59.

8 Constantin Ardeleanu, *The European Commission of the Danube, 1856–1948: An Experiment in International Administration* (Leiden: Brill, 2020), 62–4.

9 Ardeleanu, *European Commission of the Danube*, 56.

10 Glen A. Blackburn, 'International Control of the Danube', *Current History* 32:6 (1930), 1154; Ardeleanu, *European Commission of the Danube*, 56.

11 Ardeleanu, *European Commission of the Danube*, 56, 75; Blackburn, 'International Control of the Danube', 1154.

12 'Length of the Rhine (Update 2015)', International Commission for the Hydrology of the Rhine Basin, https://www.chr-khr.org/en/news/length-rhine-update-2015 [accessed 29.03.25].

13 Rady, *Habsburg Empire*, 4–5; Hans A. Schmitt, 'Germany without Prussia: A Closer Look at the Confederation of the Rhine', *German Studies Review* 6:1 (1983), 10; M. Rowe, 'France, Prussia, or Germany? The Napoleonic Wars and Shifting Allegiances in the Rhineland', *Central European History* 39:4 (2006), 611–40.

14 E.M. Arndt, *Deutschlands Fluss, aber nicht Deutschlands Gränze* (1813), Translation by UvA Talen / Study Platform on Interlocking Nationalisms (SPIN), https://ernie.uva.nl/upload/media/08b5d331dbd8e9157f61e017c52b-f7af.pdf [accessed 07.08.22]; Mark Cioc, 'The Political Ecology of the Rhine', in Christof Mauch (ed.), *Nature in German History* (New York/Oxford: Berghahn Books, 2004), 31, 33; Martijn van der Burg, *Napoleonic Governance in the Netherlands and Northwest Germany: Conquest, Incorporation, and Integration* (Cham: Springer International Publishing, 2021), 37.

15 Howard, *First World War*, 114.

16 From French Convention of 16 November 1792, translated in Mark Cioc, 'The Rhine as a World River', in Edmund Burke and Kenneth Pomeranz (eds), *The Environment and World History* (Berkeley/Los Angeles: University of California Press, 2009), 170; L. Kunz, 'The Danube Régime and the Belgrade Conference', *The American Journal of International Law* 43:1 (1949), 104; Joep Schenk, *The Rhine and European Security in the Long Nineteenth Century: Making Lifelines from Frontlines* (London/New York: Routledge, Taylor & Francis Group, 2021), 22–5.

17 Kennedy, *Concise History of the Netherlands*, 264.

18 Quoted in Simon Schama, *Patriots and Liberators: Revolution in the Netherlands, 1780–1813* (New York: Knopf, 1977), 2; B.H.M. Vlekke, *Evolution of the Dutch Nation* (New York: Roy Publishers, 1945), 1.

19 'Der Rheinische Courier verliert auf der Heimreise von der Leipsiger Messe alles' (1813–1814), The British Museum, Prints & Drawings, Registration number 1989,1104.121; Schenk, *Rhine and European Security*, 21.

20 Ardeleanu, *European Commission of the Danube*, 53, 56; Central Commission for the Navigation of the Rhine (CCNR), https://www.ccr-zkr.org/11010100-en.html [accessed 25.08.24]; Cioc, 'Political Ecology of the Rhine', 33.

21 Somervell, 'Navigation Problems on the Danube', 304, 307–8; Mazower, *Balkans*, 22; Coates, *Story of Six Rivers*, 58–9; Blackburn, 'International

Control of the Danube', 1157; George Kiss, 'TVA on the Danube?', *Geographical Review* 37:2 (1947), 282.

22 Ardeleanu, *European Commission of the Danube*, 309–11.

23 Kunz, 'Danube Régime', 108; Ardeleanu, *European Commission of the Danube*, 312.

24 Ardeleanu, *European Commission of the Danube*, 312; Blackburn, 'International Control of the Danube', 1156.

25 Paul Halpern, 'Troubridge, Sir Ernest Charles Thomas (1862–1926), naval officer', *Oxford Dictionary of National Biography* [*ODNB*]; Alice Teichova and Penelope Ratcliffe, 'British Interests in Danube Navigation after 1918', *Business History* 27:3 (1985), 286.

26 E.g. *Percy Sanderson*, Dredgepoint.org, https://dredgepoint.org/dredging-database/equipment/percy-sanderson [accessed 05.03.25]; Somervell, 'Navigation Problems on the Danube', 308.

27 Teichova and Ratcliffe, 'British Interests in Danube Navigation', 286; G.K.S. Hamilton-Edwards, 'Weir, Andrew, first Baron Inverforth (1865–1955), shipowner', *ODNB*.

28 Teichova and Ratcliffe, 'British Interests in Danube Navigation', 285, 289–91; Walker D. Hines and Brehon Burke Somervell, *Report on Danube Navigation: Submitted to the Advisory and Technical Committee for Communications and Transit of the League of Nations* (Geneva: League of Nations, 1925), 101–4, 111.

29 Blackburn, 'International Control of the Danube', 1157.

30 Somervell, 'Navigation Problems on the Danube', 310; Blackburn, 'International Control of the Danube', 1157; Hines and Somervell, *Report on Danube Navigation*, 101–4, 111; Teichova and Ratcliffe, 'British Interests in Danube Navigation', 289–91; Marie-Janine Calic, *A History of Yugoslavia*, trans. Dona Geyer (West Lafayette, Indiana: Purdue University Press, 2019), 66.

31 Somervell, 'Navigation Problems on the Danube', 307; Ardeleanu, *European Commission of the Danube*, 310, 312–16.

32 Teichova and Ratcliffe, 'British Interests in Danube Navigation', 284, 294, 296.

33 Kunz, 'Danube Régime', 108; Ardeleanu, *European Commission of the Danube*, 316.

34 Ardeleanu, *European Commission of the Danube*, 316–18.

35 The Mauthausen Concentration Camp 1938–1945, Mauthausen Memorial, https://www.mauthausen-memorial.org/en/About-us/Organisation [accessed 08.08.22].

36 Árpád Von Klimó, *Remembering Cold Days: The 1942 Massacre of Novi Sad and Hungarian Politics and Society, 1942–1989* (Pittsburgh, PA: University of Pittsburgh Press, 2018), 23–7.

37 Sheryl Silver Ochayon, 'The Shoes on the Danube Promenade – Commemoration of the Tragedy', Yad Vashem: The World Holocaust Remembrance Centre, https://www.yadvashem.org/articles/general/shoes-on-the-danube-promenade.html [accessed 05.03.25]; Coates, *Story of Six Rivers*, 33–4.

38 'Murder of the Jews of Romania', Yad Vashem: The World Holocaust Remembrance Centre, https://www.yadvashem.org/holocaust/about/final-solution-beginning/romania.html [accessed 08.08.22].

39 Árpád von Klimó, '1956 and the Collapse of Stalinist Politics of History: Forgetting and Remembering the 1942 Újvidék/Novi Sad Massacre and the 1944/45 Partisan Retaliations in Hungary and Yugoslavia (1950s–1960s)', *The Hungarian Historical Review* 5:4 (2016), 739–66.

40 Quoted in Kunz, 'Danube Régime', 111; Kiss, 'TVA on the Danube?', 274–302; Coates, *Story of Six Rivers*, 34, 54; Ardeleanu, *European Commission of the Danube*, 319–22.

41 Ardeleanu, *European Commission of the Danube*, 317.

42 Kunz, 'Danube Régime', 113; H. Briggs, 'Josef L. Kunz, 1890–1970', *American Journal of International Law* 65:1 (1971), 129.

43 David T. Cattell, 'The Politics of the Danube Commission under Soviet Control', *American Slavic and East European Review* 19:3 (1960), 388; Ardeleanu, *European Commission of the Danube*, 321.

44 Ardeleanu, *European Commission of the Danube*, 322.

45 Thomas De Waal and Balázs Jarábik, 'Bessarabia's Hopes and Fears on Ukraine's Edge', *Carnegie Europe*, Blog (24 May 2018), https://carnegieeurope.eu/2018/05/24/bessarabia-s-hopes-and-fears-on-ukraine-s-edge-pub-76445; Irina Marica, 'New National Holiday in Romania: The Union with Bessarabia Celebrated on March 27', Romania-Insider.com (15 March 2017) [both accessed 02.06.22].

46 'Russia Announces Troops Withdrawal from West Bank of Dnipro River', *Business Standard* (10 November 2022); Oleksiy Goncharenko, 'Odesa Rejects Catherine the Great as Putin's Invasion Makes Russia Toxic' (14 November 2022), *Atlantic Council*, Blog, https://www.atlanticcouncil.org/blogs/ukrainealert/odesa-rejects-catherine-the-great-as-putins-invasion-makes-russia-toxic/ [accessed 18.11.2022].

47 Andrew Roth et al., 'Russia's War in Ukraine: Complete Guide in Maps, Video and Pictures', *The Guardian* (15 May 2022); Vincent Mundy, 'Ukraine's "hero river" Helped Save Kyiv: But What Now for its Newly Restored Wetlands?', *The Guardian* (11 May 2022).

48 'Turkey Pushes for Ukraine Grain Exports Deal as Key Meeting Due', *Daily Sabah* (7 June 2022).

49 Danube Commission, https://www.danubecommission.org/dc/en/

danube-commission/; Iván Gyurcsík (ed.), *Danube Commission 70* (Budapest: Institute for Foreign Affairs and Trade, 2019), https://www.danubecommission.org/uploads/doc/2019/Danube_Commission_70.pdf [both accessed 08.08.22].

50 'Press Release' (12th Extraordinary Session of the Danube Commission, 17 March 2022), https://www.danubecommission.org/uploads/doc/2022/press/en_12_ext_session.pdf; 'Russia's Powers in Danube Commission Terminated – Ministry of Infrastructure', *Interfax – UKRAINE* (18 March 2022), https://interfax.com.ua/news/general/815445.html [both accessed 29.03.25].

51 Peter Beaumont, '"Trying to make the world starve": Russian Drones Destroy Grain Warehouses at Ukraine Ports', *The Guardian* (24 July 2023); Dinara Khalilova, 'Kuleba: Russia Excluded from Danube Commission due to its Attacks on Odesa Oblast', *The Kiev Independent* (1 March 2024).

Chapter 7: Numinous Rivers

1 Rabindranath Tagore, 'Brahmā-Viṣṇu-Śiva', *Rabindranath Tagore: Selected Poems*, trans. William Radice (Harmondsworth: Penguin Books, 1985), 45–7.

2 G.S. Mudur, 'ISRO Sheds Light on Adam's Bridge', *The Telegraph Online* (7 July 2024), https://www.telegraphindia.com/india/isro-sheds-light-on-adams-bridge-submerged-ridge-a-continuity-from-india-to-sri-lanka/cid/2032049 [accessed 05.03.25].

3 'Ganges River', in Paul Robbins (ed.), *Encyclopedia of Environment and Society* 5 (SAGE Publications, 2007), 723, https://sk.sagepub.com/ency/edvol/environment/chpt/ganges-river.

4 The Ganges, World Wildlife Fund [WWF], https://www.wwf.org.uk/where-we-work/ganges [accessed 05.03.25]; M.M. Hossain, A.M. Zaman and Fulco Ludwig, 'Climate Change Impact on the Discharge of Ganges-Brahmaputra-Meghna (GBM) River Basin and Bangladesh', International Conference on Climate Change in relation to Water and Environment (I3CWE-2015), Dhaka University of Engineering & Technology, Gazipur, 2015, 45; Md. Munsur Rahman et al., 'Ganges-Brahmaputra-Meghna Delta, Bangladesh and India: A Transnational Mega-Delta', in Robert J. Nicholls et al. (eds), *Deltas in the Anthropocene* (Cham: Springer International Publishing, 2020), 23–51.

5 Gagan Matta et al., 'Repercussions of Tourism on Water Quality of River Ganga in Lower Himalayas', *ESSENCE: International Journal for Environmental Rehabilitation and Conservation* (2018), 93; TOI Lifestyle

Desk, 'Beyond death: How Haridwar helps Souls Find Peace', *The Times of India*, 20 March 2025.

6 Kim Knott, *Hinduism: A Very Short Introduction*, 2nd edn (Oxford: Oxford University Press, 2016), 13, 51, 113; R.S. Sharma, *India's Ancient Past* (Delhi: Oxford University Press, 2005), 3–5.

7 Sudipta Sen, *Ganges: The Many Pasts of an Indian River* (New Haven, CT: Yale University Press, 2019), 7, 50–60; Sugata Ray, 'Water Is a Limited Commodity: Ecological Aesthetics in the Little Ice Age, Mathura, ca. 1614', in Sugata Ray and Maddipati Venugopal (eds), *Water Histories of South Asia: The Materiality of Liquescence* (Abingdon, Oxon/New York: Routledge, 2020), 37.

8 Sunil Amrith, 'Land of Sacred Waters: The Quests and Trades that Flowed from the Ganges', *Lapham's Quarterly* (3 January 2019).

9 Lawrence A. Babb, *Absent Lord: Ascetics and Kings in a Jain Ritual Culture* (Berkeley, CA: University of California Press, 1996), 5; Malise Ruthven, *Islam: A Very Short Introduction*, 2nd edn (New York: Oxford University Press, 2012), 38–9.

10 Knott, *Hinduism*, 3–4.

11 Sharma, *India's Ancient Past*, 260; Amit Kumar, 'Mapping Multiplicity: The Complex Landscape of Bodh Gaya', *Sociological Bulletin* 64:1 (2015), 40; Sen, *Ganges*, 167–8; Knott, *Hinduism*, 113; *Ficus Religiosa*, Royal Horticultural Society, https://www.rhs.org.uk/plants/7213/ficus-religiosa/details [accessed 30.03.25].

12 Frankopan, *Silk Roads*, 27–31.

13 Sabina Knight, *Chinese Literature: A Very Short Introduction* (Oxford/New York: Oxford University Press, 2012), 8-9; 'Receding Water Levels of China's Yangtze Reveal Ancient Buddhist Statues', Reuters (20 August 2022), https://www.reuters.com/business/environment/receding-water-levels-chinas-yangtze-reveal-ancient-buddhist-statues-2022-08-20/ [accessed 05.03.25].

14 Sen, *Ganges*, 146–7; Frankopan, *Silk Roads*, 27.

15 Sen, *Ganges*, 197–8.

16 Kama Maclean, 'Seeing, Being Seen, and Not Being Seen: Pilgrimage, Tourism, and Layers of Looking at the Kumbh Mela', *CrossCurrents* 59:3 (2009), 320.

17 Sen, *Ganges*, 217–19; Sharma, *India's Ancient Past*, 261–3.

18 Sharma, *India's Ancient Past*, 140, 253, 260; Sen, *Ganges*, 221, 222.

19 Indira Gandhi, Address to the Plenary Session of the United Nations Conference on Human Environment at Stockholm, Sweden, on 14 June 1972, reproduced in 'Poverty and Pollution' in Indira Gandhi, *The Spirit of India: Volumes presented to Shrimati Indira Gandhi by the Indira Gandhi*

Abhinandan Samiti: Volume One (Bombay: Asia Publishing House, 1985), 272.

20 Richard M. Eaton, 'Temple Desecration and Indo-Muslim States', *Journal of Islamic Studies* 11:3 (2000), 295–6.

21 Eaton, 'Temple Desecration', 313.

22 William Dalrymple, *The Last Mughal: The Fall of Delhi, 1857* (London: Bloomsbury, 2006), 81; Sen, *Ganges*, 35.

23 Eaton, 'Temple Desecration', 313; Sen, *Ganges*, 244–9; Richard H. Davis, *Lives of Indian Images* (Delhi: Motilal Banarsidass Publishers, 1999), 75.

24 Vivek Nanda, 'Kumbakonam: The Ritual Topography of a Sacred and Royal City of South India', *Archaeology International* 3:1 (2012), 43–8; Diana L. Eck, *India: A Sacred Geography* (New York: Harmony Books, 2012), 156–7.

25 Morna Livingston, *Steps to Water: The Ancient Stepwells of India* (Princeton, NJ/Oxford: Princeton Architectural Press, 2002); Amanda M. Gaggioli et al., 'Early Water Management in South Asia: Geochronology and Micromorphology of Rock Pools and Small-Scale Water Catchment Features in Karnataka, India', *Geoarchaeology* 36:5 (2021), 780–8.

26 Tim Mackintosh-Smith (ed.), *The Travels of Ibn Battutah* (London: Picador, 2003), 210–11, 318n; Tamara I. Sears, 'Following River Routes and Artistic Transmissions in Medieval Central India', *Ars Orientalis*, 45 (2015), 43–5.

27 Iqtidar Husain Siddiqui, 'Water Works and Irrigation System in India during Pre-Mughal Times', *Journal of the Economic and Social History of the Orient* 29:1 (1986), 52–77.

28 Iqtedar Alam, 'Transitioning Waterscapes of the Two Great Tanks of Delhi: Hauz-i-Shamsi & Hauz-i-Khas', in Q. Irshad and M. Juned (eds), *Ekistics: An Approach to Urban-Regional Planning & Development, Vol. 2: Urban Transformation* (New Delhi: Jamia Publishing House, 2020), 64; Siddiqui, 'Water Works and Irrigation System', 53–4.

29 Mackintosh-Smith (ed.), *Travels of Ibn Battutah*, 163.

30 Mehrdad Shokoohy and Natalie H. Shokoohy, 'Tughluqabad, Third Interim Report: Gates, Silos, Waterworks and Other Features', *Bulletin of the School of Oriental and African Studies, University of London* 66:1 (2003), 45; Siddiqui, 'Water Works and Irrigation System', 72; Alam, 'Transitioning Waterscapes of the Two Great Tanks of Delhi', 65–6; India Habitat Centre, 'Hauz Khas – the tomb of Feroz Shah Tughlaq and the Madrasa complex' (2016), https://www.indiahabitat.org/themes/ihc/img/gallery/14430/14430.pdf [accessed 31.03.25]; 'The Lat of Firozshah Tughlaq [Delhi]', Photograph by Samuel Bourne, 1860 (British Library), https://it.m.wikipedia.org/wiki/File:The_Lat_of_Ferozeh_Shah_-Delhi-..jpg [accessed 31.03.25].

31 Justin Marozzi, *Tamerlane Sword of Islam, Conqueror of the World* (London: Harper Perennial, 2005), 204; Elizabeth B. Moynihan, *Paradise as a Garden in Persia and Mughal India* (New York: George Braziller, 1979), 95.

32 Babur, *Baburnama: A Memoir*, trans. Annette Susannah Beveridge (New Delhi: Rupa Publications India Pvt Ltd, 2017), 326–7.

33 Babur, *Baburnama*, 318.

34 Moynihan, *Paradise as a Garden*, 1; Margrit Pernau, 'Mapping Emotions, Constructing Feelings: Delhi in the 1840s', *Journal of the Economic and Social History of the Orient* 58:5 (2015), 646.

35 Moynihan, *Paradise as a Garden*, 49.

36 Moynihan, *Paradise as a Garden*, vii, 102–4.

37 Moynihan, *Paradise as a Garden*, 98.

38 Sen, *Ganges*, 292.

39 Asoka Pillar Edict V quoted in Sen, *Ganges*, 147; N.A. Nikam and Richard McKeon, *The Edicts of Asoka* (Chicago/London: The University of Chicago Press, 1959), 2, 15, 55–6; A. Ghosh, 'The Pillars of Aśoka – Their Purpose', *East and West* 17:3/4 (1967), 273.

40 Ray, 'Water is a Limited Commodity', 42.

41 'Krishna Janmasthan temple, (Krishna Jàmbhoomi), Mathura | Lord Kirshna's birthplace', The Gaudiya Treasures of Bengal, https://thegaudiyatreasuresofbengal.com/2022/10/14/krishna-janmbhoomi-sri-krishna-janmasthan-temple-mathura/ [accessed 28.08.24].

42 Knott, *Hinduism*, 13, 34–5, 52; Sharma, *India's Ancient Past*, 246–7.

43 Ray, 'Water is a Limited Commodity', 37, 42, 43.

44 Quoted in Eaton, 'Temple Desecration', 303.

45 Ray, 'Water is a Limited Commodity', 43.

46 Ray, 'Water is a Limited Commodity', 43, 46, 53; Salim Zaweed, 'Salient Features of Bundela Architecture at Orchha', *Proceedings of the Indian History Congress* 68 (2007), 1409, 1411.

47 'Aurangzeb's Id-gah at Mathura by Sita Ram c. 1814–15' (British Library), https://commons.wikimedia.org/wiki/File:Aurangzab%27s_red_sandstone_mosque_on_the_birthplace_of_Krishna_-_British_Library_Add.or.4844.jpg [accessed 01.04.25]; Michael H. Fisher, *An Environmental History of India: From Earliest Times to the Twenty-First Century* (Cambridge: Cambridge University Press, 2018), 109.

48 Dr Mohammad Ghitreef, 'Mathura Shahi Idgah Masjid: We Should Not Be Negligent This Time, *Muslim Mirror* (15 October 2020), https://muslimmirror.com/eng/mathura-shahi-idgah-masjid-we-should-not-be-negligent-this-time/ [accessed 26.08.22].

49 Eaton, 'Temple Desecration', 305, 306–7.

50 Krishna N. Das, 'India's Holy Men to Advise Modi's Ganges River Cleanup', Reuters (New Delhi) (12 June 2014), http://reut.rs/2vnJFKN [accessed 06.03.25]; Mrigank Tiwari, 'Ganga Ties Hindus, Muslims', *Times of India* (19 January 2011); Sushmita Pathak, 'A Hindu-Muslim Dispute Tests Centuries of Interfaith Culture in India's Varanasi', *WGCU* PBS and NPR for Southwest Florida (16 September 2023), https://news.wgcu.org/2023-09-16/a-hindu-muslim-dispute-tests-centuries-of-interfaith-culture-in-indias-varanasi [accessed 06.03.25].

51 Syed Serajul Islam, 'The Tragedy of the Babri Masjid: An Expression of Militant Hindu Fundamentalism in India', *Journal of Muslim Minority Affairs* 17:2 (1997), 345; S.K. Jain, Pushpendra K. Agarwa and V.P. Singh, *Hydrology and Water Resources of India* (Dordrecht: Springer, 2007), 341; 'Ayodhya Seen from the River Ghaghara, Uttar Pradesh: Coloured Etching by William Hodges, 1785', Wellcome Collection 26802i.

52 Knott, *Hinduism*, 13, 40–3, 58; Robert P. Goldman, 'Introduction', in Robert P. Goldman (ed.), *The Rāmāyaṇa of Vālmīki: An Epic of Ancient India* (Princeton, NJ: Princeton University Press, 1990), 14.

53 Islam, 'Tragedy of the Babri Masjid', 345–6; Prashant Waikar, 'Reading Islamophobia in Hindutva: An Analysis of Narendra Modi's Political Discourse', *Islamophobia Studies Journal* 4:2 (2018), 168; Mark Tran, 'Ayodhya: Guardian Coverage of the Babri Mosque Attack', *The Guardian* (30 September 2010); Saurabh Sharma and YP Rajesh, 'India's Modi leads consecration of Ram temple in Ayodhya', Reuters (22 January 2024), https://www.reuters.com/world/india/india-counts-down-opening-grand-ram-temple-ayodhya-2024-01-22/ [accessed 01.04.25].

54 Andrew Lawler, 'Indus Collapse: The End or the Beginning of an Asian Culture', *Science* 320 (6 June 2008), 1283; G.S. Mudur, 'ISRO Sheds Light on Adam's Bridge', *The Telegraph Online* (7 July 2024), https://www.telegraphindia.com/india/isro-sheds-light-on-adams-bridge-submerged-ridge-a-continuity-from-india-to-sri-lanka/cid/2032049 [accessed 06.03.25]; A. Chatterjee, 'Do You Believe in Ram Setu? Adam's Bridge, Epistemic Plurality and Colonial Legacy', *Island Studies Journal*, 18(2) (2023), 1–25.

55 Romila Thapar, 'Imagined Religious Communities? Ancient History and the Modern Search for a Hindu Identity', *Modern Asian Studies* 23:2 (1989), 216.

Chapter 8: River under Occupation

1 *Bengal District Administration Committee, 1913–14* (Calcutta: Bengal Secretariat Press, 1914), 53.

2 Sen, *Ganges*, 310–13.

3 Chitarman, 'Shah Jahan on a Terrace, Holding a Pendant Set with his Portrait', Folio from the Shah Jahan Album, (1627–28), The Metropolitan Museum of Art, New York, Object No. 55.121.10.24.

4 Sen, *Ganges*, 315–16.

5 Sen, *Ganges*, 317–18.

6 D.A. Washbrook, 'India, 1818–1860', in Porter (ed.), *Oxford History of Empire: Vol. III*, 395–421; Sen, *Ganges*, 318.

7 Elizabeth Whitcombe, 'Irrigation', in Dharma Kumar and Meghnad Desai (eds), *The Cambridge Economic History of India, Vol. II. c.1757–c.1970* (New Delhi/Cambridge: Cambridge University Press, 1984), 690, 730.

8 British Library [BL] (Asian and African Studies): IOR/F/4/1573/64239: Refusal of Bishwanath Singh, son of the Raja of Rewah to pay the Pilgrim Tax on the Occasion of his visiting Allahabad to Bathe in the Waters of the Ganges and Jumna (October 1833–February 1835); Andrea Major, *Sovereignty and Social Reform in India: British Colonialism and the Campaign Against Sati, 1830–1860* (New York: Routledge, 2011), 61.

9 BL: IOR/F/4/1573/64239: Letter from A. Spiers to Stockwell Esq, Commissioner Revenue, Allahabad (28 September 1833). My emphasis.

10 BL: IOR/F/4/1573/64239: Letter from Spiers to Stockwell.

11 Katherine Prior, 'The British Administration of Hinduism in North India, 1780–1900' (unpublished PhD thesis, University of Cambridge, 1990), 74, 183.

12 'Kharif Crop vs Rabi Crop', EIACP PC Hub: Kerala, Kerala State Council for Science, Technology and Environment, http://www.kerenvis.nic.in/Database/Crops_2419.aspx [accessed 06.03.25].

13 S. Bhattacharya, 'Eastern India', in Kumar and Desai (eds), *Cambridge Economic History of India, Vol II*, 283; Sen, *Ganges*, 318.

14 Robin J. Moore, 'Imperial India, 1858–1914', in Porter (ed.), *Oxford History of Empire: Vol. III*, 441.

15 'No. I. Tea from Assam', *Transactions of the Society, Instituted at London, for the Encouragement of Arts, Manufactures, and Commerce* 53 (1839), 30–3; Hyde Clarke, 'On the English Settlement of the Hill Regions of India', *Journal of the Society of Arts* 6:287 (1858), 423–34; Bhattacharya, 'Eastern India', 310–12; 'The History of Tea and Twinings', Twinings Blog, https://twinings.co.uk/blogs/news/history-of-twinings [accessed 06.03.25].

16 'Water Power in India', *Journal of the Royal Society of Arts* 70:3624 (1922), 440–1; Francis Lydall, 'Hydro-Electric Development in India', *Journal of the Royal Society of Arts* 94:4726 (1946), 619–21; Whitcombe, 'Irrigation', 731–4.

17 Tom G. Kessinger, 'North India', in Kumar and Desai (eds), *Cambridge Economic History of India, Vol. II,* 242–70.
18 L.S.S. O'Malley, *Bihar and Orissa District Gazeteers: Patna*, revised by J.F.W. James (Patna: Bihar and Orissa Government Printing, 1924), 131–3; J. Johnston, *Inland Navigation on the Gangetic Rivers* (Calcutta: Thacker, Spink & Co, 1933), 7, 18.
19 O'Malley, *Bihar and Orissa District Gazeteers: Patna*, 133; Kessinger, 'North India', 245.
20 Bhattacharya, 'Eastern India', 277–79; Mohammad Ponir Hossain, 'Living along a "Dead" River in Bangladesh', Reuters (19 April 2023), https://www.reuters.com/investigates/special-report/earth-day-bangladesh-river/ [accessed 06.03.25].
21 Bhattacharya, 'Eastern India', 293–4.
22 Johnston, *Inland Navigation on the Gangetic Rivers*, 7, 28; Amitav Ghosh, *The Great Derangement: Climate Change and the Unthinkable* (Chicago: The University of Chicago Press, 2016), 104–5; 'Ghazi-ud-din Haider', Indian Culture, Government of India, https://indianculture.gov.in/artefacts-museums/ghazi-ud-din-haider#:~:text=Description%3A%20Ghazi%2Dud%2Ddin,orderlies%20standing%20on%20either%20side [accessed 04.04.25].
23 *The Imperial Gazetteer of India*, vol. 12 (Oxford: Clarendon Press, 1908), 136 [Ganges], Digital South Asia Library, https://dsal.uchicago.edu/reference/gazetteer.
24 Johnston, *Inland Navigation on the Gangetic Rivers*, 31, 34.
25 Virginia Berridge, *Opium and the People: Opiate Use and Policy in 19th and Early 20th Century Britain*, 2nd edn (New York: Free Association Press, 1999), 8–9.
26 Washbrook, 'India, 1818–1860', 403; Bhattacharya, 'Eastern India', 312–15; Berridge, *Opium and the People*, 7–8.
27 Washbrook, 'India, 1818–1860', 404; 'The Stacking Room', 'Opium Fleet Descending the Ganges on the Way to Calcutta': lithographs after W.S. Sherwill (c. 1850) text in 'The Indo-Chinese Opium Trade: Notes at an Opium Factory at Patna', *The Graphic*, 24 June 1882, 640, reproduced in Benjamin Broomhall, *The Truth about Opium Smoking* (London, 1882), 116–17.
28 Peter C. Perdue, 'Production & Consumption' in 'The First Opium War: The Anglo-Chinese War of 1839–1842', Digital Essay, MIT Visualizing Cultures, https://visualizingcultures.mit.edu/opium_wars_01/ow1_essay02.html [accessed 06.03.25]; Yangwen Zheng, *The Social Life of Opium in China* (Cambridge: Cambridge University Press, 2005), 71 (map).

29 Leela Visaria and Parvin Visaria, 'Population (1757–1947)', in Kumar and Desai (eds), *Cambridge Economic History of India: Vol. II*, 529.

30 Chetan Singh, 'Forests, Pastoralists and Agrarian Society in Mughal India', in David Arnold and Ramachandra Guha (eds), *Nature, Culture, Imperialism: Essays on the Environmental History of South Asia* (Delhi: Oxford University Press, 1995), 21–2; Mike Davis, 'The Origins of the Third World: Markets, States and Climate', Corner House Briefing 27 (30 December 2002), http://www.thecornerhouse.org.uk/resource/origins-third-world [accessed 04.04.25].

31 BL: Mss Eur F699/1/2/2/188: No. 72 'Private Secretary's Correspondence', Nos. 7101 to 7150, Mar 1860–Jun 1860, Item 7126, Letter from Baboo Kishan Lall to the Rt Hon. Lord Canning, Viceroy and Governor General of India (10 May 1860); Thomas R. Metcalf, 'Charles John Canning, Earl Canning (1812–1862), governor-general and first viceroy of India', *ODNB*.

32 P.T. Cautley, *Report on the Ganges Canal Works: From their Commencement until the Opening of the Canal in 1854. Vol. I*, Printed by Order of the Secretary of State for India in Council (London, 1860), 67.

33 Quoted in Whitcombe, 'Irrigation', 689–90.

34 Visaria and Visaria, 'Population (1757–1947)', 492–3; Mike Davis, *Late Victorian Holocausts: El Niño Famines and the Making of the Third World* (London/New York: Verso, 2001), 7.

35 Visaria and Visaria, 'Population (1757–1947)', 493.

36 Cautley, *Report on the Ganges Canal Works, Vol. I*, 124, 131; Victor Mallet, *River of Life, River of Death: The Ganges and India's Future* (Oxford: Oxford University Press, 2017), 166–7; 'The Ganges Canal', The Ganges, India Institute of Civil Engineers [ICE], https://www.ice.org.uk/what-is-civil-engineering/infrastructure-projects/the-ganges-canal [accessed 06.03.25]; Georgina Drew, 'Transformation and Resistance on the Upper Ganga: The Ongoing Legacy of British Canal Irrigation', *South Asia: Journal of South Asian Studies* 37:4 (2014), 674–6.

37 'Opening of the Ganges Canal', *Illustrated London News* (5 August 1854), 117–18.

38 Cautley, *Report on the Ganges Canal Works, Vol. I*, 130–1.

39 P.T. Cautley, *Report on the Ganges Canal Works: From their Commencement until the Opening of the Canal in 1854, Vol. II*, Printed by Order of the Secretary of State for India in Council (London, 1860), 403, 433; Sen, *Ganges*, 222.

40 Washbrook, 'India, 1818–1860', 418–19; Barbara D. Metcalf and Thomas R. Metcalf, *A Concise History of Modern India*, 3rd edn (Cambridge/New York: Cambridge University Press, 2012), 101–3; Dalrymple, *Last Mughal*, 2.

41 Metcalf and Metcalf, *Concise History of Modern India*, 103; The Memorial Well, Cawnpore, Statue by Marochetti, albumen print by Samuel Bourne 1865–6, University of Michigan Museum of Art, https://umma.umich.edu/objects/the-memorial-well-cawnpore-statue-by-marochetti-1984-1-308/; 'Mutiny Memorial in New Delhi', National Army Museum, Blog and photograph, https://collection.nam.ac.uk/detail.php?acc=1980-04-37-31 [both accessed 06.03.25].

42 Ghalib, quoted in Dalrymple, *Last Mughal*, 80.

43 'Maharaja Shri Ishwari Prasad Narayan Singh Bahadur of Benares (1822–89) c. 1887', Royal Collection Trust, Albumen print and description, https://www.rct.uk/collection/2107688/maharaja-shri-ishwari-prasad-narayan-singh-bahadur-of-benares-1822-89 [accessed 06.03.25].

44 Isle of Wight Record Office: OG/CC/2301: Letter from Joan Kennard, Grand Hotel, Darjeeling, India, to her father, John H. Oglander [c/o H.H. Maharajah of Benares Guest House, Benares] (6 March 1910).

45 Hugh Tinker, *The Foundations of Local Self-Government in India, Pakistan and Burma* (London: Pall Mall Press, 1954), 58; Sandria B. Freitag, 'State and Community: Symbolic Popular Protest in Banaras's Public Arenas', in Sandria B. Freitag (ed.), *Culture and Power in Banaras: Community, Performance, and Environment, 1800–1980* (Berkeley and Los Angeles, CA/Oxford: University of California Press, 1989), 220–3; John Broich, 'Engineering the Empire: British Water Supply Systems and Colonial Societies, 1850–1900', *Journal of British Studies* 46:2 (2007), 359–60.

46 Freitag, 'State and Community', 222–3.

47 *Bengal District Administration Committee, 1913–14* (Calcutta: Bengal Secretariat Press, 1914), 10, 12; East India *(Sedition Committee, 1918). Report of Committee appointed to Investigate Revolutionary Conspiracies in India* (London: HMSO, 1918), 11–12, 18–19.

48 Curzon, Speech on 20 July 1904, quoted in Moore, 'Imperial India, 1858–1914', 443; Robin J. Moore, 'Curzon and Indian Reform', *Modern Asian Studies* 27:4 (1993), 719–40; Raja Deen Dayal, 'Just after Shooting: Lord and Lady Curzon Posed with Tiger Shot at 70 Yards, near Nekonda, Warangal District, Hyderabad, c.1902 (b/w photo)', British Library archive/Bridgeman Images, Image no. BL6867170; 'Lord Curzon and Maharaja Scindia Madhavrao II Scindia, with Tigers, 1911 (c)', Photograph, India c. 1911, National Army Museum, Accession no. NAM.1964-08-20-34.

Chapter 9: Dividing the Waters

1 Dadabhai Naoroji, 'Ninth Congress – Lahore – 1893', in *Speeches and Writings of Dadabhai Naoroji* (Madras: A. Natesan & Co., 1918), 57.

2 O.H.K. Spate, 'The Partition of the Punjab and of Bengal', *The Geographical Journal* 110:4/6 (1947), Fig. 6 (map).
3 From Taslima Nasrin, 'Denial', *Ay Kosto Jhenpe, Jiban Debo Mepe* (1994), translated by Subhoranjan Dasgupta in Ranabir Samaddar (ed.), *Reflections on Partition in the East* (Calutta/New Delhi: Calcutta Research Group/Vikas Publishing House, 1997), 210.
4 Sharma, *India's Ancient Past*, 3.
5 Lawler, 'Indus Collapse', 1283.
6 Sharma, *India's Ancient Past*, 3; Thapar, 'Imagined Religious Communities?', 222.
7 Babur, *Baburnama*, 316.
8 O.H.K. Spate, 'The Boundary Award in the Punjab', *The Asiatic Review* (Jan 1948), 8.
9 Muhammad Ali Jinnah, 1940, quoted in Anita D. Raman, 'Of Rivers and Human Rights: The Northern Areas, Pakistan's Forgotten Colony in Jammu and Kashmir', *International Journal on Minority and Group Rights* 11:1/2 (2004), 210.
10 W.H. Auden, 'Partition', *The Atlantic* (1966), in *The Complete Works of W.H. Auden: Poems, Volume II 1940–1973*, ed. Edward Mendelson (Princeton: Princeton University Press, 2022), 610–11; 'Never set eyes on the Land', Nutkhut Exhibition, University of Greenwich 2019, https://www.nutkhut.co.uk/projects/never-set-eyes/ [accessed 31.12.20].
11 Ian Copland, 'The Master and the Maharajas: The Sikh Princes and the East Punjab Massacres of 1947', *Modern Asian Studies* 36:3 (2002), 658n.
12 Spate, 'Partition of the Punjab and of Bengal', 202–3.
13 'Building a City from Scratch – The New Town of Milton Keynes' (1967), ITN Archive, https://www.youtube.com/watch?v=8nP5YtIuAJg [accessed 26.08.24].
14 Tim Marshall, *Prisoners of Geography: Ten Maps Telling You Everything You Need to Know about Global Politics* (London: Elliott and Thompson Limited, 2016), 200–2; Daniel Haines, '(Inter)Nationalist Rivers?: Cooperative Development in David Lilienthal's Plan for the Indus Basin, 1951', *Water History* 6:2 (2014), 138.
15 Food and Agriculture Organization of the United Nations [FAO]. *AQUASTAT Transboundary River Basins – Indus River Basin* (Rome, Italy: FAO, 2011), Table 1.
16 'Know Punjab', Government of Punjab, India, https://punjab.gov.in/know-punjab [accessed 06.03.25].
17 James M. Douie, 'The Punjab Canal Colonies', *Journal of the Royal Society of Arts* 62:3210 (1914), 611; Khushwant Singh, *A History of the Sikhs: Volume 2: 1839–2004*, 2nd edn (New Delhi: Oxford University Press, 2004), 116.

18 Spate, 'Partition of the Punjab and of Bengal', 208; F.J. Fowler, 'Some Problems of Water Distribution between East and West Punjab', *Geographical Review* 40:4 (1950), 591; Mahesh Rangarajan, 'Environmental Histories of India: Of States, Landscapes, and Ecologies', in Edmund Burke and Kenneth Pomeranz (eds), *The Environment and World History* (Berkeley/Los Angeles, CA: University of California Press, 2009), 240.
19 Spate, 'Partition of the Punjab and of Bengal', 209; Amjad Iqbal, 'Over 2,500 Indian Sikhs Attend Annual Pilgrimage', *The Dawn* (22 November 2015), https://www.dawn.com/news/1221378 [accessed 28.08.22].
20 Navtej K. Purewal and Virinder S. Kalra, 'Adaptation and Incorporation in Ritual Practices at the Golden Temple, Amritsar', *Journal of Ritual Studies* 30:1 (2016), 75–6.
21 Quoted in Stephen C. McCaffrey, 'The Harmon Doctrine One Hundred Years Later: Buried, Not Praised', *Natural Resources Journal* 36:4 (1996), 972.
22 Quoted in McCaffrey, 'Harmon Doctrine', 981; Haines, 'Disputed Rivers', 641.
23 McCaffrey, 'Harmon Doctrine', 967, 1002.
24 Haines, '(Inter)Nationalist Rivers?', 134, 138, 142; Haines, 'Disputed Rivers'.
25 Joya Chatterji, 'The Fashioning of a Frontier: The Radcliffe Line and Bengal's Border Landscape, 1947–52', *Modern Asian Studies* 33:1 (1999), 188, 199.
26 Md. Munsur Rahman et al., 'Ganges-Brahmaputra-Meghna Delta, Bangladesh and India: A Transnational Mega-Delta', in Robert J. Nicholls et al. (eds), *Deltas in the Anthropocene* (Cham: Springer International Publishing, 2020), 23–51.
27 Sundarbans Biosphere Reserve (National Park). Bird Life International, Data Zone. Site Description (2004 Baseline). https://datazone.birdlife.org/site/factsheet/sundarbans-biosphere-reserve-(national-park)-iba-india; Kazi Ahsan Habib et al., 'An Overview of Fishes of the Sundarbans, Bangladesh and Their Present Conservation Status', *Journal of Threatened Taxa* 12:1 (2020), 15156.
28 Habib et al., 'Overview of Fishes of the Sundarbans', 15160, 15165.
29 Chatterji, 'Fashioning of a Frontier', 222.
30 Chatterji, 'Fashioning of a Frontier', 210, 215; Kimberley Anh Thomas, 'The River-Border Complex: A Border-Integrated Approach to Transboundary River Governance illustrated by the Ganges River and Indo-Bangladeshi Border', *Water International* 42:1 (2017), 43, 45.
31 Chatterji, 'Fashioning of a Frontier', 221–5.
32 Amitav Ghosh, *The Great Derangement: Climate Change and the Unthinkable* (Chicago, IL: The University of Chicago Press, 2016), 6; Rohan D'Souza, 'Event, Process and Pulse: Resituating Floods in Environmental Histories of South Asia', *Environment and History* 26:1 (2020), 31–49.

33 Chatterji, 'Fashioning of a Frontier', 224; Haines, 'Disputed Rivers', 640.
34 Thomas, 'River-Border Complex', 44.
35 Thomas, 'River-Border Complex', 43–4; Punam Pandey, 'Revisiting the Politics of the Ganga Water Dispute between India and Bangladesh', *India Quarterly: A Journal of International Affairs* 68:3 (2012), 267–81.
36 Sikander Abu Jafar, 'This Struggle Will Go On', in *Poems for Bangla Desh: The Voice of a New Nation.* Translated from the Bengali by Pritish Nandy. Selected by Tambimuttu (London: Lyrebird Press, 1972), 50.
37 Shaheedulla Qaiser, 'To the Mother of a Martyr', in *Poems for Bangla Desh*, 30–1.
38 Humayun Azaad, 'The Blood Bank', in *Poems for Bangla Desh*, 66.
39 Sen, *Ganges*, 349.
40 Indira Gandhi, 'Address to the Plenary Session of the United Nations Conference on Human Environment at Stockholm, Sweden, on 14 June 1972', reproduced in 'Poverty and Pollution', *The Spirit of India: Volumes Presented to Shrimati Indira Gandhi by the Indira Gandhi Abhinandan Samiti: Volume One* (Bombay: Asia Publishing House, 1985), 272.
41 Sen, *Ganges*, 343.
42 Archana Chaudhary, 'A Journey Down the Ganges in the Age of Modi', Bloomberg (2 May 2019), https://www.bloomberg.com/features/2019-ganges-journey/ [accessed 28.08.22]; John Irwin, 'The Ancient Pillar-Cult at Prayāga (Allahabad): Its Pre-Aśokan Origins', *Journal of the Royal Asiatic Society of Great Britain and Ireland* 2 (1983), 253.
43 Hannan McCormick et al. (eds), *State of the Thames 2021: Environmental Trends of the Tidal Thames* (London: Zoological Society of London, 2021).
44 Tseqaye Gabre-Medhin, 'Nile' (written in English, 1997), in Beckett and Tebeje (eds), *Songs We Learn from Trees*, 71–3.
45 Rohan D'Souza, 'Water in British India: The Making of a "Colonial Hydrology"', *History Compass* 4:4 (2006), 621–8.
46 B.L. Verma, 'Delhi Water Supply and Sanitation', *India International Centre Quarterly* 9:3/4 (1982), 311, 314, 317.
47 John Vidal, 'Himalayas Hydroelectric Dam Project Stopped after Scientist on Hunger Strike against the Project Almost Dies', *The Guardian* (13 March 2009); Georgina Drew, 'Transformation and Resistance on the Upper Ganga: The Ongoing Legacy of British Canal Irrigation', *South Asia: Journal of South Asian Studies* 37:4 (2 October 2014), 670–83; Ramachandra Guha, *The Unquiet Woods: Ecological Change and Peasant Resistance in the Himalaya*, expanded edn (Delhi: Oxford University Press, 1991), 173; Sen, *Ganges*, 347.
48 Guha, *Unquiet Woods*, 155–7, 162, 166, 170, 178; D'Souza, 'Event, Process and Pulse', 31–2.
49 Guha, *Unquiet Woods*, 177.

50 See e.g. Guha, *Unquiet Woods*, 178ff; Sen, *Ganges*, 346–53; Georgina Drew, 'Mountain Women, Dams, and the Gendered Dimensions of Environmental Protest in the Garhwal Himalaya', *Mountain Research and Development* 34:3 (2014), 235–42; 'The Tehri Dam, India – Stumbling Toward Disaster', *Cultural Survival* (24 February 2010), Catastrophe, https://www.culturalsurvival.org/publications/cultural-survival-quarterly/tehri-dam-india-stumbling-toward-catastrophe [accessed 06.03.25].

51 'Save the Ganga Movement' – An Initiative to Protect River Ganga (4 September 2009), India Water Portal, https://www.indiawaterportal.org/articles/save-ganga-movement-initiative-protect-river-ganga [accessed 06.02.25]; Nandini Oza, *The Struggle for Narmada: An Oral History of the Narmada Bachao Andolan, by Adivasi Leaders Keshavbhau and Kevalsingh Vasave* (Hyderabad: Orient BlackSwan, 2022).

52 Ganges River Dolphin, WWF, https://www.worldwildlife.org/species/ganges-river-dolphin; Indus River Dolphin, WWF https://www.worldwildlife.org/species/indus-river-dolphin; Amazon River Dolphin, WWF, https://www.worldwildlife.org/species/amazon-river-dolphin [all accessed 06.05.25].

53 DG Correspondent, 'Dolphin Declared the National Aquatic Animal of India', Blog, Delhi Greens (27 May 2010) [accessed 06.05.25].

54 DG Correspondent, 'Dolphin Declared the National Aquatic Animal of India'; Government of Pakistan Tweet (24 February 2019), 4:10 p.m., https://twitter.com/GovtofPakistan/status/1099703121058717697?s=20&t=nXmpRDjYLjjnQeEniM_WVw [accessed 06.05.25]; 'Indus River Dolphin', WWF.

55 Rita Brara and Maria Valeria Berros, 'A World Parliament of Rivers', *Springs: The Rachel Carson Center Review* 1 (2022), https://springs-rcc.org/attributing-legal-personhood-to-rivers/ [accessed 24.04.25]; Isabella Kaminski, 'River Ouse May Become First in England to Gain Legal Rights', *The Guardian* (1 March 2023).

56 *Rights of Rivers: A Global Survey of the Rapidly Developing Rights of Nature Jurisprudence pertaining to Rivers* (Cyrus R. Vance Centre/Earth Law Centre, International Rivers, undated, c. 2021), Section 4.4.1 India, https://www.internationalrivers.org/resources/reports-and-publications/rights-of-river-report/ [accessed 06.05.25].

57 Bushra Quasmi, 'Rivers as Legal Persons: A Regressive Step', *Economic and Political Weekly* 52:30 (2017), 26.

Chapter 10: Birth of a River

1 Mr and Mrs S.C. Hall, *The Book of the Thames: From Its Rise to its Fall* (London, 1859), 4.

2 Jonathan Schneer, *The Thames: England's River* (London: Little, Brown,

2005), x; Thames River Trust, 'The Thames River Basin', https://www.thamesriverstrust.org.uk/the-thames-river-basin/; '"Water and Wetland Index – Critical Issues in Water Policy across Europe (2003)": Results Overview for the Thames River Basin (United Kingdom)', WWF (2003), 1, https://awsassets.panda.org/downloads/wwithamesuk.pdf [both accessed 12.05.25].

3 'Early Ice Age', GeoEssex' [accessed 15.07.22]; Andrew S. Goudie and Denys Brunsden, *The Environment of the British Isles: An Atlas* (Oxford: Clarendon Press 1994), 2, 5.

4 Margaret E. Collinson, *Fossil Plants of the London Clay* (London: The Palaeontological Association, London, 1984); 'Introduction', in *British Regional Geology: London and the Thames Valley*, compiled by M.G. Sumbler, 4th edn (London: HMSO for the British Geological Survey, 1996), 3–4; R.A. Ellison and J.A. Zalasiewicz, 'Palaeogene and Neogene', in *British Regional Geology* (1996), 94, 103–4.

5 'Introduction', in *British Regional Geology*, 4; Ellison and Zalasiewicz, 'Palaeogene and Neogene', 92.

6 Samuel Pepys, *The Diary of Samuel Pepys* (22 September 1665), https://www.pepysdiary.com/diary/1665/09/22/; 'East India Company ships at Deptford', Royal Museums Greenwich, https://www.rmg.co.uk/collections/objects/rmgc-object-13352; Jon Cotton, 'The Early River Thames: The Iron Age and Before' (24 February 2017), Brewminate: A Bold Blend of News and Ideas [all accessed 06.03.25].

7 M.G. Slumbler et al., 'Quaternary', in *British Regional Geology*, 132; Cotton, 'Early River Thames'; Walter Thornbury, 'Bagnigge Wells', in *Old and New London: Volume 2* (London, 1878), 296–8, in *British History Online*, http://www.british-history.ac.uk/old-new-london/vol2/pp296-298; 'John Conyers', The British Museum, https://www.britishmuseum.org/collection/term/AUTH233374 [both accessed 18.04.25].

8 'A letter to the publisher, written by the ingenious Mr. John Bagford', in Leland's *Collectanea* (1715): *Joannis Lelandi Antiquarii de Rebus Britannicis Collectanea: cum Thomae Hearnii Praefatione Notis et Indice ad Editionem Primam* (London, 1770), lxiii–lxvi.

9 D.P. McCarthy, 'The Biblical Chronology of James Ussher', *Irish Astronomical Journal* 24 (1997), 73–82; Handaxe, British Museum Cat. No. SLAntiq.246. https://www.britishmuseum.org/collection/object/H_SLAntiq-246 [accessed 18.04.25].

10 Lisa Hendry, 'First Britons', Natural History Museum (NHM) Blog https://www.nhm.ac.uk/discover/first-britons.html [accessed 15.02.25].

11 L.C. Dale, 'An Analysis of the Furze Platt Handaxes at the Royal Ontario Museum, Toronto', *Lithics: The Journal of the Lithic Studies Society* 41

(2020), 66; Slumbler et al., 'Quaternary', 129, 130, 132; Derek Hodgson, 'The First Appearance of Symmetry in the Human Lineage: Where Perception Meets Art', *Symmetry* 3:1 (2011), 45.

12 L.C. Dale, 'Early Neanderthal Social and Behavioural Complexity during the Purfleet Interglacial: Handaxes in the Latest Lower Palaeolithic' (unpublished PhD thesis, Durham University, 2022), 16–17; Dinnis and Stringer, *Britain*, 53.

13 Ian Sample, 'First Humans Arrived in Britain 250,000 Years Earlier than Thought', *The Guardian* (7 July 2010); Nick Ashton et al., 'Hominin Footprints from Early Pleistocene Deposits at Happisburgh, UK', *PLoS ONE* 9:2 (2014), 1–13; Chris Gosden, *Prehistory: A Very Short Introduction*, 2nd edn (Oxford: Oxford University Press, 2018), 29–30.

14 Josie Mills, 'Migration Event: When Did the First Humans Arrive in Britain?', University College London [UCL] Blog (24 February 2019), https://blogs.ucl.ac.uk/researchers-in-museums/2019/02/24/migration-event-when-did-the-first-humans-arrive-in-britain/ [accessed 23.04.22]; 'First Pioneers in Northern Europe 900,000 Years Ago', British Museum Blog, https://www.britishmuseum.org/research/projects/first-pioneers-northern-europe [accessed 21.04.22].

15 Ancient Human Occupation of Britain (AHOB) Database: Happisburgh 1 Epoch: Middle Pleistocene; Biozone: 'Cromerian'; MIS: 13, https://www.ahobproject.org/database/showSite.php?View=FAUNA&LocNum=25; AHOB Database: Happisburgh 3 Epoch: Early Pleistocene; Biozone: 'Cromerian'; MIS: 21, https://www.ahobproject.org/database/showSite.php?View=FAUNA&LocNum=745 [both accessed 07.03.25]; Dinnis and Stringer, *Britain*, 43; Song Xing et al., 'Middle Pleistocene Hominin Teeth from Longtan Cave, Hexian, China', *PLoS ONE* 9:2 (2014), 2, 4; Yang-heshan Yang et al., 'Last Record of Trogontherium Cuvieri (Mammalia, Rodentia) from the Late Pleistocene of China', *Quaternary International* 513 (2019), 30–6.

16 Dinnis and Stringer, *Britain*, 81–3.

17 Slumbler et al., 'Quaternary', 110.

18 'Mammoth Bones at Trafalgar-Square', *The Times* (21 November 1924), 17; Chris Manias, 'Hippos of the Thames', *History Today*, 66:4 (2016).

19 Slumbler et al., 'Quaternary', 110, 129; 'First Pioneers in Northern Europe 900,000 Years Ago', British Museum Blog.

20 Luc Amkreutz and Sasja van der Vaart-Verschoof (eds), *Doggerland: Lost World under the North Sea* (Leiden: Sidestone Press, 2022).

21 Dinnis and Stringer, *Britain*, 93; Cunliffe, *Europe between the Oceans*, 36–7; Olav Odé et al., 'Mapping a Drowning Land', in Amkreutz and van der Vaart-Verschoof (eds), *Doggerland*, 38–41.

22 Cunliffe, *Europe between the Oceans*, 37 (maps); Odé et al., 'Mapping a Drowning Land'.

23 Dinnis and Stringer, *Britain*, 143; 'Cheddar Man FAQ', NHM Blog, https://www.nhm.ac.uk/our-science/research/projects/human-adaptation-diet-disease/cheddar-man-faq.html [accessed 15.02.25].

24 Richard Bradley, *The Prehistory of Britain and Ireland*, 2nd edn (Cambridge: Cambridge University Press, 2019), 7.

25 Dominic Perring, 'London's Hadrianic War?', *Britannia*, 48 (2017), 42–3.

26 Battersea Shield, British Museum no. 1857,0715.1, https://www.britishmuseum.org/collection/object/H_1857-0715-1; The Waterloo Helmet, British Museum no. 1988,1004.1, https://www.britishmuseum.org/collection/object/H_1988-1004-1; La Tène, British Museum, https://www.britishmuseum.org/collection/term/x111161 [all accessed 07.05.25].

27 Bradley, *Prehistory of Britain and Ireland*, 166.

28 Salway, *Roman Britain*, 16, 19; Barry W. Cunliffe, *The Celts: A Very Short Introduction* (Oxford/New York: Oxford University Press, 2003), 80.

29 William Shakespeare, *The Life and Death of Richard the Second*, Act 2, Sc. 1, http://shakespeare.mit.edu/richardii/richardii.2.1.html [accessed 15.02.25].

30 Michael B. Charles and Michael Singleton, 'Claudius, Elephants and Britain: Making Sense of Cassius Dio 60.21.2', *Britannia*, 53 (2022), 175; A.A. Barrett, 'Claudius' British Victory Arch in Rome', *Britannia* 22 (1991), 1; Salway, *Roman Britain*, 13, 24–5.

31 John Schofield and Tony Dyson, *Archaeology of the City of London* (London: City of London Archaeological Trust, 1980), 6; Cunliffe, *Celts*, 18–21, 88–9; Salway, *Roman Britain*, 8, 19–21.

32 Quote from *The Panegyrick Oration, Ascribed to Mamertinus, in Praise of the Emperours Dioclesian and Maximian; Intituled only to Maximian*, in Aylett Sammes, *Britannia Antiqua Illustrata*, Vol. I (London: 1676), 310; Salway, *Roman Britain*, 12; Cunliffe, *Celts*, 89.

33 Tacitus, 'Agricola', *Agricola* and *Germania*, no. 11, page 9.

34 Tacitus quoted in Salway, *Roman Britain*, 33.

35 Barry Cunliffe, 'The Temple of Sulis Minerva at Bath', *Archaeology* 36:6 (1983), 16–23; Salway, *Roman Britain*, 54–5.

36 M. Rhodes. 'The Roman Coinage from London Bridge and the Development of the City and Southwark', *Britannia* 22 (1991), 179–90; 'London Span', *Arizona Republic* (19 April 1968), 18.

37 J.N. Adams, '"Romanitas" and the Latin Language', *The Classical Quarterly* 53:1 (2003), 184–205.

38 Peter Ackroyd, *Thames: Sacred River* (London: Vintage Books, 2008), 23–4.

39 Peter Rowsome and Mark Burch, *Londinium: A New Map and Guide to Roman London* (London: Museum of London Archaeology, 2011); Ian Blair and Jenny Hall, *Working Water: Roman Technology in Action* (London: Museum of London, 2003), 13–14.

40 Rowsome and Burch, 'Londinium: A New Map'; BHM Aquincumi Museum and Archaeological Park, http://www.aquincum.hu/en/aktprogram/beporzok-napja-2025; 'Roman Amphitheatre', Alexandria Portal, http://www.alexandria.gov.eg/Alex/english/Roman%20Amphitheater.html [both accessed 15.02.25].

41 Stephen D. Myers, 'The River Walbrook and Roman London' (unpublished PhD thesis, University of Reading, 2016), 1–2; Rowsome and Burch, 'Londinium: A New Map'.

42 Rowsome and Burch, 'Londinium: A New Map'.

43 Isca Howell et al., *Roman and Medieval Development South of Cheapside: Excavations at Bow Bells House, City of London, 2005–6*, MOLA Archaeology Studies Series 26 (London: Museum of London Archaeology, 2013), 9, 76, 87.

44 Barbara West and Gustav Milne, 'Owls in the Basilica', *London Archaeologist* 7 (2002), 31–5.

45 A.J. Parker, 'The Birds of Roman London', *Oxford Journal of Archaeology* 7:2 (July 1988), 197, 212, 217; Peter Holden and Tim Cleeves, *RSPB Handbook of British Birds*, 3rd edn (London: Christopher Helm, 2010), 120; Bailleul-Lesuer, 'Exploitation of Live Avian Resources in Pharaonic Egypt', 9–10.

46 Parker, 'Birds of Roman London', 208.

47 Salway, *Roman Britain*, 26–7.

48 Cunliffe, *Celts*, 88–91; Salway, *Roman Britain*, 30–1; Hazel Muir, 'Boudicca Rampaged through the Streets of South London', *New Scientist* (21 October 1995) [accessed 06.03.25]; Rowsome and Burch, 'Londinium: A New Map'.

49 Salway, *Roman Britain*, 26–7; 'History of Hadrian's Wall', English Heritage, https://www.english-heritage.org.uk/visit/places/hadrians-wall/hadrians-wall-history-and-stories/history/; 'The Antonine Wall', https://www.antoninewall.org/ [both accessed 06.03.25].

50 Blair and Hall, *Working Water*, 9; Bronze head of Hadrian (117–138 CE), British Museum, no. 1848,1103.1, https://www.britishmuseum.org/collection/object/H_1848-1103-1 [accessed 06.03.25].

51 'Archaeologists Reveal Details of Huge Fort Built by Romans on Route into London 2,000 Years Ago', Museums.EU, The European Museums Network, 17 May 2016, https://museums.eu/article/details/116222/archaeologists-reveal-details-of-huge-fort-built-by-romans-on-route-

into-london-2000-years-ago [accessed 06.03.25]; Blair and Hall, *Working Water*, 16, 23; Ian Blair et al., 'Wells and Bucket-Chains: Unforeseen Elements of Water Supply in Early Roman London', *Britannia* 37 (2006), 8; Salway, *Roman Britain*, 32; Myers, 'River Walbrook and Roman London', 202.

52 London Museum, 'Lost Rivers: The Walbrook', https://www.londonmuseum.org.uk/collections/london-stories/lost-rivers-the-walbrook/; Mithraeum, Bloomberg Philanthropies, https://www.bloomberg.org/arts/advancing-the-arts-around-world/mithraeum; Danubian Riders, London Museum, https://www.londonmuseum.org.uk/collections/v/object-448174/danubian-riders [all accessed 05.04.25]; John Schofield and Tony Dyson, *Archaeology of the City of London* (London: City of London Archaeological Trust, 1980), 22–3.

53 Rowsome and Burch, 'Londinium: A New Map'.

54 Nick Bateman, 'Death, Women, and the Afterlife: Some Thoughts on a Burial in Southwark', in John Clark et al. (eds), *Londinium and Beyond: Essays on Roman London and its Hinterland for Harvey Sheldon*, CBA Research Report 156 (Council for British Archaeology, 2008), 162–6.

55 Martin Henig, 'Glass and Copper-Alloy Pendant', in Howell and Blackmore, *Roman and Medieval Development South of Cheapside*, 58–9.

56 Salway, *Roman Britain*, 98–101; David Williams and César Carreras, 'North African Amphorae in Roman Britain: A Re-Appraisal', *Britannia* 26 (1995), 240.

57 John Blair, *The Anglo-Saxon Age: A Very Short Introduction* (Oxford/New York: Oxford University Press, 2000), 23–4; Ian Wood, 'The Mission of Augustine of Canterbury to the English', *Speculum* 69:1 (1994), 16.

58 John Schofield and Tony Dyson, *Archaeology of the City of London* (London: City of London Archaeological Trust, 1980), 20–9; Dominic Perring, *London in the Roman World* (Oxford: Oxford University Press, 2022), 350–70.

59 Victoria Ridgeway, *Secrets of the Gardens: Archaeologists Unearth the Lives of Roman Londoners at Drapers' Gardens* (Brockley: Pre-Construct Archaeology, 2009), 56–65; James Gerrard, 'Wells and Belief Systems at the End of Roman Britain: A Case Study from Roman London', *Late Antique Archaeology* 7:1 (2011), 551–72; Peter Guest, 'The Hoarding of Roman Metal Objects in Fifth-Century Britain', in F.K. Haarer (ed.), *AD 410: The History and Archaeology of Late and Post-Roman Britain* (London: Society for the Promotion of Roman Studies, 2014), 117–29; Salway, *Roman Britain*, 78; Rowsome and Burch, *Londinium: A New Map*.

60 Cunliffe, *Celts*, 99.

61 Derek Keene, 'The Walbrook Study: A Summary Report. Social and

Economic Study of Medieval London' (London: Centre for Metropolitan History, Institute of Historical Research, 1987), 2; Douglas Killock, 'London's Middle Saxon Waterfront: Excavations at the Adelphi Building', *Transactions of the London and Middlesex Archaeological Society* 70, Supplement (2019), 129–65; R. Cowie, 'Lundenwic – "unravelling the Strand"', *Archaeology Today* 8:5 (1987), 30–4.

62 Historic England Research Records: Blackfriars Ship I, Hob Uid: 405065, Heritage Gateway, https://www.heritagegateway.org.uk/Gateway/Results_Single.aspx?uid=405065&resourceID=19191 [accessed 06.05.25]; Historic England, *Kent: Building Stones of England* (Swindon: Historic England, 2023).

63 R.L. Terrington et al., 'Quantifying Anthropogenic Modification of the Shallow Geosphere in Central London, UK', *Geomorphology* 319 (2018), 15–34.

Chapter 11: Shadows of an Imperial River

1 British Library: T. Milles, *Custumers Alphabet and Primer. Conteining their creede . . . their Ten Commandements . . . and Forme of Prayers. Togither with a pertinent Answere to All such as . . . would faine perswade others that the bringing home of Traffique must needes decay our shipping, etc* (1608).

2 E. Spenser, *The Faerie Queen*, Book IV, Canto XI, from *The Complete Works in Verse and Prose of Edmund Spenser* (London, 1882), compiled by Risa S. Bear, University of Oregon, https://scholarsbank.uoregon.edu/server/api/core/bitstreams/5792a02b-164d-4de4-98a9-37ab8c8463bc/content [accessed 06.03.25]; A. MacColl, 'The Temple of Venus, the Wedding of the Thames and the Medway, and the End of *The Faerie Queene*, Book IV', *The Review of English Studies* 40:157 (1989), 39.

3 Spenser, *Faerie Queen*, Book IV, Canto XI.

4 John Denham, 'Cooper's Hill' (*Poems and Translations*, 1668), available at https://jacklynch.net/Texts/cooper.html [accessed 07.03.2025]; T.H. Banks, 'Sir John Denham's "Cooper's Hill"', *The Modern Language Review* 21:3 (1926), 269–77.

5 'The Thames or the Triumph of Navigation (caricature)', Royal Museums Greenwich, https://www.rmg.co.uk/collections/objects/rmgc-object-147312 [accessed 27.05.24].

6 Campbell, *Rivers and the Powers of Ancient Rome*; Ackroyd, *Thames: Sacred River*, 24; Vanessa Taylor, 'Water and Its Meanings in London: 1800–1914', in Bill Luckin and Peter Thorsheim, *A Mighty Capital under Threat: The Environmental History of London, 1800–2000* (Pittsburgh,

PA: University of Pittsburgh Press, 2020), 166; M@, 'Who Is Old Father Thames', *Londonist* Blog, 2017, https://londonist.com/2015/07/who-was-old-father-thames [accessed 15.02.25].

7 David Garrioch, '1666 and London's Fire History: A Re-Evaluation', *The Historical Journal* 59:2 (2016), 319–38.

8 S. Healy, 'Newcastle-upon-Tyne, Borough', in A.D. Thrush and J. Ferris (eds), *The House of Commons, 1604–1629* (Cambridge/New York: published for the History of Parliament Trust by Cambridge University Press, 2010), https://www.historyofparliamentonline.org/volume/1604-1629/constituencies/newcastle-upon-tyne [accessed 07.03.25].

9 Francis Sheppard, *London: A History* (Oxford: Oxford University Press, 1998), 126; The National Archives [TNA], 'Hearth Tax return for Pudding Lane (Book 4), August 1666', digitized at TNA Education Service, 'The Great Fire of London: How London Changed. What Happened?', https://nationalarchives.gov.uk/documents/education/fire-of-london.pdf [accessed 30.10.20]; Matthew Davies et al., *London and Middlesex Hearth Tax, Part 1 and Part 2* (London: British Records Society, 2014); Dorian Gerhold, 'Where Did the Great Fire Begin?', *London and Middlesex Archaeological Society Transactions*, 66 (2015), 1–7.

10 Garrioch, '1666 and London's Fire History', 330–1; Margaret Makepeace, *The East India Company's London Workers: Management of the Warehouse Labourers, 1800–1858,* new edn (Woodbridge, Suffolk: Boydell & Brewer, 2010), 17–39; Hazel Forsyth, *Butcher, Baker, Candlestick Maker: Surviving the Great Fire of London* (London: I.B. Tauris, 2016), 11.

11 Pepys, *Diary of Samuel Pepys* (2 September 1666), https://www.pepysdiary.com/diary/1666/09/02/ [accessed 26.05.24].

12 James W.P. Campbell, 'The Supply of Stone for the Rebuilding of St Paul's Cathedral 1675–1710', *Construction History* 28:2 (2013), 26–7, 35, 37, 41.

13 Eric Robinson and Martin Litherland, *Holiday Geology Guide – Greenwich* (British Geological Society/NERC, 1999).

14 Vanessa Harding, 'Recent Perspectives on Early Modern London', *The Historical Journal* 47:2 (2004), 435; Elizabeth McKellar, *The Birth of Modern London: The Development and Design of the City, 1660–1720* (Manchester/New York: Manchester University Press, 1999), 13.

15 Robert Hooke, England's Leonardo, 'Architecture', http://roberthooke.org.uk/?page_id=166 [accessed 15.02.25]; School of Samuel Scott, 'Entrance to the Fleet River' (1750), London Picture Archive (City of London Corporation), accession no. 46.

16 Robert Hooke's London, 'A Week in the Life of Robert Hooke: Sunday 23 March to Saturday 29 March 1673' (posted 30 March 2013), [accessed 15.02.25]; Carry van Lieshout, 'London's Changing Waterscapes: The

Management of Water in Eighteenth-Century London' (unpublished PhD thesis, King's College, University of London, 2012); Nicholas Barton, *The Lost Rivers of London: A Study of Their Effects upon London and Londoners* (New Barnet, Herts: Historical Publications Ltd, 1962), 76–8; David Fathers, *London's Hidden Rivers: A Walker's Guide to the Subterranean Waterways of London* (London: Francis Lincoln, 2017), 61; UCL River Fleet Restoration Team, 'The History of the River Fleet' (2009), 7–8, https://www.camden.gov.uk/documents/20142/1458280/River+Fleet.pdf [accessed 15.02.25].

17 Coates, *Story of Six Rivers*, 171–4.

18 I.E.S. Edwards, 'Notable Acquisitions of Egyptian Antiquities in the Years 1753–1853', *The British Museum Quarterly* 18:1 (1953), 15; 'Everything You Ever Wanted to Know about the Rosetta Stone', British Museum Blog (14 July 2017) [accessed 07.05.22].

19 Andrew Phillips and J.C. Sharman, *Outsourcing Empire: How Company-States Made the Modern World* (Princeton, NJ/Oxford: Princeton University Press, 2020); Michael Talbot, *British-Ottoman Relations, 1661–1807: Commerce and Diplomatic Practice in Eighteenth-Century Istanbul* (Woodbridge, Suffolk/Rochester, New York: Boydell & Brewer, 2017); William A. Pettigrew and David Veevers (eds), *The Corporation as a Protagonist in Global History, c. 1550–1750* (Leiden/Boston: Brill, 2018); Makepeace, *East India Company's London Workers*, 17, 24.

20 John Blake, *The Sea Chart: The Illustrated History of Nautical Maps and Navigational Charts* (London: Conway Maritime, 2009), 74.

21 'Text of HBC's Royal Charter' (2 May 1670), Hudson's Bay Company. https://www.hbcheritage.ca/things/artifacts/the-charter-and-text [accessed 31.05.24].

22 Bryony Coles, 'The European Beaver', in Terry O'Connor and Naomi Sykes (eds), *Extinctions and Invasions: A Social History of British Fauna* (Oxford: Oxbow Books/Windgather Press, 2010), 112, 115.

23 A.M. Carlos and F.D. Lewis, *Commerce by a Frozen Sea: Native Americans and the European Fur Trade* (Philadelphia, PA: University of Pennsylvania Press, 2010), 4, 15–35; E.E. Rich, 'Russia and the Colonial Fur Trade', *The Economic History Review*, 7:3 (1955), 310.

24 TNA: MPG 1/221 (map) item extracted from CO 267/11: West Africa, 'A Draught of the Coast of Africa from the Streights Mouth to Cape Bona Esprance' [1663–1681]; William Pettigrew, *Freedom's Debt: The Royal African Company and the Politics of the Atlantic Slave Trade, 1672–1752* (Chapel Hill, NC: University of North Carolina Press, 2013), 11.

25 P.W. Mapp, *The Elusive West and the Contest for Empire, 1713–1763* (Chapel Hill, NC: University of North Carolina Press, 2011); J.W. Gerard, *The*

Peace of Utrecht: A Historical Review of the Great Treaty of 1713–14, and of the Principal Events of the War of the Spanish Succession (New York/ London, 1885), 292.

26 Jane Glover, *Handel in London: The Making of a Genius* (London: Picador, 2019), 47, 72, 87–8, 95; Antonia Quirke, 'In Search of the Black Mozart: A Revealing Look at Handel's Investment in the Slave Trade', *New Statesman* (4 June 2015); D. Hunter, 'Handel and the Royal African Company', Musicology Now website (14 June 2015), https://musicologynow.org/handel-and-the-royal-african-company/ [accessed 07.03.25]; David Conn, 'The British Kings and Queens who Supported and Profited from Slavery', *The Guardian* (6 April 2023). See also the Centre for the Study of the Legacies of British Slavery, UCL, https://www.ucl.ac.uk/lbs.

27 Pettigrew, *Freedom's Debt*, 12; Kenneth Morgan, *Edward Colston and Bristol* (Bristol: The Bristol Branch of the Historical Association, 1999); 'Liverpool: The Castle and Development of the Town', in W. Farrer and J. Brownbill (eds), *A History of the County of Lancaster: Volume 4* (London, 1911), 4–36; Madge Dresser (with contributions from Bristol Museums Black History Steering Group), 'Bristol and the Transatlantic Slave Trade', Bristol Museums, https://www.bristolmuseums.org.uk/stories/bristol-transatlantic-slave-trade/; *Discovering Britain: Making Connections: A Self-Guided Walk in Falkirk* (Royal Geographical Society with IBG, 2014), 4, https://www.discoveringbritain.org/content/discoveringbritain/walk%20booklets/Falkirk%20walk%20-%20written%20guide.pdf [both accessed 07.03.25].

28 Jörg Vögele, *Urban Mortality Change in England and Germany, 1870–1913* (Liverpool: Liverpool University Press, 1998), 37, Table 3.

29 Fariborz Nasr-Azadani et al., 'Downscaling River Discharge to Assess the Effects of Climate Change on Cholera Outbreaks in the Bengal Delta', *Climate Research* 64:3 (2015), 257–74.

30 'Cholera', *Evening Mail* (London) (16 November 1831), 1; E. Ashworth Underwood, 'The History of Cholera in Great Britain', *Proceedings of the Royal Society of Medicine, Section of Epidemiology and State Medicine* (3 November 1947), 165–73; Bill Luckin, *Pollution and Control: A Social History of the Thames in the Nineteenth Century* (Bristol: Adam Hilger, 1986).

31 Luckin, *Pollution and Control*, 81, 83, 87.

32 Newcastle University, Rare Book Collection: RB616.932 BEL: Gateshead Board of Health, Cholera Morbus, Collections relative to the Cholera at Gateshead, in the county of Durham (1831–32); J.P. Kay, 'Letter to The Revd Thomas Chalmers', *The Moral and Physical Condition of the Working Classes Employed in the Cotton Manufactories in Manchester*, facsimile 2nd edn (Manchester: E.J. Morten, 1832, 1969), 8.

33 Luckin, *Pollution and Control*, Chapter 4.
34 Luckin, *Pollution and Control*, 18.
35 S. Halliday, *The Great Stink of London: Sir Joseph Bazalgette and the Cleansing of the Victorian Metropolis* (Stroud, Glos: Sutton Publishing Ltd., 1999).
36 Thames Water's Tideway Tunnel, https://www.tideway.london.
37 Barton, *Lost Rivers of London.*
38 Halliday, *Great Stink*, 145, 148; Dale H. Porter, *The Thames Embankment: Environment, Technology, and Society in Victorian London* (Akron, OH: University of Akron Press, 1998).
39 M. Bawtree, 'The City of London Coal Duties and Their Boundary Marks', *London Archaeologist* 1:2 (1969), 27–30.
40 Stawell Heard, 'Drowning in Sewage: The Forgotten Story of the Principe Alice Disaster', Royal Greenwich Museums Blog (1 June 2021), https://www.rmg.co.uk/stories/blog/library-archive/drowning-sewage-sinking-princess-alice [accessed 07.03.25].
41 Leslie B. Wood, *The Restoration of the Tidal Thames* (Bristol: Adam Hilger, 1982); McCormick et al. (eds), *State of the Thames 2021*, 59.
42 *Report to Board of Trade by Inspector of Fisheries on Injury to Fisheries by Deposit of Rubbish in Estuary of River Thames.* House of Commons, Reports of Commissioners, C. 5394 (1888), 4–5.
43 J. Vernon, *Modern Britain 1750 to the Present* (Cambridge: Cambridge University Press, 2017), 230.
44 T. Wiles, '[Introduction]', *Journal of the Royal Society of Arts* 77:3972 (1929), 186.
45 J.H. Estill, 'The Port of London', *Journal of the Royal Society of Arts* 77:3972 (1929), 191–6; S. Abrevaya Stein, '"Falling into Feathers": Jews and the Trans-Atlantic Ostrich Feather Trade', *The Journal of Modern History* 79:4 (2007), 802–4; Beaver House, London Picture Archive: SC_PHL_01_014_83_3415.
46 John A. Burton, *The Naturalist in London* (Newton Abbot/London: David & Charles, 1974), 87; Joint Nature Conservation Committee (JNCC), 'Non-Native Marine Species in British Waters: A Review and Directory' (JNCC, 1997), 94, http://jncc.defra.gov.uk/page-1700 [accessed 20.07.22]; GB Non-Native Species Information Portal (GNNNSIP) (http://www.nonnativespecies.org [accessed 07.03.25]; P.F. Clark et al., *The Commercial Exploitation of Thames Mitten Crabs: A Feasibility Study.* A Report for the Department for Environment, Food and Rural Affairs by the Department of Zoology, The Natural History Museum, London DEFRA. Ref FGE 274 (2008). See also Neal Ascherson, *Black Sea: The Birthplace of Civilisation and Barbarism* (London: Vintage 2007), Chapter 11.
47 Nigel Watson, *Port of London Authority: A Century of Service 1909–2009*

(Gravesend: St Matthew's Press, 2009), 221; 'House Flag, Shell Mex and B. P. Ltd', Royal Greenwich Museums, https://www.rmg.co.uk/collections/objects/rmgc-object-383 [accessed 07.09.25]; A. Cochrane and G. Jones, 'Samuel, Marcus, first Viscount Bearsted (1853–1927), petroleum entrepreneur', *ODNB*; T.S. Eliot, 'The Waste Land', *Selected Poems* (London: Faber and Faber, 1961), 61.

48 'Loss of the Maria Lee', *The Times* (22 October 1873); Exploring Kent's Past: Maria Lee, Kent County Council: HER No. TQ 57 NE 38, https://webapps.kent.gov.uk/KCC.ExploringKentsPast.Web.Sites.Public/SingleResult.aspx?uid=MKE12492 [accessed 28.04.24]; 'Fatal Explosion', *The Times* (20 July 1889); 'Naptha Vessel Struck by Lightning', *Northern Guardian* (Hartlepool) (6 July 1900); 'Great Fire at Purfleet', *Morning Post* (12 January 1897).

49 C.T. Marvin, *The Region of the Eternal Fire: An Account of a Journey to the Petroleum Region of the Caspian in 1883* (London, 1891) 318, also 236; Helen Thompson, *Disorder: Hard Times in the 21st Century* (Oxford: Oxford University Press, 2023), 18–23, 67–8.

Chapter 12: Thames Gateway

1 Charles Dickens Jr, *Dickens's Dictionary of the Thames, From Its Source to the Nore, 1885: An Unconventional Handbook* (London, 1885), 49.

2 Ramesh Kallidai, quoted in Mark Gould, 'Riddle of the Hindu Relics in the Thames', *The Guardian* (2 November 2005); Nikola Burdon, 'Hindu Finds from the Thames', *London Archaeologist* 10:10 (2004), 276–9; Ackroyd, *Thames*, 81.

3 'Double-Edged Sword', London Museum, Object ID A2373, https://www.londonmuseum.org.uk/collections/v/object-37092/double-edged-sword/ [accessed 15.02.25]; see also 'The Bridges that Built London', BBC Four, 2012, extract on YouTube, https://www.youtube.com/watch?v=MFB26RwHK6U [accessed 07.03.25].

4 'A Pestilential River', *The Times* (9 August 1897); 'Reservoir Finds', *The Times* (8 October 1959).

5 Dr Jane Kershaw quoted in I. Kwai, 'This Treasure Hunter's Latest Find? A 1,000-Year-Old Viking Sword', *The New York Times* (15 March 2024). Thanks to Diane Bramble for this.

6 Charles Dickens, 'Bound for the Great Salt Lake', *All the Year Round* 9 (4 July 1863), 444–9; A.J. Lloyd, 'Emigration, Immigration and Migration in Nineteenth-Century Britain', *British Library Newspapers* (Detroit, MI: Gale, 2007), https://www.gale.com/binaries/content/assets/gale-us-en/primary-sources/intl-gps/intl-gps-essays/full-ghn-contextual-essays/

ghn_essay_bln_lloyd1_website.pdf [accessed 24.07.22]; Raphael Samuel, 'Comers and Goers', in H.J. Dyos and M. Wolff (eds), *The Victorian City, Vol. 1* (London: Routledge & Kegan Paul, 1973), 123–60.

7 Curators' Note, No. 9, 'Metal Statuettes of Vishnu, 20th Century', 'Secret Rivers' Exhibition, London Museum (2019).

8 'Swaminarayan Jayanti', BBC Religions (28 August 2009), https://www.bbc.co.uk/religion/religions/hinduism/holydays/swaminarayanjayanti.shtml; 'Yogiji Maharaj', https://www.swaminarayan.org/yogijimaharaj/life/29.htm; Putney Bridge (28 June 1970), Petersham Meadows (29 September 1974), *UK Prasadi Yatra Guidebook* (London: BAPS Swaminarayan Sanstha, 2015), nos. 2, 7, http://download.baps.org/Data/Sites/1/Media/OtherPDFs/UK_Prasadi_Yatra_Guidebook__web__001.pdf; 'Jal-Jhilani Celebrations on the River Thames, London UK' (15 September 2013), BAPS Swaminarayan Sanstha website, https://www.baps.org/Photos/2013/Jal-Jhilani-Utsav-7167.aspx?mid=49459 [all accessed 15.02.25].

9 'Islington Temple', *Illustrated London News* (20 June 1970); Public Invitation, Opening of Yogi Hall, 14 June 1970, in 'Yogiji Maharaj in the UK: 50th Anniversary Celebrations, UK & Europe', BAPS Swaminarayan Sanstha (14 June 2020), https://www.baps.org/Photos/2020/Yogiji-Maharaj-in-the-UK-A-Photo-Story-22179.aspx?mid=210982 [accessed 15.02.25].

10 *UK Prasadi Yatra Guidebook*, no. 19.

11 'Awards & Accolades', Shree Swaminarayan Mandir, https://londonmandir.baps.org/the-mandir/awards/ [accessed 15.02.25].

12 'HH Pramukh Swami Maharaj's Asthipushpa Visarjan at Hudson River, New York, New York, USA' (7 September 2017), BAPS Swamimarayan Sanstha, https://www.baps.org/News/2017/Asthipushpa-Visarjan-NY-12012.aspx [accessed 15.02.25].

13 D. Majumdar, 'Hindu Idols to be Immersed in Thames', BBC News (27 September 2006), http://news.bbc.co.uk/1/hi/england/london/5382200.stm; 'In Pictures: Making a Deity', BBC News (28 September 2006), http://news.bbc.co.uk/1/hi/in_pictures/5386404.stm; 'Thames Immersion for Hindu Idols', BBC News (2 October 2006), http://news.bbc.co.uk/1/hi/england/london/5401122.stm; Kalyan Majumdar in 'Statue of Hindu Goddess Immersed in River in Religious Festival', AP Archive (3 October 2006/23 July 2015), https://www.youtube.com/watch?v=XP1gVi4TeGQ [all accessed 07.03.25].

14 'A Sense of Belonging', Hounslow Ganeshotsav Mandal, https://www.hgmlondon.co.uk/about; Thames Ganeshotsav Mandal, 2015, https://thamesfestivaltrust.org/whats-on/thames-ganeshotsav-mandal-2015-1093/ [both accessed 15.02.25].

15 S. Rait, 'Sikh Mourning', Remembrance Exhibition, Abbey House Museum & University of Leeds (25 June 2018) [accessed 15.06.24]; 'Demand for Funeral Pyres for Hindus, Sikhs', *Hindustan Times* (14 January 2006); 'River May Become UK "Ganges"', BBC News (21 August 2002), http://news.bbc.co.uk/1/hi/england/2205913.stm [accessed 14.06.24]; Ackroyd, *Sacred River*, 81.

16 G.R. Sims, 'Sweated London', in G.R. Sims (ed.), *Living London*, vol. 1 (London, 1902), 50–1; Newman, 'The Poor Jews' Temporary Shelter'; Culiner, *Finding Home*; David Feldman, 'Jews in the East End, Jews in the Polity, "The Jew" in the Text', *19: Interdisciplinary Studies in the Long Nineteenth Century* 13 (2011), https://doi.org/10.16995/ntn.630.

17 British Brothers League poster (January 1902), https://commons.wikimedia.org/wiki/File:BritishBrothersLeaguePoster(1902).jpg [accessed 15.02.25]; Henry Norman quoted in 'England for the English', *Tower Hamlets Independent and East End Local Advertiser* (18 January 1902), 8.

18 Aliens Act 1905 c. 13; Krista Maglen, 'Intercepting Infection: Quarantine, the Port Sanitary Authority and Immigration in Late Nineteenth and Early Twentieth Century Britain' (unpublished PhD thesis, Glasgow University, 2001), Chapter 5.

19 Royal British Legion, 'Charles Wotten (1895–1919)' (31 October 2021) [accessed 24.07.22]; J. Jenkinson, *Black 1919: Riots, Racism and Resistance in Imperial Britain* (Liverpool: Liverpool University Press, 2009), 166–8; Gerwarth and Manela, 'Great War as a Global War'.

20 Special Restriction (Coloured Alien Seamen) Order (1925), Open University, Making Britain Database, https://www.open.ac.uk/researchprojects/makingbritain/content/special-restriction-coloured-alien-seamen-order-1925 [accessed 24.07.22]; M. Pearsall, 'Enemy Aliens in Great Britain 1914–1919', TNA Blog (24 March 2017) [accessed 24.07.22]; L. Tabili, 'The Construction of Racial Difference in Twentieth-Century Britain: The Special Restriction (Coloured Alien Seamen) Order, 1925', *Journal of British Studies* 33, 1 (1994), 54–98; M. Matera, *Black London: The Imperial Metropolis and Decolonization in the Twentieth Century*, (Oakland, CA: University of California Press, 2015), Chapter 1.

21 J. Salter, *The Asiatic in England: Sketches of Sixteen Years' Work among Orientals* (London, 1873).

22 Bank of England Inflation Calculator, https://www.bankofengland.co.uk/monetary-policy/inflation/inflation-calculator [accessed 06.09.24].

23 D.P. Patel, 'The Grand Old Man: Dadabhai Naoroji and the Evolution of the Demand for Indian Self-Government' (unpublished PhD thesis, Harvard University, 2015), 68, 86–7, 221–2.

24 R.M. Hughes, 'Conclusion', in Salter, *Asiatic in England*, 296–303; John

Marriott, *The Other Empire: Metropolis, India and Progress in the Colonial Imagination* (Manchester: Manchester University Press, 2003).

25 Hughes, 'Conclusion', 299.

26 Dadabhai Naoroji, Open University, Making Britain Database, https://www.open.ac.uk/researchprojects/makingbritain/content/dadabhai-naoroji; Bhikaiji Rustom Cama, Open University, Making Britain Database, https://www.open.ac.uk/researchprojects/makingbritain/content/madame-cama [both accessed 14.05.22]; R. Visram, *Asians in Britain: 400 Years of History* (London/Sterling, VA: Pluto Press, 2002); R. Visram, *Ayahs, Lascars and Princes: The Story of Indians in Britain 1700–1947* (London: Routledge, 1986, 2016).

27 'Strangers' Home for Asiatics, Africans and South Sea Islanders', Open University, Making Britain Database, https://www.open.ac.uk/researchprojects/makingbritain/content/strangers-home-asiatics-africans-and-south-sea-islanders; 'Nathalal Jagivan Upadhyaya', Open University, Making Britain Database, 'https://www.open.ac.uk/researchprojects/makingbritain/content/nathalal-jagivan-upadhyaya [both accessed 07.03.25]; Jenkinson, *Black 1919*, 77–8.

28 'Jomo Kenyatta', Open University, Making Britain Database, https://www5.open.ac.uk/research-projects/making-britain/content/jomo-kenyatta; 'Ports, British Shipping (Assistance) Act (1935)', Open University, Making Britain Database, https://www.open.ac.uk/researchprojects/makingbritain/taxonomy/term/640 [both accessed 07.03.25]; Matera, *Black London*; L. James and D. Whittall, 'Ambiguity and Imprint: British Racial Logics, Colonial Commissions of Enquiry, and the Creolization of Britain in the 1930s and 1940s', *Callaloo* 39:1 (2016), 166–84; E.F. Evans, 'Reverse Imperial Ethnography and C.L.R. James's London Writing', *Modernism/modernity* 28:2 (2021), 311–32.

29 British Nationality Act, 1948 c. 56; 'The Story of the Windrush', Royal Museums Greenwich Blog, https://www.rmg.co.uk/stories/windrush-histories/story-of-windrush-ship; David Olusoga, 'The Windrush Story Was Not a Rosy One Even Before the Ship Arrived', *The Guardian* (22 April 2018); Naomi Oppenheim, 'The Forgotten Voyages: Beyond Windrush', British Library Blog (5 July 2018), https://blogs.bl.uk/americas/2018/07/the-forgotten-voyages-beyond-windrush.html; National Windrush Museum, https://www.nationalwindrushmuseum.com/ [all accessed 07.03.25].

30 Commonwealth Immigration Act, 1968 c. 9; Immigration Act, 1971 c. 77. Jessica Elgot, 'Theresa May's "hostile environment" at Heart of Windrush scandal', *The Guardian* (17 April 2018); Diane Taylor, 'UK Removed Legal Protection for Windrush Immigrants in 2014', *The Guardian* (16 April

2018); Amelia Gentleman, 'Windrush: Only One in Four Applicants Have Received Compensation', *The Guardian* (22 June 2022); 'Windrush Generation: Who Are They and Why Are They Facing Problems?', BBC News (24 November 2021), https://www.bbc.co.uk/news/uk-43782241 [accessed 24.07.22].

31 M. Levinson, *The Box: How the Shipping Container Made the World Smaller and the World Economy Bigger*, 2nd edn (Princeton, NJ: Princeton University Press, 2016).

32 'A City Fit for Wildlife', *New Scientist* (28 March 1985), 30–3; K. Allen and A. Massoudi, 'Qatar and Brookfield Win Battle to Take Over Canary Wharf', *Financial Times* (28 January 2015); Phil Pinch, 'Waterspace Planning and the River Thames in London', *London Journal* 40:3 (2015), 272–92.

33 Rachael Burford, 'Campaigners Vow to Protest Outside Robert Milligan Slave Trader Statue "Every Day" Until it Is Torn Down', *The Standard* (9 June 2020).

34 'Minnesota Protesters Pull Down Columbus Statue at Capitol', MPR News (10 June 2020), https://www.mprnews.org/story/2020/06/10/minnesota-protesters-pull-down-columbus-statue-at-capitol; O. O'Connell, 'New Orleans Protesters Rip Down Statue of Slave Owner and Throw it in Mississippi River', *The Independent* (14 June 2020), https://www.independent.co.uk/news/world/americas/new-orleans-slave-owner-john-mcdonogh-statue-protest-mississippi-river-a9565666.html [all accessed 16.06.24].

35 Morgan, *Edward Colston and Bristol*; D. Hayton et al. (eds), 'Colston, Edward II (1636–1721), of Mortlake, Surr.', in *The House of Commons, 1690–1715* (Cambridge/New York: Cambridge University Press, 2002), http://www.historyofparliamentonline.org/volume/1690-1715/member/colston-edward-ii-1636–1721 [accessed 16.02.25]; J. Grey, 'Bristol George Floyd Protest: Colston Statue Toppled', BBC News (7 June 2020), https://www.bbc.co.uk/news/uk-england-bristol-52955868 [accessed 14.05.22]; H. Siddique and C. Skopeliti, 'BLM Protesters Topple Statue of Bristol Slave Trader Edward Colston', *The Guardian* (7 June 2020); David Olusoga, 'The Toppling of Edward Colston's Statue Is Not an Attack on History. It Is History', *The Guardian* (8 June 2020); @BristolCouncil Twitter (11 June 2020, 6:10 a.m.), https://twitter.com/BristolCouncil/status/1270946469864931328?ref_src=twsrc%5Etfw%7Ctwcamp%5Etweetembed%7Ctwterm%5E1270946469864931328%7Ctwgr%5E%7Ctwcon%5Es1_&ref_url=https%3A%2F%2Fwww.theguardian.com%2Fuk-news%2F2020%2Fjun%2F11%2Fedward-colston-statue-retrieved-bristol-harbour-black-lives-matter [accessed 13.05.22]; M. Shed,

'The Colston Statue: What Next?' (4 June 2021–3 January 2022), https://www.bristolmuseums.org.uk/whats-on/m-shed/the-colston-statue-what-next/ [accessed 16.02.25]; S. Morris, 'Statue of Slave Trader Edward Colston to Go on Display in Bristol Museum', *The Guardian* (28 May 2021).

36 M. Fry, 'Dundas, Henry, first Viscount Melville (1742–1811), politician', *ODNB*; @MuseumofLondon Tweets (9 June 2020), https://threadreader-app.com/thread/1270360552343326726.html [accessed 12.05.22]; BBC News, 'Robert Milligan: Slave Trader Statue Removed from Outside London Museum' (9 June 2020), https://www.bbc.co.uk/news/uk-england-london-52977088 [accessed 16.02.25]; A. Gray and D. Thom, '"The Surrounding Great Work": Memory, Erasure, and Curating the Built Environment of the West India Docks, 1802–2022', *British Art Studies* 22 (2022).

37 Rose George, *Ninety Percent of Everything* (New York: Metropolitan Books, 2013); Watson, *Port of London Authority*, 222; 'Our History', Port of London Authority, https://pla.co.uk/our-history; Nigel Spearing MP, Port of London (Financial Assistance) Bill' (2nd Reading), HC Deb, Hansard, vol. 982, 16 April 1980, https://hansard.parliament.uk/Commons/1980-04-16/debates/1d75adf5-da68-466f-bf74-474134ced029/PortOfLondon(FinancialAssistance)Bill#contribution-e7395e08-4c91-40d4-96a9-a07c56aa7398 [both accessed 07.03.25].

38 Institute of Employment Rights, 'Anger as Public Contract for DP World, the Firm behind P&O Sackings, is Confirmed' (27 March 2023), https://www.ier.org.uk/news/anger-as-public-contract-for-dp-world-the-firm-behind-po-sackings-is-confirmed; 'Our History', Forth Ports, https://www.forthports.co.uk/forth-ports-group/our-history/; 'Our Ownership Structure', Thames Water, https://www.thameswater.co.uk/about-us/governance/our-structure]; 'Macquarie Backed Thames Water's Upgrades to London's Water and Wastewater Infrastructure', Macquarie, https://www.macquarie.com/au/en/insights/thames-water-upgrading-londons-water-and-wastewater-infrastructure.html [all accessed 15.02.25]; K. Allen and A. Massoudi, 'Qatar and Brookfield Win Battle to Take Over Canary Wharf', *Financial Times* (28 January 2015).

39 Watson, *Port of London*, 223; David E. Sanger, 'Under Pressure, Dubai Company Drops Port Deal', *The New York Times* (10 March 2006); DP World, 'London Gateway Welcomes Europe's Largest Quay Cranes to Service Mega Vessels' (22 February 2024), https://www.dpworld.com/london-gateway/news/latest-news/london-gateway-welcomes-largest-quay-cranes-to-service-mega-vessels; DP World, 'DP World Launches a Premium Barge Service between the Upper Rhine Region and Rotterdam

World Gateway' (17 January 2022), https://www.dpworld.com/en/eu-intermodal/News-and-Press-Releases/News/New-Premium-Barge-Service; DP World, 'Antwerp Gateway', https://www.dpworld.com/en/belgium/services/antwerpgateway; Lilia Khovrak, '80+ Terminals of DP World', Offers (26 October 2021), SeaRates by DP World, https://www.searates.com/blog/post/80-terminals-of-dp-world [all accessed 08.06.24].

40 Jeffrey Harrison and Peter Grant, *Thames Transformed: London's River and its Wildfowl* (London: Andre Deutsch, 1976), 37; Alwyne Wheeler, *The Tidal Thames: A History of a River and its Fishes* (London: Routledge & Kegan Paul, 1979), 90; Vanessa Taylor, 'Whose River? London and the Thames Estuary, 1960–2014', *The London Journal* 40:3 (2015), 249; McCormick et al. (eds), *State of the Thames 2021*, 31–3, 59.

41 Wheeler, *Tidal Thames*, 67–9; 'The Heart of the Huchen Population Beats on the Balkans', ICPDR Danube Watch (February 2015), https://www.icpdr.org/publications/heart-huchen-population-beats-balkans [accessed 23.06.24].

42 McCormick et al. (eds), *State of the Thames 2021*, 58–9.

43 Harrison and Grant, *Thames Transformed*, 80; Wheeler, *Tidal Thames*, 61; Clean Rivers Trust, *State of the Urban Environment, Environment Agency Report* (July 2021), https://www.cleanriverstrust.co.uk/state-of-the-urban-environment-environment-agency-report-july-2021/; 'Complex Life Cycle of an Eel', Thames River Trust, https://www.thamesriverstrust.org.uk/thames-catchment-community-eels-project/life-cycle-of-an-eel/ [accessed 16.02.25]; Peter Coates, 'Eurofisch: Hyper-Mobility, Cosmopolitanism and the European Eel's Appeal', Migration Mobilities People Blog (6 June 2022), https://migration.bristol.ac.uk/2022/06/06/eurofisch-hyper-mobility-cosmopolitanism-and-the-european-eels-appeal/; European Eel Anguilla, Anguilla, Taxonomic Notes, IUCN Red List, https://www.iucnredlist.org/species/60344/12353365; McCormick et al. (eds), *State of the Thames 2021*, 55; 'East Atlantic Flyway UNESCO Nomination is "tremendous news"', BBC News (12 April 2023), https://www.bbc.co.uk/news/uk-england-suffolk-65242387 [all accessed 06.03.25].

Chapter 13: Disappearances?

1 Francis La Flesche, *A Dictionary of the Osage Language* (Washington DC: United States Government Printing Office, 1932), in Bureau of American Ethnology Bulletin 109, 111; The Osage Nation, Resource Page: https://www.osageculture.com/language/learn-osage/resource-page) [accessed 25.04.25].

2 Friends of the Chicago Portage, 'A Canal of but Half a League? (LaSalle Gets it Right)', The Chicago Portage Blog, http://drupal.library.cmu.edu/chicago/node/95 [accessed 08.07.24]; Adam Shoalts, *A History of Canada in Ten Maps: Epic Stories of Charting a Mysterious Land* (Toronto: Penguin Canada, 2018), 114–18.

3 R. Gross, 'Mapping the Chicago Portage: Seventeenth-Century Explorations by Jolliet, Marquette, La Salle, and Joutel', *Terrae Incognitae* 54:2 (2022), 176; Chet Van Duzer, *Frames That Speak: Cartouches on Early Modern Maps* (Leiden: Brill, 2023), 97–102; Library of Congress, 'Map of Northern America and Part of Southern America from the Mouth of the Saint Lawrence River to Cayenne Island with the New Discoveries of the Mississippi River or Colbert River', attrib. Abbé Claude Bernou (1681). https://www.loc.gov/resource/gdcwdl.wdl_15489/?r=-0.355,0.479,1.326,0.604,0 [accessed 04.03.25].

4 Quoted in I.J. Cox, *The Journeys of Rene Robert Cavelier Sieur de La Salle, Volume 1* (1905; New York: Allerton Book Co., 1922), 167–8.

5 Shoalts, *History of Canada*, 118; P.H. Wood. 'La Salle: Discovery of a Lost Explorer', *The American Historical Review* 89:2 (1984), 294–323; Gross, 'Mapping the Chicago Portage', 182.

6 'Treaty of Paris, 1763', State Department, USA, https://history.state.gov/milestones/1750-1775/treaty-of-paris [accessed 21.02.25].

7 C.F. Williams, 'The Louisiana Purchase and Arkansas: Reflections on State and National Development', *The Arkansas Historical Quarterly*, 62:4 (2003), 361–9; 'On this day, the Louisiana Purchase is completed', National Constitution Center, NCC Staff Blog (20 December 2022), https://constitutioncenter.org/blog/on-this-day-the-louisiana-purchase-is-completed [accessed 08.07.24].

8 Idaho State Historical Society Reference Series, 'The Lewis and Clark Trail across Idaho', no. 49, https://history.idaho.gov/wp-content/uploads/2018/08/0049.pdf [accessed 08.07.24]; Williams, 'Louisiana Purchase and Arkansas', 368.

9 Zebulon Pike, *An Account of a Voyage up the Mississippi River*, c. 1806 (The War College Series, undated), 40–1; M. Sioli, 'When the Mississippi Was an Indian River: Zebulon Pike from St Louis to its Sources 1805–1806', *Revue Française d'Études Américaines* 98 (2003/4), 9–19; W. Upham, *Minnesota Geographic Names: Their Origin and Historic Significance* (1920; Minnesota Historical Society, 1969), 94–6.

10 'Mississippi River Facts', National Park Service, https://www.nps.gov/miss/riverfacts.htm [accessed 22.02.25]; Keith A. Baca, *Native American Place Names in Mississippi* (Jackson, MI: University of Mississippi, 2007).

11 'Mississippi River Flood History 1543–Present', National Weather Service,

National Oceanic and Atmospheric Administration (NOAA), https://www.weather.gov/lix/ms_flood_history [accessed 22.02.25].

12 M. Gonzalez, 'Continental Divides in North Dakota and North America', *North Dakota Geological Survey* 30:1 (2003), 4–5.

13 Ron Redfern, *Origins: The Evolution of Continents, Oceans and Life* (London: Weidenfeld & Nicolson, 2002), 118–19.

14 Thomas Madigan (Hemisphere Field Services), 'The Geology of the MNRRA Corridor', *River of History – A Historic Resources Study*, Chapter 1, National Park Service (last updated 22 November 2019), https://www.nps.gov/miss/learn/historyculture/river-of-history-chapter-1.htm [accessed 22.02.25].

15 Louise Humphrey and Chris Stringer, *Our Human Story* (London: National History Museum, 2019), 144–5; 'The Cerutti Mastodon Discovery', Blog, San Diego Natural History Museum [accessed 05.07.24].

16 National Park Service, 'Bering Land Bridge', https://www.nps.gov/bela/learn/beringia.htm [accessed 22.02.25]; 'Native American Populations Descend from Three Key Migrations', University College London (12 July 2012), https://www.ucl.ac.uk/news/2012/jul/native-american-populations-descend-three-key-migrations [accessed 05.07.24].

17 T. Garlinghouse, 'Revisiting the Mound-Builder Controversy', *History Today* 51:9 (September 2001); Cahokia Mounds State Historic Site, UNESCO World Heritage Convention, https://whc.unesco.org/en/list/198 [accessed 19.02.25].

18 'Cahokia Mounds State Historic Site: World Heritage Site', National Park Service, https://www.nps.gov/articles/000/cahokia-mounds-state-historic-site-world-heritage-site.htm; A.B. Weil and A.A. Hunter, 'Saving Sugarloaf Mound in St. Louis, Missouri', *CRM: The Journal of Heritage Stewardship* (Winter 2010), 78, http://npshistory.com/newsletters/crm/journal-v7n1.pdf [both accessed 04.07.22]; Gosden, *Prehistory*, 95.

19 A.J. White et al., 'After Cahokia: Indigenous Repopulation and Depopulation of the Horseshoe Lake Watershed AD 1400–1900', *American Antiquity* 85:2 (2020), 264–5, 272.

20 E.J. Neiburger, 'The Mississippian Indians and Copper', *Central States Archaeological Journal* 57:4 (2010), 174–6; Felipe Fernández-Armesto, *The Americas: The History of a Hemisphere* (London: Phoenix, 2004), 36; W.R. Iseminger, 'Culture and Environment in the American Bottom: The Rise and Fall of Cahokia Mounds', in Andrew Hurley (ed.), *Common Fields: An Environmental History of St. Louis* (St. Louis, MO: Missouri Historical Society Press, 1997), 41; Glossary, Illinois State Museum (2000), https://www.museum.state.il.us/muslink/nat_amer/pre/htmls/gloss.html [accessed 22.02.25].

21 White et al., 'After Cahokia', 264.

22 'Cahokia Mounds State Historic Site: World Heritage Site', National Park Service, https://www.nps.gov/articles/000/cahokia-mounds-state-historic-site-world-heritage-site.htm [accessed 04.07.22]; 'The Egyptian Pyramid', Smithsonian National Museum of Natural History, Blog (revised February 2005), https://www.si.edu/spotlight/ancient-egypt/pyramid [accessed 22.02.25].

23 Cyrus Thomas, 'Report on the Mound Explorations of the Bureau of Ethnology', in Twelfth Annual Report of the Bureau of Ethnology, 1890–1891 (Bureau of American Ethnology, 1894), 615; Smithsonian Research Online, https://repository.si.edu/handle/10088/91661; B. Keel, 'Cyrus Thomas and the Mound Builders', *Southern Indian Studies* (1970), 7, 8–9; Garlinghouse, 'Revisiting the Mound-Builder Controversy'.

24 Cahokia Mounds State Historic Site: World Heritage Site', National Park Service, https://www.nps.gov/articles/000/cahokia-mounds-state-historic-site-world-heritage-site.htm [accessed 04.07.22]; Gosden, *Prehistory*, 95.

25 'Research Club Hunts History of a Lost Race', *Detroit Free Press* (2 July 1944); 'The Mound Builders', Detroit Urbanism, Blog, (21 December 2015), http://detroiturbanism.blogspot.com/2015/12/the-mound-builders.html [accessed 19.02.25].

26 'Dickson Mound (Lewistown, IL) Memorabilia, ca. 1940–1945', American Philosophical Society, https://as.amphilsoc.org/repositories/2/resources/935 [accessed 25.05.25].

27 D. Guillory, 'The Dilemma of Dickson Mounds', *Illinois Issues* 25, Northern Illinois University Libraries (1990), https://www.lib.niu.edu/1990/ii901221.html [accessed 22.02.25]; US National Park Service, 'Native American Graves Protection and Repatriation Act, Facilitating Respectful Return', https://www.nps.gov/subjects/nagpra/index.htm [accessed 04.07.22]; D. Pollack, *Caborn-Welborn – Constructing a New Society after the Angel Chiefdom Collapse* (Tuscaloosa, AL: University of Alabama Press, 2004), 101–8.

28 Mr Inouye (Select Committee on Indian Affairs), 'Providing for the Protection of Native American Graves and the Repatriation of Native American Remains and Cultural Patrimony', US Senate Report 101–473, 1990, 6; K. Coody Cooper, *Spirited Encounters: American Indians Protest Museum Policies and Practices* (Lanham, MD: AltaMira Press, 2008), 96; D.S. Murphree (ed.), *Native America: A State-by-State Historical Encyclopedia* (Santa Barbara, CA: Greenwood, 2012), 428.

29 US National Park Service, 'Facilitating Respectful Return'; 'Dickson Mounds Reopens', Illinois State Museum: Story of the Illinois State Museum (Illinois Digital Archives), 1994, http://www.idaillinois.org/digital/collection/p16614coll28/id/333 [accessed 04.07.22].

30 Thompson quoted in Guillory, 'Dilemma of Dickson Mounds'.

31 H. Dellios and R. Pearson, 'Neighbors Mourn Dickson Mounds' Demise', *Chicago Tribune* (26 November 1991); H. Dellios, 'Controversy Laid to Rest as Dickson Mounds Closes', *Chicago Tribune* (4 April 1992); Chip Colwell, *Plundered Skulls and Stolen Spirits: Inside the Fight to Reclaim Native America's Culture* (Chicago, IL: University of Chicago Press, 2017).

32 Patricia Cleary, *Mound City: The Place of the Indigenous Past and Present in St. Louis* (Columbia, MO: University of Missouri Press, 2024); C.J. Ekberg and S.K. Person, *St. Louis Rising: The French Regime of Louis St. Ange de Bellerive* (Champaign, IL: University of Illinois Press, 2015), 187–205; Weil and Hunter, 'Saving Sugarloaf Mound', 78.

33 The Osage Nation, 'Sugar Loaf Mound', https://www.osageculture.com/culture/geography/sugarloaf-mound [accessed 07.07.24]; Weil and Hunter, 'Saving Sugarloaf Mound', 78–81; Iseminger, 'Culture and Environment in the American Bottom', 57.

34 B. Broom, 'Grandmothers, Grandfathers "from long ago": Miss. Returns Remains to Chickasaw Nation', *Clarion Ledger* (n.d.); N. McGreevy, 'Mississippi Returns Hundreds of Native Americans' Remains to Chickasaw Nation', *Smithsonian Magazine* (2 April 2021); Associated Press, 'Mississippi State Receives Grant to Return Native Remains', US News (14 November 2021), https://www.usnews.com/news/best-states/mississippi/articles/2021-11-14/mississippi-state-receives-grant-to-return-native-remains [accessed 06.07.22]; cf. L. Jaffe et al., 'The Repatriation Project. America's Biggest Museums Fail to Return Native American Human Remains', *ProPublica* (11 January 2023), https://www.propublica.org/article/repatriation-nagpra-museums-human-remains [accessed 16.02.25].

35 Indian Removal Act (1830), National Constitution Center, https://constitutioncenter.org/the-constitution/historic-document-library/detail/indian-removal-act-1830 [accessed 07.07.24].

36 'Removal of Tribal Nations to Oklahoma', Oklahoma Historical Society, https://www.okhistory.org/research/airemoval [accessed 08.07.24]; Theda Perdue, 'The Legacy of Indian Removal', *The Journal of Southern History* 78:1 (2012), 3–36.

37 Donald Worster, *Rivers of Empire: Water, Aridity, and the Growth of the American West* (Oxford: Oxford University Press, 1986), 14–15; M. Saikku, 'Down by the Riverside: The Disappearing Bottomland Hardwood Forest of Southeastern North America', *Environment and History* 2:1 (1996), 86, 94n; J. Baeten, 'Making Wet Places Drier: Mapping the Evolution of Drainage Technology in the U.S.', NiCHE (14 July 2020), https://niche-canada.org/2020/07/14/making-wet-places-drier-mapping-the-evolution-of-drainage-technology-in-the-u-s [accessed 22.02.25].

38 L. Hurley, 'Supreme Court Agrees to Weigh Navajo Nation Water Rights

Battle', NBC News (4 November 2022), https://www.nbcnews.com/politics/supreme-court/supreme-court-agrees-weigh-navajo-nation-water-rights-battle-rcna55281 [accessed 19.02.25]; M.L. Lawson, *Dammed Indians: The Pick-Sloan Plan and the Missouri River Sioux, 1944–1980* (Norman, OK: University of Oklahoma Press, 1994).

39 D. Eller, 'Pollution and Habitat Loss Make Mississippi River among Nation's Most Endangered', *Des Moines Register* (30 April 2019); Daniel Harris, 'Weather Tracker: Low Mississippi River Levels Take Toll on Farmers', *The Guardian* (8 December 2023).

40 E.E. Pritchard, 'The Future of Archaeology and Stewardship at TVA', in Erin E. Pritchard (ed.), *TVA Archaeology: Seventy-Five Years of Prehistoric Site Research* (Knoxville, TN: University of Tennessee Press, 2009), 299.

41 Donald Davidson, *The Tennessee: Volume Two, The New River: Civil War to TVA* (1948; Nashville, TN: J.S. Sanders & Co., 1992), 237, quoted in E.S. Shapiro, 'Donald Davidson and the Tennessee Valley Authority: The Response or a Southern Conservative', *Tennessee Historical Quarterly* 33:4 (1974), 445; also 442–4.

42 M.J. McDonald and J. Muldowny, *TVA and the Dispossessed: The Resettlement of Population in the Norris Dam Area* (Knoxville, TN: University of Tennessee Press, 1982), 4, 207–12, 267.

43 'Little Tennessee River', American Rivers, https://www.americanrivers.org/river/little-tennessee-river/ [accessed 13.07.24].

44 G.F. Schroedl, 'The Tellico Archaeological Project', in Pritchard (ed.), *TVA Archaeology*, 63, 67, 71, 91–2.

45 Schroedl, 'Tellico Archaeological Project', 89, 90–1; Robert A. Gilmer, 'In the Shadow of Removal: Historical Memory, Indianness, and the Tellico Dam Project' (unpublished PhD thesis, University of Minnesota, 2011), 263; K. McHugh, 'Facing the Past for Action in the Future: Cultural Survival in Native America', in Emily Hamilton and Kari Dodson et al. (eds), *Objects Specialty Group Postprints, The American Institute for Conservation of Historic & Artistic Works* 23 (2016), 278–90.

46 Gilmer, 'In the Shadow of Removal', 45–58, 63, 204; *United States Statutes at Large, Volume 7. Treaties between the United States and the Indian Tribes* (Boston, MA, 1846).

47 American Indian Religious Freedom Act 1978 (US).

48 Gilmer, 'In the Shadow of Removal', 204; N.F. Holly, 'The Plasticity of Place: The Lives of Cherokee Sacred Places and the Struggles to Protect Them' (unpublished History MA thesis, Western Carolina University, 2012), 66; Eastern Band of Cherokee Indians (website), https://ebci.com; United Ketooah Band of Cherokee Indians (website), https://www.ukb-nsn.gov/; American Rivers, 'Oconaluftee River', https://

www.americanrivers.org/river/oconaluftee-river [all accessed 04.03.25]; Elizabeth Giddens, *Oconaluftee: The History of a Smoky Mountain Valley* (Chapel Hill, NC: University of North Carolina Press, 2023).

49 Ammoneta Sequoyah, Richard Crowe, Gilliam Jackson, individually and Representing Other Cherokee Indians similarly Situated; the Eastern Band of Cherokee Indians; and the United Ketooah Band of Cherokee Indians, Appellants, v. Tennessee Valley Authority, Appellee, 620 F.2d 1159 (6th Cir. 1980) [accessed 21.02.25]; H. Stambor, 'Manifest Destiny and American Indian Religious Freedom: Sequoyah, Badoni, and the Drowned Gods', *American Indian Law Review* 10 (1982), 63.

50 Ammoneta Sequoyah et al. v. Tennessee Valley Authority, 480 F. Supp. 608 (1979), Affidavit of Ammoneta Sequoyah, quoted in Holly, 'Plasticity of Place', 78; Gilmer, 'In the Shadow of Removal', 200–1.

51 Affidavit of Ross Swimmer, Principal Chief of the Cherokee Nation, October 24th, 1979, quoted in Gilmer, 'In the Shadow of Removal', 171; Cheyenne Bennett, 'The Competing Narratives of Tellico: The TVA, Multivocality, and Contested Place-Making in the Little Tennessee River Valley', *Public Interest and Professional Anthropology in the South: Selected Papers from the Annual Meeting of the Southern Anthropological Society, Raleigh, North Carolina, April 2022*, 47 (2023), 5–42.

52 Sequoyah v. Tennessee Valley Authority, 620 F.2d 1159 (1980), https://law.justia.com/cases/federal/appellate-courts/F2/620/1159/394634/ [accessed 21.02.25].

53 Betsey B. Creekmore, 'Snail Darter', Volopedia (University of Tennessee, Knoxville), https://volopedia.lib.utk.edu/entries/snail-darter/ [accessed 13.07.24]; Pam Fuller and Matt Neilson, *Percina tanasi* (Etnier, 1976), Non-indigenous Aquatic Species Database, U.S. Geological Survey, revision date 16.08.11, https://nas.er.usgs.gov/queries/FactSheet.aspx?SpeciesID=827 [accessed 04.03.25].

54 'Studies on the Ecology of Maplin Sands and Coastal Zones of Suffolk, Essex, and Northern Kent', Report by the Institute of Terrestrial Ecology (Natural Environment Research Council, 1977), 1.

55 'Energy and Water Development Appropriation Act, 1980 Statement on Signing H.R. 4388 Into Law', The American Presidency Project, https://www.presidency.ucsb.edu/documents/energy-and-water-development-appropriation-act-1980-statement-signing-hr-4388-into-law; K. Kruesi, 'Snail Darter, Tiny and Notorious, Is No Longer Endangered', Associated Press (31 August 2021), https://apnews.com/article/lifestyle-environment-and-nature-fish-dams-darts-6c13a0db131573f329e1f5d26bc506e1 [both accessed 04.03.25].

56 Schroedl, 'Tellico Archaeological Project', 71.

57 Schroedl, 'Tellico Archaeological Project', 88–90, 94; Gilmer, 'In the Shadow of Removal', 76; Sequoyah Birthplace Museum, https://sequoyahmuseum.org [accessed 25.04.25].
58 McHugh, 'Facing the Past for Action in the Future', 281; Gilmer, 'In the Shadow of Removal'; Chota Memorial, Archaeological Site, https://tennesseerivervalleygeotourism.org/entries/chota-memorial/bc0a10da-46fe-4253-b674-d0aeb5ce84d6 [accessed 25.04.25].
59 Pritchard, 'Future of Archaeology and Stewardship', 301; TVA, 'Tribal Relations', https://www.tva.com/environment/environmental-stewardship/land-management/cultural-resource-management/tribal-relations; Federally Recognized Tribes, Federal Emergency Management Agency (FEMA), https://www.fema.gov/about/organization/tribal-affairs/federally-recognized [both accessed 04.03.25].
60 '7 Arrested During Healing Prayer Ceremony for Enbridge's Line 3 Pipeline Spills at the Mississippi Headwaters', Indigenous Environmental Network (IEN) Press Release (August 2021), https://www.ienearth.org/7-arrested-during-healing-prayer-ceremony-for-enbridges-line-3-pipeline-spills-at-the-mississippi-headwaters/ [accessed 05.07.24].
61 T. Montoya, 'Violence on the Ground, Violence Below the Ground' (22 December 2016), Society for Cultural Anthropology, https://culanth.org/fieldsights/violence-on-the-ground-violence-below-the-ground; IEN, 'Gulf Coast Environmental Justice Organizers Launch the L'eau Est La Vie (Water is Life) Camp, the New Hub for the Bayou Bridge Resistance' (n.d., c. 2017) [both accessed 05.07.24].
62 Joe Whittle, 'The Women Fighting a Pipeline that Could Destroy Precious Wildlife', *The Guardian* (16 January 2019); Bayou Bridge Pipeline Permit, US Army Corps (New Orleans District), https://www.mvn.usace.army.mil/bayoubridge/; 'Louisiana Appeals Court Hears Argument in Pipeline Lawsuit', *Pipeline and Gas Journal* (9 January 2020), https://www.pgjonline.com/news/2020/01-january/louisiana-appeals-court-hears-arguments-in-pipeline-lawsuit [both accessed 06.04.25].
63 Cherri Foytlin speaking in 'L'eau Est La Vie (Water is Life)', IEN YouTube Channel (23 June 2017), https://www.youtube.com/watch?v=OUd9-qcDZOo; Biloxi-Chitimacha-Choctaw of Louisiana (website), http://www.biloxi-chitimacha.com/the_confederation.htm [both accessed 04.03.25].

Chapter 14: Sold Down the River

1 William Wells Brown, *Narrative of William W. Brown, A Fugitive Slave. Written by Himself* (1847; London, 1849), 26, https://docsouth.unc.edu/fpn/brownw/brown.html [accessed 25.04.25].

2 An Act to Prohibit the Importation of Slaves, Chapter 22, 2 Stat. 426 (1807); Paul Finkelman, 'The American Suppression of the African Slave Trade: Lessons on Legal Change, Social Policy, and Legislation', *Akron Law Review* 42:2 (2015), 432, 458.

3 H.L. Gates Jr. 'What Was the Second Middle Passage?', The African Americans: Many Rivers to Cross, Blog, https://www.pbs.org/wnet/african-americans-many-rivers-to-cross/history/what-was-the-2nd-middle-passage/ [accessed 08.07.22]; Walter Johnson (ed.), *The Chattel Principle: Internal Slave Trades in the Americas* (New Haven, CT: Yale University Press, 2004); Steven Deyle, *Carry Me Back: The Domestic Slave Trade in American Life* (New York: Oxford University Press, 2005), 147–8; A.G. Carey, *Sold Down the River: Slavery in the Lower Chattahoochee Valley of Alabama and Georgia* (Tuscaloosa, AL: University of Alabama Press, 2011).

4 Leah Preble Holmes, 'Sold Down the River', *Mississippi Encyclopedia*, Center for Study of Southern Culture (11 July 2017), http://mississippi encyclopedia.org/entries/sold-down-the-river/ [accessed 25.08.19].

5 R.P. Beckinsale, 'Rivers as Political Boundaries', in Richard J. Chorley (ed.), *Water, Earth and Man: A Synthesis of Hydrology, Geomorphology and Socio-Economic Geography* (London: Methuen, 1969), 346.

6 Laura Paskus, 'Southwest Drought Desiccates Fish before Farmers', *High Country News* (8 July 2002).

7 Beckinsale, 'Rivers as Political Boundaries', 344.

8 Pettigrew, *Freedom's Debt*; 'Africans in Carolina', African Passages, Lowcountry Adaptations, Lowcountry Digital History Initiative, College of Charlston, https://ldhi.library.cofc.edu/exhibits/show/africanpassage slowcountryadapt [accessed 04.03.25].

9 'Lovisiana by de Rivier Missisipi' (c. 1720), 'Lionel Pincus and Princess Firyal Map Division', New York Public Library Digital Collections, https://digitalcollections.nypl.org/items/f7f4baa0-10dc-0135-92c9-0ab275e23d91 [accessed 16.12.22]; L. Neal, *'I Am Not Master of Events': The Speculations of John Law and Lord Londonderry in the Mississippi and South* (New Haven, CT: Yale University Press, 2012), vii, 6, death 19, 59; H.S. Burton and F. Todd Smith, 'Slavery in the Colonial Louisiana Backcountry: Natchitoches, 171–1803', *Louisiana History: The Journal of the Louisiana Historical Association* 52:2 (2011), 136, 151.

10 Neal, *'I Am Not Master of Events'*, 59, 66; Burton and Smith, 'Slavery in the Colonial Louisiana Backcountry', 151–4.

11 Burton and Smith, 'Slavery in the Colonial Louisiana Backcountry', 135, 163–4, 167–8.

12 Williams, 'Louisiana Purchase and Arkansas', 365; Charles A. Kent, 'The

North-West Territory', *Journal of the Illinois State Historical Society* 8:2 (1915), 268–80; Paul Finkelman, 'Slavery and the Northwest Ordinance: A Study in Ambiguity', *Journal of the Early Republic* 6:4 (1986), 351; 'Ohio: Local History & Genealogy Resource Guide', Library of Congress [LOC], https://guides.loc.gov/ohio-local-history-genealogy [accessed 23.02.25].

13 T. Jefferson to W. Short, Report on Negotiations with Spain (18 March 1792), Founders Online, National Archives (US), https://founders.archives.gov/documents/Jefferson/01-23-02-0259 [accessed 23.02.25].

14 T. Jefferson to R.R. Livingston (18 April 1802), Founders Online, National Archives (US), https://founders.archives.gov/documents/Jefferson/01-37-02-0220 [accessed 23.02.25].

15 Williams, 'Louisiana Purchase and Arkansas', 361, 364, 366; 'Port of New-Orleans SHUT', *Mississippi Herald* [Natchez] (28 October 1802), reproduced in C.T. Gontar, '"Port of New-Orleans Shut": A Natchez Broadside at Archivo General de Indias', *Common Place: The Journal of Early American Life* 16:2 (2016), http://commonplace.online/article/port-of-new-orleans-shut/ [accessed 23.02.25].

16 Saikku, 'Down by the Riverside', 85–6; Burton and Smith, 'Slavery in the Colonial Louisiana Backcountry', 136; R. Bailey, 'The Other Side of Slavery: Black Labor, Cotton, and Textile Industrialization in Great Britain and the United States', *Agricultural History* 68:2 (1994), 35–6.

17 Gates Jr., 'What Was the Second Middle Passage?'; Finkelman, 'The American Suppression of the African Slave Trade', 467.

18 Saikku, 'Down by the Riverside', 86, 88, 90, 94n. Charles Mohr quoted in Saikku; Baeten, 'Making Wet Places Drier'.

19 Bailey, 'Other Side of Slavery', 35; E.R. Dattel, *Cotton and Race in the Making of America: The Human Costs of Economic Power* (Chicago, IL: Ivan R. Dee, 2011), 37; H.L. Gates Jr, 'Why Was Cotton "King"?', Blog, The African Americans: Many Rivers to Cross [accessed 08.07.22].

20 Finkelman, 'American Suppression of the Slave Trade'; W. Johnson, *Soul by Soul: Life inside the Antebellum Slave Market* (Cambridge, MA: Harvard University Press, 2000), 4–5; Saikku, 'Down by the Riverside', 85–6.

21 'An Ordinance for the Government of the Territory of the United States North West of the River Ohio' (The Northwest Ordinance), LOC, https://guides.loc.gov/northwest-ordinance [accessed 23.02.25].

22 'Ursa Minor (Little Bear) and Polaris', Royal Museums Greenwich, https://www.rmg.co.uk/stories/topics/ursa-minor-little-bear-polaris [accessed 27.06.22].

23 'About the North Star', LOC, https://chroniclingamerica.loc.gov/lccn/sn84026365/; '*The North Star*, Vol. 1 No. 37', Smithsonian Digital

Volunteers, https://transcription.si.edu/project/14480; Frederick Douglass Papers at the Library of Congress, LOC, https://www.loc.gov/collections/frederick-douglass-papers/articles-and-essays/frederick-douglass-timeline/1818-to-1835/ [all accessed 26.04.25].

24 A. Hines, 'Geographies of Freedom: Black Women's Mobility and the Making of the Western River World, 1814–1865' (unpublished PhD thesis, Duke University, 2018).

25 'Missouri Compromise: Primary Documents in American History', LOC, https://guides.loc.gov/missouri-compromise; 'Kansas-Nebraska Act: Primary Documents in American History', LOC, https://guides.loc.gov/kansas-nebraska-act [both accessed 23.02.25].

26 Finkelman, 'Slavery and the Northwest Ordinance', 345.

27 J.W. Trotter, *River Jordan: African American Urban Life in the Ohio Valley* (Lexington, KY: University Press of Kentucky, 1998), xiii; M. Pasquier, 'Introduction: Religious Life on the Mississippi', in M. Pasquier (ed.), *Gods of the Mississippi* (Lexington, IN: Indiana University Press, 2013), 7; J.J.F. Sensbach, '"The Singing of the Mississippi": The River and Religions of the Black Atlantic', in Pasquier (ed.), *Gods of the Mississippi*, 18–19; J.M. Giggie, 'The Mississippi River and the Transformation of Black Religion in the Delta, 1877–1915', in Pasquier (ed.), *Gods of the Mississippi*, 116; M. Salafia, *Slavery's Borderland: Freedom and Bondage along the Ohio River* (Philadelphia, PA: University of Pennsylvania Press, 2013); John C. Inscoe, '"The Ohio River Was Not the River Jordan": A Review of Matthew Salafia's Slavery's Borderland', *Southern Spaces* (25 November 2013).

28 A. Hurley, 'Narrating the Urban Waterfront: The Role of Public History in Community Revitalization', *The Public Historian* 28:4 (2006), 34, 37; Hines, 'Geographies of Freedom', 96–7; Rachel Huffman, 'Black History Comes to Life at the Mary Meachum Celebration in St. Louis', Explore St Louis (8 September 2023), https://explorestlouis.com/whats-new/black-history-comes-to-life-at-the-mary-meachum-celebration-in-st-louis/; Mary Meachum Freedom Crossing, Great Rivers Greenway, https://greatriversgreenway.org/mary-meachum/ [both accessed 23.02.25].

29 E. Greenspan, *William Wells Brown: An African American Life* (New York: W.W. Norton & Co, 2014), 90.

30 J.W. Schuckers, *The Life and Public Services of Salmon Portland Chase* (New York, 1874), 171–6; M. Reinhardt, 'Who Speaks for Margaret Garner? Slavery, Silence, and the Politics of Ventriloquism', *Critical Inquiry* 29:1 (2002), 89; 'Map of Hamilton County, Ohio' (1856), LOC, https://www.loc.gov/resource/g4083h.la000633/?r=0.452,0.452,0.095,0.053,0 [accessed 23.02.25]; Toni Morrison, *Beloved* (New York: Alfred A. Knopf Inc., 1987).

31 Hines, 'Geographies of Freedom', 104.

32 (Untitled), Pittsburgh Gazette (25 October 1811), 3; 'Steam Boat', *Pittsburgh Gazette* (14 February 1812), 3: 'Steamboat Adventure: Down the Ohio and Mississippi Rivers with Nicholas and Lydia Roosevelt, 1811–1812: The Transportation Revolution' (Hanover College), https://history.hanover.edu/texts/1811/Web/Topic-transportation.html [accessed 23.02.25].
33 F.T. Norris, 'Where Did the Villages Go? Steamboats, Deforestation, and Archaeological Loss in the Mississippi Valley', in Hurley (ed.), *Common Fields*, 73–4; Hines, 'Geographies of Freedom', 124.
34 Finkelman, 'Slavery and the Northwest Ordinance', 356; Paul Finkelman, *An Imperfect Union: Slavery, Federalism, and Comity* (Union, NJ: Lawbook Exchange, 1981), 168.
35 State v Hoppess, Western L.J. (Ohio) 279 (1845), quoted in Finkelman, *Imperfect Union: Slavery*, 168–71.
36 Hines, 'Geographies of Freedom', 147, citing T.C. Buchanan, *Black Life on the Mississippi: Slaves, Free Blacks and the Western Steamboat* (Chapel Hill, NC: University of North Carolina Press, 2004), 10.
37 Ridgley vs Steamboat *Reindeer*, 1857, in Hines, 'Geographies of Freedom', 102–3, 121–2, 127.
38 Wells Brown, *Narrative of William W. Brown*, 13, 62–3.
39 Emphasis in original. Wells Brown, *Narrative of William W. Brown*, 64–8.
40 Wells Brown, *Narrative of William W. Brown*, 70–8.
41 Wells Brown, *Narrative of William W. Brown*, vii, 68, 94–5, 99–104.
42 Wells Brown, *Narrative of William W. Brown*, 107–8.
43 Speech by William Wells Brown, Delivered at the Town Hall, Manchester, England, 1 August 1854, from C. Peter Ripley et al. (eds), *The Black Abolitionist Papers, Vol. I: The British Isles, 1830–1865* (Chapel Hill, NC: University of North Carolina Press, 1985); Greenspan, *William Wells Brown*, 313.
44 Greenspan, *William Wells Brown*, 251.
45 William Wells Brown, A *Description of William Wells Brown's Original Panoramic Views of the Scenes in the Life of an American Slave: From His Birth in Slavery to His Death, or His Escape to His First Home of Freedom on British Soil* (London, 1849).
46 Wells Brown, *Narrative of William W. Brown*, vii–viii; Greenspan, *William Wells Brown*, 307–10.
47 W. Wells Brown, *Clotel; or, The President's Daughter: A Narrative of Slave Life in the United States* (London, 1853); Greenspan, *William Wells Brown*, 501.
48 M.K. Stallings, 'The Ghosts of Jim Crow Aboard the S.S. Admiral', Monument Lab (18 July 2020), https://monumentlab.com/bulletin/the-ghosts-of-jim-crow-aboard-the-s-s-admiral [accessed 23.02.25].

49 'How Egypt Got its Name', Illinois State Museum (n.d.), http://www.museum.state.il.us/RiverWeb/landings/Ambot/Archives/vignettes/people/How_20Egypt_20Got_20its_20Name.html [accessed 23.02.25].

50 'History & the Story of St. Louis IX', Basilica of Saint Louis, King of France, https://oldcathedralstl.org/history [accessed 09.07.22]; Montefiore, *Jerusalem*, 324–6; Stephen Humphreys, *From Saladin to the Mongols: The Ayyubids of Damascus, 1193–1260* (Albany, NY: New York Press, 1977), 301–2.

51 Book of Joshua, Hebrew Bible; Charpentier, *How to Read the Old Testament*, 33.

52 Montefiore, *Jerusalem*, 17; D. Boffey, '"From the river to the sea": Where Does the Slogan Come From and What Does it Mean?', *The Guardian* (31 October 2023).

53 Wells Brown, *Narrative of William W. Brown, Appendix*, 136.

54 K.E. Fields, 'Charismatic Religion as Popular Protest: The Ordinary and the Extraordinary in Social Movements', *Theory and Society* 11:3 (1982), 322, 338, 345, 349–50; E.D. Genovese, *Roll, Jordan, Roll; The World the Slaves Made* (New York: Pantheon Books, 1974); E. Southern, *The Music of Black Americans: A History*, 2nd edn (New York: W.W. Norton & Co., 1983), 198; Howard Thurman, *Deep River: Reflections on the Religious Insight of Certain of the Negro Spirituals* (New York: Harper and Brothers, 1955); '"I've known rivers": The Ecologies of Black Life and Resistance' (forthcoming conference: Association for the Study of the Worldwide African Diaspora, Saint Louis, Missouri, 2025), https://networks.h-net.org/group/announcements/20037498/all-us-come-cross-water-diasporic-ecological-practices [accessed 04.07.24].

55 Langston Hughes, 'The Negro Speaks of Rivers' (1921), in Langston Hughes, *The Collected Works of Langston Hughes: The Poems, 1921–1940* (Columbia, MO/London: University of Missouri Press, 2001), 36.

Chapter 15: Globalising the River Basin

1 John Wesley Powell, 'Institutions for the Arid Lands', *Century Magazine* 40 (May 1890), 114.

2 C.T. Smith, 'The Drainage Basin as an Historical Basis for Human Activity', in Chorley (ed.), *Water, Earth, and Man*, 109; Tennessee River, Tennessee Aquarium, https://tnaqua.org/app/uploads/2020/06/Tennessee_River.pdf [accessed 25.02.25].

3 TVA, *TVA: A Symbol of Resource Development in Many Countries* (Knoxville, TN: TVA Technical Library, 1952), Epigraph.

4 Daniel Macfarlane and Andrew Watson, 'Hydro Democracy: Water Power and Political Power in Ontario', *Scientia Canadensis* 40:1 (2018), 1–18.

5 R. Minami, 'The Introduction of Electric Power and its Impact on the Manufacturing Industries: With Special References to Smaller-Scale Plants', *Discussion Papers* 223 (1974), 22; D. Schaffer, 'Managing the Tennessee River: Principles, Practice, and Change', *The Public Historian* 12:2 (1990), 15–16; 'Niagara Falls Geology: Facts and Figures', Niagara Parks, https://www.niagaraparks.com/visit-niagara-parks/plan-your-visit/niagara-falls-geology-facts-figures/ [accessed 21.02.25].

6 The U.S. Army Corps of Engineers [USACE]: 'A Brief History', https://www.usace.army.mil/About/History/Brief-History-of-the-Corps/Introduction/ [accessed 21.02.25]; Bureau of Reclamation – About Us', https://www.usbr.gov/main/about/mission.html [accessed 21.02.25]; Bureau of Reclamation [BoR], 'Hoover Dam Chronology', https://www.usbr.gov/lc/hooverdam/history/articles/chrono.html [accessed 21.02.25]; M.C. Robinson, *Water for the West: The Bureau of Reclamation, 1902–1977* (Chicago, IL: Public Works Historical Society, 1979); Worster, *Rivers of Empire*.

7 David Ekblad, '"Mr. TVA": Grass-Roots Development, David Lilienthal, and the Rise and Fall of the Tennessee Valley Authority as a Symbol for U.S. Overseas Development, 1933–1973', *Diplomatic History* 26:3 (2002), 340.

8 Smith, 'Drainage Basin as an Historical Basis', 101.

9 John Wesley Powell, US Geological Survey, https://www.usgs.gov/staff-profiles/john-wesley-powell [accessed 21.02.25]; Donald Worster, 'Watershed Democracy: Recovering the Lost Vision of John Wesley Powell', *Journal of Land, Resources, & Environmental Law* 23:1 (2003); Richard Lowitt, 'The TVA, 1933–45', in Erwin C. Hargrove and Paul K. Conkin (eds), *TVA Fifty Years of Grass-Roots Bureaucracy* (Urbana, I/Chicago, IL: University of Illinois Press, 1983), 56–7.

10 F.D. Roosevelt, 11 December 1934, quoted in McDonald and Muldowny, *TVA and the Dispossessed*, 263.

11 D.E. Lilienthal, 'Navigation on the Tennessee River', *Southern Economic Journal* 4:4 (1938), 402; D.E. Lilienthal, 'Electricity: The People's Business', *The Annals of the American Academy of Political and Social Science* 201 (1939), 58–9.

12 Lilienthal, 'Navigation on the Tennessee River', 405; United States Congress. House Committee on Interstate and Foreign Commerce. Omnibus Transportation Bill, Hearings Before the Committee on Interstate and Foreign Commerce, House of Representatives, Seventy-Sixth Congress, First Session, on H.R. 2531 (1939), 1241; 'Late to the Chinese Market, Ford Aims to Catch Up', CBS News (9 July 2013). https://www.cbsnews.com/news/late-to-the-chinese-market-ford-aims-to-catch-up/ [accessed 21.02.25]; John A. DeNovo, *American Interests and Policies in the*

Middle East: 1900–1939 (St Paul, MN: University of Minnesota Press, 1963), 378.

13 Charles O. Jackson and Charles W. Johnson, 'The Summer of '44: Observations on Life in the Oak Ridge Community', *Tennessee Historical Quarterly* 32:3 (1973), 240–1; Robert Rook, 'Race, Water, and Foreign Policy: The Tennessee Valley Authority's Global Agenda Meets "Jim Crow"', *Diplomatic History* 28:1 (2004), 55–81; Richard Rhodes, *The Making of the Atomic Bomb* (New York: Simon & Schuster Paperbacks, 2012), 486–7; David M. Kennedy, *Freedom from Fear: The American People in Depression and War, 1929–1945* (New York: Oxford University Press, 1999), 664–5; Stanley Goldberg, 'Racing to the Finish: The Decision to Bomb Hiroshima and Nagasaki', *The Journal of American-East Asian Relations* 4:2 (1995), 124, 127; Justin McCurry, '"There wasn't enough about the horror": Hiroshima Survivors React to Oppenheimer', *The Guardian* (29 March 2024); BoR, Grand Coulee Dam, 'Construction History', https://www.usbr.gov/pn/grandcoulee/history/construction/index.html [accessed 12.07. 22]; USACE, 'Bonneville Lock and Dam' [accessed 12.07. 22]; 'Surrender of Japan (1945)', National Archives (US), https://www.archives.gov/milestone-documents/surrender-of-japan [accessed 22.02.25].

14 Richard G. Hewlett and Jack M. Holl, *Atoms for Peace and War, 1953–1961: Eisenhower and the Atomic Energy Commission* (Oakland, CA: University of California Press, 2023), 9; William Prather, '"The Color of this Life Is Water": History, Stones, and the River in "Suttree"', *The Cormac McCarthy Journal* 4:1 (2003), 41.

15 'A Time for Choosing' (27 October 1964), in Thomas W. Evans, *The Education of Ronald Reagan: The General Electric Years and the Untold Story of His Conversion to Conservatism* (New York: Columbia University Press, 2006), 240 (Appendix).

16 W.E. Leuchtenburg, 'Roosevelt, Norris, and the "Seven Little TVAs"', *Journal of Politics* 14 (1952), 418–41; Rosemary Feurer, 'River Dreams: St. Louis Labour and the Fight for a Missouri Valley Authority', in Andrew Hurley (ed.), *Common Fields: An Environmental History of St. Louis* (St. Louis, MO: Missouri Historical Society Press, 1997), 221–41; Karen M. O'Neill, 'Why the TVA Remains Unique: Interest Groups and the Defeat of New Deal River Planning', *Rural Sociology* 67:2 (2002), 177; Gina Bloodworth and James White, 'The Columbia Basin Project: Seventy-Five Years Later', *Yearbook of the Association of Pacific Coast Geographers*, 70 (2008), 102.

17 Rook, 'Race, Water, and Foreign Policy', 65; David Lilienthal, *TVA: Democracy on the March* (1944; New York: Harper & Bros, 1953).

18 Walter C. Lowdermilk, *Palestine, Land of Promise* (London: Victor Gollancz, 1944), 127–8; David Katz, 'Basin Management under Conditions

of Scarcity: The Transformation of the Jordan River Basin from Regional Water Supplier to Regional Water Importer', *Water* 14:10 (2022); Jan Selby, 'The Geopolitics of Water in the Middle East: Fantasies and Realities', *Third World Quarterly* 26:2 (2005), 329–49.

19 Ekbladh, '"Mr. TVA"', 351; Eric Dinmore, 'Concrete Results? The TVA and the Appeal of Large Dams in Occupation-Era Japan', *The Journal of Japanese Studies* 39:1 (2013), 28.

20 Lilienthal, *TVA: Democracy on the March*, 201–2; TVA, *TVA: A Symbol of Resource Development in Many Countries* (Knoxville, TN: TVA Technical Library, 1952), Foreword; McDonald and Muldowny, *TVA and the Dispossessed*, 229; Rook, 'Race, Water, and Foreign Policy'.

21 Dinmore, 'Concrete Results?', 2, 5, 7, 18 22, 26–8; Professor Shigeto Tsuru, 'A New Japan? Political, Economic, and Social Aspects of Postwar Japan', *The Atlantic* (January 1955), 103–7.

22 Dinmore, 'Concrete Results', 23, 26–7.

23 Lilienthal, *TVA: Democracy on the March*, 213, 217.

24 Dinmore, 'Concrete Results', 36; United Nations, Economic Commission for Asia and the Far East, 'Comprehensive Development of the Kitakami River Basin', *Ekistics* 17:98 (1964), 14–18.

25 Dinmore, 'Concrete Results', 4; 'Where Does Japan Get its Energy?', IEA, https://www.iea.org/countries/japan/energy-mix; Yoshikazu Kobayashi, 'Middle East Tensions Are a Crude Awakening for Japan's Energy Security Strategy', *East Asia Forum* (18 November 2024); Shivangi Mittal, 'Japan's Coal Imports Hit 20-month High; Exploring Alternative Markets', S&P Global (6 November 2024), https://www.spglobal.com/commodity-insights/en/news-research/latest-news/coal/110624-japans-coal-imports-hit-20-month-high-exploring-alternative-markets [all accessed 16.03.25].

26 Nick Cullather, 'Damming Afghanistan: Modernization in a Buffer State', *The Journal of American History* 89:2 (2002), 524; D. Lilienthal, *The Journals of David E. Lilienthal, Volume II: The Atomic Energy Years 1945–1950* (New York: Harper & Row, 1964), 470, 475.

27 George Kiss, 'TVA on the Danube?', *Geographical Review* 37:2 (1947), 274, 302; Coates, *Story of Six Rivers*, 54.

28 Kiss, 'TVA on the Danube?', 297.

29 Dinmore, 'Concrete Results', 26; Cullather, 'Damming Afghanistan', 522; Ekbladh, '"Mr. TVA"', 346.

30 Quoted in David Ekbladh, *The Great American Mission: Modernization and the Construction of an American World Order* (Princeton, NJ: Princeton University Press, 2010), 207; Greg Browder and Leonard Ortolano, 'The Evolution of an International Water Resources Management Regime in the Mekong River Basin', *Natural Resources Journal* 40:3 (2000), 504–5.

31 K.R. Olson and W. Frenelus, 'Environmental and Human Impacts of Lancang-Mekong Main-Stem and Tributary Dams on China, Laos, Thailand, Myanmar, Cambodia, and Vietnam', *Open Journal of Soil Science* 14 (2024), 556–8, 560, 573–4.

32 Browder and Ortolano, 'Evolution of an International Water Resources Management Regime', 505, 507, 530; Ekbladh, '"Mr. TVA"', 337, 358–61, 362, 365; Ekbladh, *Great American Mission*, 220.

33 Victor V. Nemchenok, '"That So Fair a Thing Should Be So Frail": The Ford Foundation and the Failure of Rural Development in Iran, 1953–1964', *Middle East Journal* 63:2 (2009), 264; David E. Lilienthal, 'Enterprise in Iran: An Experiment in Economic Development', *Foreign Affairs* 38:1 (1959), 135–8; Christopher T. Fisher, '"Moral Purpose Is the Important Thing": David Lilienthal, Iran, and the Meaning of Development in the US, 1956–63', *The International History Review* 33:3 (2011), 441, 446–7.

34 Cullather, 'Damming Afghanistan', 522; Christian Parenti, 'Flower of War: An Environmental History of Opium Poppy in Afghanistan', *The SAIS Review of International Affairs* 35:1 (2015), 189.

35 UN [1955–61], *Multi-Purpose River Basin Development*, Part 2D (ECAFE, 1961), quoted in Robert P. Beckinsale, 'Human Responses to River Regimes', in Chorley (ed.), *Water, Earth and Man*, 506.

36 Cullather, 'Damming Afghanistan', 521, 534, 536.

37 Cullather, 'Damming Afghanistan', 532.

38 Cullather, 'Damming Afghanistan', 528, 535–6.

39 Cullather, 'Damming Afghanistan', 525, 535–6; 'FACTBOX – Afghanistan's Battleground Kajaki Dam', Reuters (9 August 2007), https://www.reuters.com/article/world/factbox-afghanistan-s-battleground-kajaki-dam-idUSB759648/ [accessed 03.03.25].

40 Vincent Lagendijk, 'Divided Development: Post-War Ideas on River Utilisation and their Influence on the Development of the Danube', *The International History Review* 37:1 (2015), 82.

41 Quoted in Isaac Deutscher, *The Prophet Unarmed: Trotsky 1921–1929* (1959; London/New York, Verso, 2003), 178.

42 Harold Dorn, 'Hugh Lincoln Cooper and the First Détente', *Technology and Culture* 20:2 (1979), 332.

43 Dorn, 'Hugh Lincoln Cooper and the First Détente', 323, 335, 345–7.

44 *Soviet Ukraine* (1977), 13, USSR Exhibition, Los Angeles Convention Centre, 1977.

45 Richard Nelsson, 'Second World War: Dnieper Dam Blown Up by Russians – Archive, 1941', *The Guardian* (2 November 2022); Nicholas Hildyard and Josh Klemm, 'Weaponising Water – Ukraine's Dams Are Targets in Putin's War' (8 April 2022), https://euobserver.com/opinion/154675 [accessed 13.07.22].

46 TVA, 'The Global Valley', https://www.tva.com/economic-development/the-global-valley; 'Classroom for the World', https://www.tva.com/about-tva/our-history/tva-heritage/classroom-for-the-world [both accessed 03.03.25].

47 E.P. Thompson, *The Making of the English Working Class* (1963; Harmondsworth: Penguin Books, 1991), 'Preface', 12.

48 Karl August Wittfogel, *Oriental Despotism: A Comparative Study of Total Power* (New Haven, CT: Yale University Press, 1957).

49 James C. Scott, *Seeing like a State: How Certain Schemes to Improve the Human Condition Have Failed* (New Haven, CT/London: Yale University Press, 1998), 3–4; Bill Adams, 'Still Wasting the Rain?', Future Dams Blog (9 February 2021), https://www.futuredams.org/still-wasting-the-rain/ [accessed 16.02.25].

50 *Soviet Ukraine*, 19.

51 International Hydropower Association, '2024 World Hydropower Outlook', https://www.hydropower.org/publications/2024-world-hydropower-outlook [accessed 09.09.24]; Damian Carrington, 'Only a Third of World's Great Rivers Remain Free Flowing, Analysis Finds', *The Guardian* (8 May 2019).

52 Internal Displacement Monitoring Centre, 'Case Study Series – Dam Displacement' (2017), https://www.internal-displacement.org/publications/case-study-series-dam displacement/ [accessed 16.02.25].

53 e.g. James Burgess Waldram, *As Long as the Rivers Run: Hydroelectric Development and Native Communities in Western Canada* (Winnipeg, MN: University of Manitoba Press, 1988); Tina Loo and Meg Stanley, 'An Environmental History of Progress: Damming the Peace and Columbia Rivers', *Canadian Historical Review* 92:3 (2011), 399–427; Daniel Macfarlane and Peter Kitay, 'Hydraulic Imperialism: Hydroelectric Development and Treaty 9 in the Abitibi Region', *American Review of Canadian Studies* 46:3 (2016), 380–97.

54 World Hydropower Congress, Paris, 2019, International Hydropower Association, https://www.hydropower.org/events/world-hydropower-congress; 'The False Promises of Hydropower: A Joint Statement by Civil Society Organisations' (May 2019), 6–8, https://www.internationalrivers.org/wp-content/uploads/sites/86/2020/11/Optimized-English-declaration_iha2019_21x30_english_for_printing.pdf [both accessed 03.03.25].

Chapter 16: River at the Crossroads

1 *The History and Description of Africa of Leo Africanus*, Vol. I, trans. John Pory, 1600 (London: Hakluyt Society, 1896), 179.

2 Sarah Zielinski, 'The Sahara is Millions of Years Older than Thought',

Smithsonian Magazine (17 September 2014); Jasper Knight, 'Geology and Long-Term Landscape Evolution of the Central Sahara', in Jasper Knight, Stefania Merlo and Andrea Zerboni (eds), *Landscapes and Landforms of the Central Sahara* (Cham: Springer International Publishing, 2023), 9–22; Thomas L.P. Couvreur et al., 'Tectonics, Climate and the Diversification of the Tropical African Terrestrial Flora and Fauna', *Biological Reviews* 96:1 (2021), 22, 26, Fig. 2 (A).

3 Zielinski, 'Sahara is Millions of Years Older than Thought'; Kathelijn Bonne, 'The Great Bend of the Niger River: Two Separate Rivers in the Past' (30 April 2020), Gondwana Talks, https://www.gondwanatalks.com/l/niger-river/ [accessed 21.01.25]; Bernard Hugueny and Christian Lévêque, 'Freshwater Fish Zoogeography in West Africa: Faunal Similarities between River Basins', *Environmental Biology of Fishes* 39:4 (1994), 374, 376; Marina Gallinaro, 'Central Saharan Rock Art Landscapes', in Knight, Merlo, and Zerboni, *Landscapes and Landforms of the Central Sahara*, 207–17; Williams, *When the Sahara Was Green*, Map 1; Henry P. Colburn, 'Pioneers of the Western Desert', in Bleda S. Düring and Tesse D. Stek (eds), *The Archaeology of Imperial Landscapes: A Comparative Study of Empires in the Ancient Near East and Mediterranean World* (New York/Cambridge: Cambridge University Press, 2018), 90–1.

4 Kaitlin E. Allen et al., 'Rivers, Not Refugia, Drove Diversification in Arboreal, Sub-Saharan African Snakes', *Ecology and Evolution* 11:11 (2021), 6142; E. Bertuzzo et al., 'River Networks and Ecological Corridors: Reactive Transport on Fractals, Migration Fronts, Hydrochory', *Water Resources Research* 43:4 (2007), 3; Hugueny and Leveque, 'Freshwater Fish Zoogeography', 374; Timothy Avon du Feu, 'Tropical Reservoir Fisheries; Lake Kainji, Nigeria – A Case Study' (PhD thesis, University of Hull, 2003), 52, 61; *Hepsetus odoe*, Animal Diversity Web, University of Michigan [accessed 01.03.25]; *Malapterurus electricus*, Fishbase, https://www.fishbase.se/summary/Malapterurus-electricus [accessed 01.03.25].

5 Allen et al., 'Rivers, Not Refugia', 6142, 6144; Eli Greenbaum et al., 'Night Stalkers from Above: A Monograph of Toxicodryas Tree Snakes (Squamata: Colubridae) with Descriptions of Two New Cryptic Species from Central Africa', *Zootaxa* 4965:1 (2021), 1–44.

6 Bonne, 'Great Bend of the Niger River'; Noemie Arazi, 'Tracing History in Dia, in the Inland Niger Delta of Mali: Archaeology, Oral Traditions and Written Sources' (unpublished PhD thesis, University College London, 2005), 39, 40, 101.

7 Inger Anderson et al., *The Niger River Basin: A Vision for Sustainable Management* (Washington DC: The World Bank, 2005), 7.

8 Luc Descroix et al., 'Are the Fouta Djallon Highlands Still the Water Tower of West Africa?', *Water* 12:2968 (2020), 1–31; Dominique Chardon et al., 'Stabilization of Large Drainage Basins over Geological Time Scales: Cenozoic West Africa, Hot Spot Swell Growth, and the Niger River', *Geochemistry, Geophysics, Geosystems* 17:3 (2016), 1164–81; Robert P. Beckinsale, 'River Regimes', in Chorley (ed.), *Water, Earth and Maneograph*, 460; du Feu, 'Tropical Reservoir Fisheries', 56–7; Ashley Brown and Miranda Mockrin, (WWF-US) Map, Inner Niger Delta, Freshwater Ecoregions of the World, https://www.feow.org/ecoregions/details/508; Delta Intérieur du Niger, Ramsar Sites Information Service (2004), https://rsis.ramsar.org/ris/1365; Nigeria, Climate Change Knowledge Portal, https://climateknowledgeportal.worldbank.org/country/nigeria/climate-data-historical [all accessed 01.03.25].

9 Mackintosh-Smith (ed.), *Travels of Ibn Battutah*, 286; Timothy Insoll, 'A Cache of Hippopotamus Ivory at Gao, Mali; and a Hypothesis of Its Use', *Antiquity* 69:263 (1995), 330; Leo Africanus, *The Cosmography and Geography of Africa* (London: Penguin Books, 2023).

10 Insoll, 'Cache of Hippopotamus Ivory', 327, 331; Arazi, 'Tracing History in Dia', 106; J.O. Hunwick, 'The Mid-Fourteenth Century Capital of Mali', *The Journal of African History* 14:2 (1973), 201 (map); Labelle Prussin, 'The Architecture of Islam in West Africa', *African Arts* 1:2 (1968), 71; Jean-Louis Bourgeois, 'The History of the Great Mosques of Djenné', *African Arts* 20:3 (1987), 54; Felipe Fernández-Armesto, *Civilizations: Culture, Ambition, and the Transformation of Nature* (New York: Free Press, 2001), 89, 251.

11 'Profile: Timbuktu', Aljazeera (1 April 2012), https://www.aljazeera.com/news/2012/4/1/profile-timbuktu [accessed 01.03.25]; Arazi, 'Tracing History in Dia', 101, 104; John Hunwick, 'Timbuktu: A Refuge of Scholarly and Righteous Folk', *Sudanic Africa* 14 (2003), 14; Tim Insoll, 'The Archaeology of Post-Medieval Timbuktu', *Sahara* 13 (2001–2), 9.

12 Insoll, 'Archaeology of Post-Medieval Timbuktu', 9, 21; Roderick J. McIntosh, 'Before Timbuktu: Cities of the Elder World', in Shamil Jeppie and Souleymane Bachir Diagne (eds), *The Meanings of Timbuktu* (Cape Town: HSRC Press/CODESRIA/IPG, 2008), 35–6; Arazi, 'Tracing History in Dia', 105, 148, 359.

13 J. Scheele, 'Trans-Saharan Trade' (21 August 2024), *Oxford Research Encyclopedia of African History*, https://oxfordre.com/africanhistory/view/10.1093/acrefore/9780190277734.001.0001/acrefore-9780190277734-e-176 [accessed 26.01.25]; François-Xavier Fauvelle, *The Golden Rhinoceros: Histories of the African Middle Ages*, trans. Troy Tice (Princeton, NJ: Princeton University Press, 2018), 169–74; Mackintosh-Smith (ed.), *Travels*

of Ibn Battutah, 281; Ivor Wilks, 'Wangara, Akan and Portuguese in the Fifteenth and Sixteenth Centuries. 1. The Matter of Bitu', *The Journal of African History* 23:3 (1982), 340–1, 344; Fernández-Armesto, *Civilizations*, 89.

14 L.C. Beadle, *The Inland Waters of Tropical Africa: An Introduction to Tropical Limnology*, 2nd edn (London/New York: Longman, 1981), 207; Williams, *When the Sahara Was Green*, 1; D.T. Niane, 'Relationships and Exchanges among the Different Regions', in Niane (ed.), *General History of Africa*, 616.

15 Tim Mackintosh-Smith, 'Foreword', in Mackintosh-Smith (ed.), *Travels of Ibn Battutah*, x–xi; Mackintosh-Smith (ed.), *Travels of Ibn Battutah*, 325n; J.E.G. Sutton, 'The African Lords of the Intercontinental Gold Trade Before the Black Death: Al-Hasan Bin Sulaiman of Kilwa and Mansa Musa of Mali', *The Antiquaries Journal* 77 (1997), 221–42.

16 Mackintosh-Smith (ed.), *Travels of Ibn Battutah*, 281–4; Wilks, 'Wangara, Akan and Portuguese', 340–1; Maurizio Dioli, 'Dromedary (Camelus Dromedarius) and Bactrian Camel (Camelus Bactrianus) Crossbreeding Husbandry Practices in Turkey and Kazakhstan: An In-Depth Review', *Pastoralism* 10:1 (2020), 6; Teka, Tegegne. 'Introduction: The Dromedary in the East African Countries: Its Virtues, Present Conditions and Potentials for Food Production', *Nomadic Peoples* 29 (1991), 6–7.

17 V. Fernandes translated in Wilks, 'Wangara, Akan and Portuguese', 340–1.

18 Prussin, 'Architecture of Islam in West Africa', 71; Bourgeois, 'History of the Great Mosques of Djenné', 54.

19 Mackintosh-Smith (ed.), *Travels of Ibn Battutah*, 284, 293; H.A.R. Gibb and C.F. Beckingham (eds), *The Travels of Ibn Battuta*, Vol. IV (London: Hakluyt Society, 1994), 974–6.

20 K. Kone, 'The Soninke in Ancient West African History', *Oxford Research Encyclopedia of African History* (28 March 2018), https://oxfordre.com/africanhistory/view/10.1093/acrefore/9780190277734.001.0001/acrefore-9780190277734-e-160 [accessed 26.01.25]; D.T. Niane, 'Mali and the Second Mandingo Expansion', in Niane, *General History of Africa*, 126, 128, 131, 133–5.

21 D.T. Niane, *Sundiata: An Epic of Old Mali*, trans. G.D. Pickett; additional material by David W. Chappell and James Jones (1960/1965; Pearson Education Ltd., 2006), 85n.

22 Quoted in Niane, *Sundiata*, 82.

23 Niane, 'Mali and the Second Mandingo Expansion', 145; Niane, *Sundiata*, 85n.

24 Fernández-Armesto, *Civilizations*, 91–2.

25 Mackintosh-Smith (ed.), *Travels of Ibn Battuta*, 287, 292, 325n; Gibb and Beckingham (eds), *Travels of Ibn Battuta*, 965; John O. Hunwick,

'An Andalusian in Mali: A Contribution to the Biography of Abū Ishāq al-Sāhilī, c. 1290–1346', *Paideuma* 36 (1990), 59; 'Timbuktu', UNESCO World Heritage Convention, https://whc.unesco.org/en/list/119/; 'Mithqal', n., *OED*; The Royal Mint, 1000g bar, https://www.royalmint.com/invest/bullion/bullion-bars/gold-bars/royal-mint-1kg-gold-bar-cast/ [accessed 01.03.25].

26 Peter Russell, *Prince Henry 'the Navigator': A Life* (New Haven, CT: Yale University Press, 2000), 118; J.M. Massing, 'Observations and Beliefs: The World of the Catalan Atlas', in J.A. Levenson (ed.), *Circa 1492: Art in the Age of Exploration* (New Haven, CT: Yale University Press, 1991), 27, 28, 118–19; Clara Estow, 'Reflections on Gold: On the Late Medieval Background of the Spanish "Enterprise of the Indies"', *Mediaevistik* 6 (1993), 92; Clara Estow, 'Mapping Central Europe: The Catalan Atlas and the European Imagination', *Mediterranean Studies* 13 (2004), 14; John Man, *Xanadu: Marco Polo and Europe's Discovery of the East* (London: Bantam Press, 2009), 140–1; Catalan Atlas Legends (and translations), The Cresques Project (Source gallica.bnf.fr / BnF), https://www.cresquesproject.net/catalan-atlas-legends [accessed 01.03.25]: Panels III, IV, VI.

27 'Abd al-Raḥmān ibn 'Abd Allāh Sa'dī, 'Introduction', in John O. Hunwick (ed.), *Timbuktu and the Songhay Empire: Al-Sa'di's Ta'rīkh al-Sūdān down to 1613, and Other Contemporary Documents* (Leiden: Brill, 1999); David C. Conrad, *Empires of Medieval West Africa: Ghana, Mali, and Songhay* (2005; New York: Chelsea House, 2010), 70–3, 117.

28 Russell, *Prince Henry 'the Navigator'*, 118–19, 131–2, 200–1; The Cresques Project, Panel III.5', https://www.cresquesproject.net/catalan-atlas-legends/panel-iii [accessed 31.08.22].

29 Ivana Elbl, 'Cross-Cultural Trade and Diplomacy: Portuguese Relations with West Africa, 1441–1521', *Journal of World History* 3:2 (1992), 170, 177; J. Devisse and S. Labib, 'Africa in Inter-Continental Relations', in Niane (ed.), *General History of Africa IV*, 667; P.E.H. Hair, 'The Falls of Félou: A Bibliographical Exploration', *History in Africa*, 11 (1984), 119.

30 Ricardo Pelizzo, 'Timbuktu: A Lesson in Underdevelopment', *Journal of World-Systems Research* 26 (2001), 273–4; John Craig, *The Mint: A History of the London Mint from A.D. 287 to 1948* (Cambridge: Cambridge University Press, 2010), xvi, 166; Craig, *The Mint*, Royal African Company seal with coat of arms, British Museum Reg. no. 1838,0125.2, https://www.britishmuseum.org/collection/object/H_1838-0125-2 [accessed 24.12.22]; Pettrigrew, *Freedoms Debt*, 11–12. Ricardo Pelizzo, 'Timbuktu: A Lesson in Underdevelopment', *Journal of World-Systems Research* 26 (2001), 273–4; John Craig, *The Mint: A History of the London Mint from A.D. 287 to 1948* (Cambridge: Cambridge University Press, 2010), xvi, 166;

Craig, *The Mint*, Royal African Company seal with coat of arms, British Museum Reg. no. 1838,0125.2, https://www.britishmuseum.org/collection/object/H_1838-0125-2 [accessed 24.12.22]; Pettrigrew, *Freedoms Debt*, 11–12.

31 Dubois 1897, translated in Insoll, 'Archaeology of Post-Medieval Timbuktu', 14; Abd al-Rahman al-Sadi translated in Hunwick, 'Timbuktu', 13.

32 Rosa De Jorio, *Cultural Heritage in Mali in the Neoliberal Era* (Urbana, IL: University of Illinois Press, 2016), 15; Bourgeois, 'History of the Great Mosques of Djenné', 55–7, 60, 62; 'Timbuktu', UNESCO World Heritage Convention; Thomson Reuters, 'Timbuktu Tombs Destroyed by Mali Islamists', *The World, Global Post* (31 July 2016), https://theworld.org/stories/2016/07/31/timbuktu-tombs-destroyed-mali-islamists [accessed 04.08.24].

Chapter 17: Oil Rivers

1 British Treaty with Opobo (4 January 1873), quoted in K. Onwuka Dike, *Trade and Politics in the Niger Delta 1830–1885: An Introduction to the Economic and Political History of Nigeria* (Oxford: Oxford University Press, 1956), Appendix C, 223.

2 William Neville Geary, *Nigeria Under British Rule* (1927; New York: Barnes & Noble, 1965), 282–3; Letter from Johnston to JaJa, 18 September 1887, and Ultimatum, 19 September 1887, quoted in Okpete Kanu, 'The Life and Times of King Jaja of Opobo, 1812–1895' (MA thesis, Dalhousie University, 1970), 182–4, http://hdl.handle.net/10222/76501.

3 Geary, *Nigeria Under British Rule*, 284.

4 Geary, *Nigeria under British Rule*, 9–11; Sir Harry H. Johnson, *The Story of My Life* (Indianopolis, IN: Bobbs-Merrill Co., 1923), 181–2.

5 Geary, *Nigeria Under British Rule*, 284, 291, 292; Kanu, 'Life and Times of King Jaja', 193; Michael Lobban, *Imperial Incarceration: Detention without Trial in the Making of British Colonial Africa* (Cambridge: Cambridge University Press, 2021), Chapter 6.

6 Dike, *Trade and Politics in the Niger Delta, 1830–1885: An Introduction to the Economic and Political History of Nigeria* (Oxford: Oxford University Press, 1956), 23–5, 225; Kanu, 'Life and Times of King JaJa', 205–6; K.C. Murray, 'A List of Sites, Buildings and Other Antiquities Declared to be Monuments under the Antiquities Act from February 1956 to December 1964', *Journal of the Historical Society of Nigeria* 4:1 (1967), 167. M. Osifuye photograph, King Jaja's Statue, 2007, https://en.wikipedia.org/wiki/File:King_Jaja_Opobo_statue_2.jpg; 'A Visit to Opobo, 1961', from R. Henderson, 'A Mighty Tree: Onitsha History, Kingship, and Changing Cultures', https://amightytree.org/visit-to-opobo-december-1961/ [both accessed 01.03.25].

7 Dike, *Trade and Politics in the Niger Delta*, 183–90.
8 Geary, *Niger under British Rule*, 292.
9 'British Treaty with Opobo, 4 January 1873'; quoted in Dike, *Trade and Politics in the Niger Delta*, Appendix C, 215–16.
10 'A Note by Sir Harry Johnston', Geary, *Niger under British Rule*, Appendix C, 288, 290 (emphasis in original); Johnson, *Story of My Life*, 182.
11 Thomas Fowell Buxton, *The African Slave Trade and its Remedy* (London, 1840); 'Narrative of the Niger Expedition', *Colburn's United Service Magazine and Naval and Military Journal*, Part III (London, 1843), 223ff; Philip D. Curtin, *The Image of Africa: British Ideas and Action, 1780–1850*, Vol. 2 (Madison, WI: University of Wisconsin Press, 1973), 303–4.
12 'Oil Palm', Food and Agriculture Organisation, https://www.fao.org/3/y4355e/y4355e03.htm [accessed 29.12.22]; Freda Wolfson, 'A Price Agreement on the Gold Coast-The Krobo Oil Boycott, 1858–1866', *The Economic History Review* 6:1 (1953), 70.
13 C. Fyfe, 'Mungo Park (1771–1806), traveller in Africa', *ODNB*; Fyfe, 'Alexander Gordon Laing' (1794–1826), army officer and explorer in Africa', *ODNB*; E. Baigent, 'Richard Lemon Lander (1804–1834), traveller in Africa', *ODNB*; Dike, *Trade and Politics in the Niger Delta*, 60, 63, 172–3.
14 Dike, *Trade and Politics in the Niger Delta*, 61n, 206; Geary, *Niger under British Rule*, 288, 290.
15 T. Maluwa, 'The Origins and Development of International Fluvial Law in Africa: A Study of the International Legal Regimes of the Congo and Niger Rivers from 1885 to 1960', *Netherlands International Law Review* 29:3 (1982), 376; Dave Keating, 'How Belgium is Being Forced to Confront the Bloody Legacy of King Leopold II', *New Statesman* (9 June 2020, updated 5 October 2023); Frans Buelens and Stefaan Marysse, 'Returns on Investments during the Colonial Era: The Case of the Belgian Congo', *The Economic History Review*, 62 no. S1 (2009), 140.
16 Granville to Plessen, 8 October 1884, quoted in Maluwa, 'Origins and Development of International Fluvial Law', 372.
17 Maluwa, 'Origins and Development of International Fluvial Law'.
18 Maluwa, 'Origins and Development of International Fluvial Law'.
19 Kapnist quoted in Maluwa, 'Origins and Development of International Fluvial Law', 380.
20 'Memorandum on the "Niger Question" by H.P. Anderson' (1884), quoted in Maluwa, 'Origins and Development of International Fluvial Law', 377, see also 374. Emphasis in original.
21 Peter Burroughs, 'Imperial Institutions and the Government of Empire', in Porter (ed.), *Oxford History of Empire: Vol. III*, 194.
22 Maluwa, 'Origins and Development of International Fluvia Law', 375, 382;

Thomas Uwadiale Obinyan, 'The Annexation of Benin', *Journal of Black Studies* 19:1 (1988), 29–40; 'Benin Bronzes', British Museum, https://www.britishmuseum.org/about-us/british-museum-story/contested-objects-collection/benin-bronzes [accessed 29.12.22].

23 Geary, *Nigeria Under British Rule*, 286; David Pratten, *The Man-Leopard Murders: History and Society in Colonial Nigeria* (Edinburgh: Edinburgh University Press, 2007), 63; Parliamentary Papers (PP), *Southern Nigeria. Report for 1908*, Colonial Reports – Annual. No. 630. Southern Nigeria 1910. Cd. 4964–4, page 32.

24 *Southern Nigeria. Report for 1908*, 30, 32; J.A.A. Le Prince, 'Control of Malaria: Oiling as an Antimosquito Measure', *Public Health Reports (1896–1970)* 30:9 (1915), 599–600.

25 Listed in John M. Carland, *The Colonial Office and Nigeria, 1898–1914* (Basingstoke: Macmillan, 1985), 108.

26 PP (1920), *Nigeria. Report by Sir F.D. Lugard on the Amalgamation of Northern and Southern Nigeria, and Administration, 1912–1919*. Cmd. 468, page 67; O.U. Kalu, 'Waves from the Rivers: The Spread of the Garrick Braide Movement in Igboland, 1914–1934', *Journal of the Historical Society of Nigeria* 8:4 (1977b), 95–110; Pratten, *Man-Leopard Murders*, 101, 109.

27 PP (1902), *Northern Nigeria: Report for the Period from 1st January 1900 to March 31st, 1901 by the High Commissioner of Northern Nigeria*, Colonial Reports – Annual No. 346, 1902, Cd. 788–16, page 5; E. de C. Duggan. 'Notes on the Munshi ('Tivi') Tribe of Northern Nigeria: Some Historical Outlines', *Journal of the Royal African Society* 31:123 (1932), 176, 177n, 178, 179; E. de C. Duggan, 'The Cotton-Growing Industry of Nigeria', *Journal of the Royal African Society* 21:83 (1922), 199, 201.

28 Susan M. Martin, *Palm Oil and Protest: An Economic History of the Ngwa Region, South-Eastern Nigeria, 1800–1980* (Cambridge: Cambridge University Press, 1988), 2, 106–14, 116.

29 Aba Commission, quoted in Martin, *Palm Oil and Protest*, 116, 117, 187n.

30 PP (1920), *Nigeria. Report by Sir F.D. Lugard*, 6; K. Dike Nworah, 'The Politics of Lever's West African Concessions, 1907–1913', *The International Journal of African Historical Studies* 5:2 (1972), 248; Unilever, *United Africa Company: A Brief Guide* (Port Sunlight, Unilever Archives & Record Management; undated), https://archives-unilever.com/media/_file/website-documents/uac%20-%20united%20africa%20company%20booklet.pdf; Geoffrey L. Baker, *Trade Winds on the Niger: The Saga of the Royal Niger Company, 1830–1971* (London/New York: Radcliffe Press/St. Martin's Press, 1996); Brian Lewis, *So Clean: Lord Leverhulme, Soap and Civilisation* (Manchester: Manchester University Press, 2017).

31 Toyin Falola and Matthew M. Heaton, *A History of Nigeria* (Cambridge: Cambridge University Press, 2008), Chapter 6.

32 George Awoonor Williams [Kofi Awoonor], *Afro-Asian Poems: Anthology*, Vol. 1 Part 2 (Colombo: Afro Asian Writers' Bureau, 1965), 44; Duncan Yoon, 'Cold War Africa and China: The Afro-Asian Writers' Bureau and the Rise of Postcolonial Literature' (unpublished PhD thesis, UCLA, 2014), 94–8.

Chapter 18: Who Are the Masters Now?

1 Germaine Dieterlen, 'The Mande Creation Myth', *Africa: Journal of the International African Institute* 27:2 (1957), 135.

2 Dieterlen, 'Mande Creation Myth'; Jan Jansen and James R. Fairhead, 'The Mande Creation Myth, by Germaine Dieterlen, as a Historical Source for the Mali Empire', *Journal of West African History* 6:2 (2020), 93–114; 'Glossary', in B.A. Ogot (ed.), *General History of Africa, Vol. V: Africa from the Sixteenth to the Eighteenth Century* (Oxford/Berkeley, CA: UNESCO/Heinemann/University of California: 1992), 969.

3 Anderson et al., *Niger River Basin*, 8.

4 David Kinnersley, *Troubled Water: Rivers, Politics and Pollution* (London: Hilary Shipman Ltd., 1988), 2; Quasmi, 'Rivers as Legal Persons', 25; G. Hardin, 'The Tragedy of the Commons', *Science* 162 (1968), 1243–8; du Feu, 'Tropical Reservoir Fisheries', 289; Susan Himmelweit and Roberto Simonetti, 'Nature for Sale', in Steve Hinchliffe and Kath Woodward (eds), *The Natural and the Social: Uncertainty, Risk, Change*, 2nd edn (London: The Open University, 2004), 101–3.

5 E. Wymenga et al., 'Ecological Hotspots in the Upper Niger Basin and Inner Niger Delta. II. Existing Data and Information. A&W-report 2253b', Altenburg & Wymenga Ecological Consultants, Feanwâlden, 'Summary/Résumé' (2017), https://www.altwym.nl/wp-content/uploads/2020/05/Wymenga-cs-2017.-Preliminary-ecological-hotspots-Upper-NIger-Basin-and-Inner-NIger-Delta-def.pdf [accessed 11.01.25].

6 Anderson et al., *Niger Basin*; Tiyanjana Maluwa, 'Legal Aspects of the Niger River under the Niamey Treaties', *Natural Resources Journal* 28:4 (1988), 671–97; M.K. Mahlakeng and Hussein Solomon, 'An Analysis of Regime Capacity and a Nascent Environmental Conflict in the Niger River Basin', *Journal for Contemporary History* 2:2 (2017), 193; du Feu, 'Tropical Reservoir Fisheries', 46; 'The History of NBA', Autorité du Bassin du Niger, http://www.abn.ne/index.php?option=com_content&view=article&id=1:historique&catid=1:labn&lang=fr&Itemid=0 [accessed 05.09.22].

7 Articles 2, 12 in 'Cameroon, Ivory Coast, Dahomey [Benin], Guinea, Upper Volta [Burkina Faso], Mali, Niger, Nigeria and Chad. Agreement concerning the Niger River Commission and the Navigation and

Transport on the River Niger. Done at Niamey, on 25 November 1964', UN Treaties No. 8507 (1967).

8 'Inner Niger Delta', GeoVille, http://globwetland-africa.org/wp-content/uploads/2022/05/12.-FactSheet_IR_InnerNigerDelta_final.pdf; Fact Sheet, Inner Niger Delta, Ramsar Convention on Wetlands, https://www.ramsar.org/sites/default/files/documents/library/wwd2004_rpt_mali_press_e.pdf; Sabrina Beeler Stücklin and Karin Frei, 'Between Water Spirits and Market Forces: Institutional Changes in the Niger Inland Delta Fisheries among the Somono and Bozo Fishermen of Wandiaka and Daga-Womina (Mali)', in Tobias Haller (ed.), *Disputing the Floodplains* (Leiden: Brill, 2010), 83; 'Announcement to Build Guinea Dam Bypasses Regional Collaborative Process', Wetland International Blog (26 July 2017), https://www.wetlands.org/blog/announcement-build-guinea-dam-bypasses-regional-collaborative-process/; Chris Baker, Peter de Koning and Mori Diallo, 'Sustaining the Inner Niger Delta Lifeline', Alliance for Global Water Adaptation (AGWA) (22 March 2023), https://www.alliance4water.org/wr4er-cases/sustaining-the-inner-niger-delta-lifeline; Inner Niger Delta, Freshwater Ecoregions of the World, https://www.feow.org/ecoregions/details/508; Anderson et al., *Niger River Basin*, 24; Jansen and Fairhead, 'The Mande Creation Myth', 100, 101, 103; 'Caspian Tern', The Mediterranean Science Commission (CIESM), https://ciesm.org/marine/programs/seabirds/caspian-tern/; 'The Niger River – Four Ecoregions, One Refuge', WWF, https://wwf.panda.org/wwf_news/?2218/The-Niger-River-four-ecoregions-one-refuge; Water, Peace and Security Partnership, *Water and Conflict in the Inner Niger Delta: A Governance Challenge* (1 June 2022), 9, https://waterpeacesecurity.org/files/227 [all accessed 28.02.25].

9 D.T. Niane, 'Mali and the Second Mande Expansion', in J. Ki-Zerbo and D.T. Niane (eds), *General History of Africa: Africa from the Twelfth to the Sixteenth Century, Vol. IV*, Abridged Edition (Oxford/Berkeley, CA: UNESCO/James Currey Ltd/University of California, 1997), 56; 'Manden Charter, Proclaimed in Kurukan Fuga': Decision of the Intergovernmental Committee: 4.COM 13.59, UNESCO Intangible Cultural Heritage, https://ich.unesco.org/en/decisions/4.COM/13.59 [accessed 28.02.25]; Mary Jo Arnoldi, 'Cultural Patrimony and Heritage Management in Mali: The Old Towns of Djenné and the Sanké Mon Festival', *Africa Today* 61:1 (2014), 48.

10 De Jorio, *Cultural Heritage in Mali*, 145.

11 Manden Charter, Proclaimed in Kurukan Fuga: Mali, 'Nomination for Inscription on the Representative List in 2009 (Reference No. 00290)', Convention for the Safeguarding of the Intangible Cultural Heritage, Intergovernmental Committee for the Safeguarding of the Intangible

Cultural Heritage, UNESCO, Fourth Session, Abu Dhabi, United Arab Emirates, 28 September to 2 October 2009', p. 3, s. 2, UNESCO, https://ich.unesco.org/en/RL/manden-charter-proclaimed-in-kurukan-fuga-00290 [accessed 28.02.25]; Jansen and Fairhead, 'The Mande Creation Myth'.

12 'Dream mandé – Djata' Festival d'Avignon' (2017), https://festival-avignon.com/en/edition-2017/programme/dream-mande-djata-7181 [accessed 28.02.25].

13 Established in 1998. De Jorio, *Cultural Heritage in Mali in the Neoliberal Era*, 78, 80–1.

14 'The Sanké Mon: Collective Fishing Rite of the Sanké, Mali' [UNESCO Nomination by Mali Government]. Convention for the Safeguarding of the Intangible Cultural Heritage. Intergovernmental Committee for the Safeguarding of the Intangible Cultural Heritage. Fourth Session Abu Dhabi, United Arab Emirates, 28 September to 2 October 2009. Nomination for Inscription on the Urgent Safeguarding List in 2009 (Reference No. 00289), https://ich.unesco.org/en/USL/sanke-mon-collective-fishing-rite-of-the-sanke-00289 [accessed 28.02.25]; Arnoldi, 'Cultural Patrimony and Heritage Management in Mali'; Water, Peace and Security Partnership, *Water and Conflict in the Inner Niger Delta*, 11–12.

15 Stücklin and Frei, 'Between Water Spirits and Market Forces', 78, 82–5, 116.

16 'Kainji Hydroelectric Dam', ICE, https://www.ice.org.uk/what-is-civil-engineering/what-do-civil-engineers-do/kainji-hydroelectric-dam [accessed 05.09.22]; Salah El-Din El-Zarka, 'Kainji Lake, Nigeria', in William C. Ackermann, C.F. White and E.B. Worthington (eds), *Man-Made Lakes: Their Problems and Environmental Effects* (Washington DC: American Geophysical Union, 1973), 200, 205; du Feu, 'Tropical Reservoir Fisheries', 55, 57, 61, 85, 197.

17 du Feu, 'Tropical Reservoir Fisheries', 286.

18 du Feu, 'Tropical Reservoir Fisheries', 54, 70, 274–6, 284, 290, 313; Mansur Abubakar Wara, 'The Sorko Expansion in the Waters of the Niger to the End of the 20th Century', *Annals of Global History* 1:1 (2019), 1; Frank Salamone, 'The Serkawa of Yauri: Class, Status or Party?', *African Studies Review* 18:1 (1975), 88–101.

19 du Feu, 'Tropical Reservoir Fisheries', 45; Ian Goldin, *Development: A Very Short Introduction* (New York/Oxford: Oxford University Press, 2018), 77.

20 Abubakar Tafawa Balewa quoted in Edmund Chilaka, 'Nigeria's Lower Niger Dredging Campaigns, 1909–2014: The Politics of a Lugardian Inland Water Transport Project versus the Global Playbook', *Water History* 15:2 (2023), 271.

21 31 August 1964 speech by Abubakar Tafawa Balewa quoted in Salihu Mohammed Niworu, 'The Politics of Neglect in the Resettled Communities of Borgu: A Recipe for Armed Struggle', *African Research Review* 11:2 (2017), 73.

22 El-Zarka, 'Kainji Lake, Nigeria', 200, 211; du Feu, 'Tropical Reservoir Fisheries', 54, 70; Niworu, 'Politics of Neglect', 73; Wara, 'The Sorko Expansion in the Waters'; Ruth Shinenge Gyuse and Timothy Terver Gyuse, 'Kainji Resettlement Housing: 40 Years Later', *Journal of Urbanism: International Research on Placemaking and Urban Sustainability* 1:3 (2008), 247–64.

23 Niworu, 'Politics of Neglect', 73, 74–5, 79.

24 'Kainji Hydroelectric Dam', ICE; Ogaga Ariemu, 'Epileptic Electricity Supply: Majority of Power Plants Performing Below Capacity – NERC', *Daily Post* (2 April 2024).

25 15 February 1969 speech by Yakubu Gowon quoted in Niworu, 'Politics of Neglect', 73.

26 Adaobi Tricia Nwaubani, 'Remembering Nigeria's Biafra War that Many Prefer to Forget', BBC News (15 January 2020), https://www.bbc.co.uk/news/world-africa-51094093 [accessed 28.02.25].

27 Martin Williams, *Nile Waters, Saharan Sands: Adventures of a Geomorphologist* (Cham: Springer International Publishing, 2016), 17; Lirong Dou et al., 'Early Cretaceous (Aptian to Albian) Vegetation and Climate Change in Central Africa: Novel Palynological Evidence from the Doseo Basin', *Geological Journal* 59:2 (2024), 442–4, 463–4; T.J.A. Reijers, S.W. Petters and C.S. Nwajide, 'The Niger Delta Basin', in R.C. Selley (ed.), *Sedimentary Basins of the World*, Vol. 3 (Elsevier, 1997), 151–72; Michele L. Tuttle, Ronald R. Charpentier and Michael E. Brownfield, *The Niger Delta Petroleum System: Niger Delta Province, Nigeria, Cameroon, and Equatorial Guinea, Africa*, U.S. Geological Survey Open File Report 99–50H (1999).

28 'The Secession that Failed', *Time Magazine*, 26 January 1970, 19; Nigeria, *Hansard* HC Deb, vol. 779, cc. 1571–1636, 13 March 1969; Nigeria and Biafra (Supply of Arms), *Hansard* HC Deb, vol. 782, cc. 926–7, 28 April 1969; Chibuike Uche, 'Oil, British Interests and the Nigerian Civil War', *The Journal of African History* 49:1 (2008), 113–16, 122, 129–30. See also Chijoke Uwasomba and Victor S. Alumona, 'Militancy in the Niger Delta and the Deepening Crisis of the Oil Economy in Nigeria', *Africa Development / Afrique et Développement* 38:3–4 (2013), 24; Dr Raji et al., 'Shell D'Arcy Exploration and the Discovery of Oil as Important Foreign Exchange Earnings in Ijawland of Niger Delta, C. 1940s–1970', *Arabian Journal of Business and Management Review (OMAN Chapter)* 2:11

(2013), 24; Meredith Coffey, 'Ethnic Minorities and the Biafran National Imaginary in Chukwuemeka Ike's Sunset at Dawn and Chimamanda Ngozi Adichie's Half of a Yellow Sun', in Toyin Falola and Ogechukwu Ezekwem (eds), *Writing the Nigeria-Biafra War* (Woodbridge, Suffolk: Boydell & Brewer, 2016), 265–83.

29 John Vidal, 'Niger Delta Oil Spills Clean-Up Will Take 30 Years, says UN', *The Guardian* (4 August 2011); United Nations Environment Programme, Environmental Assessment of Ogoniland: Site Factsheets, Executive Summary and Full Report (2 August 2011), https://www.unep.org/resources/assessment/environmental-assessment-ogoniland-site-factsheets-executive-summary-and-full; Domale Keys, 'Ogoni Women's Climate Justice Was Decades Ahead of Today's Debates', *Ms [Magazine]* (8 March 2022); Neil Munshi and William Clowes, 'One of World's Most Polluted Spots Gets Worse as $1 Billion Cleanup Drags On', Bloomberg UK (31 August 2022), https://www.bloomberg.com/news/features/2022-08-31/shell-s-1b-oil-cleanup-left-one-of-world-s-most-polluted-spots-dirtier-for-now; Frank Odenthal, 'Cleaning up the Niger-Delta' [n.d.], https://www.fairplanet.org/dossier/eco-crimes-shell-and-the-niger-delta/cleaning-up-the-niger-delta/; 'Shell – Bodo', LeighDay, Cases, https://www.leighday.co.uk/news/cases-and-testimonials/cases/shell-bodo/; Keryn Tsimitakopoulos, 'The Niger Delta Basin: Reform has Finally Come, but Can it Revive Investment in the Oil and Gas Sector?', S&P Global Blog (19 January 2022), https://www.spglobal.com/commodityinsights/en/ci/research-analysis/the-niger-delta-basin-reform-has-finally-come-but-can-it-reviv.html; Shell Nigeria, 'The History of Shell in Nigeria', https://www.shell.com.ng/about-us/shell-nigeria-history.html; 'Timeline – Shell in Nigeria', Reuters (16 January 2024), https://www.reuters.com/business/energy/shell-nigeria-2024-01-16/ [all accessed 18.02.25].

30 Interview in Martin Patience, 'Why Nigeria's "Avengers" Are Crippling the Oil Sector', BBC News (22 July 2016), https://www.bbc.co.uk/news/world-africa-36846114 [accessed 30.07.24].

31 Odenthal, 'Cleaning up the Niger-Delta'; Jess Craig, 'The Village that Stood Up to Big Oil and Won', *The Guardian* (1 June 2022); BMI Bodo Cleanup, 'Bodo Cleanup: The Journey So Far and Phase 2 in Anticipation', LinkedIn (2 September 2019), https://www.linkedin.com/pulse/bodo-cleanup-journey-so-far-phase-2-anticipation-bmi-bodo-cleanup/ [accessed 28.02.25].

32 Munshi and Clowes, 'One of the World's Most Polluted Spots'.

33 Rebecca Ratcliffe, '"This place used to be green": The Brutal Impact of Oil in the Niger Delta', *The Guardian* (6 December 2019).

34 Luca Ferrini and Lucia Benavides, 'The Fomi Dam – Potential for a Project of Shared Interest', *Nexus* (29 October 2018), https://www.water-energy-food.org/ru/resources/the-fomi-dam-potential-for-a-project-of-shared-interest; 'Niger-Niandan-Milo', Ramsar, https://rsis.ramsar.org/ris/1164 [both accessed 19.01.25]; Baker, de Koning and Diallo (AGWA), 'Sustaining the Inner Niger Delta Lifeline'.

35 Monica M. van Beusekom, 'Disjunctures in Theory and Practice: Making Sense of Change in Agricultural Development at the Office Du Niger, 1920–60', *The Journal of African History* 41:1 (2000), 80–2; Office du Niger, https://maep.gouv.ml/office-du-niger/ [accessed 28.02.25]; Baker, de Koning and Diallo (AGWA), 'Sustaining the Inner Niger Delta Lifeline'.

36 'Announcement to Build Guinea Dam Bypasses Regional Collaborative Process'; Fred Pearce, 'Is China Edging Away from a Massive Dam on the River Niger?', Dialogue Earth, Blog (7 April 2021), https://dialogue.earth/en/water/is-china-edging-away-from-a-massive-dam-on-the-river-niger/ [accessed 30.07.24]; Leo Zwarts et al., *The Niger, a Lifeline: Effective Water Management in the Upper Niger Basin* (Altenburg & Wymenga Ecologisch Onderzoek BV, 2005); African Union Development Agency – NEPAD, *2nd PIDA Priority Action Plan (2021–2030) Projects Prospectus* (June 2023), 68, https://www.nepad.org/publication/2nd-pida-priority-action-plan-2021-2030-projects-prospectus [accessed 19.01.25]; Baker, de Koning and Diallo (AGWA), 'Sustaining the Inner Niger Delta Lifeline'.

37 Wymenga et al., 'Ecological Hotspots in the Upper Niger Basin and Inner Niger Delta, 'Summary/Résumé'.

38 Delta Intérieur du Niger, Ramsar Sites Information Service, https://rsis.ramsar.org/ris-search/?solrsort=area_off_d%20desc&pagetab=1 [accessed 19.01.25].

39 Radhika Nagrath, 'Good News for Enthusiasts as Migratory Birds Arrive at Ganga', *The Pioneer* (5 January 2017), https://www.dailypioneer.com/2017/state-editions/good-news-for-enthusiasts-as-migratory-birds-arrive-at-ganga.html [accessed 08.09.23]; Radhika Nagrath, 'Ornithologists, Scientists Express Concern over Adverse Impact of Climate Change on Migratory Birds (29 April 2017), https://www.dailypioneer.com/2017/state-editions/ornithologists-scientists-express-concern-over-adverse-impact-of-climate-change-on-migratory-birds.html [accessed 28.02.25]; 'Yangtze Source Sees Rising Number of Wild Geese', *Xinhua* (5 July 2018), http://www.xinhuanet.com/english/2018-07/05/c_137303629.htm [accessed 28.02.25]; R. Scott et al., 'How Bar-Headed Geese Fly Over the Himalayas', *Physiology* 30:2 (2015), 107, 108; Montagu's Harrier, Royal Society for the Protection of Birds [RSPB], 'Beatrice', 2016, https://www.rspb.org.uk/

our-work/conservation/satellite-tracking-birds/tracking-montagus-harriers. Thanks to the RSPB for their assistance.

40 Leo Zwarts, Rob G. Bijlsma and Jan van der Kamp, 'The Fortunes of Migratory Birds from Eurasia: Being on a Tightrope in the Sahel', *Ardea* 111:1 (2023), 405–6; East Atlantic Flyway: England East Coast Wetlands', UNESCO (submitted 13 September 2023), https://whc.unesco.org/en/tentativelists/6689/ [accessed 19.01.25].

41 'Mali and France, a Timeline of Mounting Tensions', Al Jazeera English (1 February 2022). https://www.aljazeera.com/news/2022/2/1/mali-france-timeline-mounting-tensions; 'Thousands in Mali Celebrate Expulsion of French Ambassador', Al Jazeera English (5 February 2022), https://www.aljazeera.com/news/2022/2/5/thousands-in-mali-celebrate-expulsion-of-french-ambassador [both accessed 24.07.24].

42 Niger Basin, Nexus Profile (October 2018), https://uploads.water-energy-food.org/legacy/nexus_profile_niger_basin__english.pdf [accessed 28.02.25].

Chapter 19: Grand Canal

1 Marco Polo in *The Travels of Marco Polo*, trans. and ed. Giovanni Battista Baldelli Boni and Hugh Murray (New York, 1845), 163.

2 Aiming Lin, Sun Zhiming, and Zhenyu Yang, 'Tectonic Relationship between the Course Change of the Yangtze River and Indo-Asia Collision', in Sean J. Landowe and Garth M. Hammler (eds), *Structural Geology: New Research* (New York: Nova Science Publishers, 2008), 2–4; Zhao Ying, 'Where is the Headstream of the Yangtze?', CGTN (updated 06 February 2020), https://news.cgtn.com/news/2020-02-05/Where-is-the-headstream-of-the-Yangtze--NNPiIVnUfC/index.html [accessed 15.02.25]; 'Yangtze Source Sees Rising Number of Wild Geese', *XinhuaNet* (5 July 2018), http://www.xinhuanet.com/english/2018-07/05/c_137303629.htm [accessed 15.02.25]; Mike Searle, *Colliding Continents* (Oxford: Oxford University Press, 2013), 271–301; Hongbo Zheng et al., 'Formation of the First Bend in the Late Eocene Gave Birth to the Modern Yangtze River, China', *Geology* 49:1 (2021), 35–9.

3 Kenneth Pomeranz, 'The Transformation of China's Environment, 1500–2000', in Burke and Pomeranz (eds), *Environment and World History*, 122–3; Siying Chen et al., 'Climate Records in Ancient Chinese Diaries and their Application in Historical Climate Reconstruction – A Case Study of *Yunshan Diary*', *Climate of the Past* 16:5 (2020), 1876.

4 Loukas Barton et al., 'Agricultural Origins and the Isotopic Identity of Domestication in Northern China', *Proceedings of the National Academy*

of Sciences 106:14 (2009), 5523–8; Yinong Xu, *The Chinese City in Space and Time: The Development of Urban Form in Suzhou* (Honolulu; University of Hawai'i Press, 2000), 15; Kenneth Pomeranz, 'Transformation of China's Environment', 125; Ch'ao-Ting Chi, *Key Economic Areas in Chinese History as Revealed in the Development of Public Works for Water-Control* (London: G. Allen & Unwin Ltd, 1936), 6.

5 Ebrey, *Cambridge Illustrated History of China*, 17, 156–7; Te-Tzu Chang and A.H. Bunting, 'The Rice Cultures [and Discussion]', *Philosophical Transactions of the Royal Society of London. Series B, Biological Sciences* 275:936 (1976), 147; Chi, *Key Economic Areas*, 65; Antonia Finnane, *Speaking of Yangzhou: A Chinese City, 1550–1850* (Cambridge, MA: Harvard University Press, 2004), 158.

6 Jie Tang, 'The Chinese Grand Canal World Heritage Site: Living Heritage in the 21st Century?' (unpublished PhD Thesis, University of Sheffield, 2018), 235, 297; The Grand Canal, Documents, 'Advisory Body Evaluation (ICOMOS)', 2014, UNESCO, 114, https://whc.unesco.org/en/list/1443/documents/ [accessed 15.02.25].

7 Ebrey, *Cambridge Illustrated History of China*, 38; Grand Canal, 'Advisory Body Evaluation (ICOMOS)', 111–14.

8 Ebrey, *Cambridge Illustrated History of China*, 51, 60–3; Sabina Knight, *Chinese Literature: A Very Short Introduction* (Oxford: Oxford University Press, 2012), 5; Robinson, *Writing and Script*, 31; I. Galambos, 'The Myth of the Qin Unification of Writing in Han Sources', *Acta Orientalia Academiae Scientiarum Hungaricae* 57:2 (2004), 181–203.

9 Brian Lander, 'Making Use of the Land: The Political Ecology of China's First Empire', *Journal of Chinese History* 71 (2023), 5–7, 13; Grand Canal, 'Advisory Body Evaluation (ICOMOS)', 113; Lingqu Canal Submission for UNESCO (National Commission of the People's Republic of China) (29 January 2013), https://whc.unesco.org/en/tentativelists/5814/ [accessed 19.08.22].

10 Ebrey, *Cambridge Illustrated History of China*, 108–9, 114; Arthur F. Wright, *The Sui Dynasty* (New York: Knopf, 1978), 143–4; Yinong Xu, *The Chinese City in Space and Time: The Development of Urban Form in Suzhou* (Honolulu; University of Hawai'i Press, 2000), 14–15; Grand Canal, 'Advisory Body Evaluation (ICOMOS)', 114.

11 Ebrey, *Cambridge Illustrated History of China*, 116.

12 *Recueil Historique des Principaux Traits de la Vie des Empereurs Chinois* (undated, 18th century). Bibliothèque Nationale de Paris, 10v and 11r. https://gallica.bnf.fr/ark:/12148/btv1b10520492s/f1.item. Translation from the French by Hélène Maloigne.

13 Bruce Connolly, 'Discovering Jiangnan – South of the River', *China*

Daily (14 November 2021); Wright, *Sui Dynasty*, 177–81; Ebrey, *Cambridge Illustrated History of China*, 114, 116; Grand Canal, 'Advisory Body Evaluation (ICOMOS)', 111–14; Jindong Cai and Jing Peng, 'Introduction of Beijing-Hangzhou Grand Canal and Analysis of its Heritage Values', *Special Issue of Historical Water Projects and Traditional Water Technologies in the Asia-Pacific Region, Selected from the Special Session at IAHR-APD 2016 Congress* 26 (2019), 2–7.

14 Tang, 'Chinese Grand Canal World Heritage Site', 166, 211–14, 235.

15 Joseph Needham, *Science and Civilisation in China. Vol. 4, Physics and Physical Technology. Pt. 3, Civil Engineering and Nautics* (London: Cambridge University Press, 1971), 350–1; Tang, 'Chinese Grand Canal World Heritage Site', Chapter 3, 226.

16 Tang, 'Chinese Grand Canal World Heritage Site', 227.

17 *Statutes of the Yuan Dynasty*, translated in Tang, 'Chinese Grand Canal World Heritage Site', 178–9.

18 Jindong Cai and Jing Peng, 'Introduction of Beijing-Hangzhou Grand Canal', 5–6; Antonia Finnane, *Speaking of Yangzhou*, 36; Tang, 'Chinese Grand Canal World Heritage Site', 269.

19 Kublai Khan, Faculty of Asian and Middle Eastern Studies, University of Cambridge, https://www.ames.cam.ac.uk/kublai-khan [accessed 15.02.25]; Ebrey, *Cambridge Illustrated History of China*, 169–71; Virgil Ciocîltan, *The Mongols and the Black Sea Trade in the Thirteenth and Fourteenth Centuries* (Leiden: Brill, 2012), 42–5, 254–79; Man, *Xanadu*, 29–30, 50–1; Tang, 'Chinese Grand Canal World Heritage Site', 156.

20 Philip Ball, *The Water Kingdom: A Secret History of China* (London: Vintage, 2017), 192–3; David Curtis Wright, 'Navies in the Mongol Yuan Conquest of Southern Song China, 1274–1279', *Mongolian Studies* 29 (2007), 207–16; Finnane, *Speaking of Yangzhou*, 23; René Grousset, *The Empire of the Steppes: A History of Central Asia* (New Brunswick, NJ: Rutgers University Press, 1970), 287.

21 Translated in Francis Woodman Cleaves, 'The Biography of Bayan of the Bārin in the Yüan Shih', *Harvard Journal of Asiatic Studies* 19:3/4 (1956), 220. Some parentheses in original omitted.

22 Ebrey, *Cambridge Illustrated History of China*, 172, 338; Jindong Cai and Jing Peng, 'Introduction of Beijing-Hangzhou Grand Canal', 3; Grand Canal, 'Advisory Body Evaluation (ICOMOS)', 114; Man, *Xanadu*, 252.

23 *Marco Polo: The Travels*, 195.

24 *Marco Polo: The Travels*, 191–2.

25 Man, *Xanadu*, 348–53.

26 Tang, 'The Chinese Grand Canal World Heritage Site', 156–7, 180–3; Man, *Xanadu*, 251; Needham, *Science and Civilisation in China*, 478.

27 Randall A. Dodgen, *Controlling the Dragon: Confucian Engineers and the Yellow River in Late Imperial China* (Honolulu: University of Hawai'i Press, 2001), 1; M.E. Lewis, *The Flood Myths of Early China* (Albany, NY: New York Press, 2006), 16-17; The Palace Museum, Beijing, 'Water Studies of Ma Yuan', https://en.dpm.org.cn/collections/collections/2011-03-31/425.html [accessed 18.06.22]; Ney Elias, 'Notes of a Journey to the New Course of the Yellow River, in 1868', *The Journal of the Royal Geographical Society of London* 40 (1870), 1–33; Ebrey, *Cambridge Illustrated History of China*, 190.

28 Antonia Finnane, 'The Origins of Prejudice: The Malintegration of Subei in Late Imperial China', *Comparative Studies in Society and History* 35:2 (1993), 218–20, 226–7.

29 Tang, 'The Chinese Grand Canal World Heritage Site', 173, 177–8; Ebrey, *Cambridge Illustrated History of China*, 190.

30 Ebrey, *Cambridge Illustrated History of China*, 190–1, 193; Ch'ao-Ting Chi, *Key Economic Areas*, 147–8.

31 Ebrey, *Cambridge Illustrated History of China*, 191; Tang, 'Chinese Grand Canal World Heritage Site', 194–201.

32 Ebrey, *Cambridge Illustrated History of China*, 190, 195, 196 (map), 210–11, 218; 'Teapots through Time', V&A Museum, https://www.vam.ac.uk/articles/teapots-through-time [accessed 25.02.25]; Stacey Loughrey Sloboda, 'Making China: Design, Empire, and Aesthetics In Britain, 1745–1851' (unpublished PhD thesis, University of Southern California, 2004).

33 Finnane, *Speaking of Yangzhou*.

34 Nie Chongzheng, 'An Imperial Commission for an Imperial Affair: On the "Kangxi Emperor's Southern Tour Scrolls"', Sotheby's Blog (30 September 2020), https://www.sothebys.com/en/articles/an-imperial-commission-for-an-imperial-affair-on-the-kangxi-emperors-southern-tour-scrolls [accessed 26.02.25].

35 Claudia Brown, 'A Western View of Kangxi's Travel to the South: Fragmentary Scroll Six of his Inspection Tour Series and its Associations', Sotheby's Blog (29 September 2020), https://www.sothebys.com/en/articles/a-western-view-of-kangxis-travel-to-the-south-fragmentary-scroll-six-of-his-inspection-tour-series-and-its-associations [accessed 16.02.25]; Mail Foreign Service, '"Give us back our treasure": Chinese Demand Cameron Returns Priceless Artefacts Looted during 19th-Century Boxer Rebellion', *Mail Online* (4 December 2013); Hui Zhong, *China, Cultural Heritage, and International Law*, Routledge Research in International Law (Abingdon: Routledge, 2018); 'Kangxi Emperor's 1689 Inspection Tour, Scroll Seven', Wuxi to Suzhou to Tiger Kill, Mactaggart Art Collection of

the University of Alberta, in 'Recording the Grandeur of the Qing: The Southern Inspection Tour Scrolls of the Kangxi & Qianlong Emperors', Asia for Educators, https://afe.easia.columbia.edu/qing/k7.html [accessed 16.02.25].

36 Gao Hao, 'The Amherst Embassy and British Discoveries in China', *History* 99:337 (2014), 571–4; Ebrey, *Cambridge Illustrated History of China*, 226–7.

37 Keneth Pomeranz, *The Great Divergence: China, Europe, and the Making of the Modern World Economy* (Princeton, NJ: Princeton University Press, 2000), 18; Maartje Abbenhuis and Gordon W. Morrell, *The First Age of Industrial Globalization: An International History 1815–1918* (London: Bloomsbury Academic, 2020), 2.

38 M.E. Haq, *Drugs in South Asia* (London: Palgrave Macmillan, 2000); Orchard, 'Shanghai', 5; Harold C. Hinton, 'The Grain Tribute System of the Ch'ing Dynasty', *The Far Eastern Quarterly* 11:3 (1952), 343.

39 Kasian Tejapira, 'Pigtail: A Pre-History of Chineseness in Siam', *Sojourn: Journal of Social Issues in Southeast Asia* 7:1 (2018), 98.

40 Pomeranz, 'Transformation of China's Environment', 125, 141; Randall A. Dodgen, 'Hydraulic Evolution and Dynastic Decline: The Yellow River Conservancy, 1796–1855', *Late Imperial China* 12:2 (1991), 56.

41 R. Davenport-Hines, 'Gordon, Charles George (1833–1885), army officer', *ODNB*; Mail Foreign Service, '"Give us back our treasure"'; Zhong, *China, Cultural Heritage, and International Law.*

42 Ch'ao-Ting Chi, *Key Economic Areas,* 147–8; Tang, 'Chinese Grand Canal World Heritage Site', 272, 277–8; Honig, *Sisters and Strangers*; Ye, 'Grand Canal in Republican China', 750–1.

43 Robert Fulton, *A Treatise on the Improvement of Canal Navigation* (London, 1796), 7, 142–3; C. Lindsey, 'Robert Fulton (1765–1815), engineer and artist', *ODNB*; National Park Service, Chesapeake and Ohio Canal, Flooding, https://www.nps.gov/choh/learn/kidsyouth/flooding.htm [accessed 16.12.24].

44 Tang, 'Chinese Grand Canal World Heritage Site', 248–51; Ye, 'Grand Canal in Republican China', 763–5.

45 D.J. Dwyer, 'The Development of China's Inland Waterways', *Geography* 46:2 (1961), 165–7; Tang, 'Chinese Grand Canal World Heritage Site', 277–8.

46 'China's Second Longest Canal Opens for Trial Operation', *Hellenic Shipping News* (21 August 2023) [accessed 16.02.25]; Jean-Paul Rodrigue, *The Geography of Transport Systems*, 6th edn (London: Routledge, 2024), Chapter 1.

Chapter 20: The Riverfly

1 *Gilgamesh* X, 312–15, in *The Epic of Gilgamesh: The Babylonian Epic Poem and Other Texts in Akkadian and Sumerian*, Translated with an Introduction by Andrew George (London: Penguin Classics, 1999), 87; Andrew George, 'The Mayfly on the River: Individual and Collective Destiny in the Epic of Gilgamesh', *Kaskal* 9 (2012), 227–42.

2 'China', WEPA Database, Water Environment Partnership in Asia, updated 8 February 2023, https://wepa-db.net/database/china [accessed 08.08.24]; Ball, *Water Kingdom*; Knight, *Chinese Literature*, 36; Lihui Yang, Deming An and Jessica Anderson Turner, *Handbook of Chinese Mythology* (Oxford/New York: Oxford University Press, 2005), 100–10; Robin McNeal, 'Constructing Myth in Modern China', *The Journal of Asian Studies* 71:3 (2012), 679–704; *The Songs of the South: An Ancient Chinese Anthology of Poems by Qu Yuan and Other Poets*, trans. David Hawkes (London: Penguin, 1985), 279n, 333n.

3 Knight, *Chinese Literature*, 3; Robinson, *Writing and Script*, 20, 31, 37, 38, 131.

4 Robinson, *Writing and Script*, 20–1.

5 Menominee/Fols Avoine Chief quoted in Pike, *Account of a Voyage up the Mississippi River*, 48–9.

6 Jeanette Winterson, *Sexing the Cherry* (London: Bloomsbury, 1989), 146–7; *The Literary Island* (London: Channel 4 Television, 1991), 59.

7 Knight, *Chinese Literature*, 2.

8 'Qian Chibi fu' ('At 'Red Cliffs', I) trans. Robert E. Hegel, in Robert E. Hegel, 'The Sights and Sounds of Red Cliffs: On Reading Su Shi', *Chinese Literature: Essays, Articles, Reviews (CLEAR)* 20 (1998), 11–30, 17.

9 Gilgamesh X, quoted in George, 'Mayfly on the River', 237–8; 'Ephemeroptera: Up-Wing Flies', The Riverfly Partnership, https://www.riverflies.org/ephemeroptera [accessed 18.02.25].

10 Knight, *Chinese Literature*, 25, 30, 40–1.

11 Trans. Liu Fei-Wen, *Gendered Words: Sentiments and Expression in Changing Rural China* (Oxford/New York: Oxford University Press, 2015), 66; Wilt L. Idema, *Heroines of Jiangyong* (Washington DC: University of Washington Press, 2009), Introduction.

12 From 'The Maiden Meng Jiang', trans. Wilt L. Idema in Idema, *Heroines of Jiangyong*, 90.

13 From Qu Yuan, 'Li Sao' (On Encountering Trouble), in Hawkes, *Songs of the South*, 76–7.

14 Alfreda Murck, 'The "Eight Views of Xiao-Xiang" and the Northern Song Culture of Exile', *Journal of Song-Yuan Studies*, 26 (1996), 114–16; Idema, *Heroines of Jiangyong*, 162n; Igor Iwo Chabrowski, 'Rivers as Prisms of

Urban Imagining: Eastern Sichuan Work Songs', in Martin Knoll, Uwe Lübken and Dieter Schott (eds), *Rivers Lost, Rivers Regained: Rethinking City-River Relations* (Pittsburgh, PA: University of Pittsburgh Press, 2017), 177–99.

15 Murck, '"Eight Views of Xiao-Xiang"', 114; 'About Hunan', Hunan Provincial Department of Culture and Tourism, https://whhlyt.hunan.gov.cn/whhlyt/english/AboutHunan/202205/t20220524_24630094.html [accessed 09.08.24]. Thanks to Alfreda Murck for correspondence on Xiao and Xiang rivers.

16 Murck, '"Eight Views of Xiao-Xiang"', 113–14; Alfreda Murck, *Poetry and Painting in Song China: The Subtle Art of Dissent* (Cambridge, MA: Harvard University Asia Center for the Harvard-Yenching Institute, 2000), 8–10; Knight, *Chinese Literature*, 32–3; Hawkes, *Songs of the South*, Introduction, 32–7.

17 Jung Chang and Jon Halliday, *Mao: The Unknown Story* (London: Cape, 2005), 229.

18 Mao Zedong, 'Repel the Attacks of the Bourgeois Rightists (July 9, 1957)', in Michael Y.M. Kau and John K. Leung (eds), *The Writings of Mao Zedong, 1949–1976: Vol. II January 1956 – December 1957* (Armonk, NY: M.E. Sharpe 1993), 630; Ball, *Water Kingdom*, 41.

19 Chinese Posters Foundation: 'Rain is no Dragon's Spit' (BG E37/35), https://chineseposters.net/search/search?keys=no+dragon+spit; 'There is no "Dragon's Palace" or "Dragon King" under the Sea' (BG E37/32), https://chineseposters.net/posters/e37-32 [both accessed 26.02.25]. Thanks to Stefan Landsberger for translations for Chinese posters.

20 Tang, 'Chinese Grand Canal World Heritage Site', 266; Landsberger, '"Eliminate Superstition" Campaign (1965)', Chinese Posters Foundation, https://chineseposters.net/themes/eliminate-superstition [accessed 26.02.25]; Maura Elizabeth Cunningham, 'Q&A with Denise Y. Ho, 'Author of Curating Revolution: Politics on Display in Mao's China', *Association for Asian Studies* (29 May 2018), https://www.asianstudies.org/qa-with-denise-y-ho-author-of-curating-revolution-politics-on-display-in-maos-china/ [accessed 26.02.25].

21 Judith Shapiro, *Mao's War against Nature: Politics and the Environment in Revolutionary China* (Washington DC: Cambridge University Press, 2009); Ball, *Water Kingdom*, 293–5.

22 Chinese Posters Foundation: 'Cleave the Peak', 1973 (PC-1973-003), https://chineseposters.net/posters/pc-1973-003; 'The New Look of Mountains and Rivers', 1972 (PC-1972-003), https://chineseposters.net/posters/pc-1972-003 [both accessed 18.02.25].

23 Ball, *Water Kingdom*, 237–40.

24 Mao Zedong, 'Swimming' (1956), from *Ten Poems and Lyrics by Mao Tse-tung: Translation and Woodcuts by Wang Hui-Ming* (Amherst: University of Massachusetts Press, 1975), 63.

25 'Chairman Mao Swims in the Yangtse', *Peking Review* (29 July 1966), 4; Ball, *Water Kingdom*, 218–19; S. Poon, 'Embodying Maoism: The Swimming Craze, the Mao Cult, and Body Politics in Communist China, 1950s–1970s', *Modern Asian Studies* 53:5 (2019), 1450–85.

26 Mao Zedong quoted in 'Chairman Mao swims in the Yangtse', 5.

27 'Chairman Mao swims in the Yangtse', 4; 'Follow Chairman Mao and Advance in the Teeth of the Great Storms and Waves', *Peking Review* 9:31 (29 July 1966), 7.

28 Quotations from 'Chairman Mao Swims in the Yangtse', 5–7; 'Chairman Mao's Swim in the Yangtse Inspires the People of China and the World', *Peking Review* 33 (12 August 1966), 17–19; Yoon, 'Cold War Africa and China: The Afro-Asian Writers' Bureau and the Rise of Postcolonial Literature'.

29 Kaiya Zhou and Xingduan Zhang, *Baiji: The Yangtze River Dolphin and Other Endangered Animals of China*, trans. Luo Changyan (Nanjing: Yilin Press, 1992), 4–7.

30 Randall R. Reeves et al., *Dolphins, Whales and Porpoises: 2002–2010 Conservation Action Plan for the World's Cetaceans* (IUCN/SSC Cetacean Specialist Group, 2003), 51; Chenge An et al., 'Poyang and Dongting Lakes, Yangtze River: Tributary Lakes Blocked by Main-Stem Aggradation', *Proceedings of the National Academy of Sciences* 119:30 (2022), e2101384119, 1, 5–6.

31 Samuel T. Turvey, *Witness to Extinction: How We Failed to Save the Yangtze River Dolphin* (New York: Oxford University Press, 2009), 4–5; Amitav Ghosh, *The Hungry Tide* (London: Harper Collins, 2004).

32 Poem translated by Luo Changyan in Kaiya Zhou and Xingduan Zhang, *Baiji*, 11–12.

33 Justin Jin, 'Rebirth Along China's Yangtze River', WWF Blog (Fall 2017), https://www.worldwildlife.org/magazine/issues/fall-2017/articles/rebirth-along-china-s-yangtze-river [accessed 20.08.22].

34 Annalisa Berta, *Return to the Sea: The Life and Evolutionary Times of Marine Mammals* (Berkeley, CA: University of California Press, 2012), 9, 79; Reeves et al., *Dolphins, Whales and Porpoises*, 51–3; Healy Hamilton et al., 'Evolution of River Dolphins', *Proceedings of the Royal Society of London. Series B: Biological Sciences* 268, no. 1466 (2001), 549–56; Gillian T. Braulik et al. (eds), *Report of the Workshop on Conservation of the Baiji and Yangtze Finless Porpoise*, Institute of Hydrobiology, Chinese Academy of Sciences, Wuhan, Hubei, China (28 November–3 December

2004), Co-organised by baiji.org Foundation and Changjiang Fishery Resources Administrative Committee, Ministry of Agriculture, China, http://www.iucn-csg.org/wp-content/uploads/2010/03/Brauliketal2005.pdf; Gillian T. Braulik et al., 'Taxonomic Revision of the South Asian River Dolphins (*Platanista*): Indus and Ganges River Dolphins Are Separate Species', *Marine Mammal Science* 37:3 (2021), 1022–59; 'Rare Yangtze River Dolphin under Increasing Threat', WWF (14 December 2006), https://wwf.panda.org/wwf_news/?89780/Rare-Yangtze-river-dolphin-under-increasing-threat [accessed 17.08.22].

35 Braulik et al. (eds), *Report of the Workshop on Conservation of the Baiji*, 7; Reeves et al., *Dolphins, Whales and Porpoises*, 51; Xinhua, 'Yangtze River Dolphins under Drought Threat', *China Daily*, updated 25 November 2011; 'Chinese Paddlefish and Wild Yangtze Sturgeon Extinct – IUCN' (22 July 2022), https://www.reuters.com/business/environment/chinese-paddlefish-wild-yangtze-sturgeon-extinct-iucn-2022-07-22/; 'Calls to Save Sturgeon as "living fossil" Fish Slip towards Extinction', WWF (22 July 2022), https://www.wwf.org.uk/press-release/calls-save-sturgeon-living-fossil-fish-slip-towards-extinction [both accessed 22.02.25]; Yangtze Finless Porpoise, WWF, https://www.worldwildlife.org/species/yangtze-finless-porpoise [accessed 19.02.25]; MA Yun, 'Wuhan Yangtze Finless Porpoise Breeding and Conservation Center Inaugurated at IHB', Blog, Chinese Academy of Sciences, Institute of Hydrobiology (30 May 2022), http://english.ihb.cas.cn/newsroom/general/202206/t20220614_306477.html [accessed 26.02.25].

36 Samuel Turvey et al., 'Rapidly Shifting Baselines in Yangtze Fishing Communities and Local Memory of Extinct Species', *Conservation Biology* 24.3 (2010), 782–3; Daniel Pauly, 'Anecdotes and the Shifting Baseline Syndrome of Fisheries', *TREE* 10:10 (1995), 430, https://fbaum.unc.edu/teaching/articles/ShiftingBaseline.pdf.

37 Raymond Laë, 'Effect of Drought, Dams and Fishing Pressure on the Fisheries of the Central Delta on the Niger River', *International Journal of Ecology and Environmental Sciences* 20 (1994), 122; Animals in the Thames, ZSL, https://www.zsl.org/what-we-do/conservation/protecting-species/animals-in-the-thames [accessed 19.02.25]; Plants and Animals, ICPDR, https://www.icpdr.org/tasks-topics/topics/biodiversity/plants-animals [accessed 19.02.25]; Center for Biological Diversity, 'Iconic Sturgeon of Great Lakes, Mississippi River Take Step Toward Endangered Species Protection' (14 August 2019), https://biologicaldiversity.org/w/news/press-releases/iconic-sturgeon-great-lakes-mississippi-river-take-step-toward-endangered-species-protection-2019-08-14 [accessed 19.02.25]; Wildlife Institute of India, *WII-GACMC. Aquatic Fauna of Ganga River: Status and Conservation* (Dehradun: Ganga Aqualife

Conservation Monitoring Centre, 2017), 12, https://nmcg.nic.in/pdf/Status%20report%2010%2005%202018_WII%20(1).pdf [accessed 19.02.25]; WWF, 'Calls to Save Sturgeon'.

Chapter 21: Sinking City

1 Gerald M. Friedman and John E. Sanders, *Principles of Sedimentology* (New York: Wiley & Sons, 1978), 274.
2 Kate Springer, 'Soaring to Sinking: How Building Up Is Bringing Shanghai Down', *Time* (21 May 2012); Jie Yin and Dapeng Yu, 'Rising Sea Levels Could Swamp Sinking Shanghai', 360info (17 May 2023), https://360info.org/rising-sea-levels-could-swamp-sinking-shanghai/ [accessed 19.02.25].
3 S. Jevrejeva et al., 'Recent Global Sea Level Acceleration Started over 200 Years Ago?', *Geophysical Research Letters* 35:8 (2008), 1–4; S. Woodroffe, 'Coastal Landscapes', *Geographical Review* (September 2017), 3.
4 Orchard, 'Shanghai', 4; Coco Liu, 'Shanghai Struggles to Save Itself from the Sea', *Scientific American* (27 September 2011); Associated Press, 'Rising Seas Threaten Shanghai, Other Big Cities', NBC News (18 October 2009), https://www.nbcnews.com/id/wbna33368880 [accessed 23.02.25]; Duan Shaobo, 'On Some Features of Shanghai's Physical Environment', *GeoJournal* 19:2 (1989), 240; Cecile Baeteman, 'Subsidence in Coastal Lowlands Due to Groundwater Withdrawal: The Geological Approach', *Journal of Coastal Research* (1994), 61, 65, 68.
5 Orchard, 'Shanghai', 15.
6 Orchard, 'Shanghai', 3–4.
7 Orchard, 'Shanghai', 3–4, 23–5.
8 Tash Reith-Banks, 'A City Built on Water: The Hidden Rivers under Tokyo's Concrete and Neon', *The Guardian* (13 June 2019); 'Yangjingbang Creek, Shanghai', University of Bristol – Historical Photographs of China reference number: Bk05-14, https://hpcbristol.net/visual/Bk05-14 [accessed 24.02.25].
9 Orchard, 'Shanghai', 21–2; Ye, 'Grand Canal in Republican China', 740; S.R. Halsey, *Quest for Power: European Imperialism and the Making of Chinese Statecraft* (Cambridge, MA: Harvard University Press, 2015), 194.
10 Orchard, 'Shanghai', 25; Ernest O. Hauser, *Shanghai: City for Sale* (New York: Harcourt Brace, 1940), 237, 256; Emily Honig, *Sisters and Strangers: Women in the Shanghai Cotton Mills, 1919–1949* (Stanford, CA: Stanford University Press, 1986), 29, 32–3ff, 67, 118–19; Hans Derks, *History of the Opium Problem: The Assault on the East, ca. 1600–1950* (Leiden: Brill, 2012), 688.
11 Orchard, 'Shanghai', 15; Keith Clayton, *Coastal Geomorphology*

(Houndmills: Macmillan Education, 1979), 1–2; D. Kaniewski et al., 'Holocene Evolution of *Portus Pisanus*, the Lost Harbour of Pisa', *Scientific Reports* 8:11625 (2018), 10–11; Robert Dolan and H. Grant Goodell, 'Sinking Cities: A Combination of Human Activities and Geological Processes Endangers Many of the World's Largest Cities', *American Scientist* 74:1 (1986), 41–2.

12 Orchard, 'Shanghai', 19, 20 (quoting F.L. Hawks Pott, 1928), 22.

13 George B. Barbour, 'Physiographic History of the Yangtze', *The Geographical Journal* 87:1 (1936), 29; Orchard, 'Shanghai', 22–3; Irving S. Friedman, 'Whangpoo Conservancy Board Announces Resumption of Operations', *Far Eastern Survey* 9:3 (1940), 36–7; *Chien She*, Dredgepoint, https://www.dredgepoint.org/dredging-database/equipment/chien-she; Schichau Seebeck Shipyard, http://www.schichau-seebeck-shipyard.com/content/articles/000000/000029.htm; 'Little Museum of Foreign Brand Advertising in the R.O.C.', https://www.mofba.org/2021/08/02/1937-road-map-of-shanghai-yangtze-river-delta-sponsored-by-standard-vacuum-oil-co-brands-socony-gargoyle-mobiloil/ [all accessed 23.02.25]; Yongle Xue, 'Oil for the Engines of China: The Standard Oil Company and the Early Mechanization of China, 1927–1953' (unpublished thesis, Department of History, Georgetown University, 2014).

14 Advertisement, 'Menace Off Shanghai!', Socony-Vacuum Oil Company Inc., c. 1936.

15 Orchard, 'Shanghai', 23; Friedman, 'Whangpoo Conservancy Board', 36–7; 'What Happened at Pearl Harbour?', Imperial War Museum Blog, https://www.iwm.org.uk/history/what-happened-at-pearl-harbor [accessed 22.02.25].

16 Hongbin Zheng, Yiting Pan and James W.P. Campbell, 'Building on Shanghai Soil', *Construction History* 34:1 (2019), 1; Shi Luxiang and Bao Manfang, 'Case History No. 9.2. Shanghai, China, by Shanghai Geological Department, Shanghai, China', in Joseph P. Poland (ed.), *Guidebook to Studies of Land Subsidence due to Ground-Water Withdrawal* (Michigan: UNESCO, 1984), 155–6, https://unesdoc.unesco.org/ark:/48223/pf0000065167 [accessed 19.06.22].

17 Zheng, Pan, and Campbell, 'Building on Shanghai Soil', 1–3, 13, 16.

18 A.W. Skempton, 'Foundations for High Buildings', *Proceedings of The Institution of Civil Engineers* 4:4 (1955), 246, 247; Betsy McCully, 'New York Geology', New York Nature, Blog, updated 2 August 2023, https://www.newyorknature.us/new-york-geology/ [accessed 23.02.25].

19 Zheng, Pan and Campbell, 'Building on Shanghai Soil', 5, Table 3; Club Concordia, The Bund, Shanghai, Historical Photographs of China, https://hpcbristol.net/visual/oh02-03; 'German Children at the Ceremony to Lay

the Foundation Stone of the New Club Concordia, Shanghai', University of Bristol – Historical Photographs of China reference number: LD01-112, https://hpcbristol.net/visual/LD01-112 [both accessed 23.02.25]; T. Vandamme, 'The Rise of Nationalism in a Cosmopolitan Port City: The Foreign Communities of Shanghai during the First World War', *Journal of World History* 29:1 (2018), 61–2; Skempton, 'Foundations for High Buildings', 251–2; P. Chung, 'Floating in Mud to Reach the Skies: Victor Sassoon and the Real Estate Boom in Shanghai, 1920s–1930s', *International Journal of Asian Studies* 16:1 (2019), 1–31.

20 Thomas L. Holzer and Ivan Johnson, 'Land Subsidence Caused by Ground Water Withdrawal in Urban Areas', *GeoJournal* 11:3 (1985), 253; Shi Luxiang and Bao Manfang, 'Case History No. 9.2. Shanghai, China', 155.

21 Xincheng Shen, 'Engineering Shanghai: Water, Sewage, and the Making of Hydraulic Modernity' (unpublished PhD thesis, Georgia Institute of Technology, 2019), 107; Frank Hannan, 'Abstracts of Water Works Literature', *Journal (American Water Works Association)* 21:12 (1929), 1727; Holzer and Johnson, 'Land Subsidence', 253; Shi Luxiang and Bao Manfang, 'Case History No. 9.2. Shanghai, China', 159.

22 Honig, *Sisters and Strangers*, 30–1 (Table 2), 118–19; Holzer and Johnson, 'Land Subsidence', 253; Theodore Shabad, 'The Population of China's Cities', *Geographical Review* 49:1 (1959), 32; Xing Li et al., 'Rapid Loss of Tidal Flats in the Yangtze River Delta since 1974', *International Journal Environmental Research and Public Health* 17:5, 1636 (2020), 13.

23 'Shanghai Brings Surface Subsidence under Control', *Peking Review* 15:5 (14 April 1972), 5, 7; Frank Kehl, 'Approach to Environmental Problems', *Social Scientist* 5:10/11 (1977), 107.

24 'Shanghai Brings Surface Subsidence Under Control', 7–8; 'Liu Shaoqi', Chinese Poster Foundation, https://chineseposters.net/themes/liushaoqi [accessed 23.02.25].

25 'Shanghai Brings Surface Subsidence Under Control', 9; 'Yangtze River Water Conservancy Work', *Peking Review* 9 (3 March 1972), 14–15; 'Liu Shaoqi', Chinese Poster Foundation, https://chineseposters.net/themes/liushaoqi [accessed 23.02.25].

26 'Shanghai Brings Surface Subsidence Under Control', 5, 9; Kehl, 'Approach to Environmental Problems', 112.

27 Joseph F. Poland and Working Group, 'Review of Methods to Control or Arrest Subsidence', in Joseph P. Poland (ed.), *Guidebook to Studies of Land Subsidence due to Ground-Water Withdrawal* (Michigan: UNESCO, 1984), 129. https://unesdoc.unesco.org/ark:/48223/pf0000065167 [accessed 19.06.22]; Holzer and Johnson, 'Land Subsidence', 253.

28 'Shanghai's Sinking Under Control, Authorities Say', *China Daily* (13 November 2001), http://www.china.org.cn/english/2001/Nov/22063.htm [accessed 22.08.22].

29 'Shanghai is Sinking as Skyscrapers Make a Dent', eastday.com (11 December 2001), http://www.china.org.cn/english/DO-e/23452.htm; 'Shanghai Tries to Prevent Ground Sinking', *China Daily* (10 September 2002), http://www.china.org.cn/english/2002/Sep/42481.htm [both accessed 19.06.22].

30 'Shanghai is Sinking as Skyscrapers Make a Dent'; 'Shanghai to Build 333-Meter Skyscraper', *People's Daily* (29 December 2001), http://www.china.org.cn/english/24432.htm [accessed 19.06.22]; Shimao International Plaza, Council on Tall Buildings and Urban Habitats, https://www.skyscrapercenter.com/building/wd/370# [accessed 11.08.24]; 'Shanghai Still Sinking', *China Daily* (19 November 2003), http://www.chinadaily.com.cn/en/doc/2003-11/19/content_282844.htm [accessed 19.06.22].

31 Springer, 'Soaring to Sinking'; Yang Jian, 'Land Subsidence Reduced to Safe Level', *Shanghai Daily* (23 April 2016).

32 TG, 'Construction: Venice of the East', *ASEE Prism* 18:5 (2009), 19; Hou Liqiang, 'Rule to Put Limits on Skyscrapers' *China Daily* (8 May 2020), https://global.chinadaily.com.cn/a/202005/08/WS5eb4b262a310a8b2411541ad.html [accessed 19.06.22]; Shanghai Tower, Council on Tall Buildings and Urban Habitats, https://www.skyscrapercenter.com/building/shanghai-tower/56 [accessed 11.08.24].

33 Yong Jiang, Chris Zevenbergen and Yongchi Ma, 'Urban Pluvial Flooding and Stormwater Management: A Contemporary Review of China's Challenges and "Sponge Cities" Strategy', *Environmental Science & Policy* 80 (2018), 140; '"Sponge City" Theory and Practice by Kongjian Yu and his Team', Turenscape, https://www.turenscape.com/topic/en/spongecity/index.html [accessed 25.02.25]; Hannah Ospina, 'How Sponge Cities Are Keeping China's Feet Dry', *NL Netherlands* (29 June 2022), https://nlplatform.com/greener-cities-china [accessed 25.02.25].

34 D. Stanway, 'What are China's "sponge cities" and Why Aren't They Stopping Floods?', Reuters (10 August 2023), https://www.reuters.com/world/china/what-are-chinas-sponge-cities-why-arent-they-stopping-floods-2023-08-10/ [accessed 22.02.25]; Yujie Xue and Martin Choi, 'Climate Change: China's "sponge cities" Struggle to Soak up Flooding from Severe Storms Despite Billions in Investment', *South China Morning Post* (6 January 2024); Faiza Chikhi et al., 'Review of Sponge City Implementation in China: Performance and Policy', *Water, Science and Technology* 88:10 (2023), 2499–2520.

35 Coco Liu and Climate Wire, 'Shanghai Struggles to Save itself from the

Sea', *Scientific American* (27 September 2011); Josh Holder, Niko Kommenda and Jonathan Watts (Helen Roxburgh in Shanghai), 'The Three-Degree World: The Cities that Will Be Drowned by Global Warming', *The Guardian* (3 November 2017); Robert Muggah, 'How China's Sponge Cities Are Preparing for Sea-Level Rise', World Economic Forum (28 June 2019), https://www.weforum.org/agenda/2019/06/how-china-s-sponge-cities-are-preparing-for-sea-level-rise/ [accessed 20.06.22].

36 'Shanghai Still Sinking'; Karen McVeigh, '"It's absolutely guaranteed": The Best and Worst Case Scenarios for Sea-Level Rise', *The Guardian* (26 June 2023).

37 Jie Yin and Dapeng Yu, 'Rising Sea Levels Could Swamp Sinking Shanghai'; Z. Dai et al., 'Detection of the Three Gorges Dam Influence on the Changjiang (Yangtze River) Submerged Delta', *Scientific Report* 4, 6600 (2014), 4; X. Li et al., 'Rapid Loss of Tidal Flats in the Yangtze River Delta since 1974', *International Journal Environmental Research and Public Health* 17:5, 1636 (2020), 1–20.

38 Clarissa Sebag-Montefiore, 'From Red Guards to Bond Villains: Why the Mao Suit Endures', BBC Culture (2 November 2015), https://www.bbc.com/culture/article/20151007-from-red-guards-to-bond-villains-why-the-mao-suit-endures; 'Shanghai is Sinking as Skyscrapers Make a Dent'; Sally Younger, 'NASA-Led Study Pinpoints Areas of New York City Sinking, Rising', NASA (27 September 2023), https://www.nasa.gov/science-research/earth-science/earth-surface-interior/nasa-led-study-pinpoints-areas-of-new-york-city-sinking-rising/ [both accessed 22.02.25].

39 Dolan and Goodell, 'Sinking Cities', Table 1, 40, 45; 'Things That Are 9 Meters Long', Measuring Knowhow, https://www.measuringknowhow.com/things-that-are-9-meters-long/ [accessed 22.08.22]; S. Hallegatte et al., 'Future Flood Losses in Major Coastal Cities', *Nature Climate Change* 3 (2013), Table 2.

40 Jason P. Ericson et al., 'Effective Sea-Level Rise and Deltas: Causes of Change and Human Dimension Implications', *Global and Planetary Change* 50:1 (2006), 67–8; Doru Bănăduc et al., 'The Danube Delta: The Achilles Heel of Danube River–Danube Delta–Black Sea Region Fish Diversity under a Black Sea Impact Scenario Due to Sea Level Rise – A Prospective Review', *Fishes* 8, 355 (2023), 1–27.

41 Hurricane Katrina, Met Office (UK), https://www.metoffice.gov.uk/weather/learn-about/weather/case-studies/katrina [accessed 26.02.25]; 'Historical Timeline', Caesars Superdome, https://www.caesarssuperdome.com/about-us/event-highlights [accessed 23.08.22]; Dolan and Goodell, 'Sinking Cities', 45.

42 Sundiata Keita Cha-Jua, 'Introduction to The Black Scholar Special Issue

on Hurricane Katrina: High Tide of a New Racial Formation', *The Black Scholar* 36:4 (2006), 6; Robynne Boyd, 'The People of the Isle de Jean Charles are Louisiana's First Climate Refugees – but They Won't Be the Last', NRDC (23 September 2019), https://www.nrdc.org/stories/people-isle-jean-charles-are-louisianas-first-climate-refugees-they-wont-be-last; Lucy Sherriff, 'This Louisiana Town Moved to Escape Climate-Linked Disaster', BBC Future Planet (30 January 2024), https://www.bbc.com/future/article/20240130-this-louisiana-town-moved-to-escape-climate-disaster [both accessed 22.02.25].

43 Connor Ibbetson, 'Insight: What Engineers Can Do as London Sinks,' New Civil Engineer, 29 October 2018, https://www.newcivilengineer.com/latest/insight-what-engineers-can-do-as-london-sinks-29-10-2018/ [accessed 06.06.25].

44 Younger, 'NASA-Led Study Pinpoints Areas of New York City'; 'New York City Is Sinking, and Is Not Alone', The University of Rhode Island (1 June 2023); 'Umpire Rock', Central Park Conservancy, https://www.centralparknyc.org/locations/umpire-rock; 'Hot Rocks: A Geological History of New York City Parks', New York City Department of Parks & Recreation, https://www.nycgovparks.org/about/history/geology [all accessed 22.02.25].

45 F. Ceccato, P. Simonini and A. Lionello, 'Long-Term Mechanical Behavior of Wooden Pile Foundation in Venice', Conference Paper, 2nd International Symposium on Geotechnical Engineering for the Preservation of Monuments and Historic Sites, Naples 2013; N. Castelletto et al., 'Can Venice Be Raised by Pumping Water Underground? A Pilot Project to Help Decide', *Water Resources Research* 44:1 (2008), 1–11; 'Variazioni del Livello Medio del Mare', Città di Venezia (updated 5 March 2025), https://www.comune.venezia.it/it/content/variazioni-livello-medio-mare#ingl [accessed 05.05.25].

46 Mayuri Mei Lin and Rafki Hidayat, 'Jakarta, the Fastest-Sinking City in the World', BBC News (13 August 2018), https://www.bbc.co.uk/news/world-asia-44636934; Sagita Adesywi, 'A River Runs Through It: How Responsible Business Practices Can Clean Up Indonesia's Waterways', United Nations Development Programme, Blog (21 March 2023), https://www.undp.org/indonesia/blog/river-runs-through-it-how-responsible-business-practices-can-clean-indonesias-waterways; 'West Java Administration Expands Citarum River Clean-Up Campaign', *The Jakarta Post* (19 June 2024); Emily Cassidy, 'Nusantara: A New Capital City in the Forest', https://earthobservatory.nasa.gov/images/152471/nusantara-a-new-capital-city-in-the-forest [all accessed 12.08.24].

47 'Will Rising Sea Levels Wipe Countries off the Map?', The Insight,

BBC Podcast (8 December 2022); Amy Houston, 'Tuvalu Became a Digital Nation to Spark Global Action for Climate Change Mitigation', The Drum, Blog (10 January 2024), https://www.thedrum.com/news/2023/05/30/tuvalu-became-digital-nation-spark-global-action-climate-change-mitigation [accessed 22.02.25].

48 Rémi Thiéblemont and Mélanie Becker, 'Rising Sea Levels and Subsiding Towns: A Double Threat to the Coastline', Polytechnique Insights (18 October 2023) [accessed 26.02.25]; Oliver Milman, 'New York City is Sinking due to Weight of its Skyscrapers New Research Finds', *The Guardian* (19 May 2023); Sandra Laville, 'Human-Made Materials Now Outweigh Earth's Entire Biomass – Study', *The Guardian* (9 December 2020); Andreas Malm, 'Sea Wall Politics: Uneven and Combined Protection of the Nile Delta Coastline in the Face of Sea Level Rise', *Critical Sociology* 39:6 (2013), 803–32; Matthew Kelly, 'The Thames Barrier: Climate Change, Shipping and the Transition to a New Envirotechnical Regime', in Jon Agar and Jacob Ward (eds), *Histories of Technology, the Environment and Modern Britain* (London: UCL Press, 2018), 206–29; Dipesh Chakrabarty, 'Whose Anthropocene? A Response', in Robert Emmett and Thomas Lekan (eds), 'Whose Anthropocene? Revisiting Dipesh Chakrabarty's "Four Theses"', *RCC Perspectives: Transformations in Environment and Society* 2 (2016), 103–13.

Conclusion

1 McCormick et al. (eds), *State of the Thames 2021*, 40.

2 Michael Wagreich et al., 'The Urban Sediments of Karlsplatz, Vienna (Austria) as a Reference Section for the Anthropocene Series', *The Anthropocene Review* 10:1 (2023), 316–29; 'Crawford Lake Chosen as the Primary Marker to Identify the start of the Anthropocene Epoch' (12 July 2023), University of Southampton News, https://www.southampton.ac.uk/news/2023/07/crawford-lake-anthropocene.page [accessed 02.03.25].

3 Alexander Farnsworth quoted in Damian Carrington, 'Canadian Lake Chosen to Represent Start of Anthropocene', *The Guardian* (11 July 2023).

4 Zwarts, Bijlsma and van der Kamp, 'Fortunes of Migratory Birds from Eurasia'.

5 William Gibson, Quote Investigator, http://quoteinvestigator.com/2012/01/24/future-has-arrived/ [accessed 15.03.25]; Tim Chatterton and Georgia Newmarch, 'The Future Is Already Here—It's Just Not Very Evenly Distributed', *ACM Interactions*, XXIV.2 (March/April 2017), 42.

6 Jan C. Semenza and Albert I. Ko, 'Waterborne Diseases that are Sensitive to Climate Variability and Climate Change', *New England Journal of Medicine* 389:23 (2023), 2175–87.

7 'Enfield's Baby Beaver Is Another First for London', Enfield Council (28 September 2023), https://www.enfield.gov.uk/news-and-events/2023/09/enfields-baby-beaver-is-another-first-for-london [accessed 02.03.25].

8 'Eastern Band of Cherokee Indians', https://www.ebci.gov/; 'Oconaluftee River', American Rivers, https://www.americanrivers.org/river/oconaluftee-river/; 'Sicklefin Redhorse Swims Toward Success', TVA (25 July 2024), https://tvawcma.com/the-powerhouse/stories/sicklefin-redhorse-swims-toward-success; Bill Fontenot and Richard DeMay, 'Wings over the Wetlands: Wading Birds in Louisiana (Barataria-Terrebonne National Estuary Program, 2008), 15, https://btnep.org/wp-content/uploads/2017/07/WadingBirdsinLa.pdf; Restore the Mississippi Delta, 'Wildlife', https://mississippiriverdelta.org/whats-at-stake/wildlife; 'Mississippi Flyway: Reelfoot to Lake Itasca', Free Passage, https://northamericancorridors.com/home/the-mississippi-flyway-reelfoot-to-lake-itasca/ [all accessed 07.04.25]; Will Dunn, 'The Great Stink: How Privatisation and Profit Polluted Britain's Waterways', *The New Statesman* (17–23 May 2024), 22–7.

Index